Theorizing
NGOs

NEXT WAVE
New Directions in Women's Studies

A series edited by
INDERPAL GREWAL,
CAREN KAPLAN, *and*
ROBYN WIEGMAN

Theorizing
NGOs

STATES, FEMINISMS,
AND NEOLIBERALISM

Victoria Bernal and Inderpal Grewal, editors

Duke University Press   Durham and London   2014

Library of Congress Cataloging-in-Publication Data
Theorizing NGOs: states, feminisms, and neoliberalism /
Victoria Bernal and Inderpal Grewal, eds.
pages cm.—(Next wave)
Includes bibliographical references and index.
ISBN 978-0-8223-5551-9 (cloth : alk. paper)
ISBN 978-0-8223-5565-6 (pbk. : alk. paper)
1. Non-governmental organizations. 2. Civil society.
3. Women—Political activity—History. I. Bernal, Victoria.
II. Grewal, Inderpal. III. Series: Next wave.
JZ4841.T44 2014
341.2–dc23   2013026388

CONTENTS

vii   ACKNOWLEDGMENTS

1   INTRODUCTION
The NGO Form: Feminist Struggles, States, and Neoliberalism
Victoria Bernal and Inderpal Grewal

19   PART I   NGOs Beyond Success or Failure

21   CHAPTER 1
The Movementization of NGOs? Women's Organizing in
Postwar Bosnia-Herzegovina
Elissa Helms

50   CHAPTER 2
Failed Development and Rural Revolution in Nepal: Rethinking
Subaltern Consciousness and Women's Empowerment
Lauren Leve

93   CHAPTER 3
The State and Women's Empowerment in India: Paradoxes
and Politics
Aradhana Sharma

115   PART II   Postcolonial Neoliberalisms and the NGO Form

119   CHAPTER 4
Global Civil Society and the Local Costs of Belonging:
Defining Violence against Women in Russia
Julie Hemment

143   CHAPTER 5

Resolving a Gendered Paradox: Women's Participation and
the NGO Boom in North India

Kathleen O'Reilly

166   CHAPTER 6

Power and Difference in Thai Women's NGO Activism

LeeRay M. Costa

193   CHAPTER 7

Demystifying Microcredit: The Grameen Bank, NGOs,
and Neoliberalism in Bangladesh

Lamia Karim

219   **PART III   Feminist Social Movements and NGOs**

221   CHAPTER 8

Feminist Bastards: Toward a Posthumanist Critique
of NGOization

Saida Hodžić

248   CHAPTER 9

Lived Feminism(s) in Postcommunist Romania

Laura Grünberg

266   CHAPTER 10

Women's Advocacy Networks: The European Union,
Women's NGOs, and the Velvet Triangle

Sabine Lang

285   CHAPTER 11

Beyond NGOization? Reflections from Latin America

Sonia E. Alvarez

301   CONCLUSION

Feminisms and the NGO Form

Victoria Bernal and Inderpal Grewal

311   BIBLIOGRAPHY

353   CONTRIBUTORS

357   INDEX

ACKNOWLEDGMENTS

When we began this project, we did not realize how long it would take us to get from start to finish, from a collaborative interest in how nongovernmental organizations (NGOs) were changing the nature of feminist organizing globally to an anthology that ended up reflecting on an already established new feminist landscape. In this process we benefited from the work of those who are included in this collection, and that of other scholars who contributed to our thinking on the topic. We read the work of, spoke to, and participated in conferences with many excellent feminist researchers who, along with us, have been thinking about the path that feminism has taken over the last couple of decades. There is a community of feminist scholars within the academy and outside it, and their writings on NGOs have changed the way we look at activism and feminism. Simultaneously they have enabled us to think about the state and civil society, and thus about culture and politics in the twenty-first century. This collection is part of the ongoing conversation in that community.

This project has benefited from the support and participation of numerous institutions, individuals, and groups. We would like to thank the Rockefeller Foundation for funding our Team Project on "Democratizing Women: NGOs, Empowerment, and Marginalization in the 21st Century," at the Bellagio Center in Italy in August 2004. Our conversations there with some superb participants—including Ambra Pirri, Surina Khan, Lamia Karim, Barbara Einhorn, Sabine Lang, Adetoun Ilumoka, Amina Jamal, and Mary John—raised important questions that are reflected in this anthology. We are also grateful both to the Humanities Research Institute of the University of California and its director, David Theo Goldberg, for supporting the Conference on Global Circuits of Feminism that we organized at the University of California, Irvine (UCI), in May 2004 and to the scholars who participated: Susan Coutin, Boatema Boateng, Angelica DeAngelis, Pheng Cheah, Maureen Mahon, Teresa Caldeira, Lisa Parks, Sabine Lang, Lamia Karim, and Denise Brennan. A grant we received from UCI's Computer and Library Collaborative Research initiative supported our collaborative research and enabled us to make further progress on this project. We received valuable research assistance from Caroline Melly at UCI and from Sarah Haley and Tina Palivos at Yale University. We extend our deep thanks to all of the contributors to the volume, whose unflagging enthusiasm for the project encouraged us, and whose patience and willingness to make changes up to the eleventh hour were crucial to its success. Thanks also to Ken Wissoker and Jade Brooks at Duke University Press, and several anonymous reviewers at the press for their interest in our project and their valuable comments on early drafts.

Individually, Victoria would most like to thank Inderpal for a wonderful collaboration. The high points of intellectual synergy were exhilarating, and the inevitable obstacles and frustrations that are part of any project were less daunting because we confronted them together. Our project was in its own way a form of feminist collaboration that involved working across disciplinary boundaries and areas of expertise, as well as across the country, from California to Connecticut. I would like to thank the Wenner-Gren Foundation for Anthropological Research and the Fulbright Foundation for supporting a year of fieldwork on NGOs, women's political activism, and donors in Tanzania. Although that research is not explicitly included here, it played an important part in shaping the contours of this anthology. I also thank the Humanities Research Institute of the University of California for supporting and hosting the quarter-long resident research group I convened in spring 2004 on "Global Circuits of Feminism." In that group Inderpal and I first began to explore our interests in the NGO form and feminism. I wish to thank the past and present members of the Women's Studies Department at UCI for the reading groups, speakers, key word events, and many conversations that have sustained and challenged me as a feminist scholar over the course of this project. I also thank my colleagues in the Anthropology Department, and my students, particularly Natalie Newton (now Dr. Newton) and Padma Govindan for our critical discussions of gender and NGOs in Vietnam and India.

Inderpal would like to thank colleagues and staff at both UCI, where this project began and took shape, and Yale University, from where it finally went to press. My thanks also go to Victoria for a collaboration that has been invigorating, generative, and also part of a wonderful friendship. We shared theories about the state, comparisons between NGOs in Africa and South Asia, ideas about diasporas, and debates about feminism—as well as discussions about daughters and college admissions. Victoria and her family became part of the wonderful years I spent at Irvine. She was also a member of the Department of Anthropology, where I found a welcoming second academic home, and where so many other colleagues (Bill Maurer, Mei Zhang, Karen Leonard, Tom Boellstorff, and Susan Coutin), encouraged and supported our project. I am also grateful to the Women's Studies Department at Irvine, where my colleagues Laura Kang and Jennifer Terry shared research, theories, and service duties with me to make this project possible. Colleagues at campuses of the University of California and California State University have nurtured and supported this project through many years; Caren Kaplan and Minoo Moallem have wondered when the anthology would be done. My thanks also to the Women's Gender and Sexuality Studies Program at Yale for its support. Yale's Program on Nonprofit Organizations invited me to present my NGO research in India— which, though unpublished, has contributed to the introduction in numerous ways—and the provost's office's sabbatical leave enabled me to complete my contributions to the anthology. Finally, I thank two organizations for teaching me about nonprofit organizations: the Asian Women's Shelter in San Francisco and Narika in Berkeley, where I learned about the possibilities and the limits of states and NGOs.

The editors and publishers would like to thank the following for permission to use copyrighted material:

Chapter 2: Lauren Leve, "Failed Development and Rural Revolution in Nepal: Rethinking Subaltern Consciousness and Women's Empowerment," *Anthropology Quarterly* 80, no. 1 (2007): 121–72.

Chapter 3: Aradhana Sharma, "The State and Women's Empowerment in India: Paradoxes and Politics," is reproduced by permission of the

American Anthropological Association from "Crossbreeding Institutions, Breeding Struggle: Women's Empowerment, Neoliberal Governmentality, and State (Re)Formation in India" in *Cultural Anthropology* 21, no. 1 (2006): 60–95. Not for sale or further reproduction.

Chapter 4: Julie Hemment, "Global Civil Society and the Local Costs of Belonging: Defining Violence against Women in Russia," *Signs*, 29, no. 3 (2004): 815–40.

Chapter 5: Kathleen O'Reilly, "Resolving a Gendered Paradox: Women's Participation and the NGO Boom in North India," *Annals of the Association of American Geographers* 97, no. 3 (2007): 613–34, reprinted by permission of Taylor & Francis (http://www.tandfonline.com).

Chapter 7: Lamia Karim, "Demystifying Micro-Credit: The Grameen Bank, NGOs, and Neoliberalism in Bangladesh," *Cultural Dynamics* 20, no. 1 (2008): 5–29, © 2008 SAGE Publications. Reprinted by permission of SAGE.

Chapter 11: Sonia Alvarez, "Beyond NGOization? Reflections from Latin America," *Development* 52, no. 2 (2009): 175–84.

Victoria Bernal and Inderpal Grewal

The NGO Form
Feminist Struggles, States, and Neoliberalism

In 2012, as we write this introduction, nongovernmental organizations (NGOs) have become normalized as key players in national
and global politics. These organizations are now well established
as an institutional form around the globe, especially in relation
to questions of women's welfare and empowerment. The "NGO
boom," as Sonia Alvarez (whose work is included here) calls it,
has been achieved (Alvarez 1999). By 2000 it was estimated that
NGOs were disbursing between twelve and fifteen billion dollars
per year (Edwards and Fowler 2002). By 2010, in some parts of the
world, the NGO sector had become more powerful than the state
itself.[1] Yet NGOs remain poorly understood despite their ubiquity,
or perhaps partly because of their rapid proliferation and diversi-
fication. However, they have created a track record over the last
three decades, and this record as well as the need to move beyond the celebratory perspective on NGOs that characterized the
1980s and 1990s has led to a more probing analytical stance. This
anthology explores what is distinctive about NGOs, and how and
with what consequences they have come to be so strongly associated with women and feminist issues.

Today feminism as a social movement seems less visible than
the plethora of NGOs addressing gender issues and women's welfare. Scholars such as Sabine Lang (also a contributor to this volume) used the phrase "the NGOization of feminism" to describe
this development (Lang 1997). As a response to these changes,
a body of feminist research has emerged that interrogates the

nature and functioning of NGOs, as well as the impact of their emergence on nations and states, feminisms, and ongoing processes and institutions that produce gender. This collection brings together feminist research concerned with global and local configurations of power and inequality to explore the relationship between feminist concerns and NGOs. The research examines NGOs that are organized by or for women and that seek to address some aspects of the welfare of women, and it aims to understand both the variety of these organizations as well as their relation to states, markets, and feminist movements in the current phase of globalization.

Clearly, the NGO is no longer seen as the panacea that it once was thought to be, yet the number and scope of NGOs—and other organizations that call themselves NGOs—continue to grow. NGOs have proliferated, some emerging from long-standing institutions (churches, for instance) and some from new social movements, corporate enterprises, or new needs (for example, NGOs focusing on global warming or other environmental issues). NGOs can be conservative or progressive, from leftist or rightist political positions. In short, it seems as if every agenda and political project has a corresponding NGO, and this diversity has complicated theorizing about NGOs as a unified field of power. Given the diversity of NGOs and the contexts in which they operate, this collection brings together a range of disciplines, research approaches, and regional expertise. The essays show the variety of NGOs that target women as well as the diversity of feminist research approaches and theoretical perspectives. We know by now that women all over the world have become prime targets of neoliberal restructuring and development. The essays collected here take that context into account but also demonstrate powerfully that neoliberalism can look very different across the world, and that neoliberal conditions do not dictate everything that an NGO does or practices. Like capitalism, neoliberalism has not eliminated all the desires and projects that might be associated with goals of social justice, equality, and democracy that can be imagined outside of its capitalist and consumer-oriented framework. Feminist struggles may be altered, but they continue to proliferate—shaped by, but not completely governed by, states, neoliberalism, and the rise of NGOs.

The contributors to this volume all work from a feminist perspective and are concerned with contemporary conditions and contexts, but they take a variety of approaches: some draw on personal experience in NGOs; some take a regional perspective, some a national one, and some conduct a fine-grained analysis of a single organization. The collection spans the range of issues with which NGOs are engaged, from microcredit to domestic violence, and explores contexts of postwar and postsocialist societies, as well as ethnic, religious, class, and rural-urban differences.

Although many of the studies focus on a particular region, country, or nation, many also address the issue of North-South relations—or, in the case of Eastern Europe, East-West histories—seeking to understand how NGOs from less powerful regions come to network with those from more powerful ones as well as how, in these transnational contexts, the state or multiple states involved provide or restrict NGOs' access to resources. Some of the research pursued here seeks to understand the impact of the search for resources on NGOs' agendas, on power differentials within and between NGOs, on the language they use to express the problems they are hoping to alleviate, and on their organizational structures. The essays suggest the relevance of specific contexts of historical and contemporary projects of colonialism and empire, geopolitical asymmetries, and old and new nationalisms that are deeply intertwined with feminist movements and with women as subjects and objects of development. Consequently, all of the essays in this collection, whether overtly or not, work in this larger framework, in which multiple states and suprastate organizations such as the United Nations intersect with particular national and local contexts.

In this introductory essay, we argue that some of the diverse perspectives and controversies surrounding NGOs—seen, for example, as agents of neoliberalism, grassroots alternatives to the state, parts of local civil society, or too tied to transnational organizations—arise from the diversity of what can be encompassed under the rubric "NGO." We develop an analysis of the NGO form that explains how such contradictory political projects can be brought under the same label, and we argue that the definition of what constitutes an NGO is profoundly gendered. An understanding of NGOs as gendered can account for the engagement of feminists and other women with and by NGOs. But before we turn to an analysis of the NGO form and the relationship between feminism and NGOs, we examine some of the key scholarship and ongoing debates about NGOs that inform our analyses and those of our contributors. It should be noted, however, that a great deal of the scholarship on NGOs pays little theoretical attention to questions of gender, and that omission provided part of the impetus for this anthology.

The scholarship on NGOs remains divided. A large body of literature has emerged that sees NGOs as providing an improved way to deliver development (Fowler 1991; Mehra 1997; Bhatia 2000; J. Fisher 2003), as vehicles that allow grassroots organizations to voice their concerns, as the organized form of social movements, and as having the ability to "empower communities and to build social capital in civil society" (Kudva 2005, 234). For some scholars, NGOs are civil society organizations that emerge in opposition to the state and provide important checks to state power (Bratton 1989; Clarke 1998). Others contend that NGOs are best understood as agents or consequences of neoliberalism, expanding globalization processes (Schuller 2007), reducing local power (Feldman 1997), and forming part of a "contemporary neoliberal aid regime" (Schuller 2009, 84).

Much of the recent literature provides more critical and contextual understandings of the relation between NGOs and development (Mercer 2002), including those by scholars who view NGOs as a form of neoliberal cooptation (Kamat 2004) and by others who locate NGOs within transnational circuits of neoliberal power (Grewal 2005). Some current scholarship, such as a special issue of *PoLAR* (*PoLAR* 2010), looks at NGOs as they are caught up in relations with funding sources, governments, and neoliberal processes that create a double bind for NGOs, situated between the powerful forces dominating them and the disenfranchised communities they intend to serve.

Debates about the impact of NGOs on states follows neoliberalism and globalization discussions in which some argue that NGOs may strengthen states while others contend that they weaken states. Those in the former group cite NGOs' contributions to stronger civil society, while those in the latter group maintain that NGOs weaken states by allowing outside influence in a country or by reducing states' sovereign power over citizens. Even within the latter line of argument, there are different approaches. Some suggest that NGOs are agents of neoliberalism or imperialism (Funk 2006; Kamat 2004; Hearn 2007) and that they undermine states' sovereignty by weakening the social contract between states and citizens. Yet others suggest that it is in the accounting practices and entrepreneurial strategies adopted by NGOs, rather than in the weakening of the state, that we see a move into neoliberalism. For instance, a number of scholars have drawn attention to the ways NGOs are marketized, engaging in entrepreneurial strategies to compete for funding (Feldman 1997; Paley 2001; Elyachar 2002).

The theorizing around NGOs is thus deeply tied to theories of the state, globalization, and neoliberalism. Scholars seem divided between classical liberal theory and more poststructuralist ideas of the state. For example, theorizations using the former make a clear distinction between private and public, civil society and state, with boundaries between the nation-state and what is outside it. Liberal scholars argue for NGOs as "transnational civil society" (Batliwala and Brown 2006, 2), as a "new paradigm of civil society" (Stromquist 2002), or as a "sub-species of civil society organization" (Eade 2000, 12). Habermasian theories of the "public sphere" also fall into this category of theorizations, suggesting that NGOs are separated from the state. According to such theories, NGOs lie within the private sphere that is separate from the state, and feminist NGOs are seen as potentially oppositional to the state.

In contrast, a poststructuralist approach to the state relies on contested state boundaries, transnational connections forged through the globalization of finance and corporations, ambiguous and dynamic constructions of public and private, and a more Foucauldian idea of governmentality that sees continuities between the state and civil society. Here there is a focus on the everyday practices of NGOs, their strategies of rule and expertise, and struggles both within them and between staff, donors, and clients. This allows a focus on the professionalization that takes place in NGOs and on the production of entrepreneurial subjects within capitalist ideologies, even in the nonprofit sector. It may also make visible the unintended effects of NGOs. As Lauren Leve shows in this volume, such uncertainties mean that NGOs should be understood in light not only of their own ostensible goals, but also of the kinds of subjects they produce.

Scholars have attempted to understand NGOs through a variety of approaches, some through classifying their target populations and others through the nature of their relationship with the state; their mode of organization, degree of professionalization, and/or scale; their resources and relations with donors; their specific goals; or their ideology or political economy. Clearly the question of resources plays a role in NGOs' goals, practices, and strategies. Thus the research tells us that some NGOs are local, remaining steadfast in connecting to local resources and setting their own agendas, and to their resource base, thus suggesting authenticity and allegiance to grassroots or local goals and a resistance to institutionalization. Other research may show that NGOs can become vehicles used to accomplish goals for established authorities or to pursue agendas determined by donors and other powerful institutions, rather than agendas driven by feminist activism (Silliman 1999). Many NGOs have become transnational, linking themselves to international donors or professional networks and receiving not only resources but also agendas, practices, and discourses through these mainly European and American foundations (Aksartova 2009). Research on funding and resource strategies reveals great diversity, from the blatant example in Mexico where political candidates create NGOs "whose sole purpose was to purchase goodwill and name recognition" (Richard 2009, 176) to the intermediary type of organization that serves to mediate among different scales and institutions (Schuller 2009; Richard 2009). These NGOs negotiate between agendas, concerns, and local and translocal institutions and languages.

The scholarly feminist work on NGOs collected here reveals the fluidity between the supposedly separate domains of state and society. Public and private partnerships have come into existence even as states have increasingly incorporated transnational and neoliberal governmentalities. Initial ideas that feminist NGOs stood outside of and in opposition to the state are no longer tenable. Some NGOs have enabled feminist advocacy and activism, while others have professionalized feminist agendas in collaboration with states and corporate-style bureaucracies. These alterations have occurred in tandem with changes in governmentalities and geopolitics within and between states since the 1980s as transnational corporations, humanitarian aid networks, and structural adjustment programs became increasingly powerful in the new economic order of neoliberal policies adopted by the US and European states (Williamson 1989).

For us, the key question is not to debate the pros and cons of NGOs or to perform policy-oriented assessments of their accomplishments, though readers interested in those issues will certainly find our collection informative. Rather, we explore the nature of the NGO as a form of organizing, how NGOs have altered relations between feminisms and the state, and the ways NGOs are contributing to new constructions of gender and changing relations among women as well as between women and men.

The NGO Form

Since NGOs are diverse and heterogeneous, even if they share a focus on women or gender, what is important to note is how NGOs have nonetheless come to be seen as a unified phenomenon. NGOs seem present in every country and associated with every social issue and political debate. NGOs of varying types now make up a large share of the organizations and bodies undertaking welfare and empowerment work among women. However, despite their variety, NGOs are often understood as an alternative to the state as well as to corporations, taking the place of the state in the work on development and welfare, and providing services free or at much lower costs than private businesses (Richard 2009). NGOs seem to be a unified domain, crucially in terms of their distinction from the state and the market. Moreover, many NGOs work to maintain this distinction as a central feature of their institutional identities, even as they develop state-like and/or corporate aspects and influences. This is true especially in the so-called developing world and the global South. Even in more developed contexts and the global North, we find that much welfare work is understood as the domain of NGOs. In the United States, for instance, such organizations were often called nonprofit organizations and thus were positioned in relation and opposition to the private corporate sector. Increasingly, however, they are now understood and designated as NGOs, a label that highlights their distinction from the state rather than from market-driven organizations.

We contend that the term "NGO" has come to make sense through an articulation of a negative form: it is defined by something that it is not—in other words, it is assumed to be not the state. Yet this negative form means that the term has a capaciousness that may be responsible for its popularity and widespread usage globally. This umbrella term covers over many differences among NGOs so that all kinds of organizations can be brought together under one label; those practicing more conservative and regressive politics can exist under the same label as their political opponents. The negative form of the NGO has the capacity to encompass many different political projects. The negative aspect of the form—that which is not the government—comes to be normative, and it supports a clear divide between public and private realms of power that is consistent with models of the normative liberal state. The NGO, therefore, obscures the contingent nature of such domains of struggle.

Thus NGOs may even help produce the state, through what Timothy Mitchell (1999) has called their "state effect." They make the state visible by emphasizing that they are not the state, even as forms of governmentality proliferate within them. For instance, the Indian government has a set of rules and regulations for NGOs, which have to register with the government even as it continues to subcontract out welfare and other projects to them. Thus, although the distinction between state and NGO disappears in relation to many state projects, the construct of NGOs as a separate sector is kept alive.

One important contradiction masked by the broad umbrella term is that despite the diversity of states, markets, and institutions through which NGOs come to be legible as different, NGOs are not separate from the state or from markets. The designations "nonprofit" and "nongovernmental" should be taken instead as pointing to complex relationships that need to be investigated and analyzed. Such relationships are complex not simply because of the diversity of NGOs or states, but also because NGOs exist in a geopolitical context of the knowledge and power frameworks of the expanding modern West. This context includes new and old networks of finance, communication, and knowledge that take for granted and promote assumptions about the nature of states, markets, and civil society, as well as other issues such as gender relations.

The United Nations conferences on women made visible the gaps between women's lives and the official representation of women. Particularly at the Beijing conference, the NGO emerged as a feminist form for representing women's interests that were not or could not be easily contained or represented through official logics or institutional frameworks. NGOs served to include as well as to manage powerful nonofficial representations. But their very name—"nongovernmental organization"—gave NGOs a kind of official, yet simultaneously nonofficial, status. The NGO, thus, came to exist in continuity with the state. We argue that the NGO form produces and converts what is outside the state into a legible form within a governmentality that parallels official state power. In this way the NGO form, somewhat paradoxically, derives power from working with the biopolitical logics of the state. Moving across what is included and excluded by the state also makes the NGO form key to neoliberal projects of privatization and state withdrawal.

These politics of official and unofficial exclusions and inclusions are profoundly gendered through divisions between public and private and through the powerful circulation of liberal democracy, which is assumed to have social and sexual contracts that define women in terms of the private sphere and as subordinate political subjects. The notion of the liberal state, as it has been globalized, assumes that such a private sphere exists everywhere and that the division between public and private is central to liberalism and also gendered. In such a context, the NGO (defined by its lack of official status and its position as outside the state) politicizes and globalizes the private as an organized entity, but also as a private entity that is not a profit-making enterprise. Since women are generally underrepresented in official positions and in the public political space, the NGO thus becomes a recognizable platform from which to make claims by and for women, and to legitimately represent them. NGOs are powerful in part because they are a recognized form of public engagement that is legible to states, donors, other NGOs, and wider publics. This recognition of the NGO form is significant given that the variation among NGOs is actually so great.

The label "nongovernmental organization" is not simply vague, it is often deceptive. If the main distinguishing characteristic of NGOs was their independence from government, then many NGOs would fall outside that designation because they are not so much separate from or dependent on states as they are entwined with states. In some settings, NGOs have become so associated with the state and with established power that some groups no longer want to be labeled as NGOs, a name now seen as tainted with the same elitism as the state. The members of one long-established NGO in India were emphatic in telling us that their group was a "civil society organization" and not an NGO. As the studies included here demonstrate, the fact that NGOs may become so intertwined with the state that their ideology and practice become less radical is a profound concern, but the integration of NGOs into the power structure is also an achievement that underlines the character of the form—which gains traction from its ability to move across borders and institutional boundaries.

Even where NGOs may seem to be separate from the state in which they are located and where they operate, they may not be separate from the states that serve as donors. It may be that some NGOs are connected to multiple states—near and distant—and that these state interests may converge or diverge. New terms have been developed to indicate government involvement, but they are either oxymoronic—government-organized, nongovernmental organization (GONGO)—or unclear. An international nongovernmental organization (INGO) could be related to a distant state, foundation, or the United Nations. Instead of new labels, what is needed is a way to categorize different types of NGOs. Our analysis of the NGO form makes sense of the ubiquity of the term and its circulation in different parts of the world.

Clearly the appeal of NGOs extends beyond women and those concerned with feminist issues. But the gendering of politics and the constructions of public and private spheres give the NGO form a particular resonance with feminism. The fact that the NGO can move across the boundaries between insider and outsider, official and unofficial, or public and private explains both the proliferation of NGOs concerned with gender issues and liberal feminist investments in the form. The state-like and state-linked, yet nonstate, form of the NGO has particular synergies with neoliberal discourses and policies. Neoliberalization fosters feminist NGOs on two levels: first, the withdrawal of state and public resources from welfare sectors creates a gap that NGOs seek to fill, taking on public roles from private positions and second, those spaces of state withdrawal were often already sites of women's paid and unpaid labor and feminist struggles for resources and services.

It is significant in this neoliberal moment to consider that the NGO is not radical in its form—which is separate from the question of whether any particular NGO is radical in its agenda or organization. Because the NGO form mimics bureaucratic state forms, NGOs are easily embraced by donors and states. Many international state or corporate donors easily switched from channeling their funds through states to channeling them through NGOs, and in that process furthered the state-like aspect of NGOs through bureaucratic accounting, reporting, and administrative requirements. Although the rationale for the shift of donor funds from states to NGOs is often framed in terms of how different NGOs are from states, we argue that it is actually their similarity that partly accounts for the ease and enthusiasm for this huge shift. NGOs appear far less threatening than mass movements, and part of their appeal to donors and states comes from the way the NGO form seems separate from the state even as it is a site of governmentality.

Partly as a result of these processes, NGOs are well ensconced within development regimes and programs of social welfare; they are not going away, and neither are neoliberal articulations of productivity, entrepreneurship, and empowerment. Also important to the rise of NGOs is the assumption that they are less hierarchical, more democratic, more devoted to welfare and to serving subordinate or minority populations, and more cost-effective than states. NGOs themselves often rely on discourses of connection to grassroots movements, efficiency of resource use, and representation of women's groups and issues. However, NGOs' disavowal of ties to states often is not borne out in their everyday practices or agendas. Their relations with states are often contentious but also dependent in many ways. Inderpal Grewal has argued that NGOs reveal that feminism has become neoliberal in both the global North and South, and that such neoliberalism has become the condition of possibility for most NGO work (Grewal 2005). Even in countries such as the United States, NGOs are part of the privatization of social work that neoliberal governments have enabled, and in other parts of the world—especially in what are called "failed states" and those that are seen as corrupt—NGOs may be the only source of welfare possible in an era of government cutbacks.

Although feminist work may become institutionalized within NGOs and is often bureaucratized within development and empowerment frameworks promoted by states and international bodies, many NGOs are working to address these problems and to maintain close ties to more progressive and movement agendas. In Tanzania we found that NGOs formed coalitions to communicate and collaborate so as to counteract the influence of donor states and foundations and the competition for funds that pit progressive NGOs against each other. Theory and practice, in some NGOs, are not separated. At the same time, it is now clear that feminist research does not support many of the claims that NGOs are more productive, more effective, and closer to grassroots movements than are states. Nonetheless, given the dominance of neoliberal policies and the fact that many states are not eager to take on social welfare burdens, the NGO form is now a well-established element of the political landscape that itself is shaping the conditions of feminist struggles.

Feminism and NGOs

The rapid global expansion of NGOs over the past two decades has profoundly changed the conditions and context of feminist activism. Many researchers have pointed out that by the end of the twentieth century, feminist activism had shifted from participation in political movements to advocacy and action in feminist and women's NGOs (Lang 1997; Alvarez 1999; Bernal 2000; Halley 2006). In the process, NGOs have participated in changing what we mean by "civil society" and "the state" and have altered the terms of feminists' engagement with states. NGOs themselves are sites of feminist struggles as they promote various constructs of "women" and as their activities produce new categories of women.

In terms of feminist struggles, NGOs' connection to women and development was catalyzed by the UN conferences on women held in Mexico City, Nairobi, and Beijing. NGOs came to world attention and to the forefront of feminist activism starting with preparations leading up to the World Conference on Women in Beijing (Timothy 2004). Feminist scholars understood the spectacle of women creating their own networks and forums outside of official institutions as heralding a new era of grassroots organizing and empowerment. NGOs emerged as a promising form of organization and a vehicle of development for an array of groups and causes.

Over the following decade such hopes were expressed by diverse scholars, activists, and organizations, as well as by development experts and international agencies (W. Fisher 1997; Appadurai 2002; Edwards and Fowler 2002).

These UN conferences explicitly included nongovernmental conferences alongside the governmental ones (Joachim 2002; Zhang 2009), so that the term "nongovernmental" became prominent for feminist activism internationally. Certainly NGOs existed prior to these landmark conferences. However, the significance of women's organizing outside of what was defined as official or governmental delegations at those conferences brought the NGO to the world stage as a form of feminist organizing. Prior to these conferences, women collectively were largely absent from official state delegations, and they perceived themselves to be excluded from state treaty making. The NGO forums at these conferences, despite the terminology of "nongovernmental," led not only to the treaties and Agreements (such as the Convention on the Elimination of All Forms of Discrimination against Women or the UN Millennium Development Goals) but also to the hope and the possibility that such goals would be carried out by the work of small organizations, so-called grassroots activists, and local feminist and women's movements (Dunlop, Macdonald, and Kyte 1996)— often with the help and support of transnational organizations.

The NGO movement in the 1980s and 1990s also heralded a more transnational turn in feminist activism, propelled by the international nature and agendas of the UN conferences, the new phase of globalization, and the emergence of technologies that made collaborations across borders easier to sustain. Margaret Keck and Kathyrn Sikkink have argued that transnational advocacy networks "helped instigate and sustain the change between 1968 and 1993" in the expansion of human rights within feminist activism (1998, ix). Despite such an expansion of and diversity in national, regional, and local projects undertaken by NGOs, many researchers point out that the kinds of issues that they have taken up have been limited. Keck and Sikkink state that by the 1990s approximately "half of all international nongovernmental social change organizations work[ed] on . . . three issues": women's rights, human rights, and the environment (1999, ix). Sally Engle Merry suggests that the activities of NGOs and the United Nations have focused on human rights and together may be seen as an international civil society" (Merry 2001). Amrita Basu argues that though women's transnational NGOs have proliferated, the results of their work are not that diverse—for example, they have been less successful in arguing for economic rights and more successful in campaigns against sexual violence (Basu 2000).

Everyday politics of NGOs may be simultaneously local, national, and transnational. Feminist activism may be inspired by movements in other parts of the world, and new communication technologies may facilitate borrowings and commonalities, but also resistances. NGOs may be funded by international donors, but they engage with and are affected by local state practices as well. Hiring staff members and deciding on priorities and political strategies may also require engaging with both nearby and distant institutions, social and cultural projects, and agendas. Although some transnational NGOs that focus on women's issues may have limited agendas based on colonial ideologies, others—whether transnational or local—may be creative in working with these ideas or may modify them to engage with specific contexts and thereby change who counts as feminist and what can be understood as benefiting women.

In addition, over the last decades, new donor states and organizations, not just those from the West, have emerged to create agendas that may be distinct in some ways but similar in other ways to existing development and welfare issues that are understood to be pertinent to women as a global target of policy and development efforts. Current struggles in the Middle East have created new kinds of female subjects of revolutionary and postrevolutionary states, supported by Islamic NGOs that work in the community. It is not just US and European foundations and states that fund such work, but groups such as the Aga Khan Foundation and conservative Saudi petrodollars support these NGOs. Such NGOs have distinct ideas about women and feminism, especially with regard to what a gendered modernity may look like. Yet, like so many other global foundations, they also focus on women's health, education, microfinance, and development. Neoliberalism may thus create a recognizably homogeneous framework for contemporary NGOs working on women's issues, but it does not control all the practices and agendas of these organizations.

The diverse research in this volume, furthermore, suggests that distinctions between public and private, foreign and local, and state and NGO are often ambiguous and always contested. These boundaries are continually shifting and dynamic, and the authors of the chapters in this volume provide a number of reasons why feminist organizing continues to work—as well as engage critically—with neoliberalism.

Feminist movements within states and in organizations linked transnationally have led states themselves to claim that they are devoted to women and to development and gender equality. Development and women's empowerment, in many states, is now a state enterprise, sometimes done in collaboration with NGOs, as Aradhana Sharma shows in this volume. NGOs may be subcontractors for development, with benefits accruing to the state through reduced salaries and pensions because of the differential between the costs of state employees and NGO employees. However, many of the NGOs discussed in this collection are a source of employment for women. Through NGO work, middle-class women gain access to national and international networks that expand their opportunities, skill sets, and outlooks, although NGO positions are often temporary and lack the pensions and other benefits that state employment provides.

The changing state-NGO relations produce changing feminist and female subjects. Goals of development have shifted to empowerment and capacity building, involving the production of new subjects. Feminist struggles are ongoing precisely because of these fluctuating lines between public and private, of which dynamic NGOs are both a product and a catalyst. States, too, are always challenged and changing. If at one point in Western feminist theorizing, socialist feminists argued for greater state involvement in women's welfare, the fall of the Berlin Wall that signaled the end of the socialist state in Europe was followed by the emergence of new female capitalist subjects, consumers, and entrepreneurs (Ghodsee 2004). The emergence of the European Union, with its own projects of so-called gender mainstreaming was designed, as Sabine Lang argues in this volume, to propel gender politics in particular directions while foreclosing others. Long-standing feminist issues still frame NGO work, especially in poverty alleviation and health and welfare, even as international migration, wars, environmental emergencies, and new forms of resource extraction alter how these issues are experienced and dealt with. Sexual politics of contraception and reproductive rights has also been a long-standing site of struggle, and so have racial politics, but changing populations within states are now creating new agendas in these areas for NGOs. Debates about veiling in Europe, for instance, have led to anti-racism efforts by NGOs. The production of new regulations over some groups of women shows that states' engagement with women's bodies is ongoing, contingent, and negotiable. NGOs also emerge and disappear, which suggests that they are subject to the demands of new activisms and political imperatives.

Many of the debates about states and NGOs overlook the power of the market and corporate interests with which NGOs must engage. The transnational corporation has emerged as another domain of private power that can challenge NGOs and the state, though it may also collaborate with them. Many large transnational corporations support NGOs through private foundations, so it is not surprising that the language of entrepreneurial capitalism has also entered the discourse of NGOs. Because both NGOs and corporations belong to the private domain and are supposedly separated from the state, they are sometimes seen as working in tandem to challenge or bypass state power. The Soros Foundation, for example, helped support the establishment of women's studies centers and feminist NGOs in countries in the former Soviet Union and Eastern Europe, establishing a presence in newly formed nation-states and newly capitalist countries. Some of these NGOs had overtly capitalist ideologies, supporting women's empowerment through producing subjects of consumption and capitalism. Julie Hemment's essay in this volume captures some of the complexities of transnational NGO politics in Russia.

Finally, social movements and emerging political projects mean that new NGOs may be created and old ones may have to alter their existing practices. In the process, there are shifts in the relations between states and NGOs and between transnational and local NGOs. For instance, the transnational politics of lesbian, gay, bisexual, and transgender movements has given rise to NGOs that struggle for sexual rights as human rights. These universal formulations are challenged by local organizations that are contesting social ideas of sexual difference and gender binaries. In the context in which women's rights is a long-standing language of NGO activism, the new frameworks of sexual rights change existing subjects and strategies of activism.

NGOs constantly negotiate with a dynamic state and multiple contexts as well as with traditional and new ideas about feminist struggles. Questions of social justice, critiques of heteronormativity and racist and colonial practices, and the current state of capitalist market democracies also help unsettle neoliberal power relations and constructions of gender. Thus, NGOs are simultaneously neoliberal entities and sites of struggle for feminists.

The Anthology

This collection contributes to the understanding of the nature and proliferation of NGOs and provides a nuanced and complex picture of the potentials and pitfalls of the concentration of feminist action and women's welfare work in NGOs in the twenty-first century. The essays collected here do not seek to provide a history of the NGOization of feminism, since that has already been discussed in a wide range of research that covers quite a few national and state contexts (Lang 1997; Alvarez 1999; Moghadam 2000; Poster and Salime 2002; Ferree and Tripp 2006; Dolhinow 2010). Instead, we take NGOization as the starting point from which to approach the changing relations of NGOs to the simultaneously changing nature of the state and to constructions of gender and feminism. The essays demonstrate the variety of histories of NGOs relating to particular national and regional differences and to the distinct temporalities and trajectories of the emergence of NGOs and their involvement in gender issues in different contexts.

The essays ask how activism within and through NGOs empowers and/or subjugates subaltern and nonsubaltern women, exploring the ways in which NGOs transcend or perpetuate North-South inequalities and how NGOs transform or reproduce divisions among women. The feminist analyses and theorizing offered here avoid simple assessments of best practices or verdicts of success or failure for NGOs. Rather, the essays demonstrate that the intersection of feminism and NGOs has yielded unexpected results, new collaborations, struggles, and conflicts.

The three parts of the anthology focus on different aspects of feminist mobilization and NGOs. The first section, "NGOs Beyond Success or Failure," sees NGOs as deliberately or inadvertently leading to new struggles. The second part, "Postcolonial Neoliberalisms and the NGO Form," examines NGOs in relation to inequalities of class, North-South relations, urban-rural divides, and other boundaries that marginalize some groups of women while other women may benefit. This scholarship also makes visible the neoliberal logics underlying the global proliferation of NGOs and the dynamics of NGOs' relations to states. We see not only feminist struggles with the state, but also new local and transnational partnerships—involving feminists, states, and corporations—that are emerging because neoliberal logics pervade state, NGO, and development ideologies. Our final section, "Feminist Social Movements and NGOs," looks at how, despite the imbrications of NGOs in neoliberal and corporate logics (analyzed in the previous section), feminist struggles and movements remain alive—or are reinvented and restored. Perhaps, as Saida Hodžić suggests, the present has produced nostalgia for a kind of feminism that may never have really existed.

All of the essays also bring to the fore feminist questions that are now being debated widely. Some of these questions are pertinent to gender and development, since in the last two to three decades NGOs have become key institutions for delivering development. Some of the questions are about the present condition and future of feminism itself—whether the NGOization of feminism has depoliticized feminist struggles. Other questions revolve around the tensions created by NGOs' use of corporate ideologies and organizational practices, as well as state-like forms of bureaucratic management, while seeking to change society and pursue issues of social justice. The essays examine the results of feminism in collaboration with neoliberalism, states of various kinds, and international institutions such as the United Nations and the World Bank. In bringing together these essays by feminist scholars and researchers working in disparate sites around the globe, we find that NGOs are part of the geopolitical order, producing new local and transnational partnerships and conflicts that are profoundly gendered. Moreover, we argue that NGOs are engaged in representing and producing "women" as a category, while also constructing new categories of women, such as "grassroots women" and "trafficked women." Through their work, NGOs are giving rise to new divisions among women, as some are professionalized through NGO work, others are engaged as beneficiaries, and still others may be excluded or unable to participate in NGO activities. Divisions and struggles among women should not be interpreted as a failure of feminism, however, because "women" never were a homogeneous category. Feminist struggles are also struggles among differently positioned and differently subjectified women, whether in the North and the South or in urban and rural areas (as LeeRay Costa's essay shows).

The volume builds on, among other things, the exciting interdisciplinary body of work that has explored postcolonial feminisms in relation to nationalism (Alexander and Mohanty 1997; Badran 1996; Bernal, 2000; Kaplan, Alarcon, and Moallem 1999; McClintock, Mufti, and Shohat 1997; Rofel 1999; Williams 1996; Yang 1999). By asking questions regarding women's participation, activism, or empowerment, the authors included here explore crucial questions about the North-South dimensions of transnational feminist practices. Their research on NGOs provides evidence of the nature of political activism and the ideas, practices, discourses, and agendas of feminists working in NGOs. These dynamics can be understood only when viewed in the larger context of social movements, state formation, national institutions, and international bodies. The anthology takes up questions of identity, difference, the gendering of space, belonging versus exclusion, imagined communities, the naturalization of power, and the gendering of modernity and explores them in relation to contemporary feminism and the global significance of NGOs.

Notes

1. Institute for Security Studies, "NGO's and Their Quest for Legitimacy in Africa," April 8, 2010, accessed July 4, 2011, http://reliefweb.int/node/350810.

PART I   NGOs Beyond Success or Failure

The essays in Part I draw particular attention to the dynamic relations among NGOs, civil society, states, and social movements. The research demonstrates that the intersection of NGOs and feminism has surprising and diverse effects. We begin with an essay by Elissa Helms, for whom the relation between the state, feminist movements, and NGOs is rather different from what we have come to expect from much feminist research. Helms shows that NGOs may produce feminist movements instead of the other way around, thereby turning on its head the thesis that NGOs have debilitated feminist movements. Drawing on more than a decade of research in Bosnia-Herzegovina since the recent war, Helms finds that NGOs there are becoming like movements. In other words, there is a movementization of NGOs rather than an NGOization of feminism in this region. Helms's research suggests that there can be no simple linear movement that represents developments in the NGO form or its relation to various feminisms.

Lauren Leve's essay on NGOs in Nepal offers another example of the diverse and unexpected effects of NGO activities. Leve's research shows that NGOs working on education have produced revolutionary consciousness among women, who end up as Maoists, rather than the docile, capitalist subjects they were expected to become. This result cannot easily be viewed as a success or a failure of the NGO project. Examining rural women's participation and support of Maoist movements in Nepal, Leve finds that theories of resistance or empowerment often presume a particular, autonomous subject; in this case, the "Nepali woman." This

"Nepali woman" is seen through a development framework whose definitions of success and failure underlie scholarly understandings of women's participation. Leve argues that what happens to the NGO project and women's responses to it must be analyzed in relation to the specific context, culture, and historical moment. The outcomes of a project may not be contained within a "success or failure" accounting of a particular NGO, or even within a "feminist movement" narrative. As in the case Leve describes, the liberal assumptions of the NGO about women and participation may unwittingly spark more revolutionary actions by women, going beyond the project to address larger questions of social justice.

Aradhana Sharma's research in rural India explores the practices of a GONGO, the Mahila Samakhya project. Sharma discovers that this state-NGO coalition provides spaces of possibility for women to address some local problems, but it also replicates and reinforces social hierarchies. Sharma's research suggests that such partnerships are now an ongoing part of the neoliberal state as the state collaborates with NGOs to work on welfare and women's issues. NGO staff may either use this partnership or disavow it, depending on their agendas and goals, and this flexibility becomes part of how the state and NGOs operate. Sharma's examination of the goal of empowerment of women also reveals how difficult it is to settle the question of whether the Mahila Samakhya program is a success or a failure. It employs women, pushes the state to address the needs of women, and achieves some goals, but is unable to make progress in other areas. Ultimately, she argues, women's NGOs are engaged in constant struggle with the state even as they work with it, since many NGO goals and principles run counter to those of the patriarchal and masculinist state.

The Movementization of NGOs? Women's Organizing in Postwar Bosnia-Herzegovina

Bosnia's NGO Boom

During the first few years after the 1992–95 Bosnian war, nongovernmental organizations (NGOs) were "springing up like mushrooms after the rain," as it seemed to one women's organization leader in the town of Zenica, Bosnia-Herzegovina (BiH).[1] Cynical urbanites joked that any old nobody who could gather the signatures of twenty-nine of their relatives and friends (the law then required that number of signatures) could become an NGO. Indeed, although many NGOs were local spin-offs of international NGOs with professionalized staff members, there were also many groups of purely local origin. The latter were often a clutch of friends or even just one active person who registered as an NGO in the hope of garnering funding from one of the foreign and transnational donor agencies that had descended on BiH during and especially after the war. Some of these groups were the remnants of socialist-era community clubs, others had started out doing relief work during the war, and still others were forming for the first time. In a manner reminiscent of a cargo cult, people all over BiH set up NGOs hoping that the donations would come pouring in: if we build it, they will come![2] A large proportion of these organizations were women's NGOs.

Much of the hope generated around NGOs was in response to donors and foreign intervention agencies in charge of postwar reconstruction. These actors forcefully encouraged the formation of more and more NGOs that, when they appeared, were touted as evidence of the growth of civil society and ultimately democracy (Sampson 2003; Stubbs 2007). Feminist observers, citing the great numbers of women's NGOs, marveled at the extent of the Bosnian "women's movement." But there were NGOs and there were NGOs: the use of a single label masked the organizations' varying forms; motivations; conceptualizations; and engagements with communities, donors, and the state. It also hid the differing expectations of donors buried in their calls for BiH to build civil society, fight ethnonationalism, democratize, or simply "join Europe." Moreover, the terms "women's NGO" and "women's issues" were applied to, and understood as referring to, a wide range of stances and activities, from self-described feminists critical of established gender norms to those who promoted a return to traditional women's roles in the patriarchal family—as well as everything in between. Added to this variety were the many different ways in which the new rhetoric and practices were accommodated into existing society.

This essay traces the trajectory of women's organizing in BiH since the end of the war, exploring the disconnects and convergences between the discourses and practices of donors and of local women's NGOs. I unpack assumptions about women's activism and NGO work, historical patterns and the legacies of socialism, and relationships among NGOs, civil society, and the state. Instead of, or in addition to, what scholars working in other parts of the world describe as the NGOization of feminism (Alvarez 1999; Lang 1997; Silliman 1999), I argue that BiH has experienced what might be called a movementization of NGOs, although not in absolute terms. This does not mean that the negative effects of NGOization have not been strongly felt in BiH, but that more positive effects from a feminist perspective can also be identified. Like Aradhana Sharma in her work on an NGO program to empower poor women in India, I do not aim to negate existing criticisms but to "ethnographically tease out the tensions, contradictions, redefinitions, and, indeed, suppressions" (2008, xxiv) of NGO work from a feminist perspective. Although emphasis on the NGO model in BiH could be said to have impeded work toward social change in many ways, the conditions of NGO promotion—foreign intervention and the involvement of democratization and development donors—ultimately facilitated what we might now call a nascent feminist scene.

Writing about these groups is difficult to do without using the very concepts that I argue need to be scrutinized. First, because of the range of forms taken by NGOs (Klees 1998; Martens 2002), it needs to be made clear that I refer to local organizations rather than the foreign and transnational organizations also called NGOs that were perceived more in this context as donors and representatives of the international community than as local actors. This is not to say that foreign NGOs were not also participants in local processes, but to point out that they were not often referred to in these terms: usually "NGOs" referred just to local groups.[3] Second, although foreign donors and intervention agencies tended to label any independent group as an NGO and every group of women a women's NGO, everyday understandings of community engagement, organized groups, donors, and gender underpinned a more complex set of categories used to describe what groups called women's NGOs were doing. I thus argue for a more precise use of terminology, including the concepts of "NGO," "women's," and "activism."

My analysis is based on ethnographic research among women's organization participants conducted since 1997, most intensively in 1999–2000, when I was based in the town of Zenica for two years, and continuing since then in stays of several days to several months (see Helms 2013). The research included participant observation at NGO activities and gatherings where NGO leaders interacted with each other and with donor representatives; formal and informal interviews with NGO women and donor representatives; collecting written materials from NGOs and donors; and monitoring public discourses on gender and NGO activism in the local media, both television and print. Quotations given come from these interactions; first names are pseudonyms while I give the full name of one activist who requested to be identified. Translations from the Bosnian language are my own.

The organizations I studied were NGOs in that they were not governmental, although they did not all make consistent use of this label and this definition did not rule out their receiving funds or use of facilities from governmental bodies. I studied groups whose membership was made up of women and that professed, through names or mission statements, to exist for the betterment of women's lives. I began with three core NGOs in Zenica, but I soon met women from a variety of other organizations all over BiH as I accompanied the Zenica women to meetings and conferences. As I learned, being a women's organization could mean anything from helping women fulfill traditional roles as wives and mothers to pursuing feminist advocacy for the realization of women's rights and the breakdown of patriarchal ideologies and practices. Most women's groups fell somewhere in the middle. Donor organizations and representatives were similarly heterogeneous, as I discuss below. Here I explore this complicated terrain in a context that was simultaneously postconflict and postsocialist, as well as caught up in the historical moment of globalization, neoliberal trends, and European Union enlargement.

Foreign Intervention, NGOs, and Donors

Bosnia's NGO boom (Alvarez 1999) was intensified by a convergence of various forms of international attention during and especially after the war—a conflict that garnered significant media attention for the brutal way in which gender and ethnicity became central to atrocities like ethnic cleansing and mass rapes. The signing of the Dayton Peace Agreement brought the fighting to an end in late 1995 and gave BiH a new constitution, making the fragile state a signatory to every major international human rights treaty, including the Convention on the Elimination of All Forms of Discrimination against Women (see Inglis 1998). It also established a complicated, decentralized political system based on consociational power-sharing mechanisms meant to keep in check political domination by any one ethnonational group, the war being seen as a conflict among the main three (Serbs, Bosniacs [Bosnian Muslims], and Croats). These mechanisms functioned only minimally at the state level; while state institutions were gradually being strengthened, governance in practice functioned most meaningfully only at the level of the two ethnically defined "entities"—the Serb-dominated Republika Srpska and the Federation of BiH, dominated by Bosniacs and Croats. Furthermore, especially in the Federation, significant political units broke down into even smaller territories where control by one ethnonational group was undisputed. These smaller territories were cantons and—in the case of "mixed" cantons—municipalities (Bieber 1999; Gagnon 2003). The contested state was held together by a pseudoprotectorate led by the Office of the High Representative, the OSCE (Organization for Security and Cooperation in Europe), and an array of other foreign governmental, intergovernmental, UN, and nongovernmental agencies and organizations commonly referred to as the "international community" (see, for example, Bose 2002) but more accurately described as foreign intervention agencies (Jansen 2006).[4]

These actors came to BiH with a variety of projects and approaches, including crisis intervention and humanitarian aid, Third World sustainable development approaches (including gender and development), postsocialist democratization and marketization, and religious solidarity missions. Most of them shared a commitment to help build a functioning multiethnic state with a market economy and robust civil society that would eventually join the European Union.[5] BiH was part of the global neoliberal trend of promoting minimal state apparatuses, shrinking welfare programs, and touting NGOs as a new, more flexible way to administer social programs (see, for example, Edwards and Hulme 1998; Hann and Dunn 1996; Feldman 1997; Klees 1998; A. Sharma 2008; and the introduction to this volume). As was the case elsewhere, civil society came to be equated in dominant usage with the number and distribution of NGOs (see, for example, Belloni 2001; Feldman 2003; Wedel 2001). Intervention agencies pushed strongly for the establishment of as many NGOs as possible, especially in areas controlled by hard-line separatist nationalists (Sampson 2002; Stubbs 1999). In the late 1990s the OSCE actually labeled such places "neglected areas," implying that donors had not made sufficient efforts there, and as a result, NGO creation was more a product of donor attention than of local initiative. Intervention agencies (that is, governing institutions that sponsored, both logistically and financially, programs and policy initiatives) and donors (that is, those who directly funded NGOs)[6] thus set local NGOs up as an alternative to the exclusivist ethnic nationalism that reigned in the sphere of government and politics; this so-called third sector served as the great hope for the future of a peaceful, democratic BiH. There was thus a merging of global trends of NGO promotion with the practical goals specific to postwar reconstruction in BiH.[7] Local NGOs tried to make the most of the attention from donors and intervention agencies, in some cases virtually ignoring local governmental structures and even the local population (for critiques of Bosnian NGOs and notions of grassroots responsiveness, see Belloni 2001; Chandler 2000; Stubbs 1996, 2007). Such tendencies decreased during the 2000s, when many donors withdrew from the country and local governance was strengthened, but they remained a part of the operational habits of NGOs.

Although some intervention agencies focused on women's rights issues, including feminist donors and agencies in which individual feminists had initiated projects, gender issues were not high on the list of priorities for the main actors of the international community (Rees 2002). Many agencies and organizations gradually did put in place special gender units and projects, and in the early 2000s the Finnish government bankrolled the establishment of a state-level Gender Equality Agency and entity-level gender centers as part of the state apparatus.[8] On the whole, however, intervention agencies were most intent on facilitating refugee return and setting up political and financial institutions that would function in a unified state; "women's rights" and "gender" were prominent buzzwords in NGO and human rights circles but seldom appeared in high-level political discourse.

Given the polarizing nationalist politics and violence of the recent past, ethnic reconciliation and refugee return (to areas now controlled by different ethnonational groups) were major priorities. It was here, at the local level, that women were targeted, not only because they made up the majority of the surviving displaced population but also because they were believed (or at least said) to be pragmatic and forgiving peacemakers, more willing to bridge (ethnic) differences than men, especially those in power (Helms 2003, 2013). Some women's programs were even hijacked by these other priorities, as was the case with the Bosnian Women's Initiative, which was funded by the US Agency for International Development. The initiative was subcontracted out to organizations not specializing in women's issues and ultimately set aside its original women's rights goals in favor of projects focused solely on refugee return (Baines 2004). Many other projects aimed at women were also introduced, driven mostly by donor agendas; these had more to do with adapting to the neoliberal logics of a reduced state, such as numerous microcredit and other income-generating schemes as well as the provision of social services not covered by the state (see, for example, Pupavac 2005). However, despite some efforts by donors to frame these activities as responses to "transition" or steps toward rejoining Europe, most NGO projects were seen through the lens of postwar reconstruction (Jansen 2006; see also Gilbert 2006). For example, microcredit schemes were described as a way to aid internally displaced women, and small-scale crafts production was promoted as psychosocial help for women who had been traumatized by their experiences in the war.

Feminist organizations and individuals were also involved, some channeling the same government development funds as the mainstream agencies.[9] In some cases, solidarity networks made up of women activists formed NGOs in their home countries to collect donations for BiH, and several set up NGOs in Bosnia that were based on feminist principles and were later taken over by Bosnians (this was the case with Medica Zenica, discussed below). Many of these feminist donors were initially mobilized by reports of wartime sexual violence against women, although those who worked closely with Bosnians soon moved to other issues vital to local women in the postwar era, such as domestic violence, housing, and income generation. Feminists from other parts of the former Yugoslavia were also key, acting at times as consultants to donors or trainers at skills workshops and at other times as fellow recipients of foreign donor aid.

The NGO as "Claim-Bearing Label"

Not all local organizations regularly or consistently called themselves NGOs. In fact, "NGO" was not a legal category—under the socialist-era law, the term was "association of citizens," while a 2001 reform allowed groups to register as "associations" or "foundations." What the leaders of local organizations called their groups, and in which settings, was therefore telling. Especially for people who had grown up under socialism, to use the term "NGO" was at first a conscious departure from natural speech (World Bank 2002). Under socialism, community-level associations had been organized around interests like folklore, skiing, chess, or pigeon breeding. Like the socialist-era women's groups I discuss in the next section, they were apolitical at least officially and by reputation, though they functioned with communist party approval (Andjelic 2003).[10]

During and after the war, "NGO" became associated with foreign funding and other forms of support. It was the organizations associated with donor circles where the idea of NGOs as the vanguard of civil society and democracy was heavily promoted that regularly used this label and that were seen by others as a new form of association. The use of the NGO label was itself part of the language of "NGO-speak" (Wedel 2001; see also Sampson 1996). But for other organizations hoping to attract foreign funding, the claim to belong to the NGO sector was not only a plea to be included into the ranks of the funded but also to be accepted and validated—at the individual and the group level—as cultured agents of democratic tolerance, instead of being seen as the petty, tribal nationalists that they felt the media had unfairly painted them. NGOs became associated with the West and all its purported modern attributes, from cosmopolitanism and enlightened human rights standards to the material accessories of computers, mobile phones, jeeps, and nice offices.

Thus the NGO attribution operated as what Dorothea Hilhorst calls a "claim-bearing label" (2003, 6–8): what people called their organizations conveyed more about their aspirations and desired messages to specific audiences than about the organization's actual activities. Calling one's group an NGO was meant to signify that one was "doing good" (W. Fisher 1997) for society. In the Bosnian context, it was also a way to distance oneself from the widely distrusted realm of "dirty" politics, government, and corrupt business dealings. I often heard organization leaders say the words "nongovernmental organization" rather than use the acronym NGO (NVO in Bosnian), also adding "nonparty" and "nonprofit" to their list of descriptors, lest their meaning be lost. For similar reasons, it was common to stress the humanitarianism of NGOs as the polar opposite of the political. To be an NGO was to claim moral superiority, an interest in the well-being of others, and even patriotism or ethnonational pride—but by no means motivated, like politicians, by a desire for personal power or financial gain.

Women were especially credible in putting forward this claim, given the widespread association of politics and war with men, a view widely shared and also exploited by donors and intervention agencies (Helms 2003, 2007, 2013). Many NGO women thus linked humanitarianism to their being women, contrasting selfish, corrupt, and greedy men to women who cared about society because they cared about their children's future. As one woman politician put it, "women always put general interests first, common interests, while men are in it for personal interests." Furthermore, because it was taken for granted that women were mothers, I often heard at meetings of women's NGOs statements like: "If women had been in power, there would not have been a war." It followed that electing women to office, or accepting women NGO leaders as legitimate political actors, would "clean up" politics.

However, the term "nongovernmental" could also be perceived as a threat by local government officials who interpreted the label as "anti-governmental" or who regarded NGOs as irrelevant to the functions of government. This suspicion was reinforced by the fact that many NGOs received funds and support from foreign-associated sources and operated largely outside of government control, often including an avoidance of taxation. This situation also meant that NGOs were not overly concerned with how they were seen by local officials or even community members (cf., S. Henderson 2003; Hrycak 2006; Stubbs 1997). It was only later, when donors' priorities shifted, that some NGOs saw a need to cooperate with local governments and sought to win their trust and support.

The NGO label was also less effective among the general population, many of whose members were skeptical of foreign-supported NGOs and the locals who worked for them for, it was imagined, enormous salaries.[11] NGOs offering social services such as the free women's health clinic operated by Medica Zenica were evaluated much more positively than those perceived to be pursuing political goals like social or legal change

(Grødeland 2006), even though in the case of Medica, the organization also carried out activities seen as political, and its members sometimes identified themselves publicly as feminists. This meant that in everyday speech, NGOs were often referred to according to their particular reputation: an NGO offering social services might be referred to as a humanitarian organization, one that ran a youth center would be called just that, and a women's group known to organize women's social events would be called an association of women (*udruženja žena*). There was little popular sense that the NGO sector was a potential force for collective action or for serving as a watchdog on government, as donors advocated.[12] References to such functions came mainly from NGOs, their donors, and democratization officials, as well as appearing in media coverage of NGO events.

Activism and the Notion of a Women's Movement

Donors and local NGO members alike were prone to enthusiastic exclamations about the sheer number of women's organizations in so many parts of BiH, both urban and rural. This was especially true, in my experience, of feminists from Western countries on short visits to BiH. If the many women's organizations were not always proclaimed to be a women's movement, their numbers were frequently pointed to as evidence of women's desire for change, democratic participation, peace, and ethnic tolerance—for a united, multiethnic, democratic BiH where human rights, including women's rights, were respected. But there was no necessary link between the formation of women's organizations and commitment to such goals, certainly not in the way foreign agency representatives and donors imagined there to be.

The first reason for this has to do with how social activism was understood in BiH and abroad. When foreign agency representatives talked about how NGOs should operate, they often envisioned Western European and North American models of activism, nonprofit organizations, and volunteerism that assumed a level of motivation and commitment to causes that did not necessarily match those of local NGO participants. The disconnect reflected not only the legacies of socialism but also current economic realities and the way in which democracy aid and the NGO sector have developed in BiH. The starkest example was in the periodic suggestion that Bosnian NGOs might solicit funds or volunteer labor from the local population, an idea that Bosnians dismissed as ridiculous at best and immoral at worst. For an NGO to ask for time or money from an impoverished population that considered NGOs to be overflowing with foreign money was truly beyond the pale. Both foreigners and Bosnians had grown used to the presence of foreigners supplying aid (Belloni 2001). The atmosphere was a far cry from the *radne akcije* (work actions) that had been organized by the Communist party to rebuild the country after World War II, a comparison I heard from a few older people who had been drafted into such activities as youths.[13]

"Activism" thus had a different meaning in BiH than it did for many foreigners. This was so even for many members of NGOs in BiH who had a sense of working for social and political change and did refer to themselves as activists (others called themselves simply "NGO women"). It could not be taken for granted that Bosnians did NGO work out of dedication to a cause, for lower pay or even in their spare time, though few would admit to working in an NGO solely as a job.[14] Indeed, funded local NGOs offered some of the best paid and most stable work available to the average educated person (surpassed only by foreign NGOs and agencies). The few who volunteered their time for an NGO tended to be younger people who were still supported by their parents (who may have hoped that volunteering would turn into paid employment) or older women with grown or no children who, even if employed, found time to dedicate to NGO activities under a different model of social engagement (see below). One NGO in Zenica, Bosanka (the female form of "Bosnian"), fit the latter pattern of older women who treated their mostly unfunded group's activities as both a contribution to society and a personal social outlet. These activities were lower priorities for such women, however, as was the case with Edina, a core Bosanka member who eventually abandoned the group so that she could spend time with a new grandchild.

Those employed by NGOs treated it, unsurprisingly, as a job that had to be balanced with one's personal life, which for most women meant also attending to many more duties at home (much like under socialism). Such employees placed limits on how much overtime or travel they would do for their work, and especially on how far they might risk their personal well-being by speaking out on political issues or attempting to affect change. There were definite exceptions to this, but they were not the norm among those who called themselves activists.

The second reason was that there were different types of women's NGOs in terms of their dedication to changing gender norms, promoting women's rights, or advocating feminism (however defined). Some groups had been started by international humanitarian organizations and became locally run NGOs. Such organizations, along with some locally initiated NGOs, tended to provide social services and employ professionals on the basis of their skills as social workers, therapists, accountants, and so forth, rather than as social activists per se. Medica Zenica, one of my primary research sites, was one such NGO. Founded by German feminists as a therapy center to aid women war victims, especially survivors of wartime rape, it had been taken over by Bosnian women and continued to provide a range of medical, psychological, social, and vocational training services to women in the community, now through a focus on combating domestic violence (see Cockburn 1998; Helms 2013). Although there were a dozen or so Medica activists who were very strongly committed to changing existing gender norms even to feminism, including a few who turned down better paid jobs to continue working at Medica, this was not a necessary given among the nearly seventy employees of the organization working there at the time of my initial fieldwork. Medica women were by no means against goals of gender equality; indeed, they all expressed pride in Medica and its special atmosphere of an all-women organization. But this model of women helping women and their children was not so disruptive of traditional gender hierarchies as to force the employees to see the work as political. Members of Medica had not necessarily become or stayed involved out of deep conviction that the patriarchal gender order should be overturned, or because they wanted to devote significant energy to this goal through political action. Indeed, some women revealed distinctly conservative personal views on gender or a distaste for the feminist label under which the organization officially operated.

The example of Medica is a bit atypical for a service NGO, as its feminist roots infused much of its therapy work—especially the activist department called Infoteka, which in March 2009 split off to form an independent, feminist NGO. Activists from Medica have also gone on to found other feminist NGOs and to contribute in other ways to the challenging of patriarchal norms in BiH. In BiH generally, self-described feminists or even politically active women's NGOs were relatively few in number and concentrated in larger urban centers like Sarajevo, Banja Luka, Tuzla, and Zenica (see Cockburn, Hubić, and Stakić-Domuz 2001). These groups took on feminist characteristics thanks partly to individual activists who had developed a political or feminist stance and partly to personal connections among donors and other activists from Germany, Croatia, Serbia, and elsewhere. However, the general climate of disdain for vocal women with political opinions and the widespread rejection of the feminist label in BiH ensured that only the most confident women, usually those with cosmopolitan support networks and links to other feminists, adopted such stances. Most of the larger funded women's NGOs kept a low public profile and concentrated on service provision rather than issues seen as political. Moreover, the professionals employed in such NGOs did not necessarily think of themselves as activists; rather, they saw themselves as social workers, therapists, medical personnel, and the like. This trend contributed to a depoliticization of NGO work, similar to the process noted in the context of Third World development (see, for example, Escobar 1995; Ferguson 1990).

The type of NGO that most defied donor expectations for political engagement was the "association of women." Such groups were organized along the model of socialist-era women's community organizing, which in turn fit neatly into widespread gender-separate social patterns.[15] During the socialist period, after the dismantling in the early 1950s of the more vocal Anti-Fascist Women's Front (Antifašistički Front Žena, AFŽ), official women's organizing had been reduced to a loose network of community-based organizations called *aktiv žena* ("women's actives," also sometimes used in the sense of women's auxiliary), while communist party officials asserted that the "woman question" had been solved (Sklevicky 1984, 1989; see also Jancar-Webster 1990).[16] *Aktiv žena* groups were organized through local party cells but were expected to be apolitical, engaging in charity drives, community beautification projects, and social events for women such as excursions or celebrations of March 8th, International Women's Day. All-women groups were considered the most respectable social outlets for women, both married and unmarried, and were a natural outgrowth of social networks and neighborly relations in neighborhoods and villages. Women socialized at each other's houses over coffee and in evening gatherings (which sometimes included men), while men had public places like political meetings, religious services, workplaces, and pubs (Sorabji 1994; Bringa 1995).

These patterns were most pronounced in rural areas and small towns, as well as among people from such areas, though there was a range of attitudes toward women's organizing even in larger towns where gender relations were considered more modern (Denich 1976; S. Woodward 1985). The Zenica NGO Naš Most (Our Bridge) prided itself as an association of ordinary women—that is, working-class women or those with rural backgrounds). Its members expressed appreciation that this was a women's organization, because otherwise their husbands or fathers would not approve of their participating in it. A mixed-sex group would not be respectable. As I met representatives from other women's groups from around BiH, I asked them why they had chosen to be a women's organization. The majority of those from small towns and villages reacted as if this was a silly question: they formed women's organizations because they were women. It was the natural, normal thing to do, not least because men and women had different concerns (Helms 2003, 2010). "Let the men organize their own group," quipped a member of a women's group in a village in northwest BiH when I asked her why the group had organized as a women's organization.

The *aktiv žena* model also lived on in the kinds of activities that these groups imagined and organized. Naš Most carried out donor-designed projects when they won funding, such as for support of (ethnic) minority returnees or microcredit schemes for women, but their one constant activity—whether there was funding or not—was to provide a social space for women. Regular women's gatherings were held, including elaborate celebrations of March 8, which featured dinner, live music, bingo, and dancing until late in the evening. This was considered a once-a-year break from women's usual housework and family care. At the gathering I attended in 2000, the assumption that the women participants adhered to such traditionally female domestic roles was reflected in the bingo prizes, which included sets of pots and pans, cleaning gadgets, beauty products, and dishes.

Another Zenica women's group, Merjem (the Islamic version of Mary, Mother of Jesus), organized similar social activities. A conservative, religious organization, Merjem made no efforts to secure funding from Western sources (it did organize religious activities for women sponsored by Islamic groups from BiH and the Middle East). Among its activities were the type of excursions once organized by *aktiv žena* groups for the purpose of getting to know new towns and areas of BiH and "exchanging experiences" with other women. As with social gatherings, these trips were considered sufficiently respectable activities, even though they involved travel, because they were only for women. Still, when such an excursion was planned, many of the women would fret beforehand about whether their husbands or parents would allow them to go, and they scrambled to complete their domestic chores before the big day.

"Exchanging experiences" was also a phrase that Bosnian participants used to describe donor-organized NGO gatherings. Indeed, although there was a strong resemblance to older patterns and conservative gender regimes, these activities also blended into new-style NGO organizing and were mixed with the discourses of multiethnic civil society, human rights, and gender equality being promoted by intervention agencies. The March 8 celebration described above, for example, included speeches about women's rights and encouragement to vote for women political candidates, although the audience was mostly interested in the dancing and other entertainment.

Bosanka straddled these worlds. Its activities conformed to older patterns: it had been formed during the war to distribute humanitarian aid to refugees and soldiers, and its members later offered their expertise as professionals to educate village women on topics ranging from hygiene and health to voting rights and even religious or national identity (a role that, though ideologically very different, recalls the literacy courses run by the AFŽ in the late 1940s and 1950s). Bosanka also organized social gatherings and excursions with members of other women's NGOs. At the same time, its president, Šehida, became interested in democracy and civil society initiatives. Mostly on her own but always as a representative of Bosanka, she got involved in various BiH-wide NGO initiatives. This involvement may have been motivated in part by a desire to secure funding for Bosanka from the donor representatives with whom she interacted, but I believed her enthusiasm to be genuine: she herself had a respectable position as a district appeals judge and did not have to do this work.

Given this exposure to donor-led initiatives, Šehida's views and way of talking quickly diverged from those of most other members of Bosanka. At Bosanka activities, it was striking to see "old-style" activities such as excursions and social gatherings become infused with talk about democracy, civil society, and women's rights. On one occasion, Bosanka hosted a women's organization from another town on an excursion to Zenica. After showing the visitors the main shopping street, the theater, the art gallery in a former synagogue, and the Islamic pedagogical academy, nearly all on foot, Šehida had them walk nearly an hour more across town in order to show them Medica as she considered it important to point out that Zenica was home to one of the strongest women's NGOs in BiH. After this stop, Šehida talked to the visiting women about the Zenica women's contributions to people's survival during the war, aid to refugees, postwar reconstruction, and now the democratization process. The visitors, who had snapped up Medica's literature on gender-based violence, feminist therapy approaches, and women's rights, were abuzz with talk about the strength of Bosnian women and the things they were doing to make their own town a better, more democratic place despite the failings of the male-dominated political establishment. What looked from the outside like a typical women's excursion—an apolitical, unthreatening diversion for a group of married women and dutiful daughters—thus became inflected with the political language of NGO and democratization projects.

A similar mix of styles was to be found with the ubiquitous women's knitting projects. One of the first phases of donor interest during and just after the war was psychosocial therapy, which usually meant women coming together under the guidance of a psychologist to knit, weave, or sew products they could later sell. The idea was for women to discuss their war traumas and find support from each other. Foreign feminists often criticized such activities as reinforcing traditional gender roles rather than challenging them. At Medica, however, the Bosnian women defended their therapeutic knitting and sewing workshop with rural refugee women as the only way to get women together to talk and be helped. Such women would never have willingly gone to therapy due to its stigma—they weren't crazy, they said. Likewise, activists from Medica Mondiale, Medica's German donors and founders, expressed concern that Medica Zenica's vocational training in hairdressing, weaving, and sewing reinforced gender-typed professions for women (see Walsh 1998). But the Bosnians spun it differently, evoking a feminism of women's entrepreneurial independence. As the coordinator of the training project wrote in Medica's newsletter, these activities "contribute[d] to women's economic independence" and "strengthen[ed] their self-confidence and their self-reliance" rather than reinforcing gender-typed professions (Zvizdić 1996, 33):

> We are often asked why Medica, as a feminist organisation, trains the women in "typically female" activities. The reason is that we believe that traditional women's activities neither conflict with feminism, nor with the things feminism fights for and against [sic]. These activities simply have to be valued correctly. . . . When women form cooperatives or workshops together and develop an organised system for marketing their products, they are on the way to economic independence. This is why women must not allow their work to be forced into categories which are defined by men. (Ibid.)

Of course, members of the local community and even the women participants themselves were more likely to interpret such training programs as precisely the sort of occupations that were suitable for women, as the natural caregivers and homemakers of society. But the ambiguity in the two ways of reading the same activities worked to Medica's advantage, ensuring that the group would not be seen as rocking the boat too much. Organizational forms and activities were thus difficult to read, especially as many NGO women were proficient in the language of foreign intervention.

In a similar vein, foreign feminists, including those from Medica Mondiale, also asked the Bosnian women why they were not more political. They clearly thought of political activities in terms of public visibility, leading campaigns and protests, and writing letters to the media, while the Bosnians had a different vision of the political. "They [the donors] wish we'd bark [*lajati*] in public," explained Duška Andrić-Ružičić, Infoteka's president, when I asked her and her colleagues about this one day over coffee. These activists saw feminists as being "louder" in Zagreb and Belgrade, not only in Germany, than in BiH, but they were convinced that such approaches would backfire in their more conservative country. They wanted to be more muted; theirs was "feminism the Bosnian way." As one of the women put it, "it's one thing to live here and *stay* here over the long term and it's another to come here for a short time and then go back to your safe, secure country where the rule of law is in place," as the Germans would. Medica and other women's NGOs in their network were in fact working behind the scenes to improve legislation and to change the way local institutions responded to gender-based violence. This approach had often been successful: they had contributed to the passage of stronger laws against domestic violence and marital rape and of a state level gender equality law, and to efforts in many municipalities to respond in a more supportive way to women victims of violence. Meanwhile, it was some of the most conservative women's groups, the mostly female survivors of the Srebrenica genocide, who were the most public and vocal, actually demonstrating in the streets. Their message had nothing to do with women's rights or feminism, however, and in fact largely reinforced conservative nationalist gender ideals.[17]

The contrast between groups like Medica and the Srebrenica women's groups highlights one of the fundamental critiques of the NGOization of feminism. On one hand, feminist NGOs that preferred to keep a low public profile and to get things done behind the scenes challenged the expectations of feminist donors and supporters as to what women's rights (or feminist) activism should look like. Bosnian women who saw themselves as feminists maintained that they were taking a much more effective course by moving slowly and quietly, hoping for long-term change. They were also acting on their conviction that the state had an important role to play, in contrast to neoliberal trends toward the reduction of state welfare programs. It was therefore vital to pursue change on the level of law, public institutions, and state benefits.

At the same time, however, when viewed from the perspective of critiques of the NGOization of feminism (Lang 1997), Bosnian feminists were following precisely the neoliberal script that pushes NGOs toward professionalization and institutional approaches, creating dependence on the state and donors and stifling mass mobilization on issues of social justice (Alvarez 1999; Hrycak 2006; Lang 1997; Silliman 1999).[18] In this respect, Bosnian feminists were living up to the models put forth by donors and intervention agencies, including some feminist ones, that encouraged NGOs to become a link between government and society by honing their skills in policy advocacy. In fact, most Bosnian feminists considered this advocacy role to be what made their work political. They were thus caught between contradictory notions of what political activism should look like and were more inclined to choose the prevailing model of NGO advocacy that was backed by most of their donors and potential donors. They described their choice as a necessity in light of cultural norms and resistance to publicly active women, but it also helped that this way of working meant easier access to donor funds and cooperation with state institutions.

From Boom to Sputter to . . . Movement?

Most of what has been criticized as negative aspects of NGOization were also present in postwar BiH. NGOs employed small numbers of increasingly professionalized staff members, and very few thought of engaging in activism for its own sake, unpaid or in their spare time. Dependence on donor funds created disincentives to making contact with the grassroots—that is, members of local communities—except as beneficiaries of services. Indeed, even NGO agendas were donor-driven. Many avenues of funding were available for donors' priorities like refugee return, antitrafficking initiatives, and legal aid, issues that only partly or sometimes barely coincided with activists' notions of local needs. It was harder to fund initiatives with more abstract goals like influencing popular notions of acceptable gendered behavior and increasing public awareness of gender discrimination: such things were not as easily translated into "deliverables" as required by donors. It was thus difficult to see how they could meet the expectations of foreign feminists for public campaigns and political agitation. Furthermore, many NGOs were now offering services once provided by, or that could conceivably have been provided by, the state, such as shelters for victims of gender-based violence, which were never provided by the Yugoslav state but which had now come to be considered part of a state's duties according to the norms and regulations of the European Union. Not all service-providing NGOs stayed away from political initiatives, but many of them did, choosing the smoother path of professional rather than (political or feminist) activist identities, community acceptance, and often also access to local government funds. As in other parts of the world, then, in BiH NGOs were not conducive to producing forms of feminism that would emerge as a social movement or a challenge to the social and political status quo.

It is not surprising to find such characteristics in BiH, given that it has been caught up in the same global trends—led by some of the same international, governmental, and private donors and institutions—as are present in the rest of the world. At the same time, the specifics of the BiH context produced some opposing tendencies, and I argue that they arose from circumstances in which women's activism grew out of NGO creation and not the other way around. This prompts the question of whether Bosnia's is less a case of NGOization of feminism—that is, as a movement—than it is an example of the movementization of NGOs. Let us consider the trajectory of women's organizing in BiH since the initial postwar NGO boom.

As noted above, before the war and the arrival of NGOs and foreign intervention in BiH, there was no women's organizing beyond the community level, workplaces, or the communist party.[19] The Yugoslav second-wave feminist network of the late 1970s and 1980s, made up mostly of academics and journalists concentrated in Belgrade, Zagreb, and Ljubljana (Jancar 1985; Benderly 1997), was hardly noticed in the politically closed climate of socialist-era BiH.[20] It has only been since the establishment of NGOs, with the support and sometimes also at the initiative of foreign donors, that any groups or individuals emerged who could be classified as women's rights activists or feminists.

After the initial boom of the first few postwar years, NGO leaders began to worry about the survival of their organizations. There were constant troubling rumors that donors were leaving BiH and funds were drying up. Some of this was true, as humanitarian aid agencies and others, including Medica Mondiale, turned their attention to the next crisis zones, first in Kosovo and then Afghanistan and Iraq and beyond. However, the major intervention agencies did not close their offices in BiH, though their representatives began to argue that the number of NGOs in the country—which they had done so much to create—was too high for the size of the population. Only the fittest organizations would survive, and the struggle favored those with the right connections and skills, including knowledge of English, to produce fundable project proposals (see, for example, S. Henderson 2003; Hemment 2007; S. Phillips 2008). NGOs were still operating on short-term project budgets, however, and even the strongest faced uncertainty about the months ahead. For example, Medica, one of the oldest and best established NGOs in BiH, went through periods in the mid-2000s when it could only sporadically or retroactively pay some of its staff members, and in early 2007 it had to drastically cut back services and close the largest of its facilities. Eventually it found new donors, but these also made only short-term commitments. By 2009, the organization had to scale down significantly, although it continues to be a strong NGO.

Unfunded groups like Bosanka were organizing fewer and fewer activities in the late 1990s, as its members became more preoccupied with their families and the challenges of the struggling economy, as noted above in the case of Edina. Some, like Šehida, Bosanka's president, continued participating in women's rights initiatives through other funded organizations. In the run-up to the 2000 general elections, Šehida became involved with the Bosnian League of Women Voters, which had secured a grant to promote women candidates. As she traveled around BiH with this project, Šehida continued to introduce herself as representing Bosanka, although it was getting more and more difficult to engage the other members of the group in any activities aside from meeting for coffee and cakes in Zenica. Šehida complained: "These women just wait around to be told what to do, where to go. And these are housewives and pensioners who have time to do something!"

After the 2000 elections, however, even the League's activities dried up. Šehida maintained her network of NGO acquaintances and participated in a few more women's initiatives, but by 2003 she was fully immersed in some new professional activities and was no longer involved in women's issues. By 2007 Naš Most was still operating out of its president's house, organizing social gatherings and taking on funded projects when it could. NGOs in rural areas were still active where the refugee reintegration process was deemed unfinished and donor funds were still available. But many smaller groups had folded for lack of funds and/or interest.

In the meantime, the established core of the funded women's groups, among them most of those that described themselves as feminist NGOs, had strengthened their ties and come together on several entity- and state-level issues, both under donor initiatives and on their own. Cooperation was not always smooth: competition for diminishing resources brought out territorial rivalries, and there remained sensitive politicized "ethnic" issues they were not able to tackle as a collective. Still, they banded together to support legislative changes, protest acts of sexism, publicize international women's rights initiatives, and represent BiH abroad. Among other things, their work spurred the passage of a gender equality law (2003) and stricter criminalization of domestic violence (by 2005), as well as the inclusion of survivors of wartime sexual violence in the Federation law entitling civilian war victims to state benefits (2006). New organizations have been formed by now-experienced activists as well as by younger women eager to try different tactics to bring feminist voices into the public arena.

Can we call this a movement? Cynthia Cockburn and her coauthors from Medica posed this question in their research on seven Bosnian women's NGOs conducted in 2000. They found little evidence of a movement outside of NGOs and even found these lacking in their capacity for "campaigning and advocacy" (Cockburn, Hubić, and Stakić-Domuz 2001, 150). Over a decade later, what advocacy work there was had achieved some concrete results, and networks among women's NGOs, at least a select group of them, were even stronger than previously. However, as Jael Silliman argues, NGOs should not be expected to become social movements on their own, though they can be a crucial part of a broader-based movement and even function as its initiators (Silliman 1999, 46–48).

Encouragingly, then, developments outside the NGO sector have also contributed to a sense of an emerging women's, even feminist, critique of Bosnian patriarchal norms. Critical journalists, many of them women, have increasingly taken on issues such as sexual harassment, sex trafficking, the difficulties faced by women in politics, and open intolerance of homosexuality. The 2000s have seen the emergence of several women film and documentary directors whose work has taken on women's perspectives and subjects such as wartime rape (Jasmila Žbanić), fundamentalist Islam (Žbanić again), female survivors of war (Aida Begić), or the objectification of female pop singers (Danijela Majstorović). The work of female visual artists, writers, and poets has also brought forms of gender critique into public view (see Simmons 2010), as have the women's art festivals organized by the feminist foundation CURE (Girls) in Sarajevo.[21] Bosnian academics, some with graduate degrees from abroad, have begun to introduce women's and gender studies into university curricula; a master's program in gender studies was started at the University of Sarajevo in 2006 with an inaugural class that included some of the very professionals, NGO activists, and journalists who have been driving the increase in visibility of women's and gender issues. Debates about gender issues are further encouraged by increasing Internet use among younger Bosnians, including discussions about local topics through social media, chat forums, and web portals. Feminists and women's activists have also been part of a general increase in citizens' protests on the street and online (see Kurtović 2012), most encouragingly in the current "Babylution" demonstrations (as this text goes to press) sparked by government failures to provide something as basic as personal identification numbers for newborn citizens. Furthermore, besides some now-veteran women's activists, most of the women involved in these developments are from a younger generation than the majority of those active in women's NGOs, suggesting that awareness of feminist critiques and their impact on public opinion will grow. In these ways, something approaching a movement or a Bosnian feminist scene that is broader than NGOs may in fact be taking shape.

Still, most of this new activity remains within urban and highly educated circles, dealing with abstract concepts of art, representation, and academic theory. The larger public is more likely to respond to practical issues depicted in an accessible way, even when informed by theoretical principles. And there was considerable resistance in society as well as among activists to truly radical campaigns for change (Cockburn 2013). Again, the way in which NGOs developed under the tutelage of foreign intervention agencies has meant that their work is less visible to the public except where they provide services. Women providing care services fit neatly into patriarchal assumptions about what women should be doing in society and reinforced the idea of women as (nothing but) vulnerable victims in need of such services. Many foreign agencies contributed to this view; even where they encouraged campaigning and advocacy, it was mostly through quiet lobbying behind the scenes—which, though sometimes effective, did little to influence public awareness. Most crucially, there was therefore little sense of critical mass in terms of public opinion: "woman" as a mobilized identity had not been made "politically relevant" (Gal and Kligman 2000, 106).

Instead, most political initiatives on behalf of women—or using the new, poorly understood term "gender" (*džender*)—came to be seen as addressing the narrow causes of a few NGOs working at the behest of foreign donors. This was also the case when local NGO leaders or Bosnians working in international agencies appeared as the spokespeople for such initiatives: they tended to be written off as foreign stooges. After all, most successful women's activists were employed by foreign-funded NGOs, having gained the skills necessary to survive in the world of donor projects (see Hrycak 2006). With the NGO model, there was little room for new people to get involved: most NGO positions had long ago been claimed, and in any case their numbers were dwindling as funding decreased. Organizations trying new forms of activism, such as CURE's arts festival and other public events, found it difficult to engage volunteers, even among young people, precisely because the NGO model of employed activists had become the norm. Despite the rhetoric of intervention agencies about the potential of NGOs to "transform society" or act as "initiators of social and political change," to use slogans from two donor-sponsored NGO meetings I attended, the NGO model they promoted in many ways hampered the development of a more widespread or grassroots activism or movement.

Despite the drawbacks of major donor support, its subsiding has also been troublesome. Some women's NGOs have turned to state institutions as partners in their work, although they had long operated only under the scrutiny of their donors, letting the state off the hook in terms of responsibilities for social welfare. Medica Zenica enjoyed full funding from its German founders for years, a time that allowed the group's members to build up their expertise and work out their political and professional stances. When German funding dwindled, the Bosnians were forced to hone their proposal-writing skills so as to garner funds from other sources. As mentioned above, they were not always fully successful, and the NGO has struggled to stay in existence. Its members saw a need to reach out to government institutions if they were to succeed in realizing their goals. With the support of foreign institutions based in BiH (particularly one with a feminist at the helm), in 1999 they began to work with local public institutions to improve responses to gender-based violence (Helms 2006). This cooperation improved their powers of advocacy and their public visibility in ways that had a direct positive impact on the lives of women survivors of violence, many of whom did not belong to the educated elite.

At the same time that women's NGOs have turned to the state in their quest for sustainability, donors have also shifted their attention and funds to the state, as they look for exit strategies or seek to uphold standards of the European Union that make the state responsible for providing certain social services, such as those addressing gender-based violence. However, feminists like those at Medica's Infoteka were also wary. Too much merging of their activities with the state, they felt, would erase the feminist approach; they preferred to stay independent. As Medica itself, led by one group of women within the organization, moved closer to integrating its services with those of local state institutions like the Center for Social Work, another group formed Infoteka as an independent NGO in 2009. Both groups continued to see their work as feminist but in different ways (see Cockburn 2013).

Conclusion: Weighing the Effects of the NGO Boom

Bosnian women's NGOs suffered from many of the problems that characterize contemporary NGOs in general and women's NGOs in particular. However, I maintain that it is unwarranted to reject the NGO form altogether or to condemn across the board the donors and transnational agencies that promote NGOs, which Steven Sampson has cautioned against as too simplistic (2002). As the Bosnian case shows, the situation is more complex.

First, as I have discussed in this essay, what was treated by major intervention agencies as one category—the NGO—was actually a variety of organizational forms with very different modes of activity and visions of the groups' roles in society. Whereas intervention agencies expected all NGOs, and especially women's NGOs, to act as agents of social transformation, many women's NGOs were focused (nominally) on such issues only because they either had or hoped to attract funding to work in those areas. Women did not necessarily see their groups as political actors or agents of social change; rather, as in the case of those operating along the *aktiv žena* model, they saw the organizations as apolitical social outlets for their members, mutual aid societies, or service providers for the more vulnerable members of society—that is, as mitigators of the effects of postwar and postsocialist hardships. Only a handful of NGOs, however modestly, took on the tasks of working for legislative reforms, raising public awareness about forms of gender inequality, or bringing critical voices to their local communities in ways that might lead to change in dominant gendered practices and cultural expectations.

Second, precisely because of this diversity of forms, it is too much of a generalization to condemn NGOs altogether. Certainly, many women's NGOs were ineffective, short lived, coopted by state interests, or turned into professionalized service providers with little or no involvement in social or political debates. But being an NGO did not necessarily mean an organization could not have a political edge or take a cautious stance toward involvement with the state, as the handful of Bosnian NGOs like Medica/Infoteka show (see, for example, Funk 2006; S. Phillips 2008).

Critics have also attacked the NGO for its dependence on donors and foreign governments, particularly those pushing neoliberal agendas of private entrepreneurship and a scaling back of postsocialist or welfare states (see, for example, Feldman 1997, 2003; Silliman 1999; Ghodsee 2004; Hrycak 2006). Nanette Funk (2006) has offered a range of arguments showing this critique to be too simplistic and too much of a generalization when applied to postsocialist Europe. The Bosnian case, targeted by both postconflict reconstruction and development agencies as well as those promoting postsocialist democratization and marketization, only adds to the complexity that must be considered. In BiH it was more difficult to see the effects of neoliberal agendas, since processes of postsocialist economic reconstruction were often masked by discourses of postwar reconstruction and state building (Jansen 2006; Gilbert 2006). Bosnian NGOs that provided social services were indeed often stepping in where state programs had collapsed and had not been reinstated under the logic of marketizing reforms.[22] But this was not always so, especially with women's NGOs that provided aid to women war victims or, later, shelters for survivors of domestic violence and sex trafficking—the state had never addressed such issues. Without NGOs and particular officials who were specifically concerned about women, it is doubtful that such services would have appeared.

Furthermore, we cannot assume that either the intentions or the effects of all donor policies were neoliberal or even upheld the interests of Western governments. In the Bosniac-dominated areas of BiH, donors from Muslim countries financed a range of humanitarian and educational projects, including those for women that were aimed more at strengthening Bosniacs' commitment to Islam. If we consider only Western-based donors, which did share a large set of goals in BiH, there were also alternative donor organizations with environmental or feminist approaches that did not share neoliberal agendas (see Funk 2006). Indeed, as mentioned above, most aid to Bosnian women's groups, both feminist and non-feminist, was the result of a desire to help women victims of war and/or support women in peace and reconciliation efforts (a focus not without its own problems: see Helms 2003, 2010, 2013). Furthermore, if we consider the European Union as a major Western donor and policy maker, we see in the case of women's shelters that it shifted its focus from NGOs to the state: even though women's NGOs had begun the only existing shelters, EU standards now dictated that this was the responsibility of state institutions and channeled funds for such projects away from NGOs.

Feminist donors and individuals working for intervention agencies were also instrumental in fostering connections among women's activists in BiH and beyond, which Millie Thayer has argued is a powerful effect of contemporary NGO activism even in the most remote corners of the world (2010). Bosnian activists had built working relationships across a fractured BiH, the successor states of Yugoslavia, other postsocialist states in transition, and globally, leading to increased awareness of gender issues elsewhere and lessons learned from the experiences of other activists. This facet of the activists' work carried its own dangers, because connected women's activists could spend more time networking on the Internet and traveling to conferences abroad than connecting with their own local communities. Nevertheless, these connections ultimately spawned new levels of awareness and critique and fostered a sense of common cause, at least among a small group of activists. This effect may be limited, but it is not inconsequential.

In the case of BiH, it must therefore be acknowledged that most of these NGO women would not have become activists at all had it not been for foreign intervention.[23] Given the global NGO trend (Silliman 1999; A. Sharma 2008) and developments in the rest of postsocialist Europe (Wedel 2001; Mendelson and Glenn 2002), it is difficult to imagine a scenario in which NGOs would not have emerged in BiH. The wartime violence spurred many women into action, but even if there had not been a war, the burgeoning women's NGO scene in the larger cities of Yugoslavia in the 1980s would certainly have spread into BiH. However, without massive foreign intervention, it is doubtful that so many NGOs would have emerged, especially in so many smaller towns and villages. Despite the fact that the bulk of this activity eventually petered out, did nothing to challenge patriarchal norms, or became little more than professional service provision, organizations and individuals were still exposed to critiques of established gender ideologies and began to formulate their own new awareness of gender inequalities (Cockburn, Hubić, and Stakić-Domuz 2001). This was due to the great mobility of people, ideas, and resources that characterized the donor-driven NGO scene, and to the fact that intervention agencies kept women's roles visible, even if in sometimes conservative ways.

In her essay in this volume, Sonia Alvarez notes that social activists in Latin America have managed, in spite of the structural obstacles she critiqued in her earlier work (1999), to do some unseen movement work toward social change. Women's activists in BiH have also engaged in such work. The critique of NGOization must therefore be more precise in its terms. NGOs come in many forms in terms of their organization and mission and the motivation of those involved, as well as of their relationships with different kinds of donors and the state. Donors also come in different guises. The Bosnian case demonstrates that committed feminist activism or movement work, however limited, can indeed emerge from the NGO world. Although any movementization will have to encompass more than just NGOs, the possibility is there precisely because of the exposure to women's and feminist issues afforded by and through women's NGOs.

Notes

For their helpful feedback on this essay, I thank Paul Stubbs, Duška Andrić-Ružičić, Jill Benderly, and this volume's editors, Victoria Bernal and Inderpal Grewal. For financial and institutional support of various stages of the research on which this analysis is based, I thank the International Research and Exchanges Board, the Institute for the Study of World Politics, and the Central European University. A version of this text appears in Helms 2013.

1. A key informant of Sarah Phillips—an anthropologist who studied women's NGO activists in postsocialist Ukraine—used the same metaphor about the NGO boom in that country (Phillips 2008, 65).

2. Cargo cults, first described around the turn of the twentieth century by anthropologists working in Melanesia and the Pacific islands drove people to dream of riches (cargo) arriving for them by boat or plane in the same way they saw happening for colonizers and white traders. The cults' adherents imitated white behaviors, even constructing fake harbors and landing strips out of bamboo so as to lure ships and planes full of cargo.

3. Edwards and Hulme (1998) might call them GROs (grassroots organizations), distinguishing them from transnational NGOs. I avoid such terminology since the connection to grassroots or local communities was often tenuous, despite claims to the contrary.

4. Stef Jansen (2006) uses "foreign intervention agencies" as an improvement on the standard "international community," a misleading term for what is in fact a diverse group of actors and interests. I, too, refer to these actors collectively as intervention agencies, emphasizing Jansen's caveat that the "foreign" designation reflects more the ways in which these agencies were seen and sought to portray themselves than an objective reality, since such actors were well integrated into local and regional networks, employing "locals" at many levels (see Lendvai and Stubbs 2009; Pugh 2003).

5. The main exceptions to this were donors from Muslim countries that primarily worked to strengthen Bosniacs' devotion to Islam and the global Muslim community. Additionally, certain smaller donors and individual activists, including feminists, were less explicitly dedicated to free-market goals.

6. What I refer to as agencies or institutions were therefore sometimes also donors, sponsoring short-term projects, training programs, and myriad NGO meetings. Institutions like Office of the High Representative, OSCE, and the World Bank also made broad policy and set the tone for more traditional NGO donors, organizations that of course had their own sets of goals and principles. The intervention agencies were mainly responsible for maintaining the focus on ethnic reconciliation, refugee return, and the weakening of nationalist political forces, along with a less explicitly stated but equally strong emphasis on dismantling socialist economic structures and establishing a market economy that was receptive to foreign investment.

7. An interesting contrast can be drawn with Western, especially US, strategies to build civil society in other postsocialist countries. Thomas Carothers has noted that US policy in Romania in the 1990s focused specifically on "civic advocacy organizations . . . seeking to affect government policy" (1996, 65) in order to prevent a return to communism. In BiH the focus on opposing nationalists has led to sometimes blatant support of former communists, seen as a multiethnic and nonnationalist alternative.

8. The Gender Center of the Federation was established at the end of 2000, followed by the Gender Center of the Republika Srpska at the end of 2001 and the state-level Agency for Gender Equality on February 19, 2004 (see http://www.arsbih .gov.ba/, accessed June 20, 2013).

9. Prominent actors in this field were the STAR (Strategies, Training, Advocacy for Reconciliation) Project, a US-based feminist group that for a time distributed US Agency for International Development money (the project was initially part of Delphi International, though it later joined World Learning), and Kvinna til Kvinna (Women to Women), a Swedish group formed by feminist peace activists that operated with a budget from the Swedish International Development Agency.

10. The official name of the communist party was the League of Communists of Yugoslavia. I use the generic name for simplicity.

11. In a ruined economy where jobs were scarce and salaries low, NGOs were indeed a lucrative source of employment for those who could get it. They also offered travel opportunities that were less available to the general public due to both expenses and visa restrictions.

12. This function was already being attempted by the independent press, but many Bosnians noted wryly that the media's exposure of scandals, hypocrisy, and corruption rarely had any repercussions for those in power.

13. Socialist-era community organizations (the *aktiv žena* discussed below) and neighborhood-level administrative units (the *mjesna zajednica*) did occasionally

recruit volunteers—mostly youths or women—to clean up a park or distribute toys to an orphanage, but that was during more prosperous times.

14. Given these realities, it is therefore disingenuous to discount local NGO participants as cynical manipulators or insufficiently committed because they are employed in NGOs (Stubbs 2007).

15. Elsewhere, I discuss both these legacies in the context of women's roles in ethnic reconciliation and refugee return (Helms 2010).

16. Official women's organizations continued to exist under the umbrella of the National Front of the Working People. They were led by women high in the communist party hierarchy, many of whom had been active in the World War II partisan movement that spawned the AFŽ (see Dobos 1983; Sklevicky 1984). A new feminist movement began in the 1970s, flourishing in the 1980s and giving rise to the first feminist and lesbian NGOs, but these activities were little noticed in BiH (see below).

17. Positioned as grieving widows and mothers, the Srebrenica women's groups' cause was the location and burial of their missing male loved ones and the prosecution of those responsible for their deaths; they explicitly distanced themselves from feminism or any initiative concerned with women's rights (Helms 2013).

18. Among women's activists, I heard no shortage of criticism of the effects of neoliberal logics, not in such terms but as complaints about "wild capitalism" or in contrast to the positive aspects of socialism. However, there was no discussion of the role of NGOs in neoliberal formations. I heard the term "neoliberalism" for the first time in BiH in 2008, and it was used by a young progressive male activist who had been educated abroad and was plugged into transnational networks of resistance to globalization.

19. It is important to note, however, that voluntary organizations, including women's and feminist groups, were present in BiH even before the socialist era, starting in the late nineteenth and early twentieth centuries (Hadžibegović and Kamberović 1997; Sampson 2003).

20. One Sarajevo sociology professor, Nada Ler-Sofronić, who was a member of those prewar feminist networks, brought feminist critiques of Marxism into her university lectures and radio show, which no doubt influenced some people. However, I have never encountered a women's NGO activist in BiH who said she was aware of those activities before the war.

21. One could also add the Queer (arts) Festival organized in September 2008 in Sarajevo and subsequent activities of BiH's small but growing queer activist community, although public reactions to these developments have been mixed, both increasing awareness of gay rights issues but also bringing hitherto hidden homophobia into public debates.

22. At the same time, some benefits programs were thriving. These were mostly aimed at categories of people created or given new meaning by the war, usually defined by ethnicity and/or loyalty to nationalist parties, which used such benefits as clientelistic networks to maintain their power. Thus, even the World Bank

found it was politically impossible to reign in benefits to war veterans or families of fallen soldiers (see Bougarel 2006, 2007; Grandits 2007).

23. Some, particularly in the younger generation, were on this path only because they had been educated abroad, having fled the war or sought educational opportunities that were unavailable in BiH.

Failed Development and Rural Revolution in Nepal

Rethinking Subaltern Consciousness and Women's Empowerment

Humanity is a modernist figure; and this humanity has a generic face, a universal shape. Humanity's face has been the face of a man.
—Donna Haraway, 1992

If the question of female subaltern consciousness is a red herring, the question of subaltern consciousness as such must be judged a red herring as well.
—Gayatri Chakravorty Spivak, 1988

I am worried about my own country. In our country, nothing has happened besides murders and killings. Our country is our home. If the country is destroyed, our village is disturbed, and if the village is disturbed, our home is disturbed, and if our home is disturbed, then we're destroyed too.
—Padam Kumari Gorkha

On February 13, 1996, a homemade bomb exploded at the agricultural development bank in rural Gorkha district, Nepal. The blast damaged the building and its furniture; more importantly, the attack destroyed all records of the bank's agricultural loans. Within hours, nearly simultaneous attacks took place at police posts in Rolpa and Rukum districts, further west. Together, these assaults announced the commencement of a decade long armed Maoist revolt against the government of Nepal and what their instigators defined as 200 plus years of feudal exploitation of Nepal's peasantry, the beginning of the *jana yuddha*—or "People's War."

The onset of the insurrection took most Nepalis by surprise.[1] Initially dismissed by the political center as an aberrant phenomenon confined mainly to a few areas in the far western region, the movement grew by leaps and bounds; less than six years later it had penetrated almost all of Nepal's seventy-five districts, and by 2006, 70 percent of the countryside was said to be under Maoist control. As the scale of the conflict grew, so too did its casualties. By 2006, more than 13,000 people had been killed in connection with the uprising and state efforts to suppress it. Rape, kidnapping, and disappearances have become commonplace, and both the Maoists and the state have been accused of human rights abuses. Schools, health posts, and development projects have been disrupted or forced to close all over the country, and infrastructure such as airstrips, bridges, and telephone lines have been destroyed. As a result of all this, as many as 200,000 people have fled their rural homes, which are now sites of violent struggle, seeking work abroad or migrating to Nepali cities as internal refugees (IDPs).[2] Today, it is brutally clear that the insurrection and its attendant violence, insecurity, and infrastructural destruction have threatened—and in many cases destroyed—millions of rural and urban people's abilities to sustain themselves and pursue their social lives and livelihoods.

The speed and intensity with which the insurgency gained support in the countryside has inspired an abundant literature on rural life and the roots of the rebellion.[3] Almost immediately, four factors were identified as motivating popular support: (1) popular disillusionment with the failure of the Nepali state to deliver the expected democratization of local social relations and political authority after the victory of the first *jana andolan* (People's Movement) and the establishment of multiparty democracy in 1990; (2) continuing poverty and a widening gap between rural and urban quality of life despite four decades of intensive development; (3) widespread frustration with corruption at all levels of government; and (4) a backlash against the brutality of police, and later army, counterinsurgency campaigns.

The first three of these have been glossed as related elements of a broad, singularly encompassing cause: that of "failed" or "incomplete" development. Pointing to the fact that the districts at the heart of the insurrection, Rolpa and Rukum, were among the poorest in Nepal, many analysts have explained the revolt as the result of rising expectations combined with continued or even increasing deprivation.[4] Despite the fact that millions of dollars had been devoted to rural development, uneven distribution of aid benefits and political voice between urban centers and rural hinterlands, between rural districts, and between classes of rural and urban people themselves was recognized as a development failure and a threat to the state. The most common prescription for this malady—advanced at academic conferences, NGO seminars, political summits, and in a host of books, articles, and working papers on the topic—was more and better development aid.

As we will see, all of these factors are important. Yet they are all gender blind—a remarkable oversight given women's extraordinary visibility in the revolt. One of the most commented on features of the rebellion is the unprecedented degree of women's participation, and the rebels' own emphasis on women's liberation has been widely discussed.[5] One-third of all foot soldiers in Maoist strongholds are said to be women. Women occupy positions of leadership throughout the Maoist hierarchy, participate actively in village defense groups, and work as couriers and guides. It is reported that some of "the most violent actions against local 'tyrants' are associated with all women-guerrilla groups" (Gautam, Banskota, and Manchanda 2001, 236–37). Indeed, the journalist-scholar and human rights activist Rita Manchanda has suggested that Gorkhali women's active support for the Maoists reflects not the absence or failure of development activities there, but, to the contrary, their surprising success. In an essay titled "Empowerment with a Twist" (1999), she proposes that, at least in Gorkha district, the insurrection has benefited from two decades of development work. In particular, she and her colleagues Shobha Gautam and Amrita Banskota propose that women's presence among the rebels has been boosted by the adult women's literacy programs run by an American INGO:

> In Gorkha district, it is literate women and men who are joining the struggle. Ironically, it is the success of the adult literacy campaign which has paved the way for women to become active in the public life of the community, for girls to go to schools and for girls politicized in school to be drawn into the armed struggle. (Gautam, Banskota, and Manchanda 2003, 121)

By this theory, far from discouraging violence, development activities have actually helped catalyze it: "Literacy campaigns . . . designed to promote the empowerment of women inadvertently encouraged many conscientised young women to choose subsequent empowerment through armed struggle" (Gautam, Banskota, and Manchanda 2003, 121).[6]

The contrast between this hypothesis and the "failed development" account raises questions about the relationship between development and rural insurrection in Nepal, especially given the industry's concern to promote "participation" and "empowerment." Does popular support for the rebellion reflect the incompleteness or failure of the development enterprise, or is it an inadvertent result? What is "empowerment," and how is it related to democracy—and/or violent resistance to the developmental state? Are women different types of social actors than men? What are the relations between—and/or results of—transformations in political, developmental, or gendered consciousness? As we will see, addressing these questions requires ethnographic engagement with development as both ideological practice and practical enterprise. It also demands a critical rethinking of conventional understandings of subaltern subjectivity and its relation to oppositional political consciousness.

This study is focused on the same Gorkhali women Manchanda referred to above, women who participated in an INGO-run rural women's literacy and empowerment program in the mid-1980s—and who are for the most part actively sympathetic to the uprising now, even as they criticize the violence and lament lives lived in fear—and lives lost. It is important to note at the outset that the women on whose experiences my reflections are based are not official members of the rebel cadre. They have not left their homes to join the People's Army in the forest; nor are they party activists or members of the local militia, on the whole. Yet they support the rebels by feeding them, housing them, and, most importantly, not informing the government about their activities or whereabouts. As in other parts of the country, such help can tax already stretched food supplies and inspire violent retribution from military forces, so this intimate proximity is also a source of fear, which is a reality that shaped all the communications on which this chapter is based.[7] But without their support, these women told me, the insurgents would be lost. And as I have learned through my observations of daily life in this "conflict zone," the notion that there are two distinct and opposed sides is mostly an illusion anyway (Leve 2004).[8]

My approach reflects the difficulties of doing direct ethnography with the Maoists themselves. It is also, however, a result of circumstance. I first learned of Manchanda's article when it was forwarded to me by the director of the INGO she credited for helping to catalyze Gorkhali women's revolutionary consciousness. A note attached concluded with the question: "Interested?"

Given my relationship to the program and its participants, it was hardly surprising that the director thought I might be interested. At the point that Manchanda made her trip to Gorkha and published her article, I'd known the women from the program she was talking about for nine years and had published two commissioned studies on the effects of the program, one specifically focused on the question of women's empowerment. My first research trip to Gorkha was in 1991, at which time I did ethnographic interviews and organized a quantitative survey of women who had taken part in the course in order to understand the effects of the program five years after it was completed. On the basis of this report, the INGO, which I will henceforth refer to as DFA (Development for All),[9] asked me to return in 1995–96 to do a ten-year retrospective evaluation. Women's empowerment was a particular concern in the development world at that time—as well as a personal interest of mine—so I centered my next round of research on this. What all this meant when the director contacted me was that I had a decade of longitudinal data on the effects of the program on its participants as individuals and the community as a whole.

Plus, I'd made friends—the women I'd stayed with and worked with while doing the research, field-based employees of DFA who helped me at every stage, the teachers, keepers of tea stalls and shopkeepers that I'd interviewed or bantered with on the path, and, of course, the women themselves, plus various of their parents, husbands, brothers, sisters, mothers-in-law, and children I'd met along the way. When I returned in early 2001 during a ceasefire, Gorkha was officially classified as a "severely affected area," and I wondered how—and whether—I'd be received. The fact that people remembered me and the relationships that DFA had built meant that I was welcomed, however, and I found familiar faces willing to work with me again. Since then, I've stayed with participants and their families every time I've returned to Gorkha, and, when the war made it impossible for me to go there myself, local women who'd worked with me in the past—including some who had learned to read in the program I'll be discussing—continued the interviewing for me. At those times, I also worked with Gorkhali migrants to Kathmandu and met others in the district center.

This chapter attempts to bring what I have learned from them to bear on the "failed development" thesis—and Manchanda's ironic "successful development" one. It seeks to understand participants' understandings of development and its relation to social and gender justice, the forms of consciousness that participants took from their experience of literacy study, and their redeployment of these against the state in the context of changes in the material realities and human expectations of men, women, and families in the region. At the end, we will see that while there is no single reason for the support Gorkhali women feel for the insurrection—understandings of it and affinities for it reflect multiple circumstances and subjectivities—all their own stories, reflections, and explanations presume a very different sort of self: a self that is not, could not be, and does not wish to be purely autonomous in the way most theories of rural empowerment presume, but rather defines itself by its relationships and, especially, its commitments. This is a self which, as Bakhtin might have put it, only exists at the point where it meets others. This insight has implications for theoretical understandings of rural empowerment and political radicalization, which in turn, has implications for imagining why some people might wish to leave their homes and take up arms, and thus what kind of human development projects are likely to support peace.

Women's Empowerment in Gorkha District

The ancestral home of the Shah dynasty, Gorkha is probably the district with the greatest name recognition beyond Kathmandu. Indeed, it was from a palace that one literally passes on the way to the villages I will be describing that Prithvinarayan Shah, tenth generation grandfather to the current king, Gyanendra, set out with his armies to conquer—nationalists say "unite"—the lands that collectively comprise the sovereign space of modern Nepal.[10] As a result of this privileged history, the district has assumed a pride of place in the nationalist consciousness. Indeed it was one of the first regions targeted for intensive development, and Gorkha Bazaar remains one of the few district centers in the mid-hills accessible by road. Nevertheless, the district has a strong leftist past, was one of the early Maoist strongholds, and remains a hotbed of insurrectionary support.

In the first eight years of the war, no fewer than twenty-one individuals from the two Village Development Committees (VDCs) that I will collectively refer to as Chorigaon left their homes to join the Maoists in the forests and underground.[11] By 2006, eleven people had been killed in the two VDCs by the state security forces (all were civilians, of whom nine were local residents, including three teenagers and two teachers), in addition to at least two others from the area who had joined the People's Army and died fighting elsewhere. For their part, the Maoists had killed more than forty police and army personnel posted there, including the dramatic massacre of twenty-three soldiers in a single attack on a police post. To get a sense of what these numbers mean in terms of the experience of violence in everyday life, consider that all of this has taken place in a community consisting of just 801 households spread out in an area of less than ten square miles (twenty-five square kilometers).[12]

Geographically, most of Chorigaon is laid out vertically: it is bordered on three sides by rivers and ranges up to about 1,230 meters in altitude at its peak. Socially, it comprises about eighteen ethnically diverse settlements, all of which are predominantly Hindu. The fastest way to reach there from Kathmandu is to take a bus or other vehicle to the district center (approximately 190 kilometers, a six- to eight-hour ride), and then walk another six to nine hours on an unpaved path down a river valley and back up the mountain and along the ridge on the other side. A twisting road to a nearby village, where the Maoists ransacked a small DFA office in 1996[13] and which now hosts a military barracks, was constructed sometime between 1996 and 2001. It remains unpaved, however, and is only motorable in the dry season. A small part of one VDC became electrified in the mid-1990s; a telephone line that was also installed then has since been destroyed in the war. What this means is little electricity, no reliable roads, and, since many of the water taps that DFA installed in the 1980s are no longer functioning, women may walk an hour or more in the dry season to get drinking water an average of nine times per day.[14]

Despite this, Chorigaon is fairly well off compared to other hill villages in other parts of Nepal. DFA's early investments in schools, health, agriculture, and microcredit programs—and especially its commitment to employing local people in the region, at its central offices and, since leaving Gorkha, at other project sites—has helped promote education, improve health and nutrition, and elevate the standard of living in the area as a whole. Moreover, its location, only a day's walk from the road head and less than a day from the capital by bus, makes it relatively accessible by rural Nepal standards. In fact, little of the mid-hill region is electrified or has road access, despite the fact that Nepal was 90 percent rural before the start of the war. Most families are subsistence farmers: in 1983, when the literacy program began, 98 percent of households owned land, although less than 55 percent were able to feed themselves from their land for more than six months in an average year.[15] Neither of these patterns has significantly changed, although cash needs have increased. Before the conflict began to force people out of the rural VDCs, most households supplemented their agricultural production with salaries and pensions earned through service in the British, Indian, or Nepali armies; through private employment in the district center, India, or Kathmandu; and/or by working others' fields, portering, or other kinds of day labor. Today, locals estimate that almost every home has at least one member living full time outside of the village whose income is critical to sustaining the household. Migration for wage labor on this scale has grown up largely since the establishment of democracy in 1990.

The history of women's development programming in the region dates to 1983 when DFA organized an evening literacy course for adults. Although the class was technically open to both men and women, the organizers found that women—few of whom had attended school as children—enrolled in the class at a much higher rate. Nonformal adult education (NFE) was a relatively new concept in Nepal at that point. The first NFE courses in that area had been introduced just the previous year in a neighboring VDC. Yet the program rapidly proved to be a popular success. In 1983–84, 1,052 people enrolled in twenty-five NFE courses in the two VDCs.[16] Eighty-seven percent of these participants were female. By the end of the program in 1986–87, more than 1,600 people had attended one or more of the literacy classes, and almost half of the participants had completed the three-year curriculum. Given that the total population of adult women (between fifteen and sixty) in Chorigaon in 1983 was about 1,634, this means that roughly two-thirds of the women in the two VDCs comprising Chorigaon participated in the NFE program.

A notable feature of these courses was their emancipatory intent. Most women's literacy courses offered in Nepal today are six or nine months that are treated primarily as a lead-in to income-generation classes, microcredit programs, or savings and loan groups. This reflects the current dominance of neoliberal ideology in development planning, which posits the market as the institution best suited to delivering overall social good and understands women's empowerment as largely a matter of facilitating women's participation in cash-yielding forms of production and consumer life (see Feldman 1997; Fernando 1997; Karim 2001; Leve 2001; Leve and Karim 2001; Rankin 2001, 2004). In contrast, DFA's program in Chorigaon was a three-year course with a participatory goal. According to the agency's first formal program evaluation—which was written by two people who went on to occupy the top two positions in the agency for many years—its main intent in teaching literacy and numeracy skills was to "assist program participants in identifying the problems faced by their families and communities" and to help them "achieve greater self-confidence so they can shape their own environment through development activities" (Sob and Leslie 1988, 3).

In prioritizing "the idea of self-help and people's participation in community development projects,"[17] the DFA program reflected fundamental ideals associated with the community-based integrated rural development (CBIRD) paradigm which was popular at that time. These ideals were also reflected in its curriculum, "Naya Goreto" (New Path), an innovative pedagogical package based on the ideas of the radical Brazilian educator Paolo Freire as adapted to Nepal by researchers at Tribhuvan University's CERID (the Center for Educational Research, Innovation, and Development) and the Boston-based INGO World Education.[18] Inspired by the Freirean ideal of "education as the practice of freedom,"[19] "Naya Goreto" aimed to combine community development, literacy learning, and critical empowerment in a way that would transform the consciousness of its participants. Freire believed that traditional educational methods dehumanize the downtrodden by reinforcing their sense of alienation and inadequacy (brought on by subjection to the hegemony of the dominant classes). He designed his pedagogy to help the people he alternately referred to as "peasants" and as "the oppressed" remake themselves as, literally, "new men" through a process of "conscientization"—a transformation whereby learners come to recognize their own value and knowledge and thus "enter the historical process as responsible Subjects," build a qualitatively "new society," and become "authentic" and "complete" human beings (Freire 1970, 18, 140, 65, 29). "Naya Goreto" followed this lead in that, "in addition to providing information," the program was designed to inspire a critical dialogue that would "help participants develop problem-solving skills, self-confidence, and a realization of their potential both as individuals and as members of a community."[20]

The DFA program also followed Freire in rejecting what he identified as the "banking" method of learning, where authoritative teachers "deposit" chunks of knowledge into passive student recipients. Instead, he—and they—advocated a "keyword" approach in which participants learned phonetic letters in the context of specific words—such as "work" (kām), "water" (pāni) and "liquor" (raksi)—which "would cause [student] participants to examine their own practices and consider changing them." As each keyword was introduced, class participants were encouraged to discuss the ways in which these terms or practices were issues in their own lives using comic-strip stories about rural women's everyday dilemmas and illustrations of people engaged in keyword-related activities. The aim of the discussions was to promote collective reflection and critical analysis of themes such as poverty, economic class and caste, environmental degradation, gender bias and inequality, bribery, and corruption.[21]

As noted, the program ran for three years consecutively. It met two hours per night five nights a week for six to eight months during the dry season. It took place in the evening so that women could finish their work before they came. Classes were held under trees, in public buildings, or in lean-to huts constructed for that purpose. Each facilitator, as NFE instructors were called, was given a packet of supplemental materials, a blackboard, and a kerosene lamp as teaching equipment. Participants received textbooks, a notebook, and one pencil each, in return for providing twenty-five *paisa* a month for kerosene and a five-rupee registration fee.[22] The first person to arrive any evening was expected to sweep out the space and/or cover it with fresh straw.

Despite a 30 percent dropout rate as a result of illness, marriage, or death, the program was highly successful. Five years after the completion of the course, 70 percent were still able to read and write their names.[23] At the end of the program, participants formed savings and loan groups, opened shops, and took up formal positions as Community Health Volunteers. A few joined local development committees, and 41 percent reported that they felt more confident speaking in public and/or asserting themselves. About a dozen girls joined the public school system in class four. Now having passed the eighth, ninth, or tenth class or studying at the university level, they formed the first cohort of educated girls in Chorigaon. Their mothers and sisters who studied at Adult Literacy Centers (ALCS) also proved more disposed to send their other daughters to school. As a result of this, along with government media messages promoting education, changing aspirations, and brute survival needs,[24] most children of both sexes attend school in Chorigaon today—or at least they did until the intensification of the conflict, which has shut down, interrupted, and made parents fearful to send their children to schools.

According to its creators, the Naya Goreto program was intended "to serve as a catalyst for development by exposing participants to new ideas and information and by giving them a vision of what was possible."[25] Did this catalyze a vision of revolutionary transformation as well? There is reason to believe that perhaps in some cases, it did. When I asked one woman about why people in Chorigaon supported the insurrection, her answer was succinct: "The Maoists work for social justice (*sāmājik nyāya*)." When I asked her if she remembered when she first began to use that term and/ or the ideals it expresses, she thought for a moment and then replied: "In the adult literacy course."

This exchange would appear to suggest that the NFE experience did indeed plant seeds that would later help to radicalize its participants. Yet as the next few sections of the chapter will show, Manchanda's thesis rests on specific assumptions about development, empowerment, and revolutionary consciousness that are not quite as suited to the situation as they may at first seem.

Underdevelopment as a Cause of Violence or Development as a Violent Process? "Empowerment" at USAID and in Theories of Conscientization

Before weighing in on what actually happened in Gorkha, we need to examine this and some other questions raised by the failed development thesis. Scholarly understandings of the relationships between violence and development have tended to fall into one of two broad perspectives. The first—which is the dominant line of analysis in mainstream development agencies and policy circles—recognizes poverty and poverty-related despair as a powerful threat to peace and stability. It therefore sees development, as a process that works to alleviate that poverty, as decreasing the chance of violent uprisings. According to this theory, "failed" or "incomplete" development is the cause of the conflict in Nepal (and many other parts of the world), and more, better, and farther-reaching interventions hold the promise of relief.

Against this, other scholars have advanced the claim that development itself is a form of structural violence—a neo-imperial enterprise through which industrialized Northern countries continue to dominate and exploit the so-called Third World (Esteva 1992; Sachs 1992; Cowen and Shenton 1995; Des Chene 1996; Rahnema and Bawtree 1997). Anthropological studies along these lines have denounced development as a governmental instrument that serves the interests of transnational corporations against postcolonial peoples and states (Gupta 1998); charged that development discourse creates new, disempowering forms of subjectivity like "underdeveloped," "illiterate" and "I.D.C." (Pigg 1992, 1997; Escobar 1995,

1996; Shrestha 1995); or deemed it an "anti-politics machine" which disguises the deeply political nature of its work beneath a seemingly objective technical-managerial discourse (1990). This is, of course, an analysis that the Maoists share.[26]

Proponents of each position agree that the solution is to promote freedom, but each works with a different idea of what freedom means.

For an example of how the first position plays out in practice, we need only turn our eyes to Washington, D.C. In its FY2004 congressional budget justification, USAID cited the unequal distribution of development's benefits between rural and urban areas as a key reason for agrarian support for the Maoists and attributed this to a dysfunctional political system that perverts development delivery:

> Poor governance and corruption, [Nepal's] forbidding terrain and lack of infrastructure all contribute to its development gains being unevenly distributed. . . . The Maoist insurgency . . . has found fertile ground largely in response to Nepal's poverty, exclusion, and poor governance.[27]

In response, the agency proposed programs that would increase national wealth by promoting and rationalizing the hydropower and forest/agricultural products sectors and expanding "good governance" to deepen democracy. The integrating theme of these goals, as they put it, was "better governance for equitable growth."[28]

A White House paper released at the end of September 2002 specifies the assumptions with which USAID was operating. It specifically linked democracy and development to the freedom of the market, and also outlined the historic role the United States sought to play in promoting neoliberal security:

> The great struggles of the twentieth century between liberty and totalitarianism ended with a decisive victory for the forces of freedom—and a single sustainable model for national success: freedom, democracy and free enterprise. In the 21st century, only nations that share a commitment to protecting basic human rights and guaranteeing political and economic freedom everywhere will be able to unleash the potential of their people and assure their future prosperity. . . . [The United States seeks] to create a balance of power that favors human freedom: conditions in which all nations and societies can choose for themselves the rewards and challenges of political and economic liberty. . . . The

United States will use this moment of opportunity to extend the benefits of freedom across the globe. We will actively work to bring the hope
of democracy, development, free markets and free trade to every corner of this world.[29]

In this model, the "political and economic freedom" guaranteed by democracy is a critical part of the development effort because it empowers
citizens to choose, participate in, and benefit from free-market policies,
thereby increasing standards of living and state security. Hence the importance of meeting "failed development" with more development—and
of generous congressional funding for USAID: "By supporting efforts to
resolve the Maoist insurgency and addressing the underlying causes of
poverty, inequality, and poor governance in Nepal, the US is making an
important contribution to fighting terrorism, promoting regional stability,
and lessening the likelihood of a humanitarian crisis."[30] Not surprisingly,
the emerging ethnographic literature on state violence and the coercive
underside of many cultures of democracy does not figure into these calculations (see Warren 1993; Tambiah 1996; Hansen 1999, 2001; Sluka 2000).

Manchanda, on the other hand, is taking the opposite approach. She
assumes that it is unregulated capitalism itself that is fueling the revolt
and supporting the various forms of violence and exploitation that led up
to it. The program models that tend to emerge from this sort of analysis
are, generally speaking, some variation on the kind of conscientization approach described earlier. The underlying assumption here is that freedom
is not merely a matter of the multiplication of choice but "the indispensable condition for the quest for human completion" (Freire 1997, 29). Likewise, justice is not seen as the natural byproduct of "conditions in which
all nations and societies can choose for themselves the rewards and challenges of political and economic liberty," as the White House paper cited
above proposed, but as the result of self-conscious human action to set
things right. In this, at least, Freirean educators and Maoist rebels share
the same, essentially Marxian, assumptions about human nature.

In theory, the two positions couldn't be more different. In practice,
however, they have had a remarkable tendency to slip into one another,
as the short-lived history of the women's empowerment unit at USAID
in Nepal reveals. In 1996, USAID-Nepal made women's empowerment a
major agency goal. As their congressional presentation explained:

The promotion of democracy through women's empowerment is a
USAID objective in Nepal. For democracy to be effective at the local

level, women must meet their basic needs and the needs of their families. . . . To organize the family through women's empowerment is to organize society, and to democratize the family is to democratize society. (Congressional Presentation 1998)[31]

The result was a huge woman-focused development offensive that enrolled over 100,000 women in six- or nine-month literacy courses in one year alone. Nearly 43,000 women "were provided legal awareness and advocacy skills," and the number of microcredit borrowers tripled between 1995 and 1996, reaching a total of 13,450.[32] This combination of literacy, legal education, and "access to productive resources" was proclaimed "critical to improving women's choices." And education came to be seen as a route to self-assertion and economic agency:

> [Our] literacy program is showing results beyond the acquisition of basic literacy and numeracy skills: women take jobs which they could not get while illiterate, thereby bringing more income into the household to support their families; they feel more confident to participate in community advocacy and user groups; and they seek additional training opportunities, such as legal and business literacy. (Congressional Presentation 1998)

It seems hard to believe that this neoliberal vision began as a Freirean ideal. By the mid-1990s "women's empowerment" had become one of the most loosely used words in the development lexicon. It had, however, emerged in the context of a very specific political and theoretical debate. Like the popular educators who designed Naya Goreto, the first women's empowerment activists were inspired by Freire's revolutionary pedagogy. They were frustrated, however, by his lack of attention to gender. If conscientization was a process by which people "leave behind the status of *objects* to assume the status of historical *Subjects*"—which sounds an awful lot like some of the more influential feminist theories of the time—Freire nonetheless never raised the question of gendered power (1997, 141; emphasis in original). Although he theorized subaltern subjectivity in terms of dependence, alienation, and dehumanization, Freire's model peasant remained sexually unmarked.

The term "women's empowerment" was born in the 1970s when feminist popular educators introduced theories of gendered power into the conscientization framework (Batliwala 1994). The concept became the focus of an international movement that eventually mainstreamed the ideal and is widely considered to have been a success. Yet I'm skeptical that its earliest advocates would recognize USAID's literacy-law-and-loan agenda as a realization of their ideal. (Nor, I suspect, would the liberal feminists at USAID acknowledge Freire's revolutionary Marxism as part of their intent.)

This shift, from the revolutionary empowerment of subaltern subjects to an instrumental empowerment for capitalist citizenship, signifies a dramatic shift in the development vision.[33] Verónica Schild (2000) has observed that "the discourse of neoliberal modernization emphasizes an active relation to the market, expressed on the part of citizens as the autonomous exercise of responsibilities, including economic self-reliance and political participation." The result, she says, is a form of governmental rationality whereby "citizens are . . . conceived—and produced—as empowered clients, who as individuals are viewed as capable of enhancing their lives through judicious, responsible choices as consumers of services and other goods." Because "the cultural contents shaping these neoliberal political subjects are none other than the liberal norms of the marketplace," she refers to these subjects as "market citizens" (2000, 276). I believe this describes USAID's program well. But from a Freirean perspective, the reduction of conscientization to consumer consciousness is a wholesale reversal of their liberatory aim. For these educators, agency is not realized through choices about what to buy, what to sell, and how to vote. Empowerment may "begin . . . by changing women's consciousness," but it should "manifest itself as a redistribution of power" (Batliwala 1994, 130). Far from a matter of freeing the market, in this model, justice follows from freeing the mind from the self-negating subjectivity that patriarchal and capitalist exploitation create.

How does this kind of slippage become possible?

One reason is because, despite dramatic differences in understanding and outlook, neoliberal and conscientization models share a number of unrecognized assumptions. First, both perceive development as a unilinear progression toward a predefined goal whereby developmental subjects become self-conscious agents, whether they express that through economic activity and disciplined participation in civil institutions or by seeking to overturn existing hierarchies and remake society. Second, both conceive of empowerment as a subjective transformation that will lead to concrete forms of action that reflect each model's analysis of "objective" reality. Third, in each of these models the developmental subject is imagined as in some way incomplete, whether what is perceived as missing is access to credit or self-knowledge and historical agency. Fourth, all of these ideas rest on the assumption that the human subject is an essentially political or else economic being who is most fully actualized at the moment of greatest autonomy. And finally, this historical agent (or "developed" modern citizen, depending on the discourse) is not usually conceived as someone who lives in a gendered body, and thus is implicitly male—even in explicitly feminist analyses.

Some of these points have been criticized as common problems in post-Enlightenment political thought (see Butler 1992; Haraway 1992; Spivak 1988a, 1988b). What I wish to emphasize here is that they unite thinkers who would otherwise be perceived as politically opposed—and who would certainly not acknowledge themselves as sharing foundational assumptions. Both the neoliberal and concientization models draw on a Hegelian legacy that looks to the uniform unfolding of an autonomous human consciousness in the direction of greater rationality, transcendence, and self-present Subjectivity. Nor are they alone in these assumptions, which structure much of the literature on peasant consciousness and rural mobilization.[34] In her critique of peasant consciousness in the work of the Ranajit Guha (1983) and the early subaltern studies collective, Gayatri Spivak suggests that "if the question of female subaltern consciousness is a red herring, the question of subaltern consciousness as such must be judged a red herring as well" (1988a, 29).

And indeed it should be.

What we will see in the next section are a series of complex relations between changing expectations and domestic reproduction, self-confidence and critical consciousness, and self-knowledge and gendered agency in Nepali social life that complicate theories that presume a teleological structure of evolving political awareness culminating in an unfettered, ungendered, autonomous (almost autochthonous) humanity. The experiences and opinions reported by NFE graduates demonstrate that the presumptions about subaltern subjectivity embedded in all of the empowerment theories above are critically out of synch with the women I met in Chorigaon.

Empowerment and Agency in Chorigaon

So how did NFE participation affect consciousness and identity? In interviews five and ten years after the conclusion of the program, women reported effects identical to those of many other literacy course graduates in Nepal: greater confidence and increased self-esteem, less shyness interacting with people outside of the family, and an expanded experience of women's ability to succeed in traditionally male domains. Overall, participants testified to a profound sense of individual and collective transformation. Statements such as "I became accustomed to speaking without feeling shy," "I'm able to express what I think; I learned to speak and I learned many other new ideas," "although we had eyes we were blind before; our eyes were opened by the ALC," and "we came out into the light from the darkness in our own homes" may sound dramatic or poetic, but such responses were exceedingly common (Leve 1993). "Before, if daughters or daughters-in-law went to meetings and spoke, people used to say that the hens were crowing," Geeta told me. "But now we're allowed to speak in meetings."

Also, by 2002, almost everyone I spoke with noted that community opinion had shifted to endorse treating sons and daughters equally.

"After we began to become educated, we came to know that sons and daughters are the same," Gyan Kumari told me. "Before this only our brothers studied, but now I know that women can study too."

"Boys and girls are naturally equal; it's society that makes a distinction between them. They are equally able to do the same work," Ram Maya said.

As a result of these sentiments, participants attested, both sons and daughters are expected to go to school today; nor do parents discriminate in providing food or medical care. "If daughters are educated as much as sons, then they can also look after their parents," Kamala affirmed, adding that she came to know this after joining the literacy class.

Given that the 24.5 percent female literacy rate in Gorkha is slightly higher than the national average,[35] and that people there credit literacy for women's intensified involvement in public life, it is not hard to imagine that DFA's programs may have "paved the way for women . . . to be drawn into the armed struggle" (Gautam, Banskota, and Manchanda 2003, 120). But the social and political subjectivities that women manifest are more complicated than the theories above would suggest. While powerful development discourses have indeed helped to extend modernist forms of thought throughout Nepal—Stacy Pigg (1992) and Laura Ahearn (2001), for instance, have both illustrated how practices and values associated with "*bikās*" have come to shape rural Nepali consciousness—the subjectivities that development produces are not the only identities that Nepali women perform.[36] To the contrary, the women I spoke with in Chorigaon conceive of themselves in quintessentially social terms, through relations that are morally inflected, often entail labor obligations, and are deeply constitutive of personal identity. In fact, the forms of self-consciousness that these "subaltern subjects" express makes me wonder whether the utopian freedom of autonomous subjectivity exists outside of the bourgeois modernist imagination at all!

Let me start with Nani Maya. Nanu, as her friends call her, is in her late twenties, the youngest of three brothers and four sisters from a middle-income farming family. She is married with two young children, and she currently lives with her husband, a sign painter, in a crowded quarter of Kathmandu. Nani Maya was in her early teens when she joined the literacy course. She'd never been to school, although all of her brothers attended, and she dreamed of studying even as she spent her days fetching water, collecting firewood, cutting grass for the buffalo, and herding the goats—gendered labor on which her household relied. When the adult literacy center opened, her parents considered it a waste of time; she was allowed to go only after her brothers intervened and then only after finishing all her regular work. She remembers that she'd often arrive late to the class, hungry and tired. But she enjoyed studying, and at the end of the course she won a scholarship from DFA to subsidize her study at the village school. There, she passed classes four, five, and six in the first division—a major accomplishment for a village girl.

"Even then," she recalled: "I could hardly find the time [to study]. I was fifteen years old and had three hours of class every morning and then more in the afternoon. I used to have to finish half my [domestic] work before the class, and the other half afterward. Somehow I convinced my parents of this schedule. . . . There was no option but to work because . . . we had lots of animals and some land and my parents couldn't finish the work alone." Despite this, she was committed to studying.

When she reached eighteen, however, her life changed: "There was gossip of my marriage, and this affected me a lot." In fact, she learned, her parents had arranged to marry her to a much older, wealthy widower. "I didn't want to marry at that time," she explained. "My plan was not to marry before [finishing class ten and earning] the S.L.C. (school-leaving certificate)":

But my parents were eager to unburden themselves of me. [They believe that] parents can only go to heaven after death if their daughters are married. Otherwise there is no chance of paradise. I protested strongly. I didn't like that man! He was already married and widowed. I was a virgin girl, and I wanted the same. "Why should I marry a widower who isn't well educated and has no personality?" I asked myself.

Finally she learned that the marriage was imminent. The plan was to bring her to a temple where the groom would apply vermillion powder (*sindhur*) to the part of her hair and then take her home—the most minimal of wedding rites. Her family was hiding this from her so she wouldn't resist. They had effectively decided to marry her by force since she refused to accept the relationship otherwise. In Nanu's mind, this was a huge betrayal. And on the night before this was to have taken place, she eloped with a boy she knew from school. Although his family was poor, he was from the same caste and otherwise a socially acceptable marriage partner. He had earned her respect by studying through class ten and passing the difficult S.L.C. exam. And most importantly, she said, he supported her dream: "My husband loves me. . . . He helped me a lot in my study. He insists on the need for education. He said if I thought there could be any future with him, he was ready to accept me. . . . I ran away from my parents' house for a better future."[37] When I last met Nanu, we talked at length about the Maoist situation. She hadn't been back to the village in three years. The last time she'd been there, when her husband had returned to see his father on his deathbed, the armed police had mistaken him for a Maoist, which, understandably, terrified her.

> I was at home cooking. Suddenly Kanchi came running in. "Why are you running inside?" I asked. Then I looked up: there was a man with a gun standing right at the door!
>
> "Is this Dil Kumar's house?" he asked. Then they searched the house from top to bottom. They were from the armed police, and they asked, "Where's Dil Kumar?" They shouted so loudly. [My] father-in-law had been sleeping. The Maoist movement had just begun.
>
> I said, "Father-in-law is sick in bed. He [her husband] came from Kathmandu to see his father who is critically ill. He's gone with our baby to play. I'll call him." But the police followed right behind me because they suspected that I might help him run away.
>
> [My husband] was at Kaila Ba's house. After reaching there, the police said, "Come on, let's go. Who are you—whose son? How long have you been living in Kathmandu? Why did you come here?" [My

husband] said, "I've been in Kathmandu for ten years, and I came here to take my sick father (for treatment), but in vain." The police were furious. When he said he was the only son they said, "You're lying." And when I said I lived in Kathmandu and not in the village, they said, "You're lying too!" Then Besar Maila's son intervened, and they beat him. Severely. With their boots, like a football. Then after beating everyone there, they were about to take my husband. He was carrying the baby, and he said to them, "Give the baby to her," to me.

Then I said [to the police], "I told you earlier that our father is sick in bed, and I showed you. You're lying! Are we lying? Or are you lying? Whatever you want to do to him, do it to me!" And I came between them so they couldn't hit my husband.

By then the old men had gathered. They told the police that [my husband] is not like that [i.e., a Maoist]. "Who gave you such information? Don't get angry. He's not like that; we would have known if he were like that," they all said. Then the police left, telling him to come to the police post at eight o'clock tomorrow morning. But when we went the next day, none of those armed police were there. They'd already left, beating some tailors on the way. The assistant subinspector said, "This is the first time that I've heard this name [her husband's]." We said, "They've already come to our home, and you're telling us this!"

If they had taken him at that time, they would've killed him. It had only been fifteen days since the teacher, Gunanidhi Sir—such a nice person—had been killed. Gunanidhi Sir had never gone for any meeting or done anything. . . . A person like that was taken from his bed and killed near the river. His wife was asked to come the next day with his clothes. She went to the police post. Then when she asked, "Where is my husband?" they said, "We don't know." When she got back to her home she came to know from some cowherd boys who saw him lying dead. He had been shot from behind. After that, she hasn't received any support from anywhere. The Maoists didn't kill him, and the police deny it. . . .

After all that, when I think of the village, I don't want to go. . . . If they'd taken him [her husband] away at that time, they would have killed him.

Given such an experience, it's hardly surprising that Nani Maya has lost faith in the putatively democratic state. Or that she favors the Maoists, who, with their promises of equality, justice, economic opportunity, and honest government, seem to offer something better. After democracy was declared in 1990, she told me, she'd expected "that there would be good facilities in the village, that there would be justice, that working people would be free to do their work, and that there wouldn't be suppression (*daman*) and exploitation (*upayog*) anymore." Instead, she's found, "the opposite has happened":

> Now the ones with power can do anything. . . . And if anyone is doing good work others try to drag them down ["pull on their legs"]. . . . There was an idea that people would become free (*swatantra*) following democracy but no such event has occurred.[38]
>
> If the king could run the government properly then these problems could be resolved. Or if the Maoists run the government . . . then people who eat by doing their duty (*kartavya*)—there would be no problem of food and clothing for those who do their duty—the government would take care of them. The rich are getting richer and the poor are getting poorer. The poor are dying on every side. But if the conflict could be resolved it wouldn't have to be like this.

This feeling, that democracy has made poor people's lives more tenuous rather than increasing their security, was widely shared and widely condemned. The phrase I've translated as "people who eat by doing their duty" expresses the understanding that social reproduction is hard work in rural Nepal. Nanu's meaning is that the people who have suffered the most under democracy are those for whom eking out a living requires painful labor (as opposed to those who live "having fun," as we will see below). If such people do as they must—as they are obliged to do in order to eat— she feels they should at least be able to feed and clothe their families. Her word choice suggests a morally grounded critique of a democracy that further impoverishes people who struggle and suffer to satisfy their most basic needs (and sends their children to die on both sides of the conflict) while "the ones with power can do anything."

Geeta, from a nearby village, expressed similar ideas: "After multiparty democracy was established, I thought, let there be development (*bikās*) in the country. Let everyone get equal opportunity. But instead, development works have stopped. Instead of building, they have destroyed . . . buildings, hospitals, bridges, drinking water, electricity, and roads. So rather than development, destruction has increased!"

At another point in the conversation, she linked these expectations to values that she traced to the literacy course:

After studying, women started to learn many things, that we too have rights and that women have been dominated by men. . . . [When democracy came,] I had hoped for equality. But what sort of development do we have now? The development is only in killings!

Perhaps because of experiences like Nani Maya's, most women told me they blamed the government more than the Maoists for the violence that had so completely transformed their lives. In part, this may have reflected a greater fear of the Maoists, who had eyes and ears in the villages in a way that the security forces did not, such that criticism whispered in one's own kitchen could bring retaliation in the middle of the night.[39] However, I think it also reflects their experiences of state violence—which has only increased since King Gyanendra inherited the throne in June 2001 and released the army, intensifying the war—and a widespread sense that the government had betrayed them. When asked what could be done to bring about peace, close to half the women interviewed expressed their desire that the government would agree to the Maoists' Forty Point Demands. These include inheritance rights for women; abolishing exploitation based on caste and ethnicity; special protections for orphans, disabled persons, and the elderly; and the provision of employment opportunities for all, in addition to forgiving rural agricultural debt, redistributing land "to the tiller," and other more familiar Marxist demands (Karki and Seddon 2003b). Indeed, not a single person suggested that the government should pursue a military victory. Rather, about 40 percent of interviewees said in exactly—or very close to—these very words: "the government (sarkār) must fulfill the wishes āvasyak or māg) of the people (janatā)."

Jamuna Devi was particularly adamant on this theme: "People's oppression and their struggles need to be recognized. . . . Poor people should be on top and the ruling rich people should be lower. Only when there is justice for the oppressed will the people have trust (bishvās) [in the state]. The government must fulfill the Maoists' demands."

Despite this clear support for the Maoist political and economic agenda, her thoughts about gender varied considerably from the rebel line. She gave a dowry (daijau) at her elder daughter's marriage, she said, so that her daughter would be appreciated and not "have to tolerate harsh words in her home." But "I felt very bad while giving it," she confessed. "I gave him my daughter, and I also gave property. Then I have no daughter to [share the] labor and no property either, and I'm left with nothing ["as if naked"], with both my daughter and my property gone!"

At the same time that she lamented the practice of giving dowry, however, Jamuna was firm in her insistence on the menstrual taboos that bar women from touching men, preparing food, or entering the house during that time. "I obey this rule very strictly because this is our women's custom. I will never abandon this tradition," she said. When I pointed out that the rebels are said to reject these observances and suggested that the practices may put women at risk—for instance, a local woman had almost died after a tiger mauled her while she was sleeping outdoors in front of her home—Jamuna responded by listing all the things that had changed:

> In the past, we used to eat and wear whatever we were given, but nowadays girls want to eat good food and wear good clothes. . . . A change has come from knowing how to read and write. Husbands, mothers-in-law, parents are also human beings. We came to know that we didn't need to treat them like gods[40] only after the literacy class. . . . [Similarly, we now know] daughters may be able to study high and stand independently (*swatantra*) on their own feet. . . . But this is our women's custom, and I won't give it up.

There is clearly something about this ritual for Jamuna that indexes an essential part of her feminine identity. I will return to this below. For now, suffice it to note that even the most adamant supporters of economic justice don't necessarily wish to do away with practices associated with gender identity, especially differences that they don't see as exploitative, but that mark the genders as distinct.

Let me conclude this section by introducing Bina, one of DFA's most dramatic success stories. Unschooled until she joined the literacy course as a young teenager, she is now married (to a policeman), with a son and a daughter, as well as holding a paying job of her own. She's been working practically since she left school. Before taking her current position at a police academy in Kathmandu, she worked for the government's community health program in her village, as an adult literacy instructor there, and, for two years, at the district hospital. In the village, she was active in community development efforts (president of her women's group, member of the forest committee and a drinking water project group) and recognized as a local leader. "Although there were people who had passed the S.L.C. in that place, they used to see me as someone who can speak, and whenever there was any problem in that area they would call me," she explained. "They'd tell me that such and such a fight has taken place, and then I had to go and resolve it."

As the wife of a policeman and someone employed by a police academy herself, Bina regrets that she can't return to the village nowadays:

> When there was no conflict, I used to go to the village once a month. I love the village. I miss it a lot. I have so much to do there. . . . I'm living here [in the city] only because I have to. Otherwise I'd prefer to be there.

But although she fears for her life, she is sympathetic to the insurrection:

> In our village, there are nine people in the police and the army. The Maoists organized a mass meeting in the village, and they read out these nine names. "These people shouldn't serve in the police and army," they said. "Ask them to leave. Instead, tell us how much salary they need; we will provide it." I came to know that they said that. "Otherwise, we know where they are and we will kill them."
>
> What can we do? It's difficult. We have to educate our children. If we'd been well educated, we wouldn't be facing so much trouble (*chintā*), would we? Who wouldn't want to live having fun (*mojmajjā*)? No one wants to face such pain (*dukkha*), do they? . . . At night when we sleep in our room, if someone knocks on the door, we feel they've come to kill us. That's the kind of fear we live with. . . .
>
> What they [the Maoists] are doing is good. They're doing it for us. It's very good to say that rich and poor will be the same. We're scared because they will kill us because of our jobs, and it shouldn't be like that. We are doing these jobs because we have to. Otherwise, though, they're not bad. Actually, if police/army recruits die and if Maoists die, it's the same—all are sons and daughters of Nepal. But they aren't fighting for personal benefit (*afno sukha, phaida*). They're fighting hoping for something for the future of the country. They're fighting without any salary, but we're fighting for our personal benefit. In a way, we're selfish (*svārthi*). Because if we don't have a job, we won't be able to feed our kids, so we've become involved. But they don't get a salary. They're fighting knowing that they may die today or tomorrow. We're fighting for our own self-interest, and they're fighting for the country.

In these comments, Bina introduces two key oppositions that structure her own and many other women's thought: self-interest versus being-for-others, and pain and trouble (*dukkha, chintā*) versus ease and fun (*sukha, mojmajjā*).

Kathryn March finds this second pattern among Tamang women in an area she calls Stupahill. One of the most characteristic aspects of Tamang self-representation, she writes, is that "life stories are told as hanging in the balance between *dukka* and *sukha*":

> Dukka is suffering: it is the physical hurt of illness, hunger, cold, or injury; it is the weight of knowing the fears, worries, wrongs, and obligations of life; and it is the sorrow, sadness, melancholy, or grief at being unable to forget hurt and hardship. Sukha is the opposite: it is the ease and comfort of health, food, warmth, clothing, and companionship; it is the feeling of uncomplicated pleasure; it is the purest as a happiness unaware even of its own good fortune. Every woman I interviewed located her life overall, and the events in her own narrative, in relation to dukka and sukha. (2002, 36)

Obviously anyone who's expected to wake every day before the cock crows, gather grass for the buffalo and fodder for the hearth, and come home and make tea before anyone else is out of bed is likely to agree that pleasure and ease are preferable to work.[41] But whereas the theories of empowerment that I analyzed above pit consciousness against unconsciousness, agency against alienation, "subjectivity" against "subalternity," and personal choice against cultural constraint, Gorkhali women conceive the freedom and independence (*swatantra*) that they aspire to in other terms. Based on my interviews, few of Chorigaon's neoliterate women would wish to live as "new [wo]men" in an altogether "new society" (as Freire proposed) or to be completely autonomous agents (with a world of choices at their fingertips). Instead, they ask for ease, security, equality of opportunity (including access to education and employment), good food and clothing, some degree of respect for their personal desires—and, as much as possible, some fun.[42] In fact, while the specific rituals that Jamuna embraces as the embodied practices of womanhood ("our women's custom") are weakening, the idea that people become themselves through gendered physical and emotional engagements—that (social) practices make (social) people—is not. While they would happily accept less work and more fun, and might very well be content to have been born as a boy, most of the women I know in Chorigaon would not choose to be disengendered—that is, socially disembedded—individuals at all.

Gendered Personhood, Generic Humanity, and Women's Suffering as Subjectivizing Force

Talal Asad's thoughts on the origins of secular personhood are helpful in making sense of all of this. Beginning from the reflection that "modern projects do not hang together as an integrated totality," but that "they do account for distinctive sensibilities, aesthetics [and] moralities," Asad suggests that "what is distinctive about modernity *as a historical epoch* includes modernity as a political economic project" which "mediates people's identities, helps shape their sensibilities and guarantees their experiences" (2003, 14; emphasis in original).

What, precisely, might these identities, sensibilities, and experiences be? Here, Asad looks to the problem of the subject. Noting the historical shifts in conceptual grammar and material life that have made it possible for secular forms of self and personhood to emerge, he observes that modernist thought presumes an "essential freedom" or "natural sovereignty" in the human subject and that it sees interests and desires as arising from this private internal space.

Characteristically, Asad links these ideas to power—in this case, theories that posit power as external to the subject—and to a post-Enlightenment "historical project whose aim is the increasing triumph of individual autonomy" (2003, 71). He argues on this basis that the movement toward "freedom from all coercive control" is rather, as Schild (2000) has already suggested, just another form of subjectification: "The paradox inadequately appreciated here is that the self to be liberated from external control must be subjected to the control of a liberating self already and always free, aware, and in control of its own desires" (Asad 2003, 73). Empowerment then "becomes a metaphysical quality defining human agency, its objective as well as its precondition" (79). Finally, he concludes that cultural theory—and here I would include development models as well—"tends to reduce [human subjectivity] to the . . . idea of a conscious agent-subject having both the capacity and the desire to move in a singular historical direction: that of increasing self-empowerment and decreasing pain" (2003, 79).

These comments go some distance toward explaining the theoretical assumptions that we encountered above. However, in reality, Asad argues, pain is not simply a biologically rooted experience that humans naturally and necessarily wish to overcome. To the contrary, it is also shaped by and rooted in particular social contexts, some of which can make it profoundly meaningful:

> What a subject experiences and how . . . *are themselves modes of living a relationship.* The ability to live such relationships over time transforms pain from a passive experience into an active one and thus defines one

of the ways of living sanely in the world. It does not follow, of course, that one cannot or should not seek to reform the social relations one inhabits, still less that pain is intrinsically a valuable thing. [But] the progressive model of agency diverts attention away from our trying to understand how this is done in different traditions, because of the assumption that the agent always seeks to overcome pain conceived as object and state of passivity. (2003, 84, emphasis in original)

In other words, *"as a social relationship,* pain is more than something unpleasant and external that impinges on someone. It is part of what creates the conditions of action and experience" (2003, 85, italics mine). And indeed in some cases, I would add, of self-realization.

Among women in Chorigaon, as throughout Nepal, certain types of pain and suffering are unambiguously condemned—particularly suffering caused by other people's irresponsibility, selfishness, thoughtlessness, or greed. But in other situations, painful struggle is seen as a normal, even normative, aspect of a woman's life; indeed, it is through certain types of suffering that the adult feminine subjectivity is produced.

For Nepali women, marriage is a socially, morally, and materially subjectifying event, an often dreaded but critical juncture at which pain and power assert themselves in girls' lives. Lynn Bennett records that her high-caste Hindu informants spoke of it as their dharma, a women's sacred duty (1983, 174–75).[43] And many ethnographers have observed that this forcible separation from the comfort of their natal homes in order to join a household of strangers in the least autonomous and most onerous domestic role is the defining experience of Nepali womanhood (Des Chene 1998; McHugh 2001; Desjarlais 2003). Not surprisingly under the circumstances, the event is paradigmatically described as a transition from *sukha* to suffering, from freedom to domination, indulgence to deprivation, easier tasks to harder work. In practice, of course, it is not always this simple, and many women spoke of miserable childhoods and/or happy married lives. But even in a Hindu-Buddhist religio-cultural setting, where a generalized experience of suffering is posited as the last word on human life, it is taken for granted that women's lives are especially filled with *dukkha* due to this dislocation and the pain of childbirth. This idea is not limited by region or ethnic group: the notion that women suffer more than men is pervasive throughout Nepal.

An important consequence of this is that women come to actualize themselves in the process of living these constraints. Suffering being common to all, it is the specifics of each woman's experience—her chance to study or lack thereof, the hunger she survived, the husband she was given, the children that she lost—that define her social persona and make her life unique.[44] Furthermore, it's through the particular ways that each woman manages the *dukkha* she is dealt that individuals exercise agency. As Robert Desjarlais notes in his analysis of a Kisang Omu's, a Yolmo woman's, life history, the choices that a women makes throughout her life will reflect on her, her siblings, her forebears, and her descendants so there is tremendous pressure to act in culturally "skillful" ways that indicate moral knowledge as well as individual creativity.

"Our lives are like links in a chain," Kisang told Desjarlais (2003, 136). After marriage, after women "grow up," "we need to eat. So I needed to tend the potatoes. I needed to do the work. Without work, we cannot eat. What to do? Sorrow means that, it turns out" (114). This statement expresses exactly what Nani Maya means by "people who eat by doing their duty" and links this labor to other kinds of productive suffering. Appearing inside an extended discussion of her marriage and the pain of moving from her father's home to a faraway place, these words reflect on the ways that social, moral, and material realities come together in the construction of female subjectivity. Despite her unhappiness at discovering that her father had arranged her marriage, Kisang emphasized that she didn't shame her family by refusing or running away. And in this way, she says, she became herself: "What to do then? My elders sent me [in marriage]. Such is the fate of the daughters. . . . *In that way, I became like this.* Nevertheless, it became nice" (131, emphasis added).

We can see similar patterns and sensibilities in the narratives of the women from Chorigaon. I have already suggested that Nani Maya eloped only after she judged her natal family to have betrayed their responsibilities to her by arranging to give her to a much older man in order to access his resources for their own benefit rather than pairing her with an appropriate partner of her own age. I would add that despite her unorthodox love marriage, she takes her role as a daughter-in-law as a matter of pride, for which reason she stayed on in the village to help her aging mother-in-law with the heavy work of carrying water, collecting firewood, and cutting grass long after her husband had left to find wage work in the city. When she tells her life story, she relates it as a narrative of suffering wherein she was wronged by her parents, her brothers, and the society's expectations for—and exploitation of—girls and women. But in her telling, she has always responded properly and responsibly, the way a good girl/woman should.

The sacrifices associated with marriage and adulthood prompted social and ethical negotiations for Bina too:

In the hills, a daughter has to get married after she grows up. She has to go to another home. . . . I was fifteen/sixteen when I got married. . . . I may have forced [my parents] to let me study, but finally I was compelled myself.

In our home, the tradition is that you get married before menstruation. . . . If you're married before menstruation, it's called *kanyadān* (the gift of a virgin), and they say that [*kanyadān* is both a religious obligation and a meritorious act]. . . . [I passed class seven living at my sister's home, helping with her children and going to school] and I had already begun my menstrual period. Then my younger brother, father, and mother discussed it. I said, "I will marry only after passing my S.L.C." But my older brother said, "No, you get married. I'll make them pledge to allow you to stay here for two more years and complete your studies. But you get married now."

She rejected this idea:

It's an impossible thing to study after getting married. You have to work in the morning and at night after becoming a daughter-in-law. When will you study? But my older brother forced me. "You have to marry," he said. . . . "If you won't marry now, then we won't send you to school." "Do what you like!" they said.

The boy who had come to ask for me was doing his BA. . . . "The boy doesn't drink or gamble and you have to marry him," was what my parents said. My older brother said, "If you don't marry that boy then I'll never tell you to get married. Go wherever you want, and do whatever you like!" After he said that, I didn't stay with him. I came to Kathmandu to stay with my younger brother. . . . [But even in Kathmandu], people kept coming to ask for me. My third sister had come to know about her marriage only three or four days after it had all been decided. . . . At that time I had said if you give me like that I'll never marry, which is why my parents consulted me. Actually, I'm the only one who's studied to class seven/eight in my family—my younger brother only studied to class three/four. . . . My parents said, "She is educated and not like the other sisters. If she commits suicide, what will we do?" So they asked for my permission because they feared I might commit suicide. But I said no.

Despite this, she acknowledges, she ultimately had to submit:

But after I came to Kathmandu, I got married anyway. He is my brother's wife's niece's son. People kept coming to my brother and asking for his sister's hand. Then my brother said, "Everyone is coming asking for you. You have to marry one." Maybe my time had come. I couldn't say no. I got married in Kathmandu, and after I'd lived here for a year and I had my daughter in my womb, I went back to the village. And life in the village was fun (*majjā*).

From *sukha* to *dukkha* to *majjā* (and now, again, *dukkha*), these events illustrate Bina's initial resistance to marriage and the life changes it would bring as well as her eventual acceptance of what she now acknowledges was inevitable ("maybe my time had come").

One way to look at this story is to focus on the relations and identities that come into play. At all points in the narrative, Bina is expected to get married and expected to marry someone her family proposed. From the religious logic of *kanyadān* and the role daughters play in fulfilling their parents' ritual obligations to her older brother's declaration that he would no longer feel compelled to feed, house, and support her if she persisted in resisting the family will ("If you don't marry that boy then I'll never tell you to get married. Go wherever you want, and do whatever you like!"), it is clear that her relatives saw her marriage as a collective concern and not as a matter of (her) individual will. Given her education, her parents made some accommodation to her exceptional status (and, perhaps, force of will). But no one assumed that her life was hers to contract as she wished; ultimately, her only real option for escaping familial power was the last resort of suicide.[45]

In evaluating this version of events, however, we must also take care to read between the lines. For while Bina frames her story in terms of parental pressure and personal resistance/accommodation—which is the expected, respectable way for women to narrate the events leading up to marriage in Nepal[46]—in fact, the family negotiated a compromise. Bina married within the bounds of normative convention, and she returned to the village to live with her mother-in-law. But she effectively selected her husband herself. Moreover, when she chose her husband, she also chose her mother-in-law, the person whose support or disapproval would most immediately affect her happiness or suffering for the next years of her life. When she says that she married her "brother's wife's niece's son," she indicates two things: one, that he was from an appropriate marriage pool and acceptable to her family, and two, that she knew, or had reliable ways of getting information about, his mother. If she'd married into a different household, they might have demanded that she limit her activities and confine herself to the fields and her home—in which case her life in the village would surely have been a lot less fun! Having accepted that marrying before completing her education was simply unavoidable, she ultimately conformed. But she also found a solution that would be bearable for her, allowing her to do what she liked to do and actualize herself in a way she enjoyed while still being a respectable wife and daughter-in-law:

> When I was working at the Community Health Program, I went for a fifteen-day training. If I'd been a daughter-in-law in another household then people would have gossiped. I was the only daughter-in-law from the area going there. But even when others used to say things, [my mother-in-law] had no such feeling. In the village, it happens that there are people who were jealous that I was working. But if anyone said anything, she would say, "Well what's wrong? My son's okay with it, and I'm okay with it, so why are you concerned about it?" She was very helpful. . . . Boys and girls would come to see me to talk about community affairs, and she would come to the field to call me and stay there while I met them at the house. She never thought, "What's this? My daughter-in-law is sitting and talking with other boys! . . ." If she hadn't been like that, I wouldn't have come here. . . . After attending the adult literacy class . . . I've done it all.

Bina's words sound like a resounding endorsement of the empowerment effects of the literacy course. Yet although she showed remarkable skill in negotiating a life for herself that is not too restrictive, her choices were made in the face of powerful constraints. What would it mean to say that Bina was empowered by her education? What would it mean to say that she was not? These stories illustrate how certain kinds of suffering are part and parcel of achieving particular forms of subjectivity.[47] To refuse this, or to defy it, is to exclude oneself from normal identity categories and, depending on the case, to court social sanction. In other words, it's not to act like a woman. And this is objectionable not primarily because defiance is condemned per se, but because social reproduction hangs on women's physical and emotional work. The *dukkha*—and dharma (religious duty)—of carrying water, cutting grass, cultivating crops, and so on is inescapably tied to the *dukkha* and dharma of social relations. This does not mean that people won't seek to minimize unpleasant obligations and maximize fun whenever possible—given, of course, that, as March's informant, Jyomo, put it, "if the work doesn't get done, no one eats" (2002, 133). Nor does it mean that women categorically lack agency to negotiate important conditions of their lives and their work. In fact, there are numerous cultural mechanisms that give individuals what we might think of as wiggling room[48]—as Bina's flight from one brother's house to another's shows (notably, this show of resistance would also have offered her older brother a way of refusing an otherwise respectable offer without offending the family from which it came). Social and material labor are both necessary if families are to reproduce themselves and individuals are to eat, and both are inescapably intertwined with the suffering that women are, in most cases, expected to bear. The alternative is not considered empowerment, but selfish individualism.[49]

Conclusion: Rethinking Empowerment and Political Consciousness

On superficial reading, the testimonies I've gathered here do little to undercut the "failed development" thesis; in fact, they might seem to support it. When the women I interviewed talked about development (*bikās*), they certainly did not see it as a form of violence. Rather, they associated violence with its absence. This was striking because they were almost certainly familiar with Maoist arguments that did indeed frame development as a form of violent imperialism. It was even more striking because almost all of them were skeptical—if not downright cynical—about what most development agencies represent as an identified political ideal—democracy. When I asked women what they hoped to see happen in their communities in upcoming years, the number two answer—after "peace"—was development. Although people mentioned specific complaints like broken water taps and smoke-outlet stoves that, once installed, turned out to be inadequate for regular cooking needs (and off the record, I learned a lot about local resentments about what were perceived as uneven distributions of the opportunities for income and upward mobility that outside projects brought), almost everyone expressed the desire to see roads, bridges, electricity, schools, and hospitals and more income-generating activities come to their area.[50] At least in the language game that we played together, no one challenged the modernization ideal.[51]

On some level, all of this is simply obvious. Just as one doesn't need elaborate social theory to explain why women who work twelve-hour days might wish to lead an easier life, it doesn't take much imagination to understand why farmers in an inaccessible rural district might want their children to have access to a modern hospital. Who wouldn't? The failed development paradigm, however, is an attempt to understand why revolutionary movements receive popular support. Or more particularly, to understand why rural women, even those who do not consider themselves Maoists and who make it clear they hate the violence and everything that has come with it, nonetheless blame politicians ("democracy") for the fact that the violence is happening, and not the Maoists themselves. It's here—at the point where the failed development paradigm is no longer simply stating the obvious—that I would argue it is genuinely dangerous, because it brings with it a whole host of tacit assumptions about what people are like and what they ought to want from life that have very little to do with these women's actual lives or what they find important in them. In fact, I would argue that almost everyone vying to influence or understand these women—foreign academics, NGO workers, and government counterinsurgency advisors alike—share the same flawed assumptions.

So why do subaltern subjects rebel? Perhaps some of the Maoist appeal is related to the dialectic of pleasure and suffering, and its intersection with the moral economy that I have described. In an argument that reflects a Gramscian turn to engagement with culture and popular consciousness, James Scott has proposed that peasants revolt when their sense of justice is violated and that this is typically when their ability to reproduce themselves—what he proposes they perceive as an implicit "right to subsistence" (1976)—is threatened. The argument is powerful, and it is also notable because it avoids some of the problems of similar Marxian-inspired analyses: Scott neither rejects local knowledge as "false consciousness" nor falls into a teleological logic that assumes a progressive model of political development in which subaltern consciousness comes increasingly to match the analysts' own (usually class-based) theory:

> The concept of false consciousness overlooks the very real possibility that the actor's "problem" is not simply one of misperception. It overlooks the possibility that he may, in fact, have his own durable standards of equity and exploitation—standards that lead him to judgments about his situation which are quite different from those of an outside observer equipped with deductive theory. To put it bluntly, the actor

may have his own moral economy. If this is the case, the failure of his views to accord with theory is not due to his inability to see things clearly, but to his values. Of course, one may choose to call these values a form of false consciousness as well. But, to the extent that they are rooted in the actor's existential needs, to the extent that they are resistant to efforts at "reeducation," to the extent that they continue to define the situation for him, it is they and not the theory which serves as reliable guides to his sentiments and behavior. (1976, 160)

In insisting that rebellions may be less matters of consciousness and more matters of morality, and that subsistence and politics meet in the realm of values, Scott's thesis reaches directly to the heart of why the Gorkhali women I worked with give the Maoists their support. Substitute "she" for "he" here, and you have a lot of my own argument. However, I don't think the difference is insignificant. I am not simply—or even particularly—offering a critique of gender-blindness in the failed development hypothesis. Rather, I'm trying to understand how theories of development, empowerment, and rural resistance reproduce their own ideological foundations by representing the modernist ideal of the autonomous self who seeks absolute freedom from the sacrifices and suffering associated with social constraints as the essence of human subjectivity. Gender specificity forces us to confront the more general problem of how we understand and theorize people.

Following the formal declaration of the end of the war and the signing of the Comprehensive Peace Agreement in November 2006,[52] it is more important than ever to try to get that understanding right. From all of these stories, it's easy to see why the Maoists have received such strong rural support. With very few dissenters, the women of Chorigaon accepted the Maoists' claim to be fighting to bring happiness and ease to people like themselves, and they contrasted this to the pain they had suffered at the hands of the state, including both the monarchy and any number of multiparty democratic governments. But why do some people leave the village to join the armed struggle while others, who may be equally sympathetic to the rebellion, stay at home?

There are doubtlessly multiple answers to this question, which is too large to take on fully here, but there may be some clues in what we have seen so far. Saubhagya Shah has proposed that one effect of the recent development rhetoric of participation is that it has created the "paradoxical subject position of agents without an agency" (2002, 145). Similarly, Judith

Pettigrew suggests that "participation in the Maoists enables village youth to participate in a new type of modernity":

> Young villagers see themselves and are seen as marginal to the "good and proper life" (McHugh 2001) offered by town living and enjoyed by those with the money to re-locate. By taking up the Maoist option, they no longer have to look to the town and "foreign" to be "at the heart of the action." Membership in the Maoists re-configures perceptions of a consumerist world that excludes them. (2003, 321)

What is apparent in both of these observations is that identification with the Maoists—in contrast to just sympathizing with them—entails at least some kind of shift in subjectivity. But even here, whatever decisions people make, or perhaps I should say, whatever commitments they decide to undertake, come from thinking of themselves as people who are constituted through relations with others and who value the social outcomes that their sacrifices help create. Recall that Bina framed the difference between the combatants on the two sides of the war in terms of selfishness versus being-for-others, and that she praised the rebels as virtuous and brave.

At the same time, selflessness and bravery may not be all that's going on here. Another way to look at this might be to acknowledge that leaving one's home to join the Maoist cadres in the forests is stepping into a new kind of social identity, which is not a universal goal. Indeed, people who actually do decide to become guerrillas, and hence, new kinds of subjects, accept a break with social traditions that may be easier for some kinds of people to make than others. This would help to explain why so many adolescents—both boys and girls—left their homes for the rebel army in Chorigaon, as elsewhere in Nepal. It would also help to explain why schools have been such effective recruiting sites—education being probably the single most powerful vehicle for social change in rural Nepal and one that changes its subjects in ways that demand new kinds of relations, as Bina's parents' recognition that, unlike her sister, she would not marry a man of their choice indicates.[53] In fact, if one is thinking specifically of the perspective of teenage girls—which my calculations suggest that at least half of the rebel recruits from Chorigaon are, or were, when they ran away—one might note that the experience of going off to a Maoist training camp might not actually be as radical a break as one might think: after all, they are fully expected, at that age, to undergo a major life change that will involve leaving their natal home for a place where they will live under others' orders, endure hardships and suffering, and, at the same time, become more complete people as a result. From the point of view of the would-be girl soldier, the main difference may be that the Maoist option involves a higher degree of physical danger, but also, perhaps, greater opportunities for fun.

If the peace process continues to go forward, a more pressing question than why they left may well become, what will happen to these girls when it's time to return? When the Maoist army decommissions them, will they be able to return to their villages and rejoin social life? Of the ten or so young women from Chorigaon proper who joined the Maoist army before 2004, at least one is dead and the whereabouts of most others are largely unknown.[54] Only one had returned home to the village before the peace agreement was signed.[55] In that situation, her marriage was immediately arranged to the son of a local family who had migrated to Kathmandu, although she was only sixteen. When I met her in the city, I saw that she acted like any young daughter-in-law and her mother-in-law seemed content. However, this is an unusual case because this girl changed her mind even before completing basic training and, in the end, spent only a few weeks away. It remains to be seen whether women who have spent years with the Maoists will be willing to return to the roles they left behind, and how their natal families and potential affines will treat this part of their history. Hisala Yami, wife of the Maoist leader Baburam Bhattarai and former head of the Women's Front, has been quoted as doubting that women, once radicalized, can ever return to their pre-Maoist homes: "Sons will be welcomed back with open arms, but for the daughters, can there be a return? When they become guerrillas, the women set themselves free from patriarchal bonds. How can they go back? That is why the women are more committed" (Gautam, Banskota, and Machanda 2003, 109).

As Nepal shifts from waging war to building peace, this will be just one of the many difficult issues that Gorkhali women and their families will face. And they will doubtless do so against a backdrop of NGOs, "experts," academics, and other well-wishers seeking to assist them in the process of reconciliation and to ensure that women's voices are heard in the transition. Indeed, this is practically guaranteed by the Comprehensive Peace Agreement itself, which commits the interim government to ending gender discrimination (3.5) and establishing a program of development that will facilitate "the socio-economic development of the country and also assist in ensuring the country's economic prosperity in a short period of time" (3.12). What this means is that programs that target Nepali women will continue, and that there will be a continued need for theories about who they are and how best to serve them. This chapter, however, is not meant to provide simple answers. Instead, what I've tried to do is to draw some connections between empowerment programs that rest on certain ideals, Gorkhali women's notorious radicalization, and a sense of what was important to them and what sort of people they think themselves to be. And I've tried to take that seriously enough to consider what it might mean to reexamine our own theoretical assumptions in that light. What happens in Chorigaon—and throughout Nepal—in the next few years will have much to teach people who are concerned with empowerment—women's or otherwise. But understanding it may require interrogating deeply held assumptions about agency, gender, development, and revolutionary consciousness.

Notes

1. Despite the fact that the government had been presented with a forty-point list of demands two weeks earlier, which it had neither acknowledged nor responded to. For more information on the political history of the CPN (Maoist) or the start of the People's War, see Karki and Seddon (2003a) and other contributions to the same volume.

2. See Kernot and Gurung (2003). This is a conservative estimate. A study carried out a year later by the Community Study and Welfare Centre (CSWC), an NGO advocating for the rights of internally displaced persons (IDPs), estimates that somewhere between 350,000 and 400,000 people have been displaced from their villages.

3. Recent anthropological and historical works alone include Hutt (2004), Karki and Seddon (2003b), Onesto (2005), Thapa (2003), Gellner (2003). Not to mention a virtual industry of reports commissioned by security concerns, aid organizations, and NGOs.

4. De Sales notes that in the two districts of Rolpa and Rukum combined there isn't a single hospital or any industry (2003, 342). Ironically, a $US 50 million, fifteen-year project in the Rapti Zone had concluded just a month and a half before the formal onset of the insurrection. On decreasing agricultural yield and increasing deprivation between 1960 and 1990, see MacFarlane (2001); see also Seddon (2001).

5. See, for instance, Parvati (2003), Pettigrew and Schneiderman (2004), Shakya (2003), Shova, Gautam and Shakya (1999), Shobha, Gautam (2001), Manchanda (1999), Onesto (2005), Maycock (2003).

6. S. Sharma (2000, 35–36) made a similar argument about USAID programs in the Rapti Zone (Gellner 2002, 21). Karki and Seddon mention this possibility as well (Karki and Seddon 2003a, 19).

7. See note 40.

8. Nepali villages comprise dense and overlapping social networks which offer those who live there various ways of positioning themselves at different times; indeed, managing different identities in different contexts is one of the skills that villagers use to get by. As Radachowsky puts it, perhaps somewhat overconfidently, "it is possible to live in the context of the 'People's War' but one must wear two or three faces. One for the Maoists. One for the State security forces. And a real face for people they trust" (Radachowsky 2003).

9. This, like all personal and institutional names in this paper, is a pseudonym I have created to protect the privacy of the people involved.

10. The "unification"—as this process is usually called—took place over the course of the eighteenth and early nineteenth centuries and brought together more than one hundred independent polities by war, marriage, or alliance/annexation. That Nepali British soldiers are called "Gurkhas" to this day reflects the fact that it was the king of Gorkha who gave the British permission to recruit within his domain, which was known at that time not as "Nepal" but as "the entire territories of the king from Gorkha." "Gurkha" is a mispronunciation of this place name. See Burghart (1984).

11. In 2001, Gorkha had a total population of 288,134 people. Although Gurungs are numerically dominant in the district, the area I'm calling Chorigaon had a relatively diverse ethnic/caste composition of Gurung, Magar, Newar, Brahmin-Chhetri, Baramu, and occupational groups. There is no one economically dominant caste in the area.

12. At the time of the 2001 census, there were 801 households with a total population of 4,234 people. See http://www.thlib.org/places/culturalgeography/nepal/census/output.php (accessed 6/20/13).

13. A local Maoist told Li Onesto, a visiting journalist, that: "We went at night and seized equipment and money. This organization gives money for education and does social work, but they direct people away from the real revolutionary solution and promote Christianity." I feel that I must state for the record here that DFA is not a Christian organization and, despite extensive interaction with both the local and national level staff, I have never seen any evidence of religious evangelism by DFA or its employees. "Hope of the Hopeless in Gorkha," http://rwor.org/a/v21/1040–049/1042/nepa122.htm.

14. Field Office Team (1983, 8).

15. Field Office Team, 28.

16. Sob and Leslie (1988, 9).

17. Sob and Leslie, 3.

18. It was released by Nepal's Ministry of Education in 1984 and immediately adopted by DFA.

19. As opposed to "education as the practice of domination" (Freire 1997, 62).
20. World Education (1989, 1).
21. World Education (1989). In addition to consciousness-raising activities, the curriculum also included concrete instruction in DFA's community development priorities such as family planning, livestock raising, planting fodder trees in landslide areas, how to prepare oral rehydration solution, and how to construct pit latrines and smoke-outlet stoves.
22. The second year, the monthly fee was raised to fifty *paisa*, and five rupees were collected for the books, raising the total cost for a year of class to thirteen rupees. The third year the monthly fee went up to one rupee and the book fee to ten rupees, bringing the total cost to twenty-one rupees (Sob and Leslie 1988, 12–13).
23. See Leve (1993).
24. For instance, the increased need for someone in the family to have a nonagricultural job; plus literate sons are believed to want literate wives.
25. World Education (1989, 2).
26. These are not the only two possibilities, of course. There's also a third approach (Grillo and Stirrat 1997; Leve 2001; Li 1991; Pigg 1993) that looks at development largely through its ironies and contradictions—noting, for example, that even neoliberal programs which explicitly aim to depoliticize populations, or to legitimate oppressive regimes, almost never succeed in doing so, or that even those sincerely intended to alleviate misery or to empower often end up inspiring or prolonging violent conflict. For instance, the massive growth of microcredit programs that provide women with gender-based access to capital resources has been documented as having actually increased violence against women in Bangladesh (Feldman 1997; Karim 2001; Rahman 1999). This paper might be said to be an example of this third approach.
27. U.S. Agency for International Development (USAID), "Budget Justification to the Congress FY 2004," http://pdf.usaid.gov/pdf_docs/PDACE110.pdf, accessed 6/20/2013.
28. http://pdf.usaid.gov/pdf_docs/PDACE110.pdf.
29. Prelude to "The National Security Strategy of the United States of America," released by the president's office, September 2002.
30. http://pdf.usaid.gov/pdf_docs/PDACE110.pdf.
31. http://www.aid/gov/pubs/cp98/ane/countries/np.htm, accessed March 21, 2005. No longer available.
32. http://www.aid/gov/pubs/cp98/ane/countries/np.htm, accessed March 21, 2005. No longer available.
33. Others have also commented on the transformation of the empowerment model from one based on the conscientization paradigm to one reflecting neoliberal norms. See, for example, Feldman (1997), Fernando (1997), Kabeer (1994), Karim (2001), Leve (2001), Tamang (2002). Katherine Rankin has also analyzed this shift through the lens of microcredit, which she blasts as a governmental strategy that

is "all the more pernicious in its approbation of feminist languages . . . to alternative (and fundamentally conservative) ends" (2001, 30).

34. This is too large an assertion to be demonstrable here, but see, for instance, Spivak (1988a, 1988b) on Guha and subaltern studies, or Laclau and Mouffe (1985) on Marx's theoretical legacies.

35. It was 0.04 percent higher in 1988, to be precise (Nepal South Asian Center, 1998).

36. See Butler (1990, 1993) for a theory of gender as performative action.

37. See Ahearn (2001) for a sensitive ethnographic study of changing marriage practices and the impact of literacy and schooling on individual aspirations and social and subjective identities in a nearby district.

38. Nanu's disillusionment with democracy was widely shared. "Democracy has done nothing but kill . . . people," Ram Maya lamented. Similarly, Sobita felt "it's due to democracy that we have no peace. . . . In my thinking the multiparty system has not fulfilled anyone's desires or expectations. . . . We thought there would be development, but now the works have either been stopped, destroyed, or burned down. Democracy has invited violence and killings, it seems."

39. To be sure, I did meet a few people who were critical of the Maoists (including the very aggrieved father of a teenage girl who had run away to join the People's Army). However, I didn't hear any reports of Maoist violence against villagers other than early "punishments" (humiliation, maiming) meted out to "class enemies," who, by 2002, had long fled the district. In contrast, I heard many complaints of police and military brutalities. As noted, this may have reflected a greater awareness of the proximity of Maoist cadres in the village itself. However, it is also likely that people who were most critical of the Maoists had left over the years and those who remained were genuinely sympathetic or else had learned to keep silent. On a related note, it's clear that people in the village were uncomfortable speaking directly about the Maoists in interviews in a way that people I interviewed in Kathmandu were not. They tended to refer to the rebels only obliquely or indirectly (for example, "he's not like that, we would have known") and, in this, made use of speech patterns that were similar to the ones that they used to refer to their husbands and other figures deserving certain kinds of formal respect—for instance, a rural woman will almost never use her husband's name, and even referring to someone as "my husband" can be regarded as excessively bold. In Nani Maya's testimony, for instance, where I have inserted "my husband," she said only "he," leaving the listener to infer whom she meant. One way of interpreting this may be that they were uncomfortable talking about such sensitive material with me or others who were writing it down, which is surely true to some degree, no matter how much they said otherwise. Yet I don't think this is all. Since honorific speech denotes distance as well as respect, I understand these practices as also reflecting their fear of either speaking too transparently or seeming to suggest intimacy, since speech could bring trouble, either from the rebels or, especially, from the security forces if it led them to think you had in-

formation that they might want. It is also true that many kinds of information are communicated much less explicitly in Nepal than in the United States and, even before the war, Nepalis were skilled at interpreting indirect speech and silences.

40. This is an allusion to the common belief that a woman should regard her husband as if he were a god and to the widespread rural practice of paying formal respect to husbands and mothers-in-law by bowing to their feet daily.

41. As Sita described the start of an average day in the village for a daughter-in-law.

42. "Development" (bikās) might also be placed on this list. If so—again based on what they told me—it would include water taps, electricity, bridges and roads, and peace.

43. I heard this many times in Chorigaon as well, and the classification always pointed to its inevitability as well as recognizing that it meant suffering.

44. See also March (2002).

45. Much of this discussion echoes analyses that feminist theorists and anthropologists working with women in South Asia have been saying for decades. See, for example, Des Chene (1998), M. Roy (1992), Kumar (1994), Skinner, Pach, and Holland (1998), McHugh (2001), March (2002), Chodorow (1989), Enslin (1998). This also parallels a more general debate about the relative individuality versus interdependence of Hindu South Asian ideas of the person as a whole (Appadurai 1986; Daniel 1987; Dumont 1970; Marriott 1989; Marriott and Inden 1977; Mines 1994).

46. It is expected that a bride will cry at her wedding and refuse to leave with the groom. Not to do so would be considered surprising, and to express enthusiasm for the marriage, shameless.

47. Although parents say it hurts them to send their daughters away knowing the hardship that is likely in store, the suffering that women experience in their new homes is accepted as an inevitable part of the next stage of their lives—that is, growing up and being a woman.

48. Veena Das has illustrated the difference between formal kinship rules and what she calls "practical kinship" and shown how the flexibility of kinship in practice offers individuals and communities options—sometimes necessary for survival—that often do not "officially" exist (1995).

49. In a project that closely parallels my own, Saba Mahmood has explored how liberal assumptions about freedom and autonomy have become naturalized in feminist scholarship. She uses the case of Muslim women in Egypt who self-consciously undertake to cultivate illiberal, seemingly disempowering, sensibilities to challenge feminist presumptions that self-realization is inimical to any kind of subjugation and that freedom consists in the ability to pursue one's own interests, which belong to an independent subject who exists prior to subjectifying power. While Mahmood is concerned with embodied practice rather than political consciousness, and the revolution she examines is conducted with ethics, not guns, we come to similar conclusions about the role of certain types

of power in constituting how women come to know themselves and be known to others in any given situation, and about the importance of this for thinking about self-realization or agency: "The women I worked with did not regard trying to emulate authorized models of behavior as an external social imposition that constrained individual freedom. Rather, they treated socially authorized forms of performance as the potentialities—the ground if you will—through which the self is realized" (2005, 31).

50. There are at least three possible explanations for this: (1) they were genuinely that invested in development as an ideal; (2) they associated me with DFA, and they were being polite; (3) despite reservations about the enterprise as a whole, they hoped that I could bring DFA back into the area and provide projects that would reinvigorate the local economy. I suspect that the truth contains elements of all three.

51. One might also argue that these women did in fact challenge development ideals in a host of practical ways, such as taking their teenage daughters out of school to get married or redeploying microcredit loans for unauthorized purposes (see Rankin n.d.). But if people were aware of these actions as acts of resistance, they certainly didn't speak of them as such to me and, even if it were pointed out to them, I'm skeptical that they would see it in that way.

52. In April 2006, King Gyanendra reinstated the elected parliament he had dissolved when he staged a palace coup in February 2005, ending fourteen months of direct rule. Among the first things the reinstated parliament did was strip the king of his power and privileges, including control of the army, and consent to the long-standing Maoist demand for a constituent assembly which would decide the fate of the monarchy and write a new constitution. Four months later, the prime minister and the Maoist supremo issued identical requests to the United Nations for peacekeepers to monitor the ceasefire and help negotiate the Maoist disarmament. On November 21, they signed a Comprehensive Peace Agreement that brought the Maoists officially into the interim government and declared the end of the ten-year People's War.

53. And indeed, schools in Chorigaon have paid a high price for their influence. While many of the local teachers did have moderate to adamant Maoist sympathies, their allegiances were hardly uniform. Nevertheless, in addition to the teacher Nani Maya mentioned, who was taken from his home at night and killed by the armed police early in the war, two others were arrested and held for over a month before being released. Another much-loved teacher (who was driven underground early in the war) was killed in the village on a holiday (Tihar) when he secretly returned to visit his mother and wife. And the first Maoist martyr in the area was a student who was shot by the police just fourteen days after the start of the war while trying to prevent the arrest of a teacher. And all this in addition to regular school closings and harassment by the security forces. While Maoist abductions of teachers and schoolchildren for forced "education" and/or induction has been widely reported in other parts of Nepal, I did not hear of this hap-

pening in Chorigaon, although people there acknowledged that Maoists often visited the schools and staged different types of "programs."

54. The mother of one girl told me that she knew her daughter was alive only because the Maoists had not yet come to tell her she was dead.

55. One local boy had a similar tale, having left for the jungle only to be fetched by his mother, who was a friend of the regional commander and not willing to risk the death of her only son. After bringing him back, that family moved to the district center and eventually to Kathmandu.

CHAPTER 3

Aradhana Sharma

The State and Women's Empowerment in India
Paradoxes and Politics

Introduction

I faced an interesting conundrum as I began research on the Mahila Samakhya program or MS (as it is commonly called), a Government of India–sponsored rural women's empowerment initiative. The source of my puzzlement was the shifting manner in which program staff introduced the program in different situations. For instance, at a meeting with Block Office[1] administrators in eastern Uttar Pradesh, Meena Rani, a program representative, introduced MS as "a [program] of the Human Resource Development Ministry of the Government of India . . . that attempts to empower women, raise their awareness and make them self-reliant."[2] However, just a few days prior to this meeting, Meena Rani had presented MS as a nongovernmental organization (NGO) to a group of village women she was attempting to recruit as program participants. When these women asked her what benefits they would receive from the program, Meena Rani responded that they would only get information, knowledge, and support; MS was a *sanstha* (NGO), and not a *sarkari* (government) program that distributed things to participants.

I had observed other field staff[3] resorting to a similar mobile positioning of MS, at times as an NGO and at other times as a government program, and wondered whether staff members were simply unclear about MS's identity. When I voiced my puzzlement to Sunita Pathak, a program administrator, she explained that

"[MS] is partly governmental, and it is also nongovernmental. . . . The national level [program in New Delhi] is strictly governmental. . . . [But] from the state level onward, [MS] is an autonomous organization." In the development world MS would be considered a Government Organized Nongovernmental Organization or GONGO, a seemingly contradictory parastatal entity. Pathak's elucidation of the program's hybrid nature cleared up some of my confusion, but it led me to question why the program was structured as a GONGO and why its personnel identified the program in a shifting either/or (NGO/GO) manner rather than as a GONGO in front of government and rural audiences.

In this essay, I take up these questions and use the MS program's hybrid organizational form and empowerment activities to point to some of the ways in which governance, the state, and women's political activism are being transformed in neoliberal India. The current regime of neoliberal governmentality, as scholars building on Foucauldian insights have argued, is characterized by the rise of novel mechanisms of self-governance (like empowerment), new institutions of rule (like NGOs and GONGOs), and the increased entanglement of such institutions with state bodies in the project of governance.[4] Grassroots empowerment, along with participation and state–civil society partnerships, have emerged as key words under neoliberalism and are being promoted by various actors, including the United Nations, the World Bank, NGOs, and states, as ideal strategies of development and governance (Sharma 2008).

How does one position the MS program and make sense of its workings in this larger transnational neoliberal context? Does the program's combination of certain critical aspects of neoliberal governance, such as empowerment and state–civil society collaboration, make MS a typical neoliberal intervention? I contend that it does not. Indeed, the MS program's alternative and layered borrowings from feminist, leftist, and radical pedagogy-based (Freire 1970) empowerment frameworks and its emphasis on women's *collective*, anti-oppression-focused political work make it difficult to qualify it as a model neoliberal initiative, writ large. What I hope to show is how MS *articulates* with the globally dominant neoliberal mantra and what this tells us about the reconfiguration of governance, the state, and subaltern and feminist struggles in postliberalization India.

I begin this essay by discussing the rationale behind the MS program's GONGO form. I then analyze how this GONGO form materializes in the work identities and lives of its personnel, describing the constraints and opportunities that MS's hybrid structure brings up. While the program's linkage with the state puts restrictions on the mobilization work its representatives do, its crossbred GONGO form and NGO affiliation also afford some maneuverability. I argue that MS functionaries' shifting usage of the two aspects of the program's identity—its government and nongovernmental labels—is a strategy that allows them to sometimes subvert state discipline and repression, and to expand the meanings and practices of empowerment.

I analyze both the discursive and material effects of the program personnel's tactical moves and unravel the paradoxes that arise when empowerment is implemented as a category of governance: it can simultaneously bureaucratize women's lives and unleash unexpected forms of empowerment. These uneven consequences of the MS program's GONGO nature raise broader questions about feminist partnerships with state agencies in postliberal India. MS began as an experiment that gave women's movement activists a testing ground for working with, rather than against, the state and implementing large-scale projects for equality and justice (Jandhyala 2001). I conclude this essay by exploring the potential of feminist-cum-state collaborations under neoliberalism. My intention is to not make easy judgments about whether feminist alliances with state agencies are good or bad (Ferguson 1990) or whether the effects of empowerment programs undertaken by such alliances are uniformly liberatory or conformist. Rather, I take my cue from many of my informants and from Foucault to argue that the governmentalization of empowerment is "dangerous" in that it is laden with risks *and* unexpected possibilities (Foucault 1982, 231; Sharma 2008). The tale I tell, therefore, is not one about the unequivocally depoliticizing effects of empowerment; rather, I tease out the forms and modalities of subaltern and feminist politics that are enabled by the governmentalization of empowerment in the neoliberal age and signal their limits (see also Chatterjee 2004).

Why a GONGO?

In 1989 the Government of India initiated the Mahila Samakhya program with Dutch funding.[5] MS was patterned after the Women's Development Programme, or WDP, then operating in Rajasthan, which had empowerment as its explicit goal. Transnational feminist scholarship and activism in the field of development identified empowerment as an ideal strategy for gender-equitable and just development (Sen and Grown 1987; Young 1993, 127–46; Kabeer 1994). Women's movement activists in India borrowed from such feminist thinking and other radical frameworks to design MS; a senior civil servant, Anil Bordia, facilitated this process (Sharma 2008). The program views social hierarchies and women's lack of awareness about their rights and about government programs as obstacles to their development. MS does not distribute material resources; rather, it mobilizes marginalized rural women through collective empowerment or "conscientization" strategies (Freire 1970), whereby they reflect on their oppressions, take action to address their problems, and come into their own as agents of change (Government of India 1997).

MS is considered innovative not only because of its nonmaterial empowerment focus but also for its crossbred GONGO structure. Why this crossbred form, and why did women's movement activists, who heretofore had had an uneasy relationship with state agencies, agree to partner with the government on an empowerment initiative?

When I posed this question to activists, some explained their willingness to work with the state as a consequence of the shifting political terrain in the 1980s. Indira Gandhi's declaration of a state of emergency in 1975, and the resultant suspension of civil rights, led to a deep suspicion of the state and the nurturing of autonomous activist spaces. However, Rajiv Gandhi's attempts to innovate government in the mid-1980s, and his promise to give greater priority to women's issues, played an important role in repositioning the state as a possible, if risky, arena for creative activist work.[6]

Feminist involvement in state development projects during the 1980s was also shaped by a realization that NGO efforts and autonomous organizational strategies were limited in their reach and results. "[Our thinking was that] we need to . . . make more impact on mainstream structures. We cannot [work] in isolation. So the question of partnerships, linkages, networks [arose in] . . . the 1980s," explained Versha Rai, a member of the core MS team. When the opportunity to collaborate with the government on designing and implementing a national-level, women's empowerment program—Mahila Samakhya—presented itself, some activists saw it as a chance to take their feminist ideas of gender equality, justice, and social change "to scale"—that is, to reach out to large groups of disenfranchised women, to use state resources to facilitate meaningful transformation, to mainstream gender within state institutions, and to perhaps reconfigure these institutions themselves (Jandhyala 2001).

In addition to noting the benefits of the state's wider reach and greater resources, many of my informants also saw state involvement in grassroots development efforts as its duty toward its most marginalized citizens, which ought not to be privatized. Furthermore, a few felt that the program's association with the Government of India gave MS authority and legitimacy in bureaucratic circles. "You write 'Government of India,' and everybody knows that you are a government program. [It] helps [with] credibility," explained Sunita Pathak, a civil servant who worked with MS.

The advantages of state participation in a women's empowerment initiative, however, were tempered by drawbacks. "The main problem is that a state, given its very nature . . . , says that if program A has three components, program A will have three components forever," claimed one bureaucrat, as he discussed the rigidity of the typical bureaucratic approach, which discouraged flexibility and innovation. Other disadvantages that my informants brought up included target-driven and top-down development strategies, red tape, political expediency, inefficiency, and corruption.

Some activists I spoke with raised more serious problems associated with government involvement in feminist and grassroots empowerment. "To be able to question issues is not something that the government and the state would like," explained Kaveri Mani. "It has a class bias. It has an urban bias. It has an elitist mode. So why should it . . . initiate a program which is going to question its own role and interest!" Nina Singh, a civil servant, added: "A government program . . . does not integrate the element of struggle that lies at the heart of empowerment. . . . That is the biggest constraint—that struggle is not understood in a government lexicon. [Bureaucrats] reduce everything to a safe thing called 'development.'" The government, hence, could not be trusted as the sole agent for women's empowerment given the inequalities it expressed and promoted, and its potential to co-opt and depoliticize struggle.

MS planners therefore desired a quasi-nongovernmental identity for MS. An NGO-like structure, they felt, would mitigate the problems with state involvement and bring in benefits, such as grassroots-level accountability and legitimacy, a bottom-up orientation, participatory and decentralized ways of working, flexibility, and a motivated workforce. In Kaveri Mani's words, "While women's groups have the advantages of being small . . . , of being close to the people, . . . [and] of having a committed staff, the advantage of the state was its outreach . . . and large scale. And so there was this feeling that it is possible to marry the two."[7]

Mahila Samakhya's GONGO structure represents this experimental "marriage" or partnership. While the national program office is part of the Department of Education of the Ministry of Human Resource Development and is headed by a bureaucrat, at the level of each participating state, MS is implemented through nongovernmental "MS Societies." The staff at the state, district, and block levels of the program is drawn from the NGO sector, and its advisory bodies are comprised of both ex officio and nongovernmental members, with the latter having at least 51 percent representation.

The MS program's crossbred structure, thus, was the result of its planners' desire to combine the positive aspects of state and NGO approaches to women's development and to preserve partial independence for the program. Because some activists were wary about collaborating with state agencies and concerned about the possible co-optation of feminist agendas of empowerment by the state, they created a semi-autonomous GONGO. But what does this GONGO form mean in practice? How does it manifest itself in the daily work lives of MS staff members, and does it, in fact, afford them relative autonomy from official dictates?

MS as a Moving Target

The program's hybrid organization raised two key conundrums for its workforce. First, they had to define their work identities. As GONGO workers, were they government employees or NGO employees? The latter received less remuneration but had more flexibility in their work, whereas the former earned more but had to work within governmental dictates. Second, MS representatives had to carefully manage their state and non-state identities in front of different audiences with varied imaginations of and expectations for state and nonstate actors. While the program's hybrid identity raised these dilemmas for its workforce, it also provided a partial resolution, as I illustrate below. Program employees mobilely positioned MS and themselves, using both GO and NGO labels to negotiate the very contradictions that the mixed GONGO form and state involvement form threw in their path, and generated unexpectedly empowering results. I also discuss what these program practices reveal about the discursive nature of the state and about the paradoxical effects of state-sponsored women's empowerment.

MS personnel rarely, if ever, identified the program as a GONGO in work-related situations, preferring instead to switch between its governmental and nongovernmental labels. Prabha Kishore, a mid-level MS employee, explained that "MS . . . wears two hats—one is a governmental hat and the other is a nongovernmental hat. We have made very good use of both these hats." She told me that she kept two letterheads. "When we write to NGOs, we use the . . . letterhead that states that Mahila Samakhya is a voluntary organization registered under the 1860 Societies Act and gives our registration number. We open [the letter] with 'Dear Colleague or Dear Friend, *Namaste*,'" she said in a sweet voice. "[But] when we need to put pressure . . . [we use] the letterhead bearing the words, 'Ministry of Human Resource Development.'" Kishore enunciated the last phrase slowly, emphasizing each word. "This letterhead evokes the reaction," she lowered her voice and stated fearfully, "'Oh God, this is a government program!' We even stamp our seal on these letters and sign them—we write them exactly like government letters are written."

To express authority, as Kishore described, MS staff members used the style, language, and voice of the state. I observed them don the governmental garb when they needed to garner the support of state administrators who might be hostile toward NGOs and women's empowerment. They also worked the bureaucratic hierarchy to their advantage by emphasizing to state, district, and block officials that MS was a program of the highest, national-level government body—the Government of India—which therefore needed to be treated with seriousness and respect.[8]

Program representatives also took on governmental personas in front of rural audiences when they wanted to perform authority. For instance, Leela Vati, a fieldworker, used the state tag to intimidate her clients. She ordered participants in some MS villages, from where the program was being phased out, to return the few things (like rugs and water pails) that their village collectives had received from the MS program. She did not have any explicit mandate from her superiors for doing so. MS participants in Bilaspur village told me that Leela Vati had threatened them when they refused to comply—"If you don't return the things, the government jeep [used by the program] will come tomorrow, forcibly take everything, and dishonor you in front of everyone!" She even took the village collective leader's signature on a blank sheet of paper. Bilaspur's women alleged that Leela Vati could easily avoid being implicated in any wrongdoing by writing a note on that piece of paper stating that the village women had voluntarily returned the things. Leela Vati thus effectively used statist symbols and practices, such as a jeep and written documentation (Gupta and Sharma 2006), to enact "official" authority, and played on the women's fear of the coercive state-as-taker.

When it was not authority but legitimacy that MS representatives desired or when they needed to justify the program's lack of resources, they wore the NGO hat. For instance, when introducing MS to potential program participants, they often identified themselves as NGO workers who were interested in building meaningful relationships with villagers, clearly distinguishing their unselfish and committed work ethic from that of state employees. NGO identification also helped when potential clients asked what tangible resources they would receive from MS. Program representatives were well aware of the popular image of the state-as-giver among rural subalterns who expected government development programs to provide for their material needs.[9] Positioning MS as a resource-poor NGO in such situations helped staff members to fend off clients' demands for concrete entitlements. Moreover, it helped explain the temporariness of the program and justify its phase-out. For example, when program participants in Seelampur block, where formal MS structures were being dismantled, charged Danu Bai, an MS fieldworker, with leaving them in the lurch, she responded that MS was a time-bound NGO project that had to end and not a government program "that [would] go on forever."

MS functionaries' shifting representation of the program in different contexts and in front of diverse audiences both catered to and shaped their interlocutors' ideas about the state and NGOs. People's imaginations of these entities are based on their social locations, on previous interactions with bureaucracies and NGOs, and on public cultural representations (Gupta 1995). For example, the subaltern actors I met often used the term "mai-baap" (mother-father) to describe the state and its functionaries; for them the "ideal" state, like good parents, was supposed to take care of their survival needs.[10] In practice, however, the local officials they encountered tended to be dishonest and uncaring. For rural subalterns, the predominantly authoritative face of the state-as-taker, which took away information, through census practices, and even fertility, compromised the legitimacy attached to the ideal parental state-as-caretaker. MS representatives had to navigate through such sedimented understandings of the state when pitching the program to differently positioned audiences. They played the apparent breach between the "G" and "NG" parts of the program's GONGO identity, thereby constructing NGOs as legitimate, time-bounded entities with no resources, and the state as an authoritative and perpetual entity flush with resources but with questionable legitimacy. Thus, by mobilely positioning the program, MS workers discursively entrenched the boundary between state and nonstate spheres.

Even though they wore different hats in different situations as a programmatic strategy, most MS functionaries allied themselves with the just and legitimate NGO world. For example, Seema Batra, an employee, told me that "[many] people who work for MS do not treat it like government service. . . . The salaries [we] get . . . are not enough for survival. So the people who work in MS do so only because they have a certain 'devotion' toward their work. You don't see that in government departments [where] people come only for the sake of their salaries." Indian public cultural discourses are rife with condemnations of the "nine to five" mentality, lack of motivation, and low productivity of government workers, and MS employees' efforts to dissociate themselves from this negativity partook of the widely prevalent critique of the state. Their careful self-positioning as NGO workers reproduced an image of the state as an entity that fosters sloth and apathy, and employs inefficient people who treat their work merely as a job. They implicitly constructed the NGO world as a distinct haven of creativity, meaningful and hard work, enthusiasm, and innovation.

The self-identification of MS personnel with the NGO sector was materially reflected in their earnings: MS employees did not receive the higher compensation and benefits associated with government jobs (Sharma 2008). Yet, like state employees, they were prohibited from leading or participating in antistate demonstrations. Ironically, most issues that MS clients took up in their quest for empowerment, such as basic needs, police matters, laws, land titles, or access to information, involved dealing with and sometimes agitating against specific state bureaucracies. But women working for MS, positioned by the government in such instances as quasi-state "GONGO" employees, were forbidden from taking part in the antistate protests of poor women they had mobilized. Seema Singh, an MS functionary, described this catch-22:

All the issues that we take up are, in some way, connected to the government. So if we come within the ambit of the government and succumb to governmental pressure, we will not be able to take up any issues. For example, the government issues licenses for *thekas* [liquor shops]. In our district we took up a big fight on this issue. In one village the police beat up women with wooden sticks as they were trying to bust the local *theka*. Many women had broken bones, but we did not back off and surrender to the government. A few days later, the *theka* closed down. . . . If we had caved in to governmental pressure, we would have never been able to take up this fight.

Singh told me that the presence of a government-licensed liquor store in the local market had increased incidents of harassment and domestic violence against women and girls, and her office took up this fight. "We got a written notice [from the government] that we could not participate in any *aandolan* [protest]," she explained. "[But] we devised ways of participating; we strategized. Can't participate? Hah! We spearheaded a big anti-alcohol campaign and shouted so many slogans against the government. During the protest, when government officials asked us who we were, we simply pretended to be village women!" Singh's team members filed properly worded leave applications at the MS office, took the day off, and protested as ordinary citizens. They circumvented state discipline and violence, and accomplished their empowerment-focused goals by identifying as local residents and carefully following written bureaucratic procedures.

Sunita Mathur, another MS staff person, demonstrated a similar subversive use of statist proceduralism. She helped women belonging to the Kol tribe in Ganna village to obtain a section of the village commons for their survival needs. This piece of land was considered prime property because it bordered a canal and a major road. Upper-caste men in the village, upset over losing this valuable land, retaliated by razing Kol huts. When Sunita Mathur heard about this, she trained the Kol women in formal, official grievance methods. She dictated to them the text of a written complaint detailing the incident. They were to bypass the block-level administration and hand in two copies of the complaint directly to the Sub-District Magistrate (SDM), a higher, district-level bureaucrat. They also had to ensure that the SDM signed and stamped "received" on both copies, and keep one copy for their records. The Kol women, under Mathur's guidance, used these standard governmental procedures and managed to retain the disputed land.

Despite its successful application in this instance, MS functionaries' use of bureaucratic proceduralism has contradictory implications for women's empowerment. On the one hand, it governmentalizes women's everyday lives and multiplies statist languages throughout society. It privileges a formalized mode of appeal that speaks to the state in its own language and requires special knowledge of bureaucratic methods; it can, therefore, delegitimize other idioms and modalities of protest. The use of such techniques can also instate problematic hierarchies between MS functionaries and participants, particularly when the former, who have more formal literacy and are better schooled in the ways of the state, use bureaucratic means to demand compliance from the very women they are meant to empower (as in Leela Vati's example above). These hierarchies can, in turn, work against the equality-oriented empowerment agenda of the MS program. On the other hand, however, encountering officials, gain-ing information about how bureaucracies work, and learning statist methods can also enable subaltern women to demand accountability and entitlements from state agencies. These methods also benefit the program's field staff, whose daily empowerment work can be dangerous. Their use of proceduralism, paper pushing, and creative positioning of themselves and the program allow them to navigate repression and violence by state and other powerful actors, as I now illustrate.

In the village of Naudia, Sunita Mathur's team assisted lower-caste women in fighting upper-caste male control over land. With its help, Naudia's MS clients called a meeting of the entire village to discuss land-related problems. At Mathur's request, Naudia's headman logged a meeting announcement in the *panchayat* (village council) register and circulated it among the residents. Upper-caste men were incensed by this notice and threatened to attack MS staff members and participants for daring to take them on. They also misinformed the local Senior Superintendent of Police, or SSP, that MS had mobilized a large group of people who were planning to *gherao* (surround or besiege) the police station in protest. On the appointed day, the forces of five police stations encircled the meeting participants. The SDM and SSP summoned Sunita Mathur to a spot some distance away from the gathering. She, however, was concerned about her safety and refused to meet the officials alone. So some village women accompanied her to the designated spot, acting as chaperones and witnesses to the exchange that ensued. Here is how Mathur described it:

The Circle Officer [a police officer] asked us a lot of questions—as a harassment tactic. He pointed to the MS jeep and asked me whose vehicle that was. I just shrugged my shoulders. "Where did you get this vehicle?" he questioned. The jeep had Government of India written on it. I avoided answering the question directly and simply stated that we got it from whoever gave it to us. . . . He asked me for my name. I said, "You can write it down—my name is Sunita and I work for Mahila Samakhya." "Is this a government program?" he asked. "Well, if the board on the jeep says Government of India, then maybe [it is] a government program. I, however, am not from the government," I answered. Then he told me that he . . . had received information that we were going to surround the local police station. "You have put a Government of India board on your vehicle and you dare to work against the Government of India! You are going against the administration!" he accused. "We are not doing anything against the administration," I replied, "and this meeting has not been called by MS. Here is the meeting announcement written by the village chief." I showed him the village council register with the recorded announcement. "The issue . . . was put forward by village women. MS staff members are not involved in this. Just like you are here to provide security, we . . . are here [as] representatives of a women's group to support the village women's cause."

The Circle Officer flaunted his official status to intimidate MS women. His performance contributed to the construction of the state as a vertically authoritative and masculinist superstructure that secures the existing social order (Mitchell 1999; Ferguson and Gupta 2002; Sharma 2008). Police functionaries and bureaucrats were present in Naudia to protect the interests of landowning upper-caste men, to defend state institutions from being challenged by subaltern women, and to secure their own positions as powerful state representatives. Their visceral display of prestige and authority enacted the prerogative dimension of state power, which rests on the state's monopoly on legitimate violence (Brown 1995). The officials' use of the language of "security" to threaten MS women also reveals how violence underwrites governmental concerns of care and protection of society (Dean 2001; Sunder Rajan 2003), and here it was being deployed to secure the welfare of some members of society over others. Sunita Mathur had to avoid getting implicated for instigating what the local administration and police saw as an antigovernment agitation and endangering the social order. Her vagueness about the MS program's nature and affiliation, self-identification as an NGO activist, and use of a meeting announcement written by the village headman were some of the tactics she used to circumvent harassment and imminent harm from state functionaries and powerful landowners. "I felt that if I really had been a government representative, then I would not have been able to accomplish anything [or] . . . do anything against the government," declared Sunita. "You see, the local mafia is supported by the administration. And we have to fight against the mafia because otherwise the issues of land and violence will never get solved and economic self-reliance will never happen. . . . That is why I have strategically decided not to use the government label."

Sunita Mathur used the word "mafia" to describe the powerful nexus between the landowning elite, local government functionaries, and organized corruption and crime. Upper-caste landowners get village commons titled in their own names with the help of local officials. These men routinely threaten low-caste women who dare to challenge them and hire goons to beat or rape them, or tear down their houses. The police and local administrators, who are in cahoots with the landowners, do not prevent land encroachment and violence; nor do they assist low-caste women in bringing cases against upper-caste men.

The Naudia incident vividly illustrates how deeply enmeshed state administrators are in the issues that concern subaltern women. The struggles that MS women take up in their empowerment efforts are directed at local structures of authority that include, and exceed, the state. This view from the bottom illustrates the difficulty of drawing a clear line between state and nonstate arenas and actors on the ground. The embeddedness of officials in local power dynamics reveals that the state is sometimes understood not so much as a spatially distinct entity but as a critical node in a network of power relations, through which other social inequalities, like those of class, caste, and gender, are channeled and reproduced. In this view, power and authority are messy and not neatly contained within the conventional boundaries of the state. The struggles of MS participants are not always directed against a clearly demarcated or abstract state, but against locally entrenched webs of power in which state representatives are key players. This blurring gives officials all the more reason to re-create the local state's distinctness, verticality, and legitimacy as the defender of law and protector of order, when needed, through exhibitions of power and prestige. Subaltern struggles for justice and entitlements thus shed light on both the evanescent "now here, now gone" nature of the boundary between the state and nonstate realms and the pressing need to draw it as a way to maintain the status quo. These mobilizations may also end up producing images of a spatially separate translocal state writ large—a just state consisting of higher up state- or national-level officials who can be called upon to discipline lower-level functionaries and intervene on behalf of the marginalized.

Mathur's story underscores the serious dilemmas associated with the MS program's linkage with the government as part of its GONGO form. To work toward their goal of just social change, field-level functionaries need to tackle local gender-, class-, and caste-based mafias that involve state representatives and also navigate official dictates and violence. This is dangerous work, which often requires them to dissociate themselves from the government label. In Seema Singh's words, "the police belong to the government, the courts belong to the government. . . . When we take up a fight, we have to fight at all these levels. If we start believing that we are working for a government project and that we are government workers, then how will we fight . . . [other] government people?"

Mathur's and Singh's decision to avoid using the state label should not be read as *disengagement* with state structures; rather, it is an innovative strategy used by MS field employees to *confront* official agencies and *challenge* hierarchies without endangering their or their clients' safety. By consciously distancing themselves from the government, mobilely positioning the program, and using bureaucratic procedures, MS employees are sometimes able to steer clear of state violence and facilitate empowering struggles.

How successful they are at negotiating governmental repression, however, is not a straightforward matter. If anything, the incidents narrated above exemplify the gendered, classist, caste-ist nature of state power described to me by Kaveri Mani and Nina Singh. They show how disciplinary and repressive forms of power work in tandem and how "the state" can operate as a "vehicle of massive domination" (Brown 1995, 174) even in the absence of any singular intention to that effect. They also unravel the illiberal underside of neoliberal governmentality (Dean 2001; Hindess 2004) that helps to reinforce the state's hypermasculinity (Sharma 2008). The state's prerogative power is used to uphold social hierarchies, to protect the institution of private property and the interests of propertied classes, to enact violence upon subaltern women and deny them justice, and, finally, to entrench the superiority and authority of state actors and institutions. MS workers encounter this patriarchal illiberality in their empowerment work with their clients, and this is where the program's GONGO nature both poses obstacles and also allows maneuverability.

Conclusion

In this essay I used ethnographic vignettes drawn from the Mahila Samakhya program to analyze how neoliberalism is altering governance and women's political struggles in India today. The MS program's organization as a state-NGO partnership, empowerment goal, and paradoxical effects provide a critical peek into the transformations that are underway. My aim was not to position MS as a neoliberal initiative but to examine how it gets entangled in the wider neoliberal project of privatizing the state and governmentalizing society through empowerment, despite its commitment to radical pedagogy and feminist goals.[11]

My analysis raises the thorny issue of how to think about feminist activism vis-à-vis the state in postliberalization India. If the state, as Mary John

(1999, 108) has argued, is the "most constitutive site of contestation" for Indian feminists, how does one make sense of novel forms of *collaboration*, however uncomfortable, between feminists and state agents at this particular moment? My point in raising this question is neither to unequivocally dismiss these partnerships as bad nor to unreflexively advocate for feminist avoidance of state structures. Indeed, the evidence I have presented illustrates how deeply state projects and actors touch subaltern women's lives and how these women's struggles are anything but disentangled with the state. The poverty-inducing and disempowering gendered consequences of liberalization programs in India and elsewhere also caution against a simplistic feminist dismissal of the state (Agnihotri and Mazumdar 1995; Menon-Sen 2001; Nagar and Raju 2003; Sparr 1994). Subaltern women, "caught in the travails of a rapidly changing society," suggests Rajeswari Sunder Rajan (2003, 91), "are desperately *in need of* the services . . . that only the state can provide in the [quantity] and at the cost that can answer to such a massive (and as yet unrecognized and unmet) demand." The important concern, then, is not *whether* feminists should engage the state, but *how*. In other words, how do Indian feminists sustain their critical engagement with the postcolonial state, honed over many years of activist work, while partnering with it? Indeed, it is with deep skepticism and self-reflexivity that some women's movements activists choose to participate in the MS program, as I have detailed above. What motivates their work is the desire to explore the possibility of whether, as Meera Srinivasan put it, "a [women's empowerment] program sponsored by the state [can] sow the seeds of some change . . ." And this requires us to delve into the *effects* of feminist-state collaborations in alternative projects of social change in the neoliberal age.

My work on the MS program illustrates the paradoxical and dangerous consequences, at once risky and enabling, of innovative partnerships in the field of women's empowerment. MS faces the threat of a bureaucratic straitjacketing and governmentalization of grassroots empowerment. In addition to its meanings as an alternative tactic for consciousness-raising, a spontaneous mobilization strategy, or a loosely defined blueprint for radical action against oppression, empowerment now exemplifies neoliberal ideals of personal capacity building and self-governance (Sharma 2008). Currently, empowerment is a mainstream, transnational development strategy widely used by NGOs and states alike. This translates into a problematic bureaucratization, hierarchization, and professionalization of empowerment as an expert intervention, which can work against the very spirit of equality and justice that empowerment is supposed to connote.[12]

The MS program's institutional structure and practices show how it becomes implicated in the spread of bureaucratic power throughout society. Even though its carefully worked out GONGO structure was an attempt, on the part of its designers, to forestall a governmental takeover of MS and of a feminist empowerment agenda, in practice, statist proceduralism has become a part of the program's fabric. Staffers use bureaucratic techniques as a subversive tactic to circumvent official repression and also train program clients in these methods. They occasionally use these techniques to discipline program participants as well, thus illustrating the dangerous slippage between tactics of resistance and strategies of domination. Governmental methods are mired in the logic of disciplinary power (Brown 1995; Foucault 1995); their proliferation through the program can institute hierarchies that might be counterproductive to its goal of empowerment.

The mainstreaming of empowerment as a category of governance also carries the risk of an official subversion of its radical possibilities. As Anil Bordia, the senior civil servant credited with getting MS under way, remarked, "the state, by definition, can only be . . . status-quoist. [In] every program [like MS], there are seeds of destruction—because the people who control the resources, who have all the say, would not . . . easily allow these things to happen. . . . The problem is [that these programs] are working in a very simmering or overt manner against a system that is rallied totally against [them]." In addition to the hurdles posed by people who monopolize state resources and who may not look kindly upon forms of empowerment that threaten their own positions of power, the bureaucratization and governmentalization of women's empowerment also imposes limits on its definition and use as an anti-oppression tactic. Quoting Anil Bordia again:

> By and large it will be true to say that empowered women would almost always take up causes which are humane, which are in conformity with law, and which are forward-looking. I would not say the same for all sections of society because the CPI-ML people and the People's War Group [radical leftist organizations] are also empowered in a sense, but they do not always take a stand which is within the framework of law. But in the case of women, I . . . know of no case where empowered women have . . . taken the law in their own hands or have acted con-

trary to . . . government policy; in fact, that is a good test of what policy should be.

Bordia's distinction between the implicitly illegitimate and violent empowerment struggles undertaken by radical leftist groups and the desirable activism of subaltern women reveals how state-sponsored empowerment initiatives can potentially serve as vehicles for turning women into law-abiding, disciplined, and responsibilized citizen-subjects (Cruikshank 1999) who use available civil-society mechanisms to fight for their rights. Marginalized women operate in the relatively unregulated, negotiational domain of subaltern political society, which, as Partha Chatterjee (2004) suggests, is not constrained by the legal norms of elite civil society. Their tutelage under state-initiated empowerment programs can be seen, perhaps cynically, as an aspect of the state's modernizing, pedagogic project that aims to turn subaltern women into proper denizens of civil society. Might this signal a *formalization* of political society dynamics and a deradicalization of its methods and goals? Some scholars have indeed used these potentially disempowering effects of governmentalization to argue against state participation in grassroots empowerment (Moser 1993) and for a careful feminist distancing from state programs (Brown 1995).[13] I offer a different reading.

My illustration of the blurring of the boundary between state and nonstate spheres under neoliberalism renders problematic easy conclusions about whether states should get involved in empowerment and whether feminists should collaborate with state institutions. The governmentalization of empowerment is not simply a reflection of direct state involvement but is also an instance of the suffusion of society at large with neoliberal practices of self-government. If we are to rethink the state conceptually so that we see state and nonstate entities as part of a complex apparatus of governance, then we need to examine the workings and effects of empowerment programs undertaken by all kinds of institutions, including GONGOS and NGOS. NGO-initiated empowerment programs, after all, do not operate in a hermetically sealed context that is unaffected by bureaucratic practices, state representatives, or international funding-agency agendas. Using the lens of governmentality also complicates the feminist debate on disentanglement with state structures. Sealing oneself off from governmental processes that permeate the entire social field may not be possible; rather, it may be more useful for activists to assume tactical positions within regimes of government.

Another way to approach these issues is to ask what kinds of subjects are being produced by the governmentalization of empowerment. Do women's "expanding relationships [to state institutions and processes] produce only active *political* subjects, or do they also produce regulated, subordinated, and disciplined *state* subjects?" asks Wendy Brown (1995, 173). My analysis of the MS program substantiates Partha Chatterjee's claim that governmental programs do not just produce bureaucratized and passive state subjects (2004). In postcolonial contexts these programs are generative in that they fashion active, sometimes dissident, political actors and provide the ground for political society mobilizations where marginalized subjects make claims on the state, tussle over entitlements, and contest social and state hierarchies through the very governmental, regulative categories made available to them. Governmentalization does not depoliticize so much as it *spawns* openings for subaltern political struggles that take novel or dangerous forms and that cannot be subsumed within the rubric of the new form of politics promoted by international development agencies, which centers on enabling civil society actors to make the state function efficiently and transparently.

My ethnography of the MS program demonstrates the interplay between depoliticization and repoliticization under neoliberalism; it points to the surprising forms of empowerment that end up happening despite constraints. MS staff and clients develop a critical awareness of structural inequalities that both implicate and exceed state bodies; they take on local mafias and connect them with gender, class, and caste hierarchies; and they learn statist languages and practices and use them to demand accountability from powerful institutions and people. These processes can be seen as empowering in that they help women formulate tactics for challenging local relations of domination in which state actors are embedded. These tactics allow women to negotiate a broader, if contingent, notion of empowerment that is not so much about changing women's individual gendered situations, narrowly construed, but about understanding and confronting multiple and overlapping structural inequalities, which shape individual and collective realities. Empowerment here is about taking up fights for issues that extend well beyond the scope of "women's" rights insofar as they focus on mechanical ideas of equality. Despite the fact that certain officials and local elites may not endorse this kind of women's empowerment, such processes, once initiated, may not be easily reined in.

Empowerment, thus, is a moving target whose meaning is constantly redefined through women's struggles. It has an ambiguous and open-ended quality that manifests itself in multiple and conflicted ways in women's lives. A governmentalization of empowerment, therefore, may not only imply a potential formalization of subaltern political society. It might also open the door for a fundamental rethinking of elite civil society and state institutions and norms, and allow for the emergence of new kinds of dissident citizens. When poor, low-caste, rural women struggle against violence or upper-caste control over land, or when they demand basic needs as entitlements, they try to make the state do what it is supposed to do—that is, guarantee their rights and survival. Subaltern women's struggles delineate the difference between the corrupted state "as is" and the ideal state "as it ought to be." The issues that women take up in their fights for justice and survival and how they implicate state officials in these issues should, as Anil Bordia hinted, serve as markers for how official policies, practices, and institutions must be altered if the promises of grassroots empowerment, substantive democracy, and justice are to be realized. How women construct the state, criticize officials and hold them accountable, and demand entitlements-as-rights point to alternative visions of state institutions and responsibilities, and of citizenship (Sharma 2008). Governmental programs, perhaps unintentionally, make it possible for women to recognize that justice-based transformation requires not only challenging social inequalities, but also reimagining the state and their relationship to it.

Empowerment, as a quasi-state-implemented project of governance, when examined through the lens of neoliberal governmentality, is a double-edged sword that is both promising and precarious. Feminist collaborations with state institutions on women's empowerment programs are clearly opening interesting vistas for challenge and change. But the dangerous underside of such projects, which MS women confront every day, means that one cannot be complacent about their liberatory potential. The context of neoliberalism in which projects like MS operate taints the language of empowerment with risks. Empowerment has layered histories and multiple avatars: a radical strategy for political conscientization, a leftist tactic for class-based politics, a feminist strategy for awareness raising and gender equality, and now a governmental strategy for development. Critical analyses of how these contentious meanings converge and clash in different contexts and how they are entangled with the dominant neoliberal ideology are crucial for scholars and activists alike

(Sharma 2008). The outcomes of these intersections are neither given nor unproblematic, and they point to the need for exerting constant vigilance when engaging the politics of empowerment.

Notes

1. A block is a subdivision of a district consisting of approximately a hundred villages. It is administered by a Block Development Officer (BDO), head of the local Block Office.
2. I follow local name conventions, omitting last names where none were used. I have changed the names of all my informants except Anil Bordia.
3. Field staff include block- and district-level MS functionaries.
4. Foucault (1991) used the concept of governmentality to explain a shift in the aim and modes of governance to a form of biopower that is centrally concerned with the welfare, care, and security of the population living in a particular territory. He drew attention to the entire ensemble of practices and institutions, including but not limited to state agencies, by which the conduct of a population is directed toward particular ends (Dean 1999). Building on Foucault, the scholarship on neoliberal governmentality examines the practices and institutions of governance under neoliberalism. For example, see Barry, Osborne, and Rose (1996), Burchell 1996, Rose 1996b, Cruikshank 1999, Ferguson and Gupta 2002, Hindess 2004, and Sharma 2008.
5. MS operates in nine Indian states.
6. For a discussion of how the Indian political context of the 1970s and 1980s impacted feminist activism, see Gandhi and Shah (1992), Philipose (2001), and Agnihotri and Mazumdar (1995).
7. In the original, longer version of this essay, I argued that these discussions about the program's GONGO structure discursively define and engender the state (Sharma 2006). Extending anthropological and feminist analyses of the state, I show how everyday development planning, in conversation with neoliberal ideas, construct the state as a distinct, vertically encompassing, and ambiguously gendered entity. Anthropological analyses of the state include Das and Poole (2004), Gupta (1995), Hansen and Stepputat (2001), Scott (1998), Sharma and Gupta (2006), and Steinmetz (1999); feminist critiques of the state include Alexander (1997), Brown (1995, 166–196), Fraser (1989, 144–60), MacKinnon (1989), Mathur (1999), N. Menon (1996), R. Menon and Bhasin (1993), Sharma (2008), and Sunder Rajan (2003).
8. Many local officials I encountered were either unaware of the program's existence or considered it insignificant. My informants explained that this was because MS had a small budget and did not distribute resources to its clients, unlike other large-scale development programs. The relative lack of significance given to a resource-poor, nonredistributive program that targets and employs women speaks to the gendered ideologies that shape state practices.
9. The image of the state-as-giver is the historical result of postindependence popu-

lism, wherein government representatives promised development for the entire nation, including food, clothing, and housing for the poor. Rural subalterns use this discourse to demand that the state fulfill its promise and ensure their entitlements (Sharma 2008).

10. This popular construction of the state as "mother-father," which alludes to the caretaking and protective roles of "good" parents, troubles any easy gendering of the state as patriarch writ large (Sharma 2008).

11. I have previously argued that the neoliberal degovernmentalization and de-welfarization of the state in India is partial (Sharma 2008). The Indian state cannot completely privatize key governmental functions like development, which legitimize its very existence. However, empowerment programs implemented by semi- and nongovernmental bodies allow the state to reconcile its developmentalist and neoliberalizing faces: they enable the state to continue performing its developmentalist duties by responsibilizing other social actors to self-develop.

12. MS representatives attempt to address education and class hierarchies among themselves and between staff members and program participants, which have resulted from the bureaucratization and professionalization of empowerment (see Nagar and Raju 2003).

13. See Jandhyala (2001) for a critical discussion of these debates in India.

PART II   Postcolonial Neoliberalisms and the NGO Form

P art II builds on some of the lines suggested by the authors in the previous section to argue that the outcomes of NGO activities are not to be understood solely through the context of the organizations' agendas, but rather through the question of their transnational form and its circulation. These essays address NGOs in relation to wider societal and geopolitical formations. They suggest that NGOs may play a part in reproducing social divisions such as class and gender precisely because these divisions are enabled by the transnational and neoliberal context of the NGO form and the way it circulates.

Julie Hemment analyzes Russian women's NGOs after socialism. She finds that these NGOs focus on the issue of violence against women in particular because they are funded by international donors who identify this issue as a global project. Although Russian women working in NGOs give the appearance of accepting this transnational agenda as their own, they also express quite divergent needs and regard critically the imposition of a global project. In the process of setting up a "crisis center," as Hemment shows, the women seek to strategically negotiate their own needs through the demands of international organizations. Hemment is particularly attentive to how the women express their distinct perspectives and criticisms, even as they comply with imposed agendas. Hemment's research reveals how women engage in new struggles as they both become the subjects of international interventions and remain the subjects of national and regional institutions.

Kathleen O'Reilly's research in India explores the contradictions between NGOs' mission to empower women and the lack of parity among the organizations' own male and female staff members. She reveals the gendered contestations taking place inside NGOs. These internal negotiations stand in contrast to the unified discourses around women's participation that appear in NGO planning documents and international development agendas. O'Reilly's analysis of an NGO working on a water project in north India makes clear that internal conflicts are not simply impediments to be overcome, but "micropolitical processes" through which women are opening up new spaces for themselves. She presents a vivid and detailed analysis of how the European donors' concern with gender parity is taken over by women NGO staff members eager to take advantage of these possibilities, who seek to insert themselves into the NGO's agenda. What is clear is that donors may have the ability to seek changes in local hierarchies, but their efforts are transformed as they encounter those hierarchies. Thus, donor-beneficiary power relations; issues of transparency and accountability; and notions of legitimacy, authenticity, and grassroots activism are not straightforward or universal but become reconfigured in different contexts through the workings of NGOs.

LeeRay Costa, in her essay on conferences of NGOs in Thailand, suggests that it is not just the North-South divide but also rural-urban and class divisions that emerge in the NGO sector. Her research shows how rural women leaders contest the cosmopolitanism of their urban counterparts, as well as the ways kinship networks operating within NGOs reproduce local hierarchies. The transnational form of the NGO is understood here as a constraint that prevents rural and subaltern women from entering the NGO, which is constructed as an elite, cosmopolitan space. Yet the circulation of the NGO form also makes subaltern women more aware of their exclusion and motivates them to resist it.

The final essay of this section is Lamia Karim's analysis of the much-vaunted and widely replicated microcredit regime in Bangladesh. Karim's research reveals that one of its major elements has been to treat women as if they are neoliberal entrepreneurs within a framework of capitalism when, in fact, women are enmeshed in sets of gendered marital and communal relationships. While women appear to be the "beneficiaries" of microcredit loans, in fact, their male relatives often control the money, while women remain vulnerable to exploitation by microcredit lenders. Karim's essay, furthermore, problematizes the production of knowledge through development frameworks and neoliberal assumptions.

These essays all raise questions about the global construction and dissemination of the empowerment project of many NGOS. They provide critical insights by analyzing these projects within the frameworks of particular and divergent articulations of local institutions as they become enmeshed with the neoliberal logics that are altering constructions of gender and states transnationally.

Global Civil Society and the Local Costs of Belonging
Defining Violence against Women in Russia

In May 1998 activists from crisis centers all over Russia gathered in Moscow for a conference to discuss the formalization of their thus far loose network into a national association. The conference was a veritable gala. I was stunned to see almost all of my Moscow-based women's movement acquaintances, as well as representatives of the main international foundations and agencies (the Ford Foundation, the Open Society Institute, the American Bar Association, the British Embassy, Amnesty International). Everybody who was anybody in the field of women's community activism and development was there.

At the conference, the theme of universalism sounded loud. The first speakers—mostly representatives of international agencies—emphasized cross-cultural commonality. One of the first to the podium was a British woman, a representative of an expatriate club and a long-time benefactor of antiviolence campaigns. As she put it, "violence against women is not a Russian problem but an international problem, affecting women of all religious and national backgrounds. We are all vulnerable to violence from men; most of us in this room will have experienced violence at some stage in their lives." She offered words of encouragement to the new network—"my point is that we were where you are now." Her remarks were intended to bring the women in the room together. They were met, however, with weary frustration by some attendees. Nadya, an activist of a Moscow-based group with whom I was well acquainted, muttered, "I always switch off when foreigners speak"; another woman groaned, "men are people too."[1] Dissent such as this erupted at the margins (in the coffee breaks, in the corridors, in whispered asides). However, this remark and these objections remained unheard.

This vignette highlights some of the key tensions of transnational women's activism that this chapter explores: the divisiveness of Western aid, the ambiguous role of nongovernmental organizations (NGOS), and the local costs of belonging in transnational or global campaigns. The campaign against violence against women is one of the most prominent campaigns of the Russian women's movement. It is one that almost all the main women's organizations participate in, in some form or another (indeed, I was attending the Moscow conference as both researcher and advocate, representing the women's group I worked with to set up a crisis center). However, the ubiquity of the issue in Russia testifies less to local perceptions of needs than to the success of transnational campaigns and the work of international donor agencies. Beyond limited, elite circles, the work of crisis centers is not understood.

This raises thorny questions about women's activism and social movements in contemporary conditions of globalization. The effectiveness of the global women's movement surely rests on its ability to heed local concerns. However, I argue that the campaigns and the logic of grants and funding that drive them impede this process. The framing of violence against women not only screens out local constructions of events, but it deflects attention from other issues of social justice, notably the material forces that oppress women. This is a troubling outcome for a movement that intends to challenge the global inequities that contribute to women's marginalization. It suggests that we need to be more attentive to the context within which feminist initiatives are nested. Examining my own participation in the campaigns as a Western scholar and activist, I argue that we need to interrogate our use of Western feminist models and concepts in order to be responsive to local knowledge and to achieve truly democratic transnational engagements.

Russia offers an interesting vantage point from which to interrogate these processes. Russian women activists are relative newcomers to the international stage; barring a few early connections during the Soviet period, they first entered into dialogue with Western feminists following the collapse of the Soviet Union in 1991.[2] As walls and boundaries were dismantled and democratization got under way, feminist scholars and activists rushed to join in solidarity with Russian women; a mass of horizontal relationships formed under the rubric of sister city schemes, academic exchanges, and, later, NGO activity. This context helps to explain the tone of the British speaker's remarks. The excitement that was generated by the democratic "revolutions" in the Eastern bloc gave rise to a dizzying sense of possibility and a climate of liberal triumphalism that legitimated this stance and these kinds of interventions.[3] However—contrary to what she supposed, we were *not* where they are now. Russian women's activism is shaped by a distinct history and a distinct set of gender alignments. What is more, activism around women's issues emerged not only in the context of the euphoria over democratic change but in the context of intense economic dislocation, too.[4] Women's groups formed in response to the devastation wrought by "shock therapy," the market-oriented economic reforms implemented in the early 1990s by democratic Russian politicians under the tutelage of US and Western European economists. These structural adjustment policies led to the dismantling of the social security system and sharp cutbacks in the healthcare system, affecting women disproportionately. This informs their perceptions of needs and definitions of problems.

The best way to scrutinize and evaluate the effectiveness of transnational campaigns is to examine their local manifestations; this "place-based ethnography" does just that (Escobar 2008:1). Drawing on nineteen months of ethnographic fieldwork conducted between 1997 and 2001, I examine the new crisis centers from the two vantage points that my research afforded me—high-profile foundation-sponsored events and interactions with provincial women's groups. Presenting insights gained in the context of an action research project that I undertook with one group, this chapter highlights local contestation about the campaigns, exploring the competing conceptions of the "crisis" facing Russian women that the campaigns have displaced. In highlighting these alternative constructions, it examines the extent to which activists have been able to translate the issue of gendered violence and to root it in their concerns.

Whence the Transnational Campaigns?

Before considering these local understandings and concerns, I will first subject the campaigns themselves to scrutiny. The presumed transparency of the issue in international development circles is interesting in itself. Since the 1990s, the campaign against violence against women has had broad resonance across locations. It is assumed to address a universal problem, the content of which is assumed and taken for granted, as my opening vignette suggests.

By the late 1990s, violence against women was not only a feminist issue that concerned women's groups; it had become an international development issue. It had won broad acceptance at the United Nations and is still prioritized by international foundations that work with women's community groups. The campaigns are determinedly transnational. The formulation (or framing, to use the language of recent social movements theory) of violence against women is deliberately inclusive, pitched in such terms as to encompass diverse social practices—from spousal abuse to female genital mutilation. How was this achieved?

Gendered violence has long been a concern of local women's movements. In the United States and Western Europe, the battered women's movement was a prominent component of second-wave organizing. The first women's crisis centers were survivor-led grassroots organizations. The provision of shelters—secret safe houses where women victims of domestic abuse could take temporary refuge—was central to these early campaigns. Elsewhere, women's groups organized around local manifestations of violence—in India around campaigns against dowry deaths, in Latin America against the state-sanctioned violence perpetrated by authoritarian regimes.

Until the late 1980s, gendered violence was a feminist issue and was not regarded with much seriousness at the international level. In the late 1980s and early 1990s this changed when, due to the efforts of activists of the international women's movement, the framing of violence against women went global.[5] In their influential account of the development of transnational advocacy networks (networks of activists that coalesce and operate across national frontiers), Margaret Keck and Kathryn Sikkink (1998) explain how the issue achieved such currency. Violence against women emerged in the 1980s as a framing that had the power to unite women from North and South. Until that point, attempts to unify in global campaigns had been largely unsuccessful. Women's activists of North and South had been deeply divided and unable to achieve a common agenda. While Northern (or "first world") feminists had been preoccupied with issues of gender discrimination and equality, Southern (or "third world") women were more concerned with issues of social justice and development, which affected both men and women, albeit in different ways. Violence against women was a framing that could encompass a broad range of practices and hence bring about dialogue between women from different locations.

Its success at the international level was largely due to the innovation of linking women's rights to human rights, bringing together two powerful constituencies for the first time—human rights activists and feminists. Feminist activists first pushed the issue to international prominence at the 1993 Vienna UN human rights conference. Their strategizing coincided with international concern about the systemic use of rape in war in Bosnia, and it was effective. In 1994, the UN High Commission on Human Rights appointed the first special rapporteur on violence against women, and rape in warfare was recognized as a crime against humanity by the Hague Tribunal.

The UN Fourth World Conference on Women in Beijing, 1995, was a pivotal moment for the success of the framing. Combating violence against women emerged as a central policy agenda both of the international women's movement and of international development. The campaigns have galvanized support across diverse constituencies, among politicians and donors. In the late 1980s major US foundations decided to make violence against women a funding priority, channeling funds to NGOs that address the issue.[6] As one American male coordinator of a crisis center training I attended explained to his Russian trainees, "[in the United States] we've found that domestic violence is an easy theme to go to the public with. People give readily. We're at the point where it's politically correct to support this type of organization."

Clearly there is much to celebrate here. Indeed, many feminist scholars regard the prominence of the campaigns as an unqualified success. The campaigns have been analyzed in terms of the increased influence and effectiveness of transnational social movements (TSMs), or transnational advocacy networks (TANs).[7] Such accounts are in keeping with celebratory accounts of NGOs and civil society; here, TSMs represent the positive, liberatory side of globalization. However, there are alternative, less sanguine ways to view this.

While it is true that transnational campaigns such as these unite women's groups across different locations, they do so at a cost. The anthropologist Aihwa Ong provides a critical reading of the "strategic sisterhood" that is the basis of this and other North-South alliances in the post-Beijing conference era. She presents it as an alliance driven by the desire of Northern women that ignores geopolitical inequalities and that is insensitive to non-first-world cultural values. She argues that transnational campaigns are based on a distinctly individualist formulation of "rights" that is Western specific.[8] The skepticism among activists that I detected in my research points toward similar frustrations in the postsocialist context.

Building on this and other critiques, I wish to introduce a note of caution in my account of the campaigns. First, I suggest that the very success of the framing can also be regarded as its weakness. Although the framing certainly yields cross-cultural clarity, it does so at a cost. At the transnational level, it works insofar as it is a catchall. However, this catchall quality screens out crucial nuances in the ways people define violence against women in different local contexts. In this chapter, I will go on to argue that in postsocialist "democratizing" contexts, as in "developing" ones, the framing deflects attention from issues of redistributive justice.

Second, it is important to consider the political economic context of the campaigns. The issue achieved prominence at a time of crucial shifts in global development agendas. The rise of NGOs and the success of the campaigns took place at a time when a neoliberal vision of development has achieved hegemony. This has introduced "a new kind of relationship between the state and civil society and advanced a distinctive definition of the political domain and its participants—based on a minimalist conception of both the state and democracy" (Alvarez, Dagnino, and Escobar 1998, 1). Concerns about these processes have been raised by both scholars and activists, in Southern or "developing" contexts as well as the postsocialist one.[9] Support for NGOs is provided within this new rubric and comes with strings attached; NGOs that accept donor support are required to take on the responsibilities of the retreating state, picking up the slack for the radical free market.[10] What is more, the sudden influx of grants and funding brings about dramatic changes in organizing. Ironically, "NGO-ization" has demobilized social movements. It has contributed to the formation of new hierarchies and allowed former elites to flourish. In many cases it also signals the triumph of Washington- or Geneva-based agendas over local concerns.[11]

The gendered violence campaigns do not operate outside this political economic context. Indeed, the forces that enable them, the logic that drives them, and their effects demonstrate their complicity. Concern about violence against women originated in the second-wave political slogan "the personal is political," which challenged the inviolability of the home and politicized it. However, the radical critique of patriarchy and gender-based economic inequality that was fundamental to the battered women's movement in the United States and Western Europe has fallen out of the transnational campaigns. In a grotesque inversion, the campaigns reprivatize the problem of domestic violence by focusing on interpersonal relations between spouses to the exclusion of structural factors outside, specifically the economic upheavals that most women believe pose the greatest threat to themselves and their families.[12] In a disturbing way, the work of the campaigns thus overlaps with the privatizing intent of neoliberalism. Indeed, this helps to explain the success of the issue among donors in the West. It is easier to garner support and international outrage around issues concerning sex and that position women as victims than around issues of social justice (Snitow 1999).

Accounting for the Rise of Crisis Centers in Russia: Foundations, Funding, and Feminists

For complex reasons, violence against women is not an issue that local groups were likely to have raised by themselves. The issue was discursively created by the meeting of Western feminists and Russian women activists in the early 1990s. These feminist-oriented Russian women set up the first crisis centers, first in Moscow and St. Petersburg, then in provincial cities. In the decade of their existence—a decade of rapid and tumultuous transformations in Russia—the crisis center network has undergone significant change. Donor support has been a key factor in its development, and feminist-oriented Russian activists have played a crucial role as brokers of ideas.

Since their arrival in Russia in the early 1990s, donor agencies have channeled a proportionally small but ideologically significant portion of civil society aid to women's groups. They met with a diverse range of women's organizations. While some set up during the mid-1980s, when Mikhail S. Gorbachev's liberalizing reforms permitted the formation of independent groups for the first time, most were founded in the early to mid-1990s in response to the dislocations of the market I have described. While some had their roots in official Soviet-era women's organizations (*zhensovety*), others regarded themselves as determinedly independent from the former regime. A small but prominent minority identified as feminist. These groups of highly educated women were mostly clustered in institutes and universities. Familiar with Western academic literature, they brought insights from Western feminism to bear on Soviet gender relations and on the effects of political and economic reform. They were also committed to practice and spearheaded attempts to bring about unity among women's groups, organizing two The Independent Russian

Women's Movement forums in 1991 and 1992. This latter group found itself particularly well positioned to take advantage of the new opportunities of democratization aid. Members' knowledge of foreign languages, experience of travel, and familiarity with liberal democratic and Western feminist concepts made for easy dialogue with the representatives of donor agencies. The crisis centers they founded, often in collaboration with Western feminist activists, were greeted enthusiastically by international donor agencies and were among the first women's projects to receive support.

However, while these initiatives won a great deal of international attention, they were less successful at home. The Independent Russian Women's Movement was marginal in Russia and did not have broad support. On the contrary, most men and women regarded women's groups with suspicion and hostility, particularly those that identified as "feminist."[13] For complex reasons, there is no commonly shared perception of gender discrimination in Russia or other former socialist states. As many scholars have noted, the commonly held notion is that the socialist state "spoiled" both men and women, emasculating men and making women too aggressive and assertive, denying them natural expression of difference and self-realization (*samorealizatsiia*).[14] Men and women perceived themselves to be equally victimized by the state. As Peggy Watson puts it, "under state socialism, society was excluded as a whole, and citizens, far from feeling excluded relative to each other, were held together in a form of political unity" (1997, 25).

I found that among feminist-oriented women's projects, crisis centers were regarded with particular incomprehension and skepticism. Indeed, even some women activists involved in the campaigns admitted that they did not think gendered violence was the most pressing issue facing Russian women and expressed concern that so many resources were put into it.

There was plenty of conflict in the private realm in the USSR. However, women with violent spouses were unlikely to recognize their experience in terms of gendered violence. Crisis centers are premised on a set of property relations that are bourgeois and on an alignment of public and private that is liberal democratic. They presume that women are both economically dependent on men and stuck in the private sphere. This was not true for Soviet women, who were brought into the workforce and guaranteed formal equality by the socialist "paternalist" or "parent" state (Verdery 1996, 63). Soviet-era property arrangements also complicate the picture. The nationalization of all property meant that there was no ideology of private ownership to give Soviet citizens the illusion of domestic inviolability. Many Soviet citizens lived in the notorious communal apartments, sharing kitchen and bathroom facilities with their neighbors. What is more, few married couples lived autonomously as nuclear families. Chronic housing shortages meant that many people lived with extended family, grandparents, in-laws, and siblings. For all these reasons, domestic conflict most commonly expressed itself in the form of tension over rights to living space, interpersonal strife, or alcoholism. Although patterns are certainly changing with the introduction of a free market, lack of housing remains the most chronic problem. Indeed, this helps to explain why women's shelters have not taken off in Russia.[15]

A further obstacle to crisis centers has been the fact that during state socialism the private sphere was constituted as a kind of "refuge" for both men and women. It was considered to be a site of authenticity against the morally compromised public sphere, and its integrity was jealously guarded by women and men alike (Verdery 1996). In the late 1990s, the private sphere remains a (reconstituted) refuge for most Russian people, a site of precious and sustaining networks that offset the violence and chaos that is perceived to be "outside" (mafia, crime, corruption, poverty). Despite the fact that levels of familial violence appear to have increased in the post-Soviet period, most women do not consider it the most pressing problem.[16] Furthermore, as many crisis center workers acknowledge, Russian women who have experienced sexual or domestic violence are commonly mistrustful of attempts from outside to intervene.

Until 1995, crisis centers were marginal offshoots of the Independent Russian Women's Movement, and although they were celebrated in international circles, their work was little understood at home. Despite this lack of fit, in the mid-1990s, the antiviolence campaigns in Russia underwent a qualitative shift. As "violence against women" became an international development issue, more funds were allocated to it and crisis centers moved from being small, rather peripheral offshoots of the women's movement to become third-sector heavyweights, a central plank of the independent women's movement and a showpiece of foundation-NGO relations.[17]

The transnational campaigns brought a key resource to Russian women's groups—a model around which to organize. This model is accompanied by skills and methods that can be transferred and taught. For activists, the crisis center model offers a blueprint and a framework. Neat, easy to learn, it has become a kind of do-it-yourself NGO kit. Foundation support has financed the production of easy-to-use materials—brochures, posters, and handbooks, including one titled "How to Create a Women's Crisis Center."[18] The Moscow-based network offers trainings, assisted by foundation support. These teach not only crisis counseling and nondirective listening skills (the hallmark skills of crisis centers), but also management, NGO development, and public relations.

Russian crisis centers have adopted what they call the "international model" and work to a specific set of standards. Through telephone hotlines and individual consultations, they provide free and confidential legal and psychological counseling to female victims of sexual or domestic violence. Counselors undergo eighty hours of training, run by staff of the most experienced centers with input from feminist psychologists, scholars, and lawyers.

What does all this mean to Russian activists? While I insist on the need to situate my study of Russian crisis centers within this "broader political geography" (Gal and Kligman 2000a, 4), I do not mean to suggest that the global blocks out the local, or to describe the flow of ideas as unidirectional. Recent scholarship of globalization has argued persuasively against this kind of determinism, and feminist scholars are prominent in the discussion.[19] Russian women activists draw on international aid and Western models as resources, translating them as necessary. In the process, projects and campaigns are transformed, not imported statically. How do these circulating discourses arrive, what are the processes of "translation" they undergo (Tsing 1997), and with what do they interact as they are "glocalized"?

In the course of my research during 1995–97, I found that the notion of crisis center did have a kind of local resonance. Once again, the violence against women framing caught on because of its catchall quality. Here, however, the keyword was not violence (*nasilie*) but crisis (*krizis*). One of the things that struck me in the course of my research was the ubiquity of the notion of crisis center (*krizisnyi tsentr*). I came across many women (out of the loop of trainings and unfamiliar with the international model) who expressed their intent to set one up, or described their work (unconnected with sexual or domestic violence) to be "something like a crisis center." I came to relate this rhetorical persistence to the fact that the whole of Russian society is perceived to be in crisis—with good cause. In addition to the perception of social and economic breakdown, the Russian crisis is also perceived to be a psychic condition—there is a great deal of talk about the neuroticization of society.

The Perspective from the Provinces:
Competing Crises and the Displacement of the Economic

Zhenskii Svet (Women's Light) is a small, university-based women's group, dedicated to women's education and consciousness-raising. It was founded in the provincial city of Tver' in 1991, long before the arrival of Western foundations, in the first wave of independent organizing in Russia. Its founder was Larisa, a professor of history who had written her dissertation on the Western women's movement, one of Russia's few self-identified feminists.[20] One of the reasons I originally made contact with this group was because it claimed to have a crisis center.[21] However, I arrived to find that this was not so. While the notion of crisis center did exist within the group, it had not quite taken root. The idea had first been introduced to the group in 1992 by some visiting German feminists; however, the project collapsed when the Germans failed to secure funding, and local interest had since waned. When I asked group members about this, they told me that sexual and domestic violence was something they had not really thought much about. It was a terrible thing, but they did not feel any real connection to it. They also insisted that women would not come together around this issue, because it was too private. They could not see how such a project could work in Tver.'

However, the idea of a crisis center had remained in the group, in diffuse forms. Katia was the custodian of one of these crisis center plans. An unemployed woman in her fifties, she attended Zhenskii Svet regularly. I met frequently with her in the course of my stay in Tver' in 1997. Katia explained that she was not concerned with dealing with the women victims of sexual violence. She intended her crisis center, or "anticrisis center" (*anti-krizisnyi tsentr*) as she preferred to call it, to be a service to assist women who encountered economic discrimination (*ekonomicheskaia diskriminatsiia*), or (gendered) discrimination in the workplace. This was a new term to refer to a new phenomenon, since the Soviet regime had had an ideological commitment to both full employment and gender equality. She understood that in the United States and Western European countries, a crisis center was a service for the victims of sexual and domestic violence but argued that in Russia such a conception did not make sense. She insisted that although sexual violence was indisputably a terrible thing, it was a much less widespread problem than economic violence and discrimination, which touched almost every woman's life.

As I pieced her story together, I came to regard it as a classic survivor's narrative. She had encountered "discrimination" in her own life and now wanted to set up a service to assist women in similar situations. Two years ago, before I met her, Katia was pressured to quit her job as a sociological analyst at the Federal Employment Service when initially generous state funding was cut back. Forced to make layoffs, her boss began to exert pressure (*davlenie*) on some members of the staff to leave. To leave, as it were, of their own volition (in order to avoid paying unemployment benefits). Although both men and women staffed the office, he targeted the women in the group. Katia experienced this as a profound shock, a profound "crisis," as did her female colleagues, who went through the same process. She told me that it was the first time she and her coworkers had had to face the idea of unemployment. She was shocked at the callous disregard of her rights. She was shocked at how her boss, a former *military officer*, she emphasized, had "pressed" her to leave. Agitated by the memory, she told me that the pressure was so intense that one woman had been "on the verge of a heart attack." Katia's account evoked the profoundly destabilizing social dislocation she and her colleagues had experienced at this time. Unemployment was not merely distressing to her on account of the financial burden it placed but because it was an attack on her dignity, on her very identity, her sense of self. It also cast a blow to her worldview. She was shaken by the fact that a person of education and high social standing (an officer) had behaved in this way.

In many ways, Katia's story is paradigmatic of women's early nongovernmental organizing in Russia. Regardless of how they described themselves, of the educational levels of their members, or of their location or ideological hue, in the early 1990s women's groups were engaged in a common purpose. They were survival mechanisms, set up for and by women who were hard hit by social and economic reform. Involvement in this activity goes beyond a concern with the gendered effects of the market and is frequently driven by a generalized perception of material, moral, and psychological crisis. In their different ways, these organizations have taken on the challenge of creating new forms of social solidarity and togetherness following the collapse of the Soviet collective.

Although Katia's conception of crisis center emphasizes structural factors—economic violence attributable to the market and shock therapy and their gendered effects—hers is neither a straightforwardly "feminist" nor anticapitalist construction. Indeed, she did not address her sense of discrimination toward men as a group or toward the institutions whose policies contributed to it (the International Monetary Fund or Russian government). Instead, she addressed herself to the absent, retreating Soviet state. She had been able to find a state agency that had overturned the decision. Although she had not been awarded material compensation, she had received symbolic recognition of the injustice of her dismissal. She intended her crisis center to be a project that would provide similar assistance to local women.

Katia's case perhaps looks idiosyncratic. In many ways, she represents a prior understanding of crisis center, one that preceded the arrival of foundation support. However, I found echoes of her understandings elsewhere. Between 1995 and 1997, before the action research project in Tver,' I visited crisis centers in St. Petersburg and several provincial cities. These visits provided alternative insights and left me with quite different impressions of the antiviolence campaigns than those I received in Moscow. Despite the fact that they formally adopt the crisis center model (the "international standard"), many of these centers had much broader programs in response to local needs. As the director of one provincial crisis center said to me over coffee, "we go to these Moscow-based seminars, workshops, and conferences, but our agendas are still driven by local concerns." Because these centers are raising the issue of violence against women for the first time, only a relatively small proportion of clients call to discuss it. All the counselors I spoke to confirmed that when they first set up, a wide range of people called their hotlines. Men called as well as women, and, strikingly, a lot of retired people—in sum, those who felt marginalized and vulnerable. I was told that people called to speak about diverse issues—unemployment, unpaid wages, loneliness, alcoholism, loss of children to the military service, as well as domestic or sexual violence. As one Petersburg-based activist put it, "there is great confusion now, the old system is broken down, but it's not clear what is emerging. People are confused, and there is a great demand for information. They don't know what to ask for, who to speak to, how to name their problems." Centers have responded to this in different ways; some speak to all callers, others only to women victims of violence. One center in Sergiev-Posad abandoned its women-only focus for a few years in response to local incomprehension.

Counselors in all the centers I visited informed me that women who do call to speak about gendered violence frequently relate it to a range of other materially based issues, such as unemployment, impoverishment, and cramped living space. In response to this, counselors focus on the woman in a broader social context, particularly on the family. Activists in provincial cities, where they may provide the only women-oriented services, conclude that it makes no sense to specialize too narrowly. They say it is impossible to separate the problem of domestic or sexual violence from other issues women face. In general, counselors afford a high priority to clients' material problems. In one St. Petersburg center, survivor support groups place great emphasis on practical steps women can take, sometimes resulting in members of a group going into business together.

These constructions could work to inform the work of the transnational feminist movement; these critiques could be the basis for dialogue. The effectiveness of the global women's movement surely rests on its ability to heed local concerns. As Ellen Dorsey puts it, we need to "carefully tread the line between building common strategies and reflecting the actual concerns and dynamism of the movement on the ground," lest the movement be discredited (1997, 355). However, there are some serious systemic impediments. First, the logic of grants and funding encourages groups to adopt the themes and terminologies prioritized by donors, making issues that fall outside this rubric unnarratable. Second, NGO staff and donor representatives are frequently not disposed to listen to these commentaries.[22] For both these reasons, crisis centers experience great pressure to conform to the "international model."

Furthermore, I found that the rubric of the crisis center and the technologies that accompanied it brought about significant changes in the ways both staff and their clients formulated the problems facing women, making the articulation of critiques and counterstrategies still less likely. In Russia, technologies and methods that are designed to empower women—such as nondirective active listening—ironically work against this insofar as they dissuade clients and counselors from articulating their material concerns. Techniques of nondirective active listening require callers to come to their own solutions. Crisis centers provide information and consultations (on legal issues and social services) but encourage clients to take part in the defense of their rights and make their own decisions. While most centers offer free legal advice, their main message is frequently what not to expect from the state. The director of one center told me: "Their first question is always 'what will the state do for me [as a battered woman] if I get divorced?' I explain that they have little realistic chance of getting help." In survivor support groups, she works to make women aware of these material and political issues, to recognize that the state is not going to help them and that the only way forward is to help themselves.

Tver' and Zhenskii Svet: Adopting the Western Model

This dynamic became clear to me in the course of my interactions with Zhenskii Svet. The action research process that I undertook with members of Zhenskii Svet brought the two models of crisis center I have outlined into competition.[23] Katia's "anticrisis center" for unemployed women was pitched against a "crisis center" for women victims of domestic and sexual violence that accepted the framing of violence against women backed by the transnational campaigns. The latter won out. It won not because it best expressed members' idea of the most important problem facing local women in Tver' but because it was considered most likely to succeed. In crucial ways, as facilitator of the seminar and as a Western outsider with resources to bring to the project, I was the arbiter.[24] The latter model had two advantages. First, it had broad legitimacy among two key constituencies—Western donor agencies and actors of the local administration. Second, it was organizationally viable. Both characteristics were consequences of international donor involvement and the success of transnational feminist campaigns.

Through the action research project, I was able to lend my energies to the group as it negotiated the contradictory nongovernmental field. In this context, my status as a Western outsider and my familiarity with donor priorities became valuable resources that group members were able to deploy. In the course of my fieldwork, I had amassed a great deal of information about women's crisis centers and realized that the network offered great possibilities for provincial women's groups. I shared this information with members of Zhenskii Svet.

Some of the women began to see the founding of a crisis center as a way to strengthen and institutionalize some of the more socially oriented programs offered by Zhenskii Svet. They saw it as a potential base from which already existing projects could be run and as a place where young women could gain work experience. A key player in this project was Tamara, a doctor and one of the newest and most enthusiastic participants of the group. An assertive, practical woman in her mid-thirties, she had recently moved to Tver' from Siberia with her family when her engineer husband lost his job. She worked part time at one of the local hospitals, renting office space with another doctor, drawing a meager salary, and offering free seminars in women's health through Zhenskii Svet.

When I met her, she was looking for a niche, a place to which she could bring her considerable energies and which would allow her independence.

"I'm not afraid of hard work," she told me. "The main thing is that I am committed to what I do." She dreamed of being able to bring about a unity between what she called her hobby (issues of women's health, the women's movement) and her career. The idea of setting up a crisis center appealed to Tamara because it most closely approximated the "concrete social project" she wanted to be involved in. Her own economic vulnerability meant that she was attuned to the plight of women in the city, and she wanted to do something practical to meet their needs. Furthermore, she was persuaded by the issue of gendered violence. As a doctor, she had noticed that many of her women patients had bruises under their clothes. "It was obvious that some of them had violent spouses, but there was no way to talk to them about it," she said.

In summer 1998, with the endorsement of other members of Zhenskii Svet, Tamara and I embarked on a preparatory project to set up a crisis center for women in Tver.' Our aims were to learn more about existing services and to locate sources of financial and material support. We met with members of the local administration and staff of the local social security services, and we traveled to Moscow and several provincial cities to visit and learn from other crisis centers. It was a successful strategy. The Tver' project coincided with a specific moment of expansion in the network of crisis centers. It was seeking to reregister itself as a national association and was eager to find more collaborators throughout the Russian Federation. To this end, its sponsors provided start-up funds for new centers and were glad to make the acquaintance of a provincial woman activist, well versed in the tenets of the international women's movement. At the same time, in Tver' local conditions were ripe. Since the mid-1990s, "women's issues" have had political currency in Russia. Throughout the regions of the Russian Federation, officials are now mandated to undertake steps to provide services for women. In this way, "crisis center" has entered the lexicon of government officials and social services personnel and is on the books. We won the support of two key political figures in the city—the mayor (who was preparing for reelection) and the president's representative to the *oblast'* (a woman journalist with an insecure political base who had begun to dabble in the "women's movement" in order to generate support for herself in the city). They were only too happy to make the acquaintance of a community group willing to undertake such an endeavor.

The center was set up in fall 1998. Tamara pulled together a group of interested women who were prepared to start work on a voluntary basis and led seminars based on the training she had received in Moscow. At the outset of the project, she acknowledged that she saw setting up a crisis center as a pragmatic move. If it took off, it would make a good umbrella project under which already existing projects could continue to run and new ones could be devised. She saw it as a pilot project through which she could discover what local women perceived their real problems to be.

As I have followed the crisis center over the last four years, I have been able to trace the shifting perceptions of its staff and volunteers. In the first months of its existence, gendered violence was very much on the periphery of the project. The first clients who came to the center were either already personally acquainted in some way with staff members or were chance passers-by. These women did not talk about domestic violence but discussed instead a variety of other, mostly materially based problems. When I asked them about their plans for the near future, Tamara and other staff and volunteers talked of setting up a variety of other projects within the center to meet local women's needs—a "work therapy" club (designed to help local women go into business together and consider economic strategies), a social club, and seminars in cosmetology and women's health. Tamara confided that in some ways she regretted focusing so directly on sexual and domestic violence. She told me: "Women who really experience this will rarely come forward to talk about it—I uncover it in conversations, it lies buried, it is very often a source of grief, but in focusing on it, we scare women away."

She gave a very different account when we met in Boston in February 2000, while she was attending a training course for Russian professionals working on domestic violence. She exhibited increasing self-confidence, both in her own position and in the validity of the crisis center narrative. She told me that much had changed since a telephone had been installed in August 1999. This enabled the center to finally open a hotline for women (*telefon doveriia*), and as soon as the service was advertised the center had been inundated with calls. There was a great appetite in the city for telephone hotlines and (particularly) for free psychological counseling. The hotline is open from 9 to 6 every day except weekends. Tamara told me that they receive between fifty and seventy calls per month, of which between six and fifteen pertain to domestic violence.

I asked her to tell me about the issues clients raised. She told me that many come to discuss problems in their relationships (*vzaimootnoshenie*) with the people they live with—alcoholism or conflicts over living space upon divorce. I asked her how many of these people had experienced domestic violence. She paused to consider and told me that in each case there is an element of domestic violence. However, this was loosely defined. One woman came to speak of problems with her mother, another about difficult relations with her sister. The rest came to discuss issues with their spouses. She told me that she was surprised that women are willing to come forward and to talk about their problems, however they define them, and that she was surprised too that people do speak about forms of domestic violence. "The need is real," she told me.

She had devised an interesting strategy to overcome the problem of women's reluctance to speak of "domestic violence." Center staff have two distinct modes of representing their work. They advertise the hotline as a generalized service, as a hotline for women (*telefon doveriia dlia zhenshchin*), "so we don't scare women away." Since fall 1999, the center has run a couple of support groups, which staff advertise as a "support group for women" (*gruppa podderzhki dlia zhenshchin*), not specifying spousal abuse. When speaking to clients, they avoid terminology that might alienate women; they do not use the term violence (*nasilie*) or violent behavior (*nasil'stvennoe povedenie*) but speak instead of controlling behavior (*kontroliruiushchee povedenie*). Likewise, they do not refer to the violator (*nasil'nik*) but the offender (*obidchik*). They discuss the myths (*mify*) and prejudices (*predubezhdeniia*) surrounding rape and domestic violence. Meanwhile, they use the language of the campaigns and speak of domestic violence, or violence against women, in their outreach and educational work, for example when speaking to the media, when lobbying the mayor, and when giving lectures to students at the university or the police academy, or to lawyers.

Tamara attributes the success of the project to the framing of violence against women. As she put it, "it was important for us to define a specific area of activity in order to achieve this. If we had chosen to deal with violence more broadly, or with economic issues, or with alcoholism as some people suggested, we wouldn't have been able to do it." She told me that the main achievement of the last six months is that the center now has a name, an image (*imadzh*) in the city. She has been able to overcome local skepticism precisely due to the international support that the project has won. The symbolic aspect of this support was as important as the material; she had used it as a bargaining chip in negotiations with local power brokers, and it had won her the grudging support of those who were very skeptical about the issue.

As is clear from her latest account, what appears to have changed most markedly is Tamara's own sense of conviction. Women come with similar problems as previously. However, she is more convinced of the efficacy of her project and more tightly socialized into the campaigns. I tried to push Tamara to reflect on this. What did these shifts in orientation mean to her? I gained no sense that she was torn by these changes. Rather, she was clearly proud about her work and its success. "We've come a long way," she told me. "There used to be no language for this kind of thing. Now the authorities have been forced to recognize the problem."

Our most recent conversations reveal a greater degree of ambivalence. When I last returned in summer 2001, I found Tamara preoccupied with new questions. Although eloquent about the importance of the work she does, she was alive to its contradictions and eager to discuss the ambivalence of collaboration with donor agencies. Together with Natasha, a crisis center colleague from a neighboring city, we discussed these issues. In the course of our conversation it became clear that the two women were dissatisfied with and baffled by foundation policies and felt unheard by foundation representatives. Although they felt that they were doing useful work, they were frustrated that so much time was taken up by bureaucratic activities. What is more, they felt constrained. Grants permit and exclude specific activities, down to the themes of trainings. Natasha explained that her center had recently been visited by agency evaluators, and it was absolutely clear to her that they were not interested in the content of the center's activities: "They just need pretty numbers, they don't need to hear my thoughts (*razmyshlenie*) about our work." Furthermore, they were concerned that donors were moving away from supporting the theme of *nasilie* (violence). The new theme, she continued, was *torgovlia liud'mi* (trafficking). Tamara nodded, saying: "We have to be like chameleons to please the foundations. Even if you don't want to take it [trafficking] on, you have to!"

Finally, they had begun to feel a sense of futility about the work they had been encouraged into. They had successfully raised an issue that both felt was real and important, but at the same time, they were aware that it was nested within a host of other concerns. As with the other crisis centers I came across, they found that their clients came to discuss a wide variety of issues. Although they were frequently able to locate (or "uncover") an element of domestic violence in clients' accounts (whether it be verbal or psychological abuse, economic pressure, or actual physical violence carried out by spouses or male relatives), clients most pressingly made reference to material problems that affected both them and their families. Their work with women uncovered issues that they felt powerless to address—problems connected with unemployment, unpaid wages, the crisis of living space. "All we can offer is psychological support. It doesn't resolve the main issues," Tamara lamented. "We can't solve the material problems." Natasha agreed, saying: "The global attention to solving women's problems must be the business of the government! Housing, the police, the law—it's too much on our shoulders!"

Conclusions

In this account so far, I have tried to convey the local meanings that get screened out by the international renditions of the violence against women campaigns. So what lessons for the transnational women's movement can we draw from this specific case?

While it is important to celebrate the success of the crisis center network in terms of the economic and political opportunities it provides local women, we also need to critically interrogate the success of the campaigns and to be aware of their discursive effects. Within contemporary conditions of globalization, transnational gender politics operates as a mode of power that constitutes some women and some issues as deserving, excluding others (Mindry 2001). Indeed, understanding these effects helps us interpret the skepticism of some of the women involved in the campaigns, such as Nadya, whose comments I began with.

Skepticism about these campaigns testifies to the fact that many people experience these campaigns and similar ones as primitivizing. In the 1990s, "violence against women" has become an international development issue, a marker to gauge the "civilization" of states. According to this yardstick, despite the collapse of the political, military, and conceptual boundaries of the Cold War, Russia remains as far away from the West as ever. In fact, ironically, rather than drawing closer, in the 1990s it has slipped backward (from Soviet gender equality to a place of "uncivilized" gender relations). I believe that it was precisely this discursive effect that many of my interlocutors objected to. Furthermore, the framing used by the international campaigns has the ideological effect of obscuring the fact that violence against women is structurally endemic within liberal democratic capitalist regimes. It is not so much the case that liberal democratic "civil" society is not violent but that the system allows for the existence (and occasionally encourages the provision) of services to mop it up.

Making gender and violence a marker of development obscures a fact that both crisis counsellors and their clients know very well—that all forms of violence, including gendered violence, have been exacerbated by structural adjustment, the very liberalizing project that was supposed to bring civility to Russia. No wonder those engaged in the ideological work of these campaigns feel ambivalent about them.

The discursive prominence of terms such as crisis center and violence and their prioritization exemplifies some troubling aspects of Western democratization aid. The prominence of the issue of violence against women can be read as part of a broader trend, marking a discursive privatization of the social dislocation accompanying transition and a depoliticization of the economic. Stopping up the gaps of the radical free market, services such as crisis centers act as mediators, educating Russian people into the new order. The individualizing, economizing discourses that these centers put out ("self-help," "self-reliance") educate people out of politics, out of expecting anything from the crumbling and retreating state. The winning out of the "international model" marks an abandonment of attempts to tackle structural problems, as my examples from Tver' reveal. Interestingly, both Tamara's and Katia's crisis center projects foreground issues of individual change and development, rather than structural issues, and there is little critical discussion of the path of democratization and development. One of the last things Tamara said to me was that women needed to be educated out of the "myth" that domestic violence has material roots. Here, she was making the feminist argument that domestic violence could not be justified as a response to economic hardship. Still, in her ready adoption of this framing, I see her as still taking on the old socialist state and its discredited, materialist ideologies, perhaps not fully aware of the implications of the new ideology that is taking its place. Meanwhile, over time the element of structural critique dropped out of Katia's "anticrisis center" plan. Whereas formerly she had at least implicitly addressed the state and the illegality of economic discrimination and dismissals, she began to speak only in terms of psychological support. Her new project description was "to afford psychological support to women who are suffering the consequences of loss of work."[25]

However, this is not the full story. My Tver' case study shows how the model of crisis center has been appropriated and embraced and deployed for various different ends. The women of Zhenskii Svet, like many other activists, made a pragmatic, strategic decision to set up a crisis center.

They were to some extent coerced into the framing, yet they have been able to reappropriate it in key ways. The crisis center meets group needs and objectives that preceded the arrival of Western funding. It has become an important discursive site where social dislocation and confusion are explored and made sense of; where needs can be defined and named, and survival strategies formulated. Like other NGOs, it is a dynamic site in which people negotiate the past and the present. No less significantly, it serves as an effective niche, a foothold for those who work there, and it contributes to the creation of new forms of solidarity and togetherness. What's more, crisis centers bring nongovernmental women's activists into dialogue with state agencies, contributing to important realignments between spheres.

I regard my colleagues' appropriation of the model as an ambivalent thing—it is part co-optation, part self-justification, and part testimony to a new formulation of gendered violence. Work conducted in the center both embraces and exceeds the gendered violence narrative. In their commentaries I see the germ of a critique and the potential formulation of a collective, or at least less individualistic response to gendered violence that could be useful to us all.

Notes

This essay is based on nineteen months of ethnographic fieldwork conducted in Moscow, Tver, and Pskov between 1995 and 2001; I dedicate it with gratitude to Valentina Uspenskaia and Oktiabrina Cheremovskaia. I am grateful to the Cornell Graduate School, the Einaudi Center for International Studies, and the Cornell University Peace Studies Program for financial support. I would like to thank Elizabeth Armstrong, Nanette Funk, Davydd Greenwood, Nancy Ries and particularly Michele Rivkin-Fish for their thoughtful and critical engagement with earlier drafts and for their encouragement of these ideas. I would also like to thank the editors of *Signs* for their support and for granting permission to reprint this material.

1. Following anthropological conventions, I make use of pseudonyms to protect the identity of the women activists I worked with in my research.

2. The official Soviet Women's Committee delegations had connections with some Western feminist activists during the Soviet period. Further, Western feminist texts circulated clandestinely via samizdat during the 1970s and 1980s, and there were limited connections between individual dissidents and Western feminist activists.

3. See, for example, Wedel (1998), Berdahl (1999), Borneman (1992), and Verdery (1996) for critical discussions of this topic.

4. Recent feminist scholarship has drawn attention to the gendered effects of democratization and transition, pointing to the ways it has marked the demotion of

women as a group in Russia and other postsocialist countries (see, for example, Bridger, Kay, and Pinnick 1996; Verdery 1996; Watson 1997; Gal and Kligman 2000a).

5. The UN Convention on the Elimination of All Forms of Discrimination against Women (CEDAW), which was adopted in 1979 and entered into force in 1981, makes no mention of violence, rape, abuse, or battery. However, by mid-1995 violence against women had become a "common advocacy position" of the women's movement and the human rights movement (Keck and Sikkink 1998, 166).

6. The Ford Foundation played a significant role in determining patterns of funding and led the way in funding campaigns against violence against women. While in 1988 major US foundations awarded eleven grants totaling $241,000, in 1993 they made sixty-eight grants totaling $3,247,800 (Keck and Sikkink 1998, 182).

7. See Keck and Sikkink 1998. Sperling, Ferree, and Risman (2001) provide a nuanced account of Russian women's activism in the context of the development of the transnational women's movement, bringing the lens of new social movement theory to bear on the changes of the last decade. Their study documents the first phase of Western donor support to Russian women's groups in the early to mid-1990s.

8. Drawing on data from China, Indonesia, and Malaysia, Ong gives examples of alternative strategies (1996). Gayatri Chakravorty Spivak has made a similar critique of the Beijing conference and its colonialist characteristics (1996).

9. See, for example, Feldman (1997), Lang (1997), Alvarez (1998), Kamat (2002), Paley (2001).

10. Alvarez, Dagnino, and Escobar introduce the concept of "APSAS" to describe the new service-oriented NGOs that are encouraged into being by international foundations and donor agencies. They regard them as Band-Aids, palliatives, hopelessly compromised by the role they play in filling up the gaps of the free market (1998, 22).

11. For discussions of how this has influenced women's movements, see, for example, Alvarez (1998), Lang (1997); for a consideration of these issues in the formerly socialist states of Central and Eastern Europe and the former Soviet Union, see Abramson (1999), Richter (1999), Snitow (1999), Sperling (2000).

12. I am grateful to Michele Rivkin-Fish for suggesting this formulation.

13. Another explanation for this skepticism is that women's organizing was enforced and managed from above by the Soviet state, in a network of official women's departments and councils. Furthermore, feminism was discredited by Bolshevik and Soviet leaders, who labeled it a Western reformist phenomenon (Noonan 1996, 77).

14. For discussions of state socialist gender arrangements and the corresponding absence of a sense of gender discrimination, see Verdery (1996), Watson (1997), Gal and Kligman (2000a).

15. I met many crisis center activists who were eager to establish shelters. However, they acknowledged that local conditions did not permit it. First, there was the dif-

ficulty of obtaining premises from local authorities. Second, it was unclear where to relocate women once they had been admitted. If in Western Europe and the United States the shelter is a temporary refuge, a stopgap for women and their families before they find their feet, in Russia people have quite literally nowhere to move on to.

16. According to data published in 1995, 14,400 cases of rape were recorded in the Russian Federation in 1993. In the same year, 14,500 women were reported to have been murdered by their husbands or male partners (Attwood 1997, 99).

17. Foundation representatives I spoke with frequently cited the crisis center network as one of the most successful women's NGO projects.

18. The Canadian Embassy funded the publication of the book. According to one of its Russian authors, five thousand copies were distributed to nascent crisis centers and women's NGOs (Zabelina 1996).

19. See, for example, Gibson-Graham (1996), Grewal and Kaplan (1994).

20. Its feminist and democratic orientation made the group unusual. However, it can be considered exemplary of the early clubs and groups founded in academic circles by women familiar with feminist texts and the Western women's movement.

21. I first learned about the group in 1995 from the Network of East-West Women electronic listserv. New women's groups, which had just been hooked up on the Internet, announced and introduced themselves and listed their interests. Groups tended to make broad declarations rather than itemize existing services. This was very much of the times, before the standardization associated with NGOs had become widespread.

22. I found that many North American or Western European feminists dismissed discussions of economic factors as a rationalization for male-perpetrated violence. The standard response was the assertion that rich men also beat their wives. While of course this is true and important, in this context it is extraordinarily dismissive of local concerns and shows little awareness of the extent of economic dislocation in Russia and its devastating effects on the lives of women and their families.

23. In brief, participatory action research (PAR) is a social change methodology, involving the participation of a community group in problem posing and solving (Maguire 1987). For helpful discussions of PAR, see, for example, Fals Borda and Rahman (1991), Maguire (1996), D. Greenwood and Levin (1998).

24. I reflect on my role and the implications of my involvement in this project elsewhere. See Hemment (2000 and 2004).

25. During my last trip to the city, in 2001, I learned that Katia had been appointed director of a newly founded, government-funded Center for Women and Families.

Resolving a Gendered Paradox
Women's Participation and the NGO Boom in North India

Introduction

Within gendered participatory approaches to development is a gendered paradox: NGOs are charged to bring women into the social and economic lives of their communities, yet they cannot accept their own women employees as full participants. Women's participation has grown popular due to gender mainstreaming trends in international development, but that has not necessarily led NGOs to embrace women's participation ideals in general or to reflect on their own internal practices. Instead, the rise of women's participation has produced an ongoing struggle among NGO staff and between staff and their constituents over meanings of women's participation and the spatial changes necessary to enable women's participation. In this chapter, I combine geographic theories of power and space with recent insights into participatory development in order to illuminate how feminist struggles among NGO staff over meanings of women's participation created opportunities for women fieldworkers' participation inside the organization. Instead of evaluating the success or failure of women's participation based on definitions of women's participation found in NGO documents, my analysis focuses on the results of dialogic exchanges (for example, conversations, heated arguments) over women's participation during project implementation. I trace the spaces where dialogic exchanges occurred *and* the spatial outcomes of dialogic exchanges in order to argue that dialogues have a practical impact on NGOs by creating space for social change.

One emphasis in recent scholarship on NGOs concerns itself with the ability of NGOs to provide alternatives to development (see, for example, Bebbington, Hickey and Mitlin 2008). NGOs have been criticized for allowing their alternative agendas to be compromised or co-opted, an outcome of their especially difficult position between dependency on state support and/or financing from international donors (Townsend, Porter, and Mawdsley 2002; Dolhinow 2005) and a simultaneous dependency on their client base (Walker, Jones, Roberts, and Froehling 2007; O'Reilly 2010). Development agendas may be resisted, incorporated and/or manipulated to fit with individual plans, both those of fieldworkers (Springer 2001; O'Reilly 2006b) and clients (Everett 1997; Bebbington 2000). The gendered paradox of participation that NGOs both contribute to and attempt to resolve is generated at the confluence of donor demands and the social context within which they are embedded (Agarwal 2001; O'Reilly 2006a). Investigation of the gendered paradox requires exploration into these organizations as central sites where discourses of participation are negotiated. The planning documents of NGOs give the impression that inside organizations discourses for women's participation are unified and uncontested. However, during fieldwork with a drinking water supply project in northern Rajasthan, India, I experienced discourses of women's participation as changing and multiple, and its associated practices as fragmented and fragile (see also Mosse 2005). Women's participation was an evolving set of contradictory meanings and practices.

In this chapter, I argue that dialogic exchanges between NGO staff over women's participation extended its meanings, thereby creating additional spaces for women's voices and concerns. As struggles unfolded over what topics and activities women's participation would contain and would not, and over the value of women's participation to the development project and the implementing NGO, the profile and relevance of women's participation was enhanced. The gendered paradox began to resolve itself as NGO staff discussed and reflected on women's participation inside their organization. As one male fieldworker said:

> Even here in this project there is no equal participation for women fieldworkers. How will she create women's participation in villages? So very slowly, whatever is in our pre-planning and written in our handbook, that much women's participation we may not get; we may do less. We keep thinking about it, between us we keep arguing and reasoning (*tarksangat ladaaii*) and we talk a lot about it. See, some way may

emerge (*nikal jaaye*). There may be a blast (*visfot*) which will bring complete participation and equality in society. (Ravinder 2000. Unpublished. Data from fieldwork)

Although Ravinder admitted that women fieldworkers did not participate in his NGO on equal footing with men and realized that, despite planning, fieldworkers might not be able to create women's participation in the management of village water resources, he was encouraged that men and women within his NGO were talking about the issues. Ravinder's words emphasize that women's participation in development was a dialogic process (for example, "arguing and reasoning") that included negotiating how women fieldworkers would participate within their own organization. He was hopeful that through these verbal exchanges—or some "explosion"—equality in society might occur. This fieldworker's awareness of the power of discussion led me to consider the ways that NGO staffs' voices emerged to produce expanded meanings and open new spaces for women's participation in the activities of the NGO.

In the pages that follow, I situate my argument within current critiques of participation and then introduce my case study NGO, Our Water, its goals, and its project area. I discuss the general condition of women in northern India that informed project goals for women's participation. This discussion is followed by an outline of geographic theories on the power struggles that cocreate language and space. I argue that our understanding of feminist struggles inside NGOs are enhanced when we consider that tensions over meanings of terms like "women's participation" are productive of new meanings and spaces. I ground these ideas in ethnographic examples that demonstrate how meanings and spaces of development are produced through the daily speech and practices of agents—in this case the many different individuals who made up the staff of Our Water. Framing dialogues as micropolitical processes that have spatial outcomes enables us to discover that although "there is no equal participation for women fieldworkers," internal struggles inside an NGO may begin to resolve the gendered paradox.

Women's Participation: Theory and Critique

Just as development planning eventually incorporated women into projects (Boserup 1970; Tinker 1990; Kabeer 1996), so too have participation programs become gendered (Tinker 1990; C. Moser 1993; Guijt and Shah 1998; C. Jackson and Pearson 1998; Cornwall 2003). Following general participatory goals (Chambers 1983, 1997) and adding women, policy makers plan that village women's participation in development projects will include them in community decision making (Guijt and Shah 1998; Agarwal 2001), lead to sustainable resource management (C. Jackson 1993), or raise women's incomes and social capital through income-generation schemes (United Nations Development Program 2003). Additionally, women's participation, it was suggested, may lead to women's empowerment, but how empowerment happens, at what scales it happens, and even *what* constitutes empowerment remains in question (Friedmann 1992; Kabeer 1996; Rowlands 1997; Guijt and Shah 1998).

Feminist scholars have criticized participatory goals by finding within them opportunities for women's exploitation (Jackson 1993; Schroeder 1999), the inability of participation to overcome existing discriminatory social contexts (Agarwal 2001), and the focus of empowerment on individuals, away from collective action (Kamat 2004). Participation has been influenced by neoliberalism, where it comes to mean achieving project efficiencies at the expense of empowerment (Dagnino 2008), a managerialist approach to the work of NGOs (Townsend, Porter, and Mawdsley 2002), a redirection of NGOs' efforts toward pleasing donors and away from client concerns (Miraftab 1997), and/or the construction of individual capability as the solution to individual problems, instead of focusing attention on collective action to address structural problems of poverty and inequality (Kamat 2004). That said, we risk stabilizing neoliberalism when we fail to question the ability of NGOs to spread neoliberalism (Bebbington 2004a). Katharine McKinnon (2007, 779) concludes that the development process should always be seen as a political struggle, and as such, the possibility of "new strategies and modes of engagement" opens.

Critics of participation charge that participatory approaches have failed to become an active practice—that is, donors, practitioners, and planners may speak the language of participation, but their actual approach during project implementation remains "top-down" (Mosse 2001).[1] Other critics claim that participatory approaches are chosen because they increase projects' cost and time efficiency by accessing local labor (Kabeer 1996; Rahnema and Bawtree 1997; O'Reilly 2006b).[2] G. Mohan and K. Stokke (2000) criticize participatory approaches for being overly "local" and therefore neglecting broader unequal relations of power within which the "local" is embedded. Samuel Hickey and Giles Mohan (2004) in their introduction continue the critique that participation has yet to deal satisfactorily with issues of power. Power is also a central focus for Bill Cooke and Uma Kothari (2001), who take a Foucauldian approach to participation in order to explore participation as a discourse through which power circulates. By framing participation as a discourse that contains "the potential for an unjustified exercise of power," Cooke and Kothari (2001, 4) argue that participation can be tyrannical in its exercise. Like any discourse, what is included and omitted in discourses of participation has important implications for project outcomes. The language and practices of participation can be deployed both to extend and to undermine power (see also Crush 1995; Escobar 1995; Kothari 2001; O'Reilly 2006b). Project documents and fieldworker trainings are intended to stabilize meanings of participation, but NGO employees generate alternative meanings of participation through their practices, which change over time and circumstances (Crewe and Harrison 1998; Mosse 2001; O'Reilly 2006b).

Recent work in critical development geography has focused on the agency of actors in making development meanings and spaces (Bebbington 2000; Nagar and Raju 2003; Laurie 2005; Page 2005). The question remains: what is the connection between project discourses and staff practices? Within development studies and critiques of participatory approaches, scholars continue to try to understand how participatory discourses link up with social processes "without even approximately determining the form or defining the logic of the outcome" (Ferguson 1990, 275). A unified discourse of participation may emerge in NGO documents, but that discourse does not reflect the multiplicity of positions and voices of staff (to say nothing of donors' or villagers' voices). Discourses may make a world, but they do not make a whole world. Beyond that world are alternative meanings (see Schech and Haggis 2002). Development plans may fail to do one thing (what they planned), but they may succeed in doing something else (usually unplanned) and "that something else has its own logic" (Ferguson 1990, 276). It is necessary, then, to go deeply into the everyday production processes of meaning creation. With this in mind, I began to notice how negative attention focused on women's participation seemed to strengthen it and encouraged the resolve of NGO staff who favored it. Staff spoke up about women's participation with more frequency and in more spaces as the project progressed.

The spatial has often been overlooked in previous work about participation, but Andrea Cornwall (2004, 75; see also Fischer 2006; Gaventa 2006) argues that framing participation as a spatial practice allows us to think about how "particular sites come to be populated, appropriated or designated by particular actors" in ways that enable or disable social transformation. Development project staff ideally create spaces for participation as a way of establishing opportunities for those on the margins to be included or for different voices to be heard. However, if we accept that space is socially and discursively produced, then it is always already imbued with social relations of power. Dominant meanings of participation will influence who enters, who speaks, and how what is said is understood within invited spaces. Existing social relationships, previous experiences, and a wider sociopolitical context are not left at the boundaries of such spaces (Cornwall 2004; see also Agarwal 2001). These dynamics are especially important given that invited spaces are designed to include a heterogeneous group of actors (Cornwall 2004, Fischer 2006). Cornwall (2004) and Frank Fischer (2006) conclude that more needs to be known about when, where, and under what conditions invited spaces work to produce what is hoped for, but also how routinized forms of participation may have transformative potential. This chapter contributes directly to those goals.

The Project and Its Area

My case study, Our Water, was a joint Indo-German development project designed to supply town and village populations in Rajasthan's *khaaraa paanii* (saline water) belt with clean drinking water. Existing groundwater is undrinkable there due to its high salt content (C. Henderson 1994). The project area covered approximately 20,000 square kilometers in three northern districts of Rajasthan: Churu, Jhunjhunu, and Hanumangarh. Phase 1 of the project (completed December 2005) covered 378 villages and two towns, reaching almost 900,000 people. Villagers harvest sweet rainwater during the rainy season (July–August) from rooftops, ground-level *kunds* (passive rainwater catchments), and other traditional sources. Before the arrival of project water, residents of the area received water twice daily at public taps through a Government of Rajasthan pipeline. The work of fetching water from public taps is predominantly the work of women and girls. Water provision by the Government of Rajasthan was sporadic, allegedly treated and free, but the Our Water supply was intended to flow twenty-four hours a day and was strictly for household consumption and livestock watering. At each village's entrance a meter records total water usage; each household pays a share of the monthly bill depending on the number of its members and heads of cattle, sheep, or camels. The underlying logic was that villagers want clean water regularly supplied, and they are willing to pay a nominal charge in order to get it. Community participation, according to *Achievements 2002* (Our Water

2002, 22) would "ensure sustainability and enhancement of the benefits" of a regular, reliable drinking-water supply.

The NGO: Our Water

Our Water comprised a technical side that was responsible for building the massive drinking-water supply infrastructure and a social side that was responsible for implementing community participation. The Government of Rajasthan employed the engineers of the technical side. The social side was a consortium of five regional NGOs that unified to form one purpose-specific NGO over the life of the Our Water project. It was charged with creating a village water committee in every village; building awareness for payment and water conservation; educating village populations about health, hygiene, and sanitation; and implementing women's participation, considered "essential across all activities" (Our Water n.d., n.p.).

The term "NGO" means many different things across contexts, and in India particularly, NGO represents a myriad of institutions, including religious organizations, trusts, fronts for other operations, and organizations contracting for social services with the state (O'Reilly 2010). I identify the social side of Our Water as an NGO because it comprised local nonprofit, nongovernmental organizations—two internationally funded organizations engaged in rural social service, and three institutions involved in field and classroom training for rural management and social work. While all the staff considered one of these organizations as a home institution, Our Water strove to act as a cohesive unit with great success.

Approximately seventy Indian staff worked for the social side of Our Water out of a main office and scattered field offices in the project area. (From this point forward, I use the name "Our Water" specifically to mean the employees working on its social side.) These members were a diverse group: some were local, some were not; their home state, first language, socioeconomic background, caste, education level, age, and marital status varied from person to person. Seven program officers (one woman, six men) managed the project from the main office and made occasional visits to the field. There was a German consultant, as required by the German donor bank. As of March 2001, there were thirty-six male fieldworkers and fourteen female fieldworkers, who lived and worked in area villages.[3] Each field team comprised one woman and two men. Women fieldworkers implemented women's participation activities, which ranged from mobilizing women's groups, to map making, to trainings on household cleanliness and safe water-handling practices. Male fieldworkers initiated village-level water management institutions, discussed payment plans, and supported latrine building. Some men (especially team leaders) concerned themselves with the work of women's participation, but for the most part, there was a fairly rigid division of labor. No man was ever assigned to the women's participation component, nor any woman to the water distribution management or sanitation component. Field teams acted as the primary link between villagers, the technical side, and Our Water program officers. Similarly, women fieldworkers formed the fundamental connection between village women and other NGO staff. Field staff worked out of village offices-*cum*-residences and met together monthly at the main office for "experience sharing" and training sessions.

From summer 1998 until winter of 2002, I visited Our Water and its project area intermittently for five periods of two months to one year. During that time, I gathered project documents and conducted participant observation with staff as they worked in the main office, field offices, and villages. I informally questioned staff about Our Water's goals, women's participation, and their practices. I recorded daily field notes, informal discussions, interactions, and practices. My research assistant, Tasneem Khan, and I recorded, transcribed, and translated twenty-two formal interviews taken in semistructured format in Hindi, Marwari, and English.

Women's Participation in a North Indian Context

In general, north India[4] can be characterized by low education levels, poorly functioning public services, and limited roles for women (Dreze and Gazdar 1998, 60). Despite recent economic growth, the region shows slow rates of poverty decline (Dreze and Gazdar 1998, 33). In Rajasthan, where socioeconomic conditions are broadly representative of the wider region of north India, liberalization and government quotas in the 1990s have led to some opportunities for women in the areas of workforce and political participation. However, compared to the rest of the country, north India lags in terms of gendered social development indicators such as mortality, fertility, morbidity, nutrition, and illiteracy (Dreze and Gazdar 1998, 33). North Indian women compare less favorably to men across human development indicators: employment, literacy, wages, age at marriage, health care access, level of education, and property rights (Mahbub ul Haq Human Development Centre 2000; S. Desai et al. 2010; United Nations Development Program 2003).

The agency of north Indian women as it relates to their reproductive health, fertility rates, and child care has been closely linked to the status and location of women after marriage (Dyson and Moore 1983; Jeffery and Jeffery 1997; L. Rahman and Rao 2004; S. Desai et al. 2010). In north India, married women usually join their husbands' families in their village (*sasuraal*) after marriage. Both older mothers-in-law and younger daughters-in-law practice *ghuunghat*—fully covering the face as a sign of modesty and respect—and *purdah* (literally, "curtain"), which involves: not leaving the house; *ghuunghat* in front of strangers, senior men, and senior women; and staying silent or lowering one's voice in the presence of these people (Luthra 1976; Joshi 1995; Unnithan-Kumar 1997; Agarwal 2001). Unmarried girls, living in their natal villages, although their work burden is greater than their brothers, do not veil or stay in seclusion. *Ghuunghat* and *purdah* are not rigid institutions, as Varsha Joshi (1995) and Gloria Raheja and Ann Gold (1994) find, but are fluid depending on a woman's age, kinship relationship to her husband's family, caste, class, religion, and marital status. While recognizing that *purdah* is a "restriction and restraint for women in virtually every activity of life" (Jacobson 1982, 82 as cited in Raheja and Gold 1994, 168; see also Nabar 1995), Raheja and Gold (1994, 169) write that *purdah* is "not a monolithic prison but a subtle, fluid, and often highly manipulatable bundle of practices and precepts" (see also U. Sharma 1978). Women find ways of expressing their agency within patriarchal systems; they accept, contribute to, *and* undermine gendered oppression. Men may be dominant, but their dominance is never complete; thus it is important to seek out how north Indian women, who often may appear powerless, destabilize male dominance (Jeffery and Jeffery 1997).

Women's Participation in the Our Water Project

The status of women in Rajasthan provided the impetus for Our Water's gendered intervention. According to NGO documents, women's participation was critical to project success in terms of its goal to improve the health conditions of the population. It was primarily married women, in their roles as mothers and household caretakers, who could learn water hygiene techniques and teach them to their children, thereby bringing about long-term health benefits. Project plans called for women to give their opinions about where neighborhood public taps should be placed, to monitor taps for water use and misuse, and to take responsibility for cleaning public taps. One or more women's representatives was required to sit on village-level water management committees to "incorporate women's concerns in the decision-making process" (Our Water 2002, 31). In addition, women's "essential" qualities of conscientiousness and commitment were required by the project to achieve sustainability (Our Water n.d., 27). Women were targeted as those who will want the system most and who would do the most toward convincing others to take care of the system. Ultimately, it was hoped that women would be empowered by participating in the project and would collectively begin to solve other problems.

Women fieldworkers—whether they were local or not, spoke Rajasthani or not, had a lot or a little education—were expected to facilitate village women's participation. The NGO's approach of hiring women to promote women's participation was in keeping with global trends of women's increasing employment in NGOs for the purpose of assisting women's development schemes (Crewe and Harrison 1998; Garcia 2001; O'Reilly 2004). However, support for women fieldworkers within the NGO and for the women's participation component was ambiguous. Some staff denigrated women's involvement, others celebrated women fieldworkers' capabilities, but a majority of NGO staff (both program officers and fieldworkers, both men and women) engaged in practices that signaled an ambivalence about women fieldworkers' importance in the project (O'Reilly 2006b). Although mixed feelings about women's participation did not break down neatly along gendered lines, often divisive problems surrounding it were conceived as women versus men. The multiple attitudes of NGO staff created the gendered paradox that NGOs marginalized their women employees even though they were charged to facilitate village women's participation.

The Micropolitics of Language, Space, and Practice

One of the aims of this chapter is to take space seriously as a realm of active political engagement within a context of unequal gender relations (see Robinson 2000). Space, as used here, is "the spatial configuration of power-imbued social relations" (Massey 2000, 283). Following Doreen Massey (2000, 282; see also Massey 1994) space may be conceived as "actively and continually practised social relations," or as Henri Lefebvre (1991, 17) puts it, as "spatial/social practice"—to suggest that space is coded with social and spatial practices *as it is produced.* Considering space as relationally constructed foregrounds the spatial "as an active force in the formulation and operation of dominance/resistance" (Massey 2000, 283; see also Sharp, Routledge, Philo, and Paddison 2000; Gaventa 2006).

Massey (2000, 284) argues that what is at issue politically is "transforming, subverting, and challenging the constitutive relations which construct spaces in the first place."

Such a politicized view of sociospatial relations is critical to an investigation of the work of development projects because projects aim to both build on *and* subvert existing spatial/social practices (see, for example, Schroeder 1999; Schroeder and Suryanata 2004; O'Reilly 2006a). NGO agendas often contain a mandate for social change; grassroots organizations set themselves the task of challenging existing social relations (see, for example, Routledge 2003). Our Water had a complementary sociospatial goal: getting women out of their houses and involving them in drinking-water supply management. Women's participation in water management was eventually supposed to lead to their empowerment (O'Reilly 2006a). Notwithstanding that such plans are fraught with tropes of colonialism, gendered private/inner spaces, and the home, they also indicate that development policies link changes in space to changes in social relations, both in the workplace and in villages. The practices of NGO field staff can be examined for their efforts to reorder gender relationships of unequal power.

Massey's argument that space is continually produced out of social relations of unequal power parallels Bakhtin's theory of meaning creation. Bakhtin suggests that social change and the creation of space may be explored by framing dialogues as fraught with micropolitics and by tracing meanings as they occur through dialogic exchange (see Bakhtin 1986; Bakhtin and Voloshinov 1994; Morris 1994). The utterances of individuals, Bakhtin posits, create direct and indirect challenges to oppressive social relations by suggesting that alternative meanings are possible (Bauer and McKinstry 1991). When individual voices suggest aloud new or different meanings of terms already defined by a dominant narrative, dialogue has occurred. His ideas allow that all meanings have some power, and some meanings dominate without having total power. Bakhtin theorizes that in social contexts of unequal power, multiple and conflicting voices are potentially productive. A dominant monologue is no longer a monologue when an individual literally gives voice to alternative meanings; alternative meanings come into play directly in conversation. Furthermore, they also engage at the scale of wider, dominant narratives, as when fieldworkers suggest village women should leave their family compound in order to attend mixed-gender village water committee meetings, discourses of women's participation compete with dominant understandings of public space as men's space. Dialogic exchange occurs between persons, but engages more broadly with prevailing narratives.

Bakhtin's ideas present development scholars with a micropolitical, discursive approach to research seeking out the processes of sociospatial change by suggesting that dialogic exchange creates new meanings of words, like "women's participation," that are potentially subversive. Extended ethnographic fieldwork is an ideal method for tracing the shifting meanings of terms over time and space. The work of fieldworkers is primarily talk—another reason to turn to Bakhtin—and as they talk, fieldworkers mobilize particular ideas about women's participation and space. Project discourses of participation are not simply read off project documents and implemented verbatim. Instead, they are interpreted and enacted by fieldworkers in a variety of ways and contexts.

In the pages below, I combine geographers' ideas about space as social relations that can both inhibit and enable particular dialogues and practices and Bakhtin's conceptualization of meaning creation in order to pry open the "black box" of NGOs (Ferguson 1990; Everett 1997). I use a variety of examples to illustrate how shifting dialogues about women's participation resulted in small changes inside NGO spaces and NGO practices of women's participation. In these dialogues, we can hear individual voices reworking meanings of women's participation, and listen for the tensions that produced spaces where voices favoring participation emerged (or did not) or where recognizable spaces for women were created (or were not). It was through dialogue that the meanings of women's participation and the spaces where it might occur expanded over the course of project implementation.

Creating Spaces for Women's Participation

In spaces where a dominant monologue is active, one subversive voice may plant the seed for dialogue, creating an opening in time-space where hegemonic meanings can be engaged dialogically. A monthly Our Water staff meeting provides an example of an opening created by the voices of two program officers, who chose to speak about the importance of women's participation. In monthly staff meetings whenever women began to speak about their work toward women's participation, most of the men would cease listening and talk softly among themselves. At such a meeting in July 2000, when the susurrus drew her notice, the women's participation program officer berated those making the noise for failing to consider the activities of women's participation important to the work that they were doing individually and to the project. A senior program officer added his voice and authority, addressing those present on the seriousness of the matter: "Seriousness *kii kamii hai. Man lenaa padegaa* but seriousness *kii kamii hai....Mahiilaa binaa yah* project *nahiin chalegaa*" (Seriousness is lacking. You have to think [about this issue] but seriousness is lacking.... Without women this project will not go forward). This was the first time to my knowledge that male fieldworkers' casualness toward women's participation was openly addressed.

Through their words the two program officers attempted to influence directly meanings of women's participation by declaring its importance and urging fieldworkers to think about it seriously. Speaking from positions of power, their authority enabled a shift to occur—suddenly the women fieldworkers in the room became visible and audible. The meeting room became a space where, temporarily, *all* voices were heard, not only those of men fieldworkers. Men began paying attention to what women were saying when they spoke. Reminders to men fieldworkers became more and more frequent in the main meeting room over the months I studied the project, and served to reinforce the growing importance of the women's participation component. If the women's participation program officer was not present when women were reporting, other program officers would speak up about the need for men's attention if it drifted away from women's remarks. The initial incident in the presence of all staff set the stage for future insistence on women fieldworkers' critical project roles.

The authority of these two program officers enabled them to challenge an existing norm that men need not concern themselves with women's participation reporting in the main meeting room. Their words challenged an existing monologue that marginalized women's participation; by speaking they created an opening for dialogic exchange about women's participation in the NGO and its importance to the project overall. However, authority does not always enable a development worker to engage those around him/her in dialogue about women's participation. For example, Ravinder often spoke in favor of women's empowerment, but he felt constrained in speaking to the women of his own family about unveiling:

I know my mother and wife should do this work [of empowering women] but I cannot make them [do it] because change in society comes slowly. I know women should not follow the veiling system (*par-*

daaprathaa) but I cannot say to them [my wife and mother], why are you covering your face (*kyon ghuunghat nikaal rahii ho*)?

Ravinder found that he *could* express his views on women's empowerment in other villages in the project area and that they meshed with Our Water's stated goals for women's participation. Despite his readiness to discuss women's empowerment when he was in other villages, he acknowledged his silence. "Change in society happens slowly," he told me, indicating that he knew his words would not, or could not, be heard. He could not open up a conversation about veiling because he was aware of the village context in which they *all* were living. Ravinder was not ready or willing to disrupt the power relations in which he was embedded. Although he did not express it, conceivably, Ravinder's awareness of his multiple positions was in part what silenced him. He knew he carried the authority of an experienced fieldworker, but he was also neighbor, son, and husband. In this particular example we hear a fieldworker realize that he cannot raise more radical meanings of women's participation within his own family/home. He spoke of it in other places, but in his own village a monological discourse spoke singularly about the practice of veiling. His own voice, which might have spoken dialogically, was silenced. The following example depicts a fieldworker introducing a more radical meaning of women's participation.

Although a naturalized, gendered division of labor existed within Our Water, over time women fieldworkers began expressing an interest in working on sanitation or water distribution management, besides women's participation. Sometimes women would unofficially take on these tasks, as male fieldworkers occasionally did with women's participation activities. Eventually a woman fieldworker named Savitri erupted in a monthly meeting, demanding tearfully that women be given the chance to form a women-only field team and prove what women fieldworkers were capable of doing in villages (O'Reilly 2004). At the time the incident was downplayed, but Savitri's indictment of the gendered inequality within Our Water stirred some fieldworkers to reflect negatively on the NGO's gendered division of labor (O'Reilly 2004). Savitri's outburst disrupted the status quo about appropriate jobs for women and men. She alerted staff to the fact that there were spaces for women's participation that extended beyond villages into their own workplace (O'Reilly 2004). She reminded those attending the meeting that women's participation was not only for village women, but something that should be happening inside Our

Water as well. She seized the monthly meeting as a platform for a feminist agenda. Savitri's words suggest that women fieldworkers reconceived particular spaces as spaces of action (Nagar 2000)—in this case the space of the meeting room. She took an opportunity in the NGO's meeting room for dialogue with those in power about greater participation in NGO activities by women fieldworkers.

When it appeared that women fieldworkers' roles might expand into the realm of previously male-only jobs, certain staff grew defensive; however, by that time an atmosphere of support for women's participation had been established inside Our Water, even if practices had not dramatically changed. Those staff opposed to women's participation could no longer claim it was not important. The tension between women's potentially expanding roles in the NGO versus men's dominance took an ironic turn during an annual visit by donor bank officers in June 2000. The most senior officer's frequent inquiries indicated to staff and to villagers that women's participation was high on the bank's agenda. There was talk that $2 million were on the table for women's participation. Some staff handled the attention to women's participation by denigrating the component, saying it was important only because it brought in funds. Together, both the positive and negative dialogues worked to establish a high profile for women's participation during the German officer's visit, which culminated in an all-staff meeting in the main office. Within the atmosphere of support for women's participation, men well known to be opposed to women's participation said that they considered women's participation an integral part of the project. Unlike how they might have denigrated women's participation in other settings, in the presence of a German bank officer, they argued that their work supported women's participation. (With the exception of Nilam, all participants are men.)

GERMAN BANK OFFICER: Do you have sufficient resources and tools for doing your jobs [of women's participation]?

RAVINDER: In our team's area, there are only two women and twenty-eight villages. The women's groups are coming up rapidly, so there should be more women fieldworkers.

GOPAL: Yes, increase the number of women fieldworkers. And they should stay in the NGO longer [in reference to high turnover of women staff].

NILAM: Why not give the women fieldworkers responsibility for sanitation? We have been restricted.

GERMAN BANK OFFICER: Do you want to do that work?

NILAM: We are accountable. Men were doing it . . .

A senior male program officer cuts her off.

VASANT: All the project components are interrelated.

RAMU: We don't take an individual approach. It's team work.

GOPAL: We work together. All do the work. Men are not seeing women's participation as separate.

GERMAN BANK OFFICER: Are men involved in women's participation?

ANAND: They do it.

KAMAL: The things are related.

VASANT: We take the microcredit groups' mission. When there were no women fieldworkers, we did this work.

ANAND: And school sanitation. We take all the activities of the NGO into the schools.

Knowing that they were expected to be working toward women's participation as part of the whole project, men who ordinarily maligned women's participation insisted it was an integral part of their work. Their statements were belied by the fact that travel for women's participation almost always came last when field teams prioritized vehicle use; male team members generally controlled the travel schedule of the team as a whole. The absence of women fieldworkers from teams was less likely to lead men fieldworkers to work toward women's participation (as suggested by Vasant in the dialogue above), as it was to enable teams to disregard those activities as significant for the project.

Similar to Savitri's words in the monthly meeting, Nilam, a woman fieldworker, attempted to argue for a change in the division of labor that would enable women fieldworkers to work on sanitation. A program officer used his authority to silence her. Perhaps he considered her remarks too subversive or simply did not want any tension to mar the German officer's visit. But the incident indicates the limits of support for women fieldworkers' participation in Our Water's activities, because so much more could have been said to support an expansion of their activities. Before this meeting, when women did work on sanitation, it was to supervise construction when the male fieldworkers were not available. Some in-the-field flexibility in the gender division of labor gave women some informal opportunities. However, women seldom got recognition for this work, which they wanted from the program officers and their male coworkers.

The words of the men who spoke after Nilam may be understood as a backlash against the increasing importance of women's participation and women fieldworkers. Most male fieldworkers resisted any intrusion of women fieldworkers into their work, and many preferred the spatial segregation between their activities. Interestingly, field staff who recognized that some men were exaggerating their activities did not call their bluff. Few wanted the work of the NGO to look bad in front of the German officers, but perhaps also the existing atmosphere of support for women's participation enabled men's activities to be viewed in a different light. For example, Anand's reference to school sanitation work may have reminded staff that access to latrines at schools enabled girls to attend. These male fieldworkers' voices ironically reinforced women's participation as a critical project component. Importantly, within a month of this meeting, program officers began discussing reassignment of women fieldworkers to sanitation and water distribution management jobs. The recognition women fieldworkers sought was now under consideration. Later that same year, women fieldworkers asked for and received training in health education, which became an education component for village women on safe water handling practices.

During the same visit of donor bank officers, women fieldworkers took an opportunity to suggest that village women's activities be expanded, and in particular to open up village water committee meetings for village women's participation.

GERMAN BANK OFFICER: Women's groups are not formal, so how can they be sustained?

SITA: This is a good question. The women's groups should be made equal to the village water committees. Even if they are informal, these groups don't feel they are weaker. They have different work but they are no weaker.

SIMA: User groups [of public tap users] are mainly women, so they feel that it is for their benefit [to participate in them].

NILAM: We have to give more and more responsibility to them.

GERMAN BANK OFFICER: Which responsibilities?

NILAM: Payment collection [of water charges]. There could also be more roles for the self-help groups.

PUSHPA: The latrine subsidy forms are filled in women's names.

SITA: The women's groups and self-help groups should be called into the village water committee meetings. Maybe they don't have legal power, but they should sit in the meetings.

These utterances are part of a larger dialogic and material struggle over village women's access to the power/space of village water committees. It was well known in Our Water that despite a guideline that every village water committee have one or more women's representatives present at meetings, meetings were often held without women present or that the women who did come were *foto sadasya* (dummy representatives). If a women's representative attended, she did not often sit with the male members. Instead she would sit silently outside of the main meeting area, but within hearing range. In this example, the German officer's question about sustainability was a verbal sanction of women's participation. It carried significant weight among staff, despite the fact that the German officers did not make decisions about Our Water's daily activities. Women fieldworkers responded by suggesting that women's participation stretch into the male spaces of village water committees by increasing the number of women invited. In their words, women's groups were placed on a par with village water committees, and the activities and spaces of user groups and self-help groups were augmented. These women fieldworkers' unstated hope was that greater numbers of women's representatives would allow women to sit with men in the main meeting room and to speak.

In the presence of all other staff, they sought the German bank officer's approval to expand village women's access to public space. Both village water committee spaces and gatherings of the NGO were conceived as further frontiers for dialogic exchange. At the same time that women fieldworkers were attempting to expand project guidelines about women's representatives in village meetings, they were also increasing their own participation in the NGO by advancing activities for women's participation at the village level that would increase their own contributions to the project overall. As the profile of women's participation grew over time, increasingly struggles surrounding women's participation in one space for one group (for example, opening village water committee meetings to women's groups) manifested themselves in other spaces for other women (for example, women fieldworkers advancing their own ideas about village women's participation). Dialogic exchange began to push for the expansion of women's participation both in the NGO and in villages.

Dialogue and the Growth of Women's Participation

In the project's early years, women's participation appeared to have little relevance to project activities. A monologue that defined women's participation as superfluous enabled the component to be considered by many staff as "some talks in a corner" (German consultant interview, 2000). I was asked when I arrived to do dissertation fieldwork the reasons I was studying the Our Water project if I were interested in women's participation. However, over the years I studied the project, dialogue about women's participation increased and formed a basis for gendered change. The more women's participation was talked about, the more presence it had—even if that presence was controversial. The more presence it had, the more women's participation became a recourse and support to those seeking gender equality within the organization and in villages. The presence of female fieldworkers was always considered critical support for producing women's participation, but a need for more women staff became pressing: "More effective and efficient support has to be given . . . mostly in the form of frequent visits by the female [staff] of the NGO, the number of which has to be increased substantially" (Our Water 2000, 12). Staff began to think reflexively about women's role in the organization; fieldworkers spoke up about women's exclusion from certain project roles. Enough momentum was generated that program officers organized a gender sensitivity training led by outside facilitators in early 2001.

As the introductory quote from Ravinder hints, these dialogues about women's participation *created* the project's women's participation goals about where village women and women fieldworkers would spend their time and who would control it. Dialogic struggles surrounding women's participation—a multiplicity of voices for it *or* against it—challenged unequal, gendered social relations and moved the conversation into new spaces. As Chik Collins (1999, 86) indicates, the "same words mobilized in different ways [. . .] make a profound impact on processes of social change." New meanings of women's participation had repercussions for gendered spaces, as nearly all of the dialogues about women's participation inherently involved a challenge to men's control of space, by tuning out women's voices or retaining village water committee meetings as male-only gatherings. Expanded meanings of women's participation resulted in an interruption of previously male-only spaces, territorial claims for women's space, or reconfigured spaces so that fieldworkers could speak in support of women's participation and be heard.

Moving past critiques that village women's participation may be in name only or make little of its intended impact (Agarwal 2001; Cleaver 2001; Mawdsley, Townsend, Porter, and Oakley 2002), this research has sought to retheorize participation through an examination of the micro-negotiations behind the intended and unintended impacts of a gendered participatory approach. Following Mike Kesby (2005), I have sought out the power dynamics behind language and practices that depoliticize women's participation. Hickey and Mohan (2004) write that through participatory approaches, the bargaining position of the poor may be strengthened—that is, that power relations may not be overturned, but within unequal relations of power the position of the poor might be rendered *less* unequal. This element of their argument is an important thread in mine, because I found that although a radical social transformation did not occur inside Our Water, women's participation as an idea gained support over time. Staff succeeded in establishing women's participation as an issue that could be spoken of, debated, reflected on, and that—despite forces against it—kept women's participation on the Our Water project agenda. The NGO's original goal of organizing village women into women's groups which would go on to solve other village problems (beyond water supply) was not realized. However, a variety of women's groups did emerge, and women fieldworkers began to raise their voices with confidence.

Can we call these newly raised voices a form of women's empowerment? If we accept Jo Rowlands's (1997) definition of empowerment as a process that increases self-confidence, agency, and a sense of dignity, then arguably feminist struggles inside Our Water over women's participation were implicated in growing empowerment for women fieldworkers. When we hear women fieldworkers taking advantage of "spaces of opportunity" (for example, the meeting room during the German bank officer's visit) to assert their desire to do other work besides women's participation, their voices sound like the voices of empowered women. The research suggests that it is through ambiguity and contradictions that women and men began to envision new roles for women in the NGO. Controversy and mixed feelings about women's participation led women and men to speak up in favor of women's increasing roles. Those ideas had support from Our Water's leadership and officers of the donor agency, but not from all. As Hickey and Mohan (2004) suggest, gender inequalities may not have been overturned, but women's position in the NGO became a little less unequal as controversy over women's participation continually put women's participation on the agenda and gave fieldworkers opportunities to speak their minds. Fieldworkers gain new insights into themselves, their situatedness in relationships of power, and their work as they talk about women's participation (Kesby 2005). Participation may lead to empowerment if through participation words and practices challenge the status quo and move *beyond* existing relations of power (Kesby

2005). This is an important consideration, given that women's empowerment for women fieldworkers was never on the project agenda—women
fieldworkers were assumed to be empowered already. The research also
shows that empowerment is a less-than-linear process: considering participation as a spatial practice lets us tell a story about women's participation in NGOs as a goal that was simultaneously supported and thwarted,
and as a practice that appears and reappears at different times and places
(Kesby 2005). What is more, women's participation grew too big to be
ignored, and the controversies that surrounded it enabled staff to think
about their own roles individually and gender roles collectively inside the
organization.

Conclusions

As Bebbington (2000, 495) suggests, development theorizing requires
"more nuanced interpretations of development that emphasize human
agency and depict what room to maneuver exists within otherwise constraining institutions and structures." This chapter illustrates that women's
participation was originally defined too narrowly, both in general and specifically with regard to space. Women's participation as defined did not encompass the many opportunities across project spaces that women fieldworkers took advantage of. Their successes were not in the creation of a
dynamic village women's program, but in their own attempts to create
greater equality inside their NGO. Bakhtin's ideas move us beyond concep-
tualizing fieldworkers' actions as "resistance" by suggesting that they work
with and against the variety of meanings of women's participation that
circulate (O'Reilly 2006b). Development policies like participation, once
NGO staffs begin discussing them and making plans for operationalizing
them, begin to take on a life of their own as meanings are struggled over
between project actors of unequal power (Collins 1999; O'Reilly 2006b; Li
2007; Mackinnon 2007). NGO fieldworkers engage in dialogic process not
just person to person, but with the overarching meanings and spaces of
women's participation that circulate within a project. Unlike policies that
seek to predetermine the meanings of terms like "women's participation,"
we see from the examples above that meanings remain open, ambiguous
and always available for re-construction (O'Reilly 2006b).

Lewis et al. (2003) demonstrated in a study of organizational cultures in
multi-agency rural development projects that the various cultures inside
organizations may lead to integration or fragmentation. They found that
breakdowns in cultural understanding explained why some ideas, espe-

cially contentious ones like 'empowerment', were never realized. Using a Bakhtinian approach, my research shows that despite a lack of shared meanings within Our Water, a highly contested idea like women's participation did gain ground, and part of what enabled the component was the tension between a stated, gendered participatory approach and the ambiguous feelings of many employees, both male and female, about women's participation's importance to the project. As Lewis (2003) indicated, norms of organizational culture cannot be read off as fixed aspects of social interaction but are instead negotiated and reshaped or even abolished within certain situations. It is these "certain situations" that a Bakhtinian analysis teases out, and particularly in this chapter, teases out with an ear to untangling the voices and power relations surrounding the production of spaces for women's participation.

This research suggests that over the course of a gendered intervention, NGO staff create a variety of opportunities where and when meanings and practices are struggled over, and where and when gendered space is in the making. Space for women's development is what is at stake territorially, but so also are those meanings that might emerge in that space. We must try to understand how power operates through language and practice, and its implications for the opening and closing of spaces (Bebbington 2004b). Our Water field staff were simultaneously influenced by and contributing to shifts in gendered domination, flexible meanings of women's participation, and spaces for newly audible voices. The gains may have been temporary and incremental, but where before there was little precedent or feeling for women's participation, over time, the issue of women's participation refracted and connected with almost every aspect of the drinking water supply project. The findings of this research indicate that development planners, policy makers and NGOs might reconsider their definitions of success for gendered participatory approaches. As the fieldworker Ravinder is aware, "change in society happens slowly," thus it is a significant step toward social change that discussions of women's participation eventually suffused the NGO. Where previously women's participation had been muted, meeting rooms, offices, and villages became spaces remade for women's participation through the words of NGO staff.

This chapter illustrates that spaces are produced by dialogues occurring in those spaces, and that dialogues can be productive of new spaces and practices. The above examples indicate that altering spaces of domination do not require an exclusive space. A space where dominant narratives can be engaged dialogically will suffice. Women fieldworkers sought to change unequal relations of power by occupying spaces and by opening up for question and feminist struggle previous understandings of those spaces as male-controlled. Even dialogues that may not have led directly to changes in NGO practices contributed to an overall atmosphere open to alternative meanings for women's participation. Continuing dialogue produced engagement with the ideas and goals of women's participation; dialogue created new spaces (e.g., meeting rooms that were not just for men's reporting) and repeatedly introduced women's participation on the agenda, which eventually led to shifts in NGO practices. The gendered paradox of women participating in their own NGO was not wholly resolved, but "arguing and reasoning" brought positive change.

Notes

This chapter is reproduced by permission of Taylor & Francis from *Annals of the Association of American Geographers* 97, no. 3 (2007): 613–34.

1. In the case of Our Water, plans for activating community participation followed trends favoring participatory approaches to natural resource management. However, community participation was fitted into preexisting large-scale plans that left scant room for local actors to maneuver. The Government of Rajasthan and the German donor bank had already decided upon the necessity of a new water supply system infrastructure and its design prior to signing cooperation agreements. Community members were given only minor roles—for example, public tap site selection, election of local management boards, and payment arrangements.

2. This criticism holds for Our Water as well, since villagers pay for water and assume responsibility for system maintenance inside village boundaries—responsibilities previously those of the Government of Rajasthan.

3. The real names of fieldworkers have not been used. As the women's participation program officer is unique in her position as the only woman manager, I have received her permission to identify her in the text.

4. North India is defined here (and elsewhere) as Madhya Pradesh, Uttar Pradesh, Bihar, and Rajasthan (see Dreze and Sen 1996; Jeffery and Jeffery 1997).

Power and Difference in Thai Women's NGO Activism

Introduction

Packed tightly into a hotel ballroom in Chiang Mai in 1996 with nearly 300 other people, I listened to the panel of seven Thai scholars, politicians, and five women and two men who represented nongovernmental organizations (NGOs). The significant presence of Thai activists at the Women's Forum of the Sixth International Conference on Thai Studies and the fact that this forum at the conference was conducted entirely in the central Thai language made the session unusual. During the forum Mae Somjit, a rural Thai woman leader from the north, stood up to speak.[1] A woman in her mid-fifties, with gray hair visible at her temples, she quickly captured the attention of the room, her lilting accent pleasing to the ear and her colorfully woven sarong a feast for the eyes. With a sweet smile and tilt of her head she said that Thai scholars had relied too much on foreign theories in analyzing women in Thailand and asserted that each society must be examined individually, with attention to difference and the particularities of place. She claimed that the concerns of village women were quite different from those of urban and upper-class women, and they too needed to be addressed. Speaking in the northern dialect (*kham muang*), Mae Somjit emphasized her regional identity and her status as a grassroots[2] woman leader from the north, thereby establishing the authenticity and authority of her claim.

Intrigued by Mae Somjit's comments that challenged status quo politeness and suggested contestation among women activists, I later went to visit her at her home. We discussed her community-based organization, the Project for Tomorrow (PFT), which works primarily with women and youth in the rural north. By the end of our meeting she had agreed to participate in my research study on Thai women's social change work. But difference and dissent among Thai women were more difficult to ascertain than I had initially and perhaps naively believed, given Mae Somjit's comments. While conducting ethnographic fieldwork in Thailand, I was struck by the amount of activism engaged in by differently located women, the diverse strategies used to achieve overlapping goals, and the reluctance of rural women activists to openly criticize or even raise questions about the approaches of more privileged women activists and NGO workers.

Such reservations should not simply be interpreted as the effect of Thai cultural norms that stress the avoidance of open confrontation and the suppression of women's opinions in political or public (read: male) spaces. Rather, they might better be understood as the effect of power relations structuring rural Thai women's entry into NGOs and spheres of activism that are simultaneously empowering and exclusionary. In addition to class, education, and age, women's differential experiences of activism were shaped by spatialized rural or urban cultural ideologies, nationalist discourses of development, and the expansion of (foreign) donor-driven projects.

In this chapter I attend to the complexity of Thai women's activism and the challenges of organizing across difference. In doing so I seek to stimulate discussion about both the commonality and heterogeneity of Thai women's concerns and methods of effecting social change, and to identify some of the fault lines that threaten to divide Thai women in their activist efforts—including those deepened by the presence of NGOs and the processes of NGOization. This may result in a more nuanced understanding of power and difference among Thai women activists as well as women activists in other geographic locations.

In Thailand, as in many countries around the globe, "women" (*phuu-ying*) is a term that activists deploy strategically, yet without explicit attention to the diversity it both subsumes and excludes. I found that factors such as class, education level, and geographic location divided women despite ongoing efforts to bring diverse women into shared spaces to work collectively. Here I identify some of the competing discourses engaged in by differently located activists and their relationship to the NGOization of women's activism in Thailand. Using feminist theories to explore Mae Somjit's claims, I argue that rural activist discourses intimately represent the situated interests of rural women as they interpret them and reflect a tacit understanding of social stratification within Thai society generally and among women specifically. Rural women's approaches to social change contest their marginalization, both in middle-class women's discourses and in NGO projects focused on the empowerment of women— even when those approaches are not explicitly articulated. At the same time, urban middle-class women's discourses reflect their own situated interests and their relative power and privilege in Thai society.

Grounding my analysis in women's actions and discourses, I draw on feminist theories of intersectionality to highlight how categories such as class, age, education, and geographic location are mutually constitutive and intimately shape Thai women's experiences (see, for example, Sacks 1989; P. Collins 1990; Mohanty 2003) and influence their understandings of social problems and social change theories that underpin women's varied forms of praxis. Similarly, feminist research on women's community activism privileges women's motivations, strategies, and redefinitions of politics (West and Blumberg 1990; Naples 1998; Naples and Desai 2002; Stein 2004). This shift in analytical attention both decenters dominant male definitions of politics and activism in Thailand and underscores the multiple and invisible ways that Thai women struggle to effect social transformation.[3] Furthermore, my analysis is informed by critical feminist work theorizing difference specifically in women's activism and how, through reflexivity and dialogue, solidarity might be achieved. In particular I bring the work of Nira Yuval-Davis (1999, 2006) on transversal politics and the work of the Sangtin Writers and Richa Nagar (2006) on collective transformation and solidarity to bear on the Thai case presented here.

Theorizing NGOization and Feminist Coalition Building

Feminist scholars have explored the contradictory effects of NGOization on women's NGOs and feminist movements in both the global North and South, in places as varied as Germany, Russia, Bangladesh, and the countries of Latin America (Alvarez 1998, 1999; Lang 2000; Nazneen and Sultan 2009; see also the chapter in this volume by Hemment). NGOization has been characterized as a complex and spatially varied process marked by one or more of the following: increasing professionalization (including emphasis on paid as opposed to voluntary labor) resulting in the creation of "experts" or "femocrats" (Lang 2000, 290), intensified hierarchization, reliance on external (state and foreign) funding, the privileg-ing of donor-driven (as opposed to locally defined) agendas, and an em-phasis on policy advocacy. In some cases, NGOization may involve closer ties between NGOs and the privatized, neoliberal state as well as a greater orientation toward self-help, development, and service provision (Lang 2000; Sangtin Writers and Nagar 2006, 159; see also the chapter in this volume by Hemment) that may cause NGOs "to lose their critical edge" (Alvarez 1999, 198). Ironically, as NGOs and their paid staff begin to re-place community-based and feminist social movement activism, they are increasingly called on as "convenient surrogates for civil society" (Alvarez 1999, 193), complicating discussions of representation and participation.

My research in Thailand[4] suggests that all of these elements of NGOiza-tion, though to varying degrees, may be found among the women's orga-nizations and NGOs that I encountered. However, here I focus mainly on processes of hierarchization and the tendency to privilege outsider (that is, expert, authoritative, or scholarly) definitions of social problems as they apply to women. The vast majority of women's workshops and confer-ences I attended were organized by middle- and upper-class Thai women, especially scholars and NGO experts, and financed by international fund-ing agencies such as the Asia Foundation and Frederich Ebert Stiftung. For rural women, participating in social and political networks with these relatively more powerful women provides crucial opportunities for edu-cation, training, and future networking, not to mention fun (*sanuk*) (Mills 1999a). Moreover, similar to the migrant women labor activists described by Mills, rural women activists who attended these events and joined NGO projects could envision themselves as "at least temporarily appropriate occupants of privileged sites of social power and knowledge production" (Mills 2008, 118).

Although in the late 1990s these women's activities were often framed by discourses of democracy and participation that sought to break down barriers of inequality and difference, organizational discourse and practice continued to rearticulate status hierarchies and to assert that rural women must learn from their urban, middle-class, educated sisters. The relation-ship of dependency that often forms between differentially located Thai women, a relationship that both metaphorically and literally mimics kin and political relations of *phii/nong* (older sibling/younger sibling), may silence rural women, rendering them invisible in the national struggle for women's empowerment.[5]

At one seminar in Chiang Mai on rural and indigenous women—

organized by the transnational organization Asia Pacific Forum for Women, Law, and Development—an urban middle-class Thai scholar commented: "We should have added 'middle class' to the title of the conference since all the women here are middle class. We need to remember the differences among rural women and their needs." Similarly, another avowed Thai feminist remarked (to a group of foreign visiting scholars): "It is still difficult for the women's movement. We are still accumulating visibility in society. We have invested so much time among ourselves, not reaching out to the constituency of the grassroots or upper-class women's groups." Although many urban, educated middle-class women are certainly aware that women's differences pose challenges for collective action, they seem less sure how to tackle them in ways that ensure empowerment for all.

NGOs in Thailand, which number in the thousands, range in size, structure, membership, goals, and practices.[6] Although Amara Pongsapich and Nitaya Kataleeradabhan trace contemporary NGOs to traditional and religious-based organizations established in the thirteenth century (1994), other scholars argue that Thai NGOs emerged as part of the pro-democracy movement in the volatile period of the 1960s and 1970s and were largely seen as oppositional to a violently oppressive state (Pasuk and Baker 1995; Connors 2003). But the challenges of securing funding following the 1980s economic boom and subsequent structural adjustment programs have resulted in a blurring of state-NGO boundaries, with NGOs increasingly engaged in development projects supportive of nation-state goals. Women's cultural, religious, and professional organizations have a significant history in Thailand, with NGOs focusing on women's equality and empowerment emerging from the 1970s onward (Pongsapich 1995, 1997). In addition to NGOs (*ongkorn eegkachon*), I refer to women's village- or community-based organizations (*ongkorn chaobaan, ongkorn chumchon*) and housewife associations (*klum maebaan*), also known as the Village Women's Development Committee (Khanakammakaan phad-thana satrii muu baan).[7] Rural women often participated in one or more of these groups and were quick to identify the differences among these three types of organizations, with the latter two characterized by voluntary membership (*NGO pen asasamak*) and NGOs defined by their career orientation (*NGO pen aachiib*). These folk categorizations reflect the increasing professionalization of community-based work experienced by rural activists that I interviewed and the proliferation of NGOs in Thailand.

As a non-Thai, outside observer commenting on the relations of Thai women activists, it is important that I situate my approach in this analysis. My intention is neither to excessively valorize nor unnecessarily romanticize the work of grassroots, rural women activists.[8] I do not mean to imply that rural women's interests are more important or that their practices are somehow more "authentic," than those of urban, middle-class women thereby constructing a hierarchy of oppression or tactics for social change that feminist scholars have rightly challenged. Neither do I mean to suggest that tensions do not exist among rural women activists or within their organizations; they do. Although space limitations preclude further examination of this issue here, I have explored these tensions elsewhere (Costa 2001, 2008). At the same time, this chapter is not intended to be a form of middle-class "NGO bashing," as one colleague put it. In fact, urban and middle-class activists and NGOs in Thailand have made innumerable significant contributions to improving the lives of Thai women both inside and outside of NGOs (Darunee and Pandey 1991; Virada 2003), and I enthusiastically support these efforts. My analysis is offered in the spirit of increasing opportunities for women's empowerment through heightened self-reflexivity and attention to difference among activists and scholars. I seek to more complexly render contemporary Thai women's activism, to examine a few of the impacts of NGOization on women's organizing, and to stimulate dialogue about processes of empowerment and solidarity within contexts shaped by processes of neoliberalism, nationalism, and globalization. Chandra Mohanty points out:

> In knowing differences and particularities, we can better see the connections and commonalities because no border or boundary is ever complete or rigidly determining. The challenge is to see how differences allow us to explain the connections and border crossings better and more accurately, how specifying difference allows us to theorize universal concerns more fully. It is this intellectual move that allows for my concern for women of different communities and identities to build coalitions and solidarities across borders. (2003, 226)

Like Mohanty, I consider my exploration a necessary component of trans-border coalition building, although I acknowledge that this analysis is less fraught for me as a feminist from the global North who writes from a privileged position. Unlike the Sangtin Writers and Richa Nagar (2006) who "played with fire" in their critical account of Indian women's NGOs and the politics of difference, my livelihood is not dependent on the organizations examined here. But as the innovative work by the Sangtin Writers demonstrates, interrogating the intersection of NGOs with women's activism is a critical step in advancing empowerment not only for rural, poor women but for all women. It is likewise a necessary move for scholars seeking to understand NGOs as spaces for the exercise of power, both liberatory and oppressive (W. Fisher 1997).

Below, I focus first on Thai women's activism in the scholarly literature. The persistent exclusion of rural women's activism in textual accounts both homogenizes women and privileges middle- and upper-class women, ironically perpetuating hierarchies that many seek to eradicate via activism and NGO work. Next I examine the discourses and practices of contemporary rural women activists observed during my fieldwork. I compare rural activists' discourses of community development, cultural preservation, and activist mothering with discourses of feminism, civil society, and human rights circulated by urban and middle-class women. In delineating these discourses and the power relations that inform them, I discuss how these narratives, while perceived as empowering in varied ways, may reproduce middle-class notions of rural Thainess (and backwardness), gender essentialism, and nationalist development rhetorics, thereby facilitating the NGOization of women's empowerment projects and reiterating global North-South disparities. Finally, I consider the implications of these discourses and practices for building political solidarity and collaborative knowledge production among diverse Thai women, implications that have resonance for feminist scholars and activists interested in women's NGO work and the dilemmas posed by difference within transnational feminist activism.

Women, Activism, and Representation in Thailand

Published work about women's activism in Thailand is scant.[9] Existing literature emphasizes the experiences and strategies of two major groups: elite women (that is, members of the Thai nobility and wives of high-ranking government officials and business leaders) and highly educated, middle-class, professional women located in urban areas and/or university settings (see, for example, Darunee and Pandey 1991; Pongsapich 1997; Doneys 2002). Following Nerida Cook, I use "middle class"

> to refer to the newly affluent middle classes which have arisen comparatively recently in Thailand. Class is a necessarily relational phe-

nomenon, and the usage here is intended to highlight the way in which many of these women contrast themselves both with the rural majority, and with a [elite] wealthy sector of urban society associated with traditional forms of power and with a conservative world view. (1998, 251)

Although elite women's activism is important and has interesting points of convergence with rural women's activism,[10] it often eclipses rural and poor women's activism because elite and highly educated, professional, urban women often have the resources, education, and time to assume leadership roles in national women's movements and formal NGOs. As Christine Walley points out, "focusing solely on formal 'feminist' organizations obscures 'indigenous' forms of feminism that do not necessarily accord with the middle-class Euro-American model" (1997, 425)—or, I would add, a middle-class Thai model. Walley continues: "For example, the activism of peasant, working-class, and minority women may be downplayed when evaluated solely in terms of gender interests rather than the intersection of gender with ethnic and class issues" (ibid.). It is precisely rural Thai women's concerns about issues of class, ethnicity, and cultural difference that situate their interests differently from those of elite and middle-class women, complicating cross-class, translocal, and transnational Thai women's organizing. Chujai, a rural activist from the North, described it this way:

> The women who come to work like this, they don't start like me. I come from the real grass roots. I come from having nothing and do this work. But for the most part, they are people who are ready for everything. They have position or rank, duty, money, a job with a salary that they are capable of doing. But we can see that those like that, it is a hobby for them.

Some rural activists, while admiring the success and prestige of their upper- and middle-class counterparts, comment that their interests diverge. I encountered such sentiments after attending a high-profile Bangkok Thai Women's Forum dismissed by some activists as a frivolous meeting of the "high heels."

Because they are the face of Thai women's activism in the sphere of transnational NGOs and women's activism (such as at the United Nations' Fourth World Conference on Women in Beijing in 1995) and because they can amass financial, organizational, and political resources, urban middle-class organizations can and do operate as gatekeepers that may prevent

Western donors and scholars from directly accessing local, community-based groups, or prevent grassroots women from accessing transnational feminist networks. Urban, middle-class women (and their handpicked rural sisters [*nong*]) have the power to decide which rural, village activists are "appropriate" and "authentic" grassroots representatives, ready to enter the sphere of transnational women's activism (see, for example, Mindry 2001). At one meeting of local NGOs and community-based groups organized by a university women's center, a visiting representative of a funding agency stated: "Our focus is on the intermediaries, the multiplicators. But without access to grassroots activities it won't work." This gatekeeping role assigned to formal women's NGOs and middle-class leaders is legitimized by funding agencies in the global North and reinforced by Thailand's social hierarchy, which privileges individuals according to education, class, urban origins, ethnicity, and age. One women's center director admitted that she struggled with this role because of the way it reinforces existing social hierarchies and concentrates power in the hands of a few. At another conference I attended, a participant spoke about how there were always the same women at the meetings. She expressed frustration with problems in getting important information out to "real villagers." After more than a year of attending women's meetings and seeing the same faces over and over again, I too began to think more critically about issues of participation, inclusion or exclusion, and the importance of connections (*sen yai*; literally, "big noodles") in Thailand and the larger NGO world.

In fact some of the best information about rural Thai women's activities comes from foreign NGOs, though distribution of their publications is limited. Unfortunately these texts emphasize women's entrée into formal politics (that is, as headmen or parliamentary representatives) rather than into civil society organizations or grassroots work, where Thai women's activities are more highly concentrated. This narrow focus reinforces definitions of politics that limit women's recognized contributions to those achieved within the existing political structure and effectively erases women's efforts within NGOs and community groups, thus reiterating the masculinist orientation of much academic work.[11] Literature on women's activism in Thailand therefore results in a partial knowledge that skews our understanding of the range and complexity of women's activism, and in particular the experiences of women in voluntary NGOs.

Discourses of Social Change and Empowerment

Based on my observations of and conversations with activists in the late 1990s, I discuss here several discourses through which women articulate and practice social change and empowerment. Although these discourses are neither exhaustive nor mutually exclusive, they do offer insights into the relations of power and difference influencing Thai women's activism. These discourses must be understood as historical artifacts intimately shaped by a range of hegemonic national and international discourses. Rural women commonly framed their activist work through discourses of community development (*phadthanaa chumchon*) and cultural preservation (*ragsaa* or *pongkan wadthanaatham*), while urban, middle-class and educated women relied on discourses of feminism, civil society (*prachaasangkhom*), and human rights *(sidthi manudsayachon)*. Though it may appear as if these are mutually exclusive, oppositional discourses, they have points of convergence in nationalist sentiments circulated during this historical moment that promote both national development and Thai culture (see, for example, Klima 2004; Costa 2008) and in transnational discourses of self-help (courtesy of the World Bank and International Monetary Fund, or IMF), decentralization, and civil society (courtesy of NGOs). I consider how identity categories such as class, education level, and geographic location contribute to activists' respective orientations and how they structure power relations within women's organizing.

Community Development and Cultural Preservation

Rural women's discourses of community development and cultural preservation underscore the specific problems they identify as most urgent (for example, economic marginalization, lack of education, cultural loss, and drug addiction), the types of activities they organize (such as income-generating activities, scholarships for girls, and cultural celebrations), the ways that they talk about social relationships (for example, the family as a building block of the community or nation), and the ways they conceptualize their roles as activists (including as mothers and as nurturers, or caretakers of children, family, community, and society). These discourses reflect and have the potential to entrench neoliberal discourses of self-help that exacerbate global North-South divisions, as well as discourses of regional and local cultural identity that perpetuate middle-class definitions of rural Thai people as simultaneously authentically Thai and backward—and therefore in need of help from middle-class or elite Thai and foreigners in the form of NGO projects.

Rural women's concern with community development and cultural preservation stresses immediate concerns, sometimes referred to in the literature as "practical gender interests," as opposed to "strategic gender interests" (Molyneux 1986, 284). I prefer to think of these as situated interests that reflect both the contingent social locations women occupy and the situated knowledges that arise from them (Haraway 1988), for what is considered practical or strategic depends on positionality and context and may shift. Furthermore, as Nancy Naples (1998) points out in her study of grassroots antipoverty activists in the United States, this distinction often breaks down in practice as women discover how the practical and strategic are intertwined.

From the perspectives of the rural Thai women I met, some of the most pressing problems in the late 1990s included the negative effects of economic restructuring and globalization. I conducted research between 1997 and 1999, at the height of the Asian economic crisis. The *baht* (Thailand's currency) fell to an all-time low, and the Thai government was forced to accept an IMF loan in the amount of $17.2 billion. Although government rhetoric claimed this economic and social burden would be shared equally by all citizens (in its "Thai help Thai" campaign), rural Thai and particularly women largely carried the load.[12] This was expressed in a local rhetoric of self-help (*chuay tua eeng*) rooted in rural Thai practices of self-reliance (*phung ton eeng*) and subsistence that conveniently dovetailed with IMF discourse as well as King Bhumipol Adulyadej's speech on his seventieth birthday, in which he extolled national self-reliance. References to globalization by rural women activists was thus largely rooted in personal experiences of economic marginalization and deprivation, though coupled with growing awareness of their political, social, and cultural marginalization as well.

Rural women were admittedly proud of their ability to seek solutions to problems of the IMF era, using what they referred to as "local wisdom" and relying on local networks. Mae Somjit's organization, PFT, hosted groups of housewives from the northern region of the country who came to observe local weaving cooperatives and other cottage industries. For these women, addressing issues of poverty, joblessness, and lack of financial resources was considered a form of activism and empowerment because it challenged the state-led (top-down) development paradigm and Thai conceptualizations of women as followers rather than leaders, evident in the oft-repeated aphorism that "women are the back legs of the elephant." Moreover, both rural and mixed women's meetings became crucial sites of activist practice in and of themselves as women shared ideas and strategies translocally. I still recall the excitement with which rural women from the north interacted with residents of a fishing village during a field visit organized by a university women's center as part of a training program for paralegals.

Not only economics captivated rural women's attention. Education of rural youth was perceived to be an important way to address poverty and offer status mobility. Rural women frequently commented on the low education levels of young people, especially girls,[13] and created scholarship programs for them. Concerns for education were reiterated in discourses of cultural preservation. Rural women identified cultural impacts that they felt were ripping apart their communities, such as drug addiction and prostitution—problems they dealt with on a daily basis and associated with the spread of Western values, especially materialism and lack of moral control. Rural women frequently spoke about the increasing licentiousness and promiscuity of village youth, their declining interest in traditional practices (such as local music, spiritual beliefs, food, and rituals), and their fascination with the foreign and modern. These youthful practices had serious implications not only for traditional gender roles and premarital sexual relations, but also for the Thai social hierarchy that privileges the aged over the young. Rural activists sought to counteract these changes through organizing cultural activities and events for village youth. The discourse of cultural preservation was particularly notable among those involved in village-based organizations such as PFT, and in village housewives' groups. For example, PFT held "local music" classes and organized groups to promote "local careers" (for example, raising fish, growing vegetables, processing and selling compost, and weaving). Mae Somjit said that she tried to act as a role model for village youth, teaching them how to live in culturally appropriate ways, including dressing in the traditional *phaasin* (sarong) crafted from locally produced fabrics.

Cultural preservation has a long history in Thailand, especially within indigenous development philosophy (that is, community culture approach; see Costa 2001) and—ironically—among elite women (Jeffrey 2002). This was evident even in 1998 in a noticeably nationalist speech delivered in the northern dialect by an elite woman for Burma Women's Day that stressed the importance of culture and the role of women in bettering the nation. But community development and cultural preservation were less a priority for urban, professional women. Although some did participate in revitalization movements for regional cultures and identities—particularly as consumers of Thai textiles—many seemed more interested in challenging culturally prescribed gender roles than in protecting culture (especially a culture that they saw as limiting women's opportunities) and in appealing to notions of civil and universal human rights. However, discourses of cultural preservation could be conveniently marshaled by middle-class NGO workers as proof of gender essentialism and rural Thai backwardness, and as evidence that rural women could benefit from development and NGO projects emphasizing human rights and women's empowerment. More than one educated activist told me with derision that rural women "think just like villagers," while a highly revered woman politician referred to the approach of her rural colleagues as "old-fashioned."

Tied to women's conventional roles as socializing agents and keepers of tradition, cultural preservation is expressed in language about protecting the family and community, not simply individual civil rights. Discourses of both community work and cultural preservation are based on an implicit homology among family, community, and nation as well as on the idea that a woman's work improves the community and culture or nation as a whole—a sentiment popular in nationalist and postcolonial movements (Chatterjee 1989; Kandiyoti 1991; McClintock 1993). This is captured in the concept of "activist mothering" (Naples 1998).

Activist Mothering

For many rural Thai women, motherhood is a primary form of identification. Problems that rural women identify frequently revolve around conflicts they experience as mothers, guardians, and providers. Many rural women first experience organizational participation through government-sponsored housewife groups at the village level, and it is interesting to note that many of the rural activists I surveyed stated "housewife" when asked their occupation, since they associate occupation with paid labor (reinforcing the voluntary-career NGO distinction). For Mae Somjit, participation in her village housewife association led to other leadership positions and her role in the 1983 establishment of a village day-care center. As a working mother of three, she observed the difficulties women faced balancing child care and wage labor outside the home, and she mobilized mothers to work with her in village and subdistrict housewife associations. In 1994 the center received national recognition from the Social Welfare

Department for its "activities which remind [villagers] of mothers' good deeds" (Phuying Geng 1998, 29).

Naples argues that activist mothering is "political activism [seen] as a central component of mothering and community caretaking of those who are not part of one's defined household or family" (1998, 11). Activist mothering includes not only women's "community work derived from concern for their children's well-being" (114), but also activism that moves beyond one's immediate family context to that of the broader community, however defined. Though coined in the context of US social welfare community action projects in the 1980s, activist mothering helps clarify both the discourses and practices engaged in by rural Thai activists.[14] Like Mae Somjit, a number of rural women leaders I met had been involved in establishing day-care centers through local housewives' associations. Despite comments by middle-class activists, NGO workers, and community development workers that local housewives' associations are simply "ladies' clubs" that accomplish little and replicate traditional gender roles, housewives' groups remain a critical space for women to obtain community organizing skills and develop vital personal relationships that may lead to participation in other village-based organizations, NGOs, and even formal politics (Nongyao 1996; Bowie 2008). It was not uncommon for rural women to rationalize their concerns for community development as a logical extension of their care for their families. One member of a district housewives' association commented: "If we are mothers and housewives, we are able to take care of our families and make them happy, and we can also help society."

Also indicative of activist mothering are linguistic practices in which well-respected rural women leaders in the north, such as Mae Somjit and Mae Malee, are referred to with the honorific *mae* (literally, "mother").[15] Not only are they mothers in their own right, but they mother, nurture, and protect their communities and, by extension, the Thai nation (Costa 2008). Activist mothering transcends the private sphere and demonstrates the interpenetration of private and public realms, challenging narrow definitions of politics and strategic versus practical interests. This redefinition of politics and celebration of women's contributions can be seen in one of the songs crafted by community activists and frequently sung during women's meetings I attended in the northern region:

What is milk? Do you know or not?
Milk is the medicine that builds our strength and power.

Anyone who drinks it will be really very satisfied and pleased.
Milk has power and strength, that is breast milk!
Milk has power and strength, that is breast milk![16]

This song plays on the double meaning of the Thai word *nom*, meaning both milk and breast. When women sing "breast milk," they motion with their hands as if they are lifting up and emphasizing their breasts. Whenever I observed (and participated in) this song, women broke into melodious laughter—expressing embarrassment and fun, but also audacity and defiance. The milk song calls attention to women's embodied difference from men—and mothers' difference from nonmothers—as well as to the unique power and strength women possess through nurturance (*liang*), a Thai practice recognized for its ability to "[display] power and hierarchy" in both public (that is, political) and private spheres (Van Esterik 1996, 23). In a gender-discriminatory society this reclamation of female power in public space is a significant act. Situated in contexts of women's conferences that brought together women from diverse social locations, the song points to rural women's embodied experiences of marginalization and struggle and is an important narrative of empowerment that women, especially mothers, tell themselves about the contributions they make to society and the larger women's movement.

Related to nurturance is the concept of sacrifice (*siasala*) that rural women activists used in descriptions of their community work, a practice that in the frameworks of both Buddhist merit making and family caregiving bestows prestige and honor on them. Sacrifice was often linked to activism as a voluntary act and opposed to activism as a paid job, reinforcing the practical and moral dilemmas faced by women in contexts of NGOization. Mae Somjit commented critically that one of her volunteers had "abandoned" her (*thing*; literally, "to throw something away") when she had the opportunity to work for money at another NGO. Mae Somjit also noted that a well-known woman leader from her area had persistently "refused" her invitations to participate in PFT activities until the organization received a large grant from a foreign donor because "she didn't think our small activities had importance." Both examples illustrate that conflicts and jockeying for status are as evident in rural women's activism as they are in women's activism generally.

The emphasis on motherhood, nurturance, and sacrifice as sites for individual and community politicization is notably absent from the discourses and practices of urban, middle-class, professional women. In fact, many middle-class activists I encountered, especially university teachers and scholars, were neither mothers nor wives and represent the growing numbers of Thai women choosing not to marry or have children (Erera et al. 2002).[17] For them, being a mother was not a primary identification through which they felt empowered to change society, and they rarely participated in singing the lively milk song, choosing instead to retreat to the edges of meeting spaces and talk among themselves.

Feminism and Human Rights

In contrast to their rural counterparts, middle-class, urban, and professional Thai women enact discourses that deconstruct conventional gender categories and challenge forms of domination using a "rights based approach to civil, political, socio-cultural and economic problems" (Virada 2003, 2).[18] Although Thai women often emphasize their high status relative to other Asian and even Western women, they are still considered inferior to men legally and in the religious sphere (Kirsch 1982, 1985; Chatsumarn 1991; Virada 1997). Moreover, a double standard structures male and female sexual relations, making it not only acceptable but inevitable that single men should "sample many flavors," as the saying goes, and that married men should have affairs, while women should remain chaste until marriage and monogamous thereafter.

For urban, middle-class women activists, gender oppression is often approached through a rather academic feminist lens—one familiar to those of us working with feminist scholarship and NGOs in the global North. A feminist analysis of Thai gender relations identifies men's undeserved social, economic, religious, and sexual privileges and the way that social norms reinforce those privileges and reward men. Discourses engaged in by middle-class women stress a "women's rights as human rights" model rooted in individual citizenship. According to Manisha Desai, during the 1995 Beijing women's conference "human rights discourse became the language for demanding women's rights" (2002, 29)—and this discourse now circulates through transnational women's networks and women's NGOs, where it is articulated "in local terms of new democracy and the role of women in nation building" (Naples and Desai 2002, 39). This was evident in Thai conference and forum titles such as "Democracy without Women?" and "The Women's Movement, Rights, Politics and Development." Notably, the word "feminism" was so new in the Thai language in the late 1990s that its translations (*satriiniyom* and *itthisaat*) were more or less meaningless to almost all of the rural women whom I met. One prominent Thai feminist told me:

> The majority would not have a chance to hear the term "feminism." Or those who have, they don't understand, or they are totally against it, or they are skeptical about it. Because they perceive feminists as those who always take matters to the street. It is against Thai culture. In Thai they always use this term *pood rong yo-yo. Yo-yo* means, you know, very annoying, you know, and noisy, very impolite, wrong.

For middle-class women, feminism might be defined as equality with men in all areas of life. The same Thai feminist stated: "We have to look at the cultural and political environment [women] are in. How do women think and act? It is the society that puts them there. They are under the dominance of male culture; women are victimized and stigmatized." For some Thai scholars, feminism also means viewing aspects of Thai culture as potential obstacles to women's activism and social change, such as social norms dictating that women should "not be aggressive in personality" but gentle and sweet. Feminism also means educating women[19]—rural women in particular—to challenge the limitations of gender ideology embedded in culture and politics. The middle-class activist Kanokwan told me: "If I educate them and let them know their rights and their duties—because if you check back in the Thai curriculum, Thais are taught to learn only duty, but they don't know their rights—it will be better I think . . . I believe education will change this country."

In her critique of Gita Sen and Caren Grown's (1987) work, Mitu Hirshman argues that implicit in statements by First World feminists that call on Third World women to "shed traditional submissiveness" and aspects of culture is "the need to show that Third World women as 'women' (i.e., victims of men and capitalism) share the same cultural space and political rationality as Western feminism and that they can be relied upon to participate in the feminist politics appropriate to the pursuit of their interests, namely women's empowerment *vis-à-vis* men and male establishments" (1995, 51). In the contexts that I describe, elite, middle-class, educated Thai women could be viewed as attempting something similar, though several were quick to tell me that their approach was distinct from Western feminism. As they seek to organize grassroots women for their own multiple purposes (that is, to put more women in formal political positions at all levels, to advance a certain vision of women's empowerment, or to maintain their own positions in NGOs), they run the risk of discursively subjecting rural Thai women to a particular kind of global Northern feminist (and development) discourse that fails to account for the specificities and diversities of women's experiences and their varied locations in shifting relations of domination.

It must be recognized that such middle-class notions of feminist activism emerge from a relative position of socioeconomic, educational, and geographic privilege—privileges that are not always explicitly acknowledged though they are ritually embodied and enacted in the diverse spaces of women's meetings. For example, rural women's relative marginalization was simultaneously reinforced and momentarily concealed during women's meetings when they could "enjoy stylish furnishings, air-conditioning, and [be] treated to the pleasures of uniformed service, restaurant-style meals and snacks—the trappings of middle-class urban privilege" (Mills 2005b, 6–7). Similar to the female Thai migrant workers and union members whom Mills describes, rural women activists at these NGO meetings were able to "lay claim to public spaces of Thai modernity, and assert their membership in 'modern' 'civil' society" in ways not generally open to them (ibid., 7; see also Mills 1999a). However, this membership was belied by other NGO practices that included seating and clothing, and—as Mills found—other "distinctly hierarchical norms of etiquette, emphasizing deferential language and bodily comportment for all but the highest status experts and officials" (2008, 118).

The fact that middle-class, educated women have access to transnational activist networks and organizations further "creates divisions at the national level between the elites who belong to such networks and the vast majority of grassroots women who don't" (M. Desai 2002, 31). I experienced this disparity in privilege and cultural capital when, during my fieldwork, several rural women on different occasions approached me privately to request help in securing foreign funding to start their own NGOs.[20] As I argue elsewhere (Costa 2001, 394–99), such requests point to the social status, prestige, and power increasingly associated with the role of NGO worker even as women struggle with the shifting meanings of community work (voluntary versus career) in contexts of NGOization.

Although many rural women are committed to the goals of feminism in theory, such as the equal rights as enshrined in the constitution, Thai women disagree over how to practice gender equality without alienating their husbands, children, and neighbors; without losing the social status or pleasure that comes with the identities of mother and wife; and without giving up aspects of traditional culture they cherish and find meaningful (see, for example, Bowie 2008). For example, some rural women find the "hard" manner with which middle-class, urban, and academic women practice their activist work problematic, according to the Thai feminist mentioned above. Mae Somjit admitted that she was a feminist but added: "not like Ajaan [a teacher]. I'm not too radical because it won't work. We need to use our tenderness, our gentle, sweet way of being a woman to get what we want." As in the United States, the term "feminist" in Thailand carries negative connotations. It may be associated with aggressiveness, confrontational behavior (typically frowned on in Thai social interaction), the dislike or hatred of men, and lesbianism. Similarly, feminism is often seen as an importation from the West, though such assertions remain hotly debated. Nevertheless, it is true that urban, professional women's discourses of feminism and social justice are shaped in significant ways by these women's education abroad in countries such as the United States, the United Kingdom, and Australia; by their frequent interaction with foreign funding agencies; and by their alliances with Thai scholars and other NGO activists working for political reform. These discourses are further configured through women's experiences in international academic and development meetings, UN and NGO conferences, and research and study programs. Given national sensitivities surrounding globalization and all things Western during the late 1990s economic crisis, it is easy to see why feminism might have been suspect for rural women. Yet for middle-class and urban women, feminism and the discourse of human rights are perceived as highly empowering, especially as they are concretized in national and transnational legal systems.

Since urban, middle-class Thai activists seek to overcome women's oppression in the spheres of marriage and divorce, employment, and politics, they often take a legal approach to instigating change. The Women's Studies Center at Chiang Mai University has instituted this approach through a paralegal training program funded by the Heinrich Böll Foundation. This program invites community-based women leaders to participate in legal training seminars so that they can in turn educate the members of their rural communities and empower rural women. Middle-class women's discourse on law and human rights was especially salient during my fieldwork, since in 1997 a new people's constitution was passed that enshrined women's equality with men. The new constitution also reformed and decentralized the country's political structure and made specific stipulations about women's political participation. Urban women's NGOs were eager not only to make rural, village women aware of these changes but also to encourage them to run for public office. Middle-class women with whom rural activists were frequently in contact consistently emphasized the importance of women's participation in formal politics. This seemed to be in part a result of the work conducted by Thai NGOs such as the Women and the Constitution Network and Women and Politics, as well as the zeitgeist of the period—which included passage of the new constitution and the ample funding available from foreign and transnational NGOs for decentralizing political structures and building civil society.

One conference brought together members of women's networks from the four regions of Thailand. Session leaders (all scholars and/or middle-class women) appeared to assume that women's local organizations and regional networks would play an active role in the upcoming elections, even though historically it has been a challenge to increase rural women's participation in politics.[21] This is because many Thai women, from rural housewives to highly educated urbanites, think of formal politics as "dirty." When I asked one urban NGO leader whose explicit goal was increasing the number of women candidates if she would ever consider running for office herself, I was surprised when she answered: "No. I know my role. Because since I was a student I decided I would not be a candidate because it's too dirty for me. I'm too clean and I know I can't—I can't be a politician. I can't play the dirty game." Similarly, it has been difficult to persuade rural women that participation in formal politics is the best way to address their concerns, since women politicians frequently face accusations of marital infidelity and promiscuity because they are constantly in male-dominated environments and transgress gendered spatial and political boundaries.[22] The rural activist Weeraya told me that when she was elected to the local district council, villagers spread rumors about her having an affair with the headman and teased her husband. The "narrowmindedness" of villagers combined with "dirty" political practices such as vote buying made her reluctant to seek office beyond the local level. Married women politicians may also face accusations of bad mothering and suffer violence at the hands of angry husbands. Clearly a politics of virtue that reinforces women's role in nurturing and sacrificing for family, community, and nation is at work here. It enforces rural women's tendency to choose community and NGO work over formal politics in a way that simultaneously empowers them because they find value in such roles and disempowers them because it reinforces middle-class views of rural women's backwardness and needs for help and development.[23] I turn now to the implications of this situation for women's solidarity and activism in Thailand.

Toward a Transborder Feminist Solidarity

Scholarship demonstrates that NGOs as spaces of civil society and dissent hold promise for women seeking empowerment and social change. In fact, women's NGOs in Thailand have in many ways enabled the progression of the women's movement and novel opportunities for women's political engagement. Nevertheless, as I and many other feminist activists and researchers have observed, the promise of NGOs is not fully realized (Mindry 2001; A. Moser 2004; Sangtin Writers and Nagar 2006). We are thus compelled to ask, as we do in this volume, how NGOs do (or do not) serve women, which women, and why, and to explore the broad ramifications of NGOization for women's empowerment and solidarity.

My analysis of contrasting discourses and practices engaged in by Thai women suggests that NGOs structure power relations in ways that both reflect the processes of colonialism and development originating in the global North and reinforce the processes of social hierarchy and difference specific to Thailand. Like colonialism, development turns on dividing practices, which categorize people into binaries such as developed or underdeveloped, knowledgeable or ignorant, progressive or backward, and modern or traditional (Foucault 1971, [1977] 1995). This provides the necessary rationale for those in the global North to help, protect, or empower those in the global South (Hobart 1993). In the late twentieth century, NGOs from the global North played a significant role in promoting this development paradigm, often reproducing its disempowering rhetoric unawares (Escobar 1995). For the women's organizations that I observed in Thailand, this transnational development discourse was articulated in the identification of target groups (rural, poor, uneducated women), in the ways that traditional practices (such as cultural preservation and mothering) valued as empowering by rural women were recast as obstacles and backwardness, and in NGOs' internal hierarchies that privileged expert urban, middle-class women's approaches and interests in a rights-based approach to social change. Mohanty's (1991) critique of Western feminist representations is appropriate here, though the "eyes" in the title of her work are no longer simply Western. Mohanty's analysis alerts us to the challenges of unacknowledged hierarchies wherever they exist—both between countries and cultures and within them. When rural Thai women become the other to urban, educated, middle-class women, then the latter can envision themselves as "liberated, and having control over their own lives" (Mohanty 1991, 74), and thus well-equipped to help their Thai sisters (*phii* or *nong*) as members of a global sisterhood. However, as Annalise Moser (2004) points out, this is not necessarily a "happy heterogeneity."

It is not surprising that urban, educated, middle-class Thai women maintain their relative privilege and power in NGOs. Neither is it unexpected that many of them fully recognize the difficulties inherent in transborder organizing. However, difference does make solidarity building more challenging, particularly when some women feel unable to voice comments or concerns that may threaten a social order that offers benefits as well as disadvantages. As I demonstrate here, identity categories of class, education level, and geographic location structure relationships between differently located women in Thailand. Class privilege allows educated, urban, middle-class women to take for granted the fact that their basic needs will be met through relatively stable jobs, incomes, and social networks and to position themselves as helpers or teachers of the rural poor by maintaining discursive control over workshops and conferences and practical control over financial resources. Similarly, education is perceived to be a critical form of knowledge and expertise that legitimizes middle-class control of NGO activities (see also Mindry 2001, 1195) and is a form of social status that compels the deference of others. Education is a crucial avenue for pursuing donor funding, as demonstrated by numerous rural women who—like Mae Somjit—returned to school in their forties, fifties, and sixties to complete their middle- and high-school education in order to work more effectively in the career NGO world. Weeraya told me that her decision to work toward her bachelor's degree resulted from "pressure—not from myself or villagers, but from when I have to associate with others outside the village who have higher education," including NGO representatives.

Differences in geographic location threaten unity among Thai women activists in their links to women's situated interests, and point to the importance of place in both enacting and theorizing social change (Harcourt and Escobar 2002; Mills 2005a; Sangtin Writers and Nagar 2006). Numerous Thai studies scholars have commented on the oppositionality between rural and urban areas and on the historically hierarchical relationship between villages and provincial or urban centers, which was exacerbated during national programs of modernization and development (Mills 1999b, 2008). At the same time, privileging urban centers and approaches belies late twentieth-century tendencies to romanticize the village, its culture, and its people as evidence of a more authentic Thainess, a tendency sometimes evidenced by NGO activists themselves who refer to "real villagers" of the "grassroots" when seeking to identify project participants or targets (see, for example, Mindry 2001).

Women's activism in Thailand has faced many challenges from historical erasure, political instability, and periodic state vilification to popular resistance against new sociocultural and gender norms introduced by activists. But one of its greatest and most implicit challenges—one familiar to women activists globally—has been that of building solidarity across differences. Mohanty argues that "solidarity is always an achievement" and a result of "mutuality, accountability, and common interests anchoring the relationships in diverse communities" (2006, xiv), while Richa Nagar writes that "solidarity is achieved through an active engagement with diversity rather than presumed from outside through the constitution of groups defined homogeneously by neediness or powerlessness" (2006, 141). My observations in late 1990s Thailand indicate that despite continuing and laudable efforts to bring diverse women into shared spaces of engagement, power and difference continue to undermine women's efforts at solidarity. NGO activists from all locations require both increased self-reflexivity and more sustained analysis of intersectionality and how NGO organizational practices and hierarchies threaten to disrupt projects for the empowerment of all women. This type of critical self-analysis is neither easy nor without risks, as the Sangtin Writers amply demonstrate, but it can have productive and rewarding results.

The challenges of exclusion and hierarchization faced by Thai women activists and intensified by NGOization are by no means unique. Feminist activists and scholars have long grappled with how to address women's diverse and at times contradictory interests in emancipatory movements, locally, nationally, and transnationally (see, for example, Grewal and Kaplan 1994; Ong 1996; Mohanty 2003; Cockburn 2007). Here I summarize two related approaches that may serve as resources for women activists in Thailand and elsewhere who are facing these challenges: transversal politics, and collective transformation and solidarity. Yuval-Davis describes transversal politics as a "dialogically situated epistemology" that rejects both assimilationist, universalizing politics and identity politics

(2006, 276; see also 281). According to her, transversal politics is based on (1) standpoint epistemology, or "a recognition that from each positioning the world is seen differently, and thus any knowledge based on just one positioning is 'unfinished'"; (2) "the encompassment of difference by equality," in which differences are recognized as important but should not be replaced by equality or hierarchized; and (3) "a conceptual—and political—differentiation between positioning, identity and values," in which shared identity does not equal shared positioning and shared positioning does not mean shared social and political values (2006, 281; 1999, 94–95). This is relevant to my discussion of Thai women's activism because in transversal politics, feminists and community activists (regardless of their status or location) are neither "representatives" nor the "authentic voice" of their communities but "advocates," and they "should be reflective and conscious of the multiplexity of their specific positionings, both in relation to other members in their constituencies and in relation to other participants in any specific encounter" (2006, 282). Furthermore, it is not necessary to be a member of a constituency for which you advocate thereby doing away with fixed boundaries and reified categories and avoiding exclusionary politics (ibid.). Transversal politics is achieved through a process of "rooting and shifting" that relies on open dialogue and the recognition that not every conflict is reconcilable (1999, 96), though Yuval-Davis (2006) notes that transversal politics is not without its own challenges.

Another approach that specifically critiques the exclusionary processes of NGOization and is relevant to the Thai case analyzed here is the methodology of collective transformation and solidarity painstakingly described by the Sangtin writers and Nagar in the context of Indian women's NGOs. This methodology is built on the collective autobiographical writing and reading of diverse women's subjective experiences as a form of "reflexive activism" (Nagar 2006, xxii) and a process of shared knowledge production that attends to intersectionality and the negotiation of power. Coming together regularly over an extended period of time, these women tackled the inequalities of class, caste, religion, and education that structured their entry into NGO work and knowledge production and challenged themselves to move beyond narrow understandings of women who were different from themselves. The honesty and vulnerability demonstrated by the Sangtin writers recalls the "rooting and shifting" stressed in transversal politics and emphasizes a "model for empowerment through dialogue" (Nagar 2006, 141).

Nagar concludes that "collaborative praxes that engage with place-based specificities of local processes and struggles can help us to articulate transnational feminist alternatives to 'global sisterhood' and 'global feminisms'" (149). By recognizing the diversity of women's approaches to social change, acknowledging the importance of their respective situated interests, and facilitating more-complex conversations about women's empowerment, both scholars and activists can move away from preconceived notions of women and their identities, habitual global North-South interactions of self and other, and the privileging of expert knowledges wherever they emerge.

As I hope this chapter has demonstrated, differently located Thai women activists have their own discourses and practices with which to address their situated interests. It is crucial that Thai women activists—as well as their activist and scholar counterparts elsewhere in the world—foster more reflexive forms of activism and opportunities for collaborative knowledge production that result in inclusive dialogue and praxis that better attend to intersectionality and relations of power. In doing so, the negative impacts of NGOization might be more adequately addressed and the empowerment of all women might become a more attainable goal.

Notes

The research on which this article is based was funded by the Fulbright Foundation, the American Association of University Women–Honolulu, the Pan-Pacific and Southeast Asian Women's Association, and the University of Hawaii. Support from the Luce Foundation allowed me to first draft some of these ideas. I would like to thank Mary Beth Mills for her careful, detailed reading of this chapter and for suggestions that greatly improved the text. I would also like to thank the volume editors, Victoria Bernal and Inderpal Grewal; and my colleagues in the faculty writing group at Hollins University.

1. The names of individuals and local Thai organizations are pseudonyms unless otherwise indicated. Names of funding agencies have not been changed. All translations from Thai are my own unless otherwise indicated.

2. Grassroots, or *raagyaa* in Thai, is a term used by activist women of all class levels to refer mainly to rural, village communities and poor urban communities.

3. Bowie (2008) offers another example of the invisible yet critical contributions of rural Thai women to formal politics at the local level. She analyzes how women mobilize kinship relations to support specific candidates, maintain village unity, and address postelection tensions.

4. I conducted fieldwork in Thailand in the period 1997–2000. Although my research focused primarily on groups in the north, I also observed and spoke with

women activists from other regions of the country at women's conferences and workshops.

5. An important exception to this invisibility is the way that rural women's bodies are mobilized in national discourses. See Costa 2008, Jeffrey 2002.

6. Dej Poomkacha (1995) counted 2,547 NGOs, while another study noted that the National Culture Commission of Thailand had registered approximately 14,000 organizations (Serrano 1994, 7).

7. Housewife groups are part of a system of women's associations at the village, sub-district, district, provincial, and national levels that was established in 1981 by the Department of Community Development to increase women's participation in local development projects.

8. Naples notes that "the privileging of the so-called grassroots can also lead to a romanticization of this site of struggle as well as a tendency to 'other' women said to be of the grassroots" (2002, 4). See also Mindry 2001.

9. Work on women in other parts of Southeast Asia is more abundant (Cook 1998, 255). Edited collections about women's activism in various nation-states often fail to include a chapter on Thailand.

10. See Cook 1998, Jeffrey 2002, Costa 2001.

11. Mills's (1999b, 2005a) work on Thai women labor activists is an important exception.

12. For example, layoffs of male workers put more pressure on women to obtain waged labor to support their families, while the negotiation of rising costs was also largely women's responsibility as the managers of household budgets.

13. Boys have access to free education by becoming monks.

14. Maternalism is evident in women's movements worldwide (West and Blumberg 1990, 22–23).

15. This is a standard honorific, not one specific to activists, though it may vary by region. Some rural women reveled in this label and role, even though it was another mark of their peasant origins and backwardness, according to some urbanites.

16. Unlike other developing countries, the Thai Ministry of Health promoted breast-feeding in the 1980s and 1990s without a prominent antiformula or anticorporate discourse (Penny Van Esterik, personal communication). Although the origin of this particular song remains uncertain, one doctor from the Thai Breast-Feeding Center notes that songs such as this were created and sung by villagers and NGO workers during the 1990s (Jiraporn Wattana, personal communication).

17. Mills made the same observation of Thai women labor activists (2005a, 133–34).

18. The discourse of rights and justice (*yudtithaam*) is also evident in Thai women's labor activism as a result of "alliances with Thai feminist and human rights groups" (Mills 2005a, 124).

19. This is done largely through consciousness-raising among "both disadvantaged women and the general public" (Cook 1998, 258).

20. Such requests underscore the power of women/NGOs from the global North in

the Thai contexts I observed, where rural women frequently assumed I was an NGO representative even when I explicitly stated that I was a graduate student.

21. Bowie (2008) offers a provocative analysis of why rural women in the north choose to forgo formal elected positions while simultaneously arguing that women are central to Thai political processes.

22. Mills found similar concerns among Thai women engaged in labor activism (2005a, 133).

23. Mindry (2001) makes a similar argument in analyzing the transnational moralizing discourses mobilized by feminists in the global North in their efforts to develop and help women in the global South.

Demystifying Microcredit
The Grameen Bank, NGOs, and Neoliberalism in Bangladesh

While economic globalization refers to the removal of trade barriers and open markets, its effects on communities are variable, contingent, and locally constructed. This chapter is an interpretation of these variable, contingent, and local expressions of grassroots globalization through an ethnographic study of globalization and neoliberalism in rural Bangladesh. It examines how globalization and neoliberalism are brought to the grass roots—the most intimate sphere of the social, the home, and women—through the modernist discourse of women's empowerment through microcredit.

Focusing on the microcredit policies and practices of the 2006 Nobel Peace Prize winner, the Grameen Bank of Bangladesh, and three other leading nongovernmental organizations (NGOs) in the country, I analyze the centrality of gender in the expansion of globalization and neoliberalism in Bangladesh.[1] I examine how Bangladeshi rural women's honor and shame are instrumentally appropriated by NGOs in the welfare of their capitalist interests. I analyze this relationship between rural women and NGOs by placing it within the political economy of shame, a concept I explain later.

Arjun Appadurai has defined grassroots globalization as:

new forms of social mobilization that proceed independently of the actions of corporate capital and the nation-state system . . . these social forms rely on strategies, visions, and horizons for globalization on behalf of the poor . . . this kind of globalization strives for a democratic and autonomous standing in respect to the various forms by which global power seeks to further its dominions. (2000, 3)

The grassroots globalization I studied in Bangladesh is contrary to Appadurai's model. It works through and not against corporate capital, donors, states, NGOs, and members of civil society and creates complex new networks of social interdependencies that are laden with the financial interests of multiple actors at the local, national, and global levels. This grassroots globalization weakens the sovereignty of the patriarchal home family and replaces it with the sovereignty of the market through NGOs, contracts, and courts. The developmental NGO is the purveyor of this new economic sovereignty that is represented by corporate and local institutional interests (NGOs) and is an architect of neoliberalism within a developmental discourse of poor women's empowerment through the market.

Neoliberalism as an ideology rests on the idea that human welfare is best served by the withdrawal of the state from welfarist policies (Harvey 2005, 64). Extending this economic definition, Aihwa Ong has termed neoliberalism a rationality of governance, stating that "governing relies on calculative choices and techniques in the domain of citizenship and of governing." It subjects citizens to act in accordance with the "market principles of discipline, efficiency, and competitiveness" (2006, 4). Neoliberalism is about the subjection of targeted populations to certain rules that inform and regulate behavior. In many postcolonial countries with weak sovereignties, the notion of citizenship as a set of entitlements is lacking. Instead, in its place, we see the emergence of a postcolonial governance authorized by NGOs whose clients are subjected to act in accordance with the values of "discipline, efficiency, and competitiveness." By postcolonial governance I refer to the subjection of targeted populations by nonstate actors such as NGOs to new technologies of market-oriented disciplinary mechanisms. It also refers to governance by NGOs that is similar to Ong's notion of "graduated sovereignties," and they seek to implement social engineering programs (population control, HIV/AIDS management, primary education, voter education, etc.) that were formerly in the domain of the state.

But neoliberalism and globalization have also created opportunities for rural people to access new routes of capital circulation and have facilitated novel movements of migrant labor. In Bangladesh, microcredit borrowers and their families have been networked into Appadurai's "finanscapes" (1998, 34). The circulations of these "finanscapes" have brought new wealth, ideas, and social identities into rural areas. For example, in Bangladesh successful rural women are sometimes able to pool their microcredit loans together to send a male kin to the Middle East or Malaysia as migrant labor who, if all goes well, repays their investment at a high interest rate to them.

In the analysis under consideration, neoliberalism and globalization operate at the grass roots through the microcredit policies of NGOs. As providers of credit, jobs, and sustenance to a financially strapped poor rural population, NGOs in Bangladesh have tremendous power to regulate people's behavior and subject them to NGO mandates and priorities. I make three arguments in this chapter. Firstly, NGOs that work with microcredit manipulate existing notions of Bangladeshi rural women's honor and shame in the furtherance of their capitalist goals and instrumentally violate local norms of cohesion and community. I call this the "economy of shame." Secondly, the work of microcredit has resulted in unanticipated neoliberal subjects, the female petty moneylender, for example, that this chapter examines. Finally, I argue that the developmental NGO operates as a shadow state in Bangladesh and is able to exercise tremendous control over the lives of the poor through a Gramscian notion of hegemony where their relationship is characterized by a "combination of force and consent, which balance each other reciprocally, without force predominating excessively over consent" (Gramsci 1971, 248). This enables the NGOs to neutralize dissenting voices in public spaces, a point I discuss in the conclusion.

The research for this article was conducted over eighteen months (1998–99), and was based on a study of the Grameen Bank and three of the largest NGOs in the country. Each of these NGOs works with microcredit, has millions of dollars in donor support, and millions of rural subscribers. These NGOs reach 80 percent of the rural population.[2] According to the Bangladesh NGO Affairs Bureau (NGOAB), from 1990 to 1998 the cumulative amount of foreign funds disbursed to NGOs stood at 1,364,421,079 *takas* ($29,030,235 @ USD 1=47 takas, 1999 rate of exchange) for 5,096 NGO projects. In 1994–95, 20 percent of foreign funds were disbursed through the NGOs (Karim 2001, 97). For western donors in Bangladesh the NGO sector is the preferred mode of developmental aid. The NGOs offer a streamlined and accountable system of aid delivery compared to the Bangladeshi state, which is bureaucratic, corrupt, and inefficient and is considered a "failed" state by Western aid agencies. The celebration of the neoliberal policies of the Grameen Bank has to be understood against this predicament of a postcolonial country

Globalization, Neoliberalism, and the NGO as a Shadow State

Globalization has been theorized as a "crisis in the sovereignty of the nation-state" with rapid movement of finance capital that lies outside the control of the state (Appadurai 2001, 4). I analyze globalization in a different context: the virtually absent state in a postcolonial country where the critical question is the emergence of a new sovereignty, the *NGO as a shadow state.* In terms of national development, many Third World countries are heavily dependent on Western aid.[3] It is precisely the lack of economic sovereignty of Third World countries that allows the International Monetary Fund (IMF), the World Bank, and Western industrialized nations and multinational corporations to exploit these countries and their populations for their corporate and political goals. This lack of economic sovereignty in developing countries gets exacerbated when NGOs with economic ties to Western capital enter development; target poor people with much-needed services that the state fails to deliver; and link together economic, political, and social life through their programs. In the absence of robust progressive social movements in many postcolonial countries,[4] these NGOs are able to set themselves up as working with the "poorest of the poor" and install themselves as *the* progressive voice in rural society. It must be emphasized that the NGO rhetoric of "working for the poorest of the poor" does not occur in a vacuum. It occurs in those instances where the state has failed or has withdrawn from the welfare of its citizens, shifting that responsibility increasingly to private charities, corporations, and developmental NGOs. Consequently, NGOs that step in to take over many of the services traditionally reserved for the state (education, healthcare, credit, employment) begin to act like a state. For example, in Bangladesh, I found that villagers often referred to the NGO as *sarkar* or the state (James Scott 2006).[5]

In the rural Bangladeshi economy, which is the focus of my analysis, the Grameen Bank and NGOs that were aided by Western donors largely facilitated the process of globalization.[6] Through microcredit operations, rural people and NGOs in Bangladesh have become mutually dependent, and credit has connected rural people with multinational corporations for the first time. Through NGOs, microcredit recipients have become consumers of products of multinational corporations such as finance capital, breeder chickens, and cell phones, and as producers, they remain dependent on multinational corporations for physical inputs such as seeds, fertilizers, and pesticides. But NGOs are not passive agents of capital. They are also active producers of new subjectivities and social meanings for people through their various economic and social programs. Thus, the relationship between rural subjects and NGOs is contradictory and varied; they instrumentally exploit each other. However, the power rests with the NGOs. That said, very little ethnographic work[7] has been done to examine how this microcredit model might intersect with local patriarchal norms and cultural practices and result in behaviors that may not correspond to building social solidarity and goodwill among targeted populations (Goetz and Sengupta 1996; A. Rahman 1999 and 2001; Ahmad 2007). It is important to note that internal NGO staff and local and international consultants hired by NGOs and aid organizations do the bulk of the research on microcredit institutions in Bangladesh (Hashemi, Schuler, and Riley 1996; Counts 1996; Bornstein 1996; Khandaker 1998; Todd 1996a and 1996b are some examples), and their employment situation often prevents them from being critical of NGO work.

Microcredit and the Political Economy of Shame

Before proceeding to an analysis of how globalization and neoliberalism operate in rural Bangladesh through microcredit operations, I would like to first introduce the two terms I use to analyze the Grameen model: microcredit and the economy of shame.

MICROCREDIT

In development rhetoric, microcredit is the extension of small loans to women for income-generating projects and has been eulogized as a magic bullet of poverty alleviation. However, according to Professor Muhammad Yunus, the Grameen Bank model of microcredit is not solely a matter of the extension of credit, it has a unique set of social objectives that it aims to implement through microcredit policies:

- It promotes credit as a human right.
- It is aimed toward the poor, particularly poor women.
- It is based on "trust," not on legal procedures and system.
- It is offered to create self-employment, income-generating activities, and housing for the poor, as opposed to consumption.

- It was initiated as a challenge to conventional banking, which rejected the poor by classifying them as "not creditworthy."
- It provides service on the doorstep of the poor based on the principle that the people should not go to the bank, the bank should go to the people.
- It gives high priority to building social capital.[8]

If we replace the term "credit" with "debt," we get the mediation of rural social relations through debt-related dependencies. In theoretical terms, debt ties the present and the future together. Debt is thus a regulator of social behavior, and present behavior determines future payoffs. By replacing credit with debt and introducing the concepts of culture and the uncertainty of the market into the equation, we can ask some difficult questions of microcredit practices of development. What happens to people in a face-to-face community when they are linked through relations of debt introduced by a modern banking system? What happens to the social position of women when they become the bearers of debt within the patriarchy of the home and the patriarchy of the modern NGO?

THE ECONOMY OF SHAME

The use of shaming as an instrument of social control of the poor, particularly of poor women, has a long history in rural Bangladesh. Women are the traditional custodians of family honor. The shaming of men through their women (mothers, wives, daughters) is a preexisting social practice. In a face-to-face society, one's ability to maintain honor (the protection of one's good name, the honor of the womenfolk, and the patriline) structures one's social acceptability. To lose face is the ultimate mark of dishonor. Rural discourse is structured around notions of honor, and any trespassing behavior (a woman seen talking to a nonkin man, for example) is spoken of in terms of the protection of the honor code—that is, our women do not do X because we are honorable people. For the poor, the discourse of honor is a symbolic covenant with God. It is a moral resource through which they view themselves as morally superior to rich and urban people.

The economy of shame refers to the appropriation of preexisting forms of shaming by a modern institution, the NGO, which instrumentally deploys various forms of shaming in its own capitalist welfare—that is, the recovery of loans. Shaming takes many forms in Bangladeshi rural society, from rude language to regulation of women's sexuality; disciplining of poor people through accusations of sexual infidelities that often result in public floggings, pouring pitch over bodies, tonsuring women's hair, and hanging a garland of shoes around one's neck; isolating one's family in the village; publicly spitting on the person every time s/he walks by; making adults hold their ears as a sign of their guilt in a public forum; breaking apart a person's house to recover money; and so on. In this context, Grameen Bank's insistence of a no-collateral loan and repayment of loans at 98 percent takes on a different meaning (for a celebratory reading of Grameen Bank, see A. Sen 1999, 201). The honor and shame codes act as the collateral of these loans. It is the honor of the family that is at stake, and that the woman represents. If the woman gets publicly shamed, the family is dishonored. In a face-to-face society, men and their families try to maintain the sanctity of their family honor by observing the honor of their women.

GOs in Bangladesh

Bangladesh, as an independent state, entered the global economy in 1971 when globalization and neoliberalism were dismantling the traditional welfare state in the West, and women-centric aid policies had become the norm for Western aid agencies. After nine months of war against Pakistani forces, Bangladesh broke away from Pakistan on December 16, 1971, and declared itself an independent state. In 1947, when the British divided India into India and Pakistan, Bangladesh was the region known as East Pakistan. The West Pakistani leadership had paid little attention to the growth of its eastern province, which was ethnically Bengali and distinct from West Pakistanis. Bangladesh (formerly East Pakistan) was an internal colony of West Pakistan that provided raw materials, such as jute, tea, paper, to West Pakistani–controlled corporations. After the war in 1971, the already fragile infrastructure of Bangladesh was in chaos (Sisson and Rose 1991; Umar 2004). It was under these circumstances that developmental NGOs stepped in as rural service providers.

NGOs began their work of war reconstruction and rehabilitation of refugees, occupying an infrastructural vacuum in the newly independent state. The developmental NGO sector soon capitalized on the women-in-development (WID) paradigm of the United Nations and Western aid organizations. The Bangladeshi state, under military leadership, also capitalized on the WID paradigm to gain development dollars and legitimacy from Western democracies.[9] The idea of women's participation in the economy was celebrated as a national goal, and developmental NGOS were given a free rein to grow and expand their rural outreach with Western aid. The Western aid organizations also preferred the NGO sector as their allies. It enabled them to bypass the bureaucracy and corruption of the Bangladeshi state[10] and to directly reach targeted segments of the rural population (Karim 2004). Over time, this developed into a lattice of dependent relationships between aid organizations, Western capital, NGOS and the Bangladeshi state.

With the transition to democracy in Bangladesh in the 1990s, NGOS have moved into the political sphere. They have begun to use their borrowers as vote banks, urging them to cast votes for political candidates who represent an NGO-friendly platform.[11] NGOS, through their partnership with Western aid agencies, USAID in particular, that emphasize "good" governance programs, have reconstituted themselves as institutions that work for grassroots democratization. In Bangladesh, the nature of democratic politics is under construction through a diverse set of actors—national political parties, NGOS, clergy—all of whom make claims on rural female subjects for their adherence. Neoliberalism has unhinged politics from the older left-identified politics, that is, the vanguard political party as the catalyst of social justice, and have introduced a new politics of grassroots mobilization of the poor organized by the NGOS. Given the dominance of NGOS over rural populations, national political parties also seek their alliance in order to win elections. Many NGOS have aggressively sponsored their female members for village-level local elections, posing a challenge to the rural patriarchal power structure through democratic means (Karim 2001, 99). For example, after winning the 2006 Nobel Peace Prize, Professor Yunus (the founder of the Grameen Bank) initially announced that he would start a new political party, a decision from which he later withdrew.[12] In the unfolding scenario, politics and development have become conjoined in the making of globalization at the grass roots.

It can be said that NGOS are remaking rural subjects as new subjects of a market-driven democratization. As Ong has pointed out, "neoliberalism can also be conceptualized as a new relationship between government and knowledge through which governing activities are recast as nonpolitical and nonideological problems that need technical solutions" (2006, 3). It must be mentioned that although NGOS can subject the poor to their will, they do not control the choices people make. For example, once empowered to vote, NGO female borrowers often cast their vote according to family preference.[13] While this grassroots mobilization unleashes new energies and potentials, and perhaps even challenges globalization at the grass roots, it remains inhibited by the financial imperatives of NGOs—that is, the management of rural populations through microcredit that tends to depoliticize political possibilities (Ferguson 1990).

There are several critical factors that allow the NGOs to play such a decisive role in rural life in Bangladesh. Firstly, there is the virtual absence of the state in the rural economy. NGOs dominate the rural economy from rural credit to telecommunications to primary education. Secondly, the NGOS provide two-thirds of the institutional credit in rural areas (Sobhan 1997, 133). In Bangladesh, neither the government banks nor the traditional moneylenders loan to the very poor because they lack physical collateral. This financial dependency of rural people on the NGOs has given them the power to act as patrons of the poor. Thirdly, the NGOs are a major source of employment in a country with limited job opportunities for its burgeoning young population. Young college graduates seek entry-level jobs with NGOs that are seen as the future—the promise of a better life and, for the better educated, an opportunity to go abroad for training. Fourthly, the NGOs have silenced dissent in the public sphere by inducting a large number of university professors and researchers as consultants in their various programs—public intellectuals who might otherwise have spoken out against the excesses of NGOs. In fact, many university professors operate as full-time NGO consultants and part-time teachers. This shift is legible in discourse. Researchers talk about NGO research as a job (*kaaj*) and not as research (*gobeshona*). Finally, the work of NGOs has fragmented the left political parties from the 1970s onward, when both groups struggled over the adherence of the poor. The resource-rich NGOs won, and they introduced loans and services that the left parties could not provide to rural constituents. Thus many people—from the rural to the urban, from the illiterate to the highly educated—are direct and indirect beneficiaries of NGO programs.

The Grameen Bank Model of Microcredit

Grameen Bank (GB) has reversed conventional banking practice by removing the need for *collateral* and created a banking system based on mutual trust, accountability, participation, and creativity. GB provides credit to the poorest of the poor in rural Bangladesh, without any collateral. At GB, credit is a cost-effective weapon to fight poverty, and it serves as a catalyst in the overall development of socioeconomic conditions of the poor who have been kept outside the banking orbit on the ground that they are poor and hence not bankable.

The Grameen Bank (or Rural Bank) was started by a local economist, Professor Muhammad Yunus, in 1976. The Bank had originally targeted rural men for its credit programs. In its early days, the Bank ran into difficulties in collecting money from men who would not allow themselves to be subjected to the Bank's strict rules. By the late 1970s, the Bank had appropriated the women-in-development (WID) paradigm of Western aid agencies and reinvented itself as a bank for poor women. By 1998, the Bank had over two million members, and 94 percent of its borrowers were poor women.

Grameen Bank has made significant contributions to rural banking. It has made credit available to the poor who were denied commercial loans due to a lack of physical collateral. It has demonstrated through its 98 percent rate of recovery that the poor are not defaulters, that the poor pay back their loans. It has taught women the importance of managing money and keeping basic accounts of expenditures. Additionally, it has introduced some new forms of social identity among rural women, such as the women's weekly meetings where women collect and discuss loan proposals, and the creation of a space where women can speak without men dominating the discourse. Moreover, Grameen women are required to say their and their husbands' names publicly (rural women do not speak their husbands' names because it is against social norms), women are taught to sign their names on loan contracts, and learn the Sixteen Decisions of the Grameen Bank that focus on social engineering (Hashemi, Schuler, and Riley 1996, 649).

Professor Yunus advocates this liberal doctrine for poor women. In many of his speeches, he claimed that not only is capitalism good for the poor, "the poor are good for capitalism."[14] Basing his claims on the 98 percent rate of return of his bank, he argues that the poor are good investments for large banks, and the financial world should take notice of that fact. Thus, the chief contribution of the bank lies in proving to the development community that the poor are "bankable"—that is, the poor repay their debts.

In my research, I found that microcredit benefited several categories of women the most: the rural middle class, women with marketable skills, women whose husbands had marketable skills—or whose husbands had regular employment and could thus pay the weekly installments—widows, and divorced and abandoned women. In the majority of the cases, the husbands and male kin of the women used the loans. In most instances, their husbands were day laborers, and this allowed them to repay the weekly installments on the loans.

The Grameen Bank model rests on the idea of the individual entrepreneur who, with the help of microcredit, becomes self-employed, owns private property (the assets she builds with the loans), and sells her labor on the market. The out-of-the-home entrepreneur links seamlessly with the ideology of neoliberalism. She is an owner of petty capital. This production of the ownership ethic is against wage labor, overtime pay, retirement benefits, and worker's compensation—that is, against the very foundations of a welfare state.[15] Failure to succeed now rests solely with the individual and not with the corporation/NGO/state.[16] In this scenario, the state withdraws from the welfare of its citizens to work for the welfare of capital.

Interestingly, microcredit policies have also shifted the discourse of poverty to a discourse of neoliberalism at the local level. Calling oneself poor[17] is now seen as pejorative in rural Bangladesh. Prior to the mass mediation of rural relations through credit, the poor felt a claim on the wealth of the rich because they were in a patron-client relationship. Thus in times of hardship, the poor could forage on the lands and ponds of the rich for sustenance. In exchange, the rural rich would make claims on the free labor and adherence of the poor. This traditional patron-client relationship has been replaced by a neoliberal discourse of self-help and individual responsibility.

While the Grameen Bank and NGOs claim that poor women are the beneficiaries of these loans, it is the husbands of the women and other male family members who really use the loans. Bangladeshi women are primarily the carriers of NGO loans; they are not their end users. In my research, I found that men used 95 percent of the loans. Even Professor Yunus has conceded as much. Commenting on the long struggle of Grameen of loaning to women over their husbands, he says, "Grameen has come a long way since then. Now Grameen lends money to husbands, but *only through the wives*. The principal borrower remains the wife" (Yunus and Jolis 1998, 91; my emphasis). In my research area, rural men laughed when they were asked whether the money belonged to their wives. They pointedly remarked that "since their wives belong to them, the money rightfully belongs to them." Women also told me that, as a Bangladeshi woman, I should know that they would give the money to their husbands who labor outside the home.

NGO officers and researchers who are connected with the microcredit industry are aware that the men control the use of the money, but in their public scripts they censor this vital information. This silencing of who really uses the money occurs for two reasons. On one level, it fulfills the Western aid mandate of targeting women in development. NGOs can show to their Western donors that women are participating in loan activities. On another level, NGOs seek out women because they are seen as docile subjects who can be coerced more easily than men.

Rural kinship relations are an important aspect of microcredit operations. Based on gender, status, and age differentiations, kin members have varying levels of obligations to each other. Into this set of existing obligatory kin relationships, the microcredit NGO has inserted the notion of collective responsibility alongside individual loans. That is, the group is both the enforcer and the guarantor of loans to the NGO. These two structures—kin obligations and collective responsibilities—are toxically synergistic, and coupled together they work to operate within an economy of shame.

The following example illustrates how these kinship obligations work. In my research area, an older woman (a widow) was returning home with her loan from the Grameen Bank when she met her nephew. He said that he knew that she had just received a loan from the bank, and as her nephew he was making a claim on her money to fund his own business. As this woman explained, as the aunt and as a woman (further complicated by the fact that she was a widow), she was obligated to give him the money. If she did not, there would be pressure from her family to do so. Thus, obligation to give to a male kin was considered by her family to be her responsibility, a higher good, and more important than her need of that money.[18]

Given the profitability of microcredit operations from the perspective of NGOs and the donor agencies (the loans of the poor are recovered), one finds too many NGOs with too much cash chasing too few creditworthy members in the rural economy. Consequently, almost every female NGO member has membership in multiple (in my area the average number was between seven to eight) NGOs. According to the Credit Development Forum (1998) out of 1,200 foreign-aided NGOs, 369 dealt specifically with credit. This had led to a routinization and simplification of NGO credit operations, from the earlier function of social engineering to the newer role as credit provider. As a result women were now unwilling to spend time learning NGO rhetoric (the Grameen Bank's Sixteen Decisions, for example), and the loan officers were under pressure from headquarters to find additional creditworthy borrowers. I found that very few Grameen women knew of any of the Sixteen Decisions.[19] At the time of getting loans, women put down on paper various projects that they would undertake with the loans. However, because of the pressure on loan officers to recover money, officers seldom had the time to monitor what the borrowers actually did with the loans. As one borrower's husband said to me with a smile:

> We took a cow loan. Fifty percent will be spent to pay off old debts, and another fifty percent will be invested in moneylending. If the manager comes to see our cow, we can easily borrow one from the neighbors.

From the perspective of the microcredit NGOs, what mattered was the maintenance of high recovery rates and not the skills training of individual borrowers. In fact, this emphasis on expanding microcredit operations had reproduced usury at multiple levels of rural society. Similarly, the availability of NGO money had encouraged many rich clients to enter the microcredit market.[20] In many instances, richer clients used poorer women as proxy members. That is, the rich client used the loan while the poor woman joined the NGO as a proxy member in exchange for a fee. If the rich client defaulted, it was still the poor proxy member who was held accountable by the NGO.

In analyzing the reasons why rural men allowed their women to become NGO members even though it brought their women in contact with nonkin men, one noticed a deep level of complicity between NGOs and rural men. Despite rural codes of honor and shame that dictated that women should not come in contact with nonkin men (and most NGOs, especially Grameen Bank, have male officers), rural men found it more useful to allow their women to join NGOs because they (rural men) work during the day. That is, poor men who lack physical collateral "give" their women in membership to NGOs as economic reassurance. In reality, *the collateral that Grameen and all other NGOs extract from the poor is the Bangladeshi rural woman's honor and shame.* The poor give their honor embodied in their women to the NGOs in exchange for the loans. It is very important to note that *this* is the pivot on which the success of the Grameen model of microcredit hinges. However, rural men are also ambivalent about the condition in which they find themselves. While they were more comfortable with microcredit because their women could stay at home, they also felt vulnerable because home enterprises do not necessarily guarantee a fixed income at the end of the month. Many rural men I spoke with said that they preferred jobs from NGOs that would offer them a guaranteed income. That is, given a choice between entrepreneurship with its associated risks and regular employment, most people I surveyed preferred the latter.

Group Versus Individual Responsibility

Group responsibility for individual loans is a fundamental organizing principle of the microcredit model. The Grameen Bank operated on this model.[21] Forty women formed a Center, which was housed in a female member's house. The women elected a leader from the group who advocated the loan proposals in their weekly meetings. These forty women formed eight smaller groups that included five women in each group. Each week, the women met in the Center and handed over their weekly installments (*kisti* in Bengali) to the bank officer.

The loans, usually between $100 and $200, were given for a year on a fixed interest rate of 16 percent, that came to 32 percent in effective or actual interest (1999 figures). The borrowers paid the interest on the original principal through the life of the loan. That is, the interest paid was not adjusted as the principal was paid down. What the borrower actually ended up paying was much higher because these loans contained many hidden costs (entrance fees, cancellation fees, late fees, mandatory savings, and often product tie-ins with loans) that raised the de facto rate to 50–60 percent for many microcredit NGOs.[22] It should be borne in mind though, that this number is still much lower than the rate charged by the rural moneylender (120 percent). Thus, of the loans that the poor could actually access, the borrowers were better off paying 60 percent to the NGOs than 120 percent to the rural moneylender.

All these women were jointly held responsible for the repayment of individual loans. Thus each woman was responsible for the repayment of all the other loans in the Center. When a default occurred, the bank (or the NGO) withheld money from the other members, forcing them to either pay up or lose access to future loans. The bank tied individual responsibility to group responsibility, using that as a mechanism to (1) maintain tight fiscal control over repayments; (2) police women borrowers' financial conduct after they received a loan; and (3) enforce payment through collective punishment for individual defaults.

This close surveillance of its women members[23] allowed the bank officers to forestall any impending default. It was the women borrowers who did the surveillance on behalf of the bank (or the NGO). Fearing potential defaults, women informed their managers about misuse of the loans by borrowers. This surveillance of conduct resulted in the daily strife that I witnessed in these group relations. Since these women and their families were linked together through loans, it was not only the women but also the community that had become part of this surveillance mechanism.

The surveillance of women already exists in rural Bangladesh, especially in the regulation of rural women's sexuality and comportment. The microcredit NGO (the Grameen Bank and other NGOs) appropriated and routinized this form of surveillance as part of its credit operating structure. NGO managers routinely told their women clients: "You are responsible for the loan and you have to make sure that no one defaults." This transference of responsibility from the NGO to the women reduced the operating costs for the NGOs (they did not have to hire additional people to monitor the borrowers), and at the same time, it created a very effective policing system whereby rural people voluntarily reported potential defaults to their managers for fear of financial reprisals. Thus, poor women policed other poor women, evicting poorer members from the group in fear of losing future income. This behavior let NGO officers off the hook, and they did not take any responsibility for the actions that the community took to enforce payments.

The picture gets complicated when one realizes that the most widespread and profitable business from microcredit is the practice of usury by women. Moneylending allows women to conduct business without leaving their homes. Women who do not possess marketable skills opt for moneylending as a profitable alternative. These women adopt the norms of the traditional moneylender and loan money at 120 percent rate of return. This notion of 120 percent interest is a form of implicit social knowledge. Rural women do not make exact interest calculations on these loans. In their universe of social knowledge, two interest rates are known, the rate charged by the NGO and that by the rural moneylender. As rational economic agents, they opt for the higher number of the traditional moneylender. Moreover, usury created a chain of dependencies that involved kin and nonkin alike, and tied multiple NGOs together. A loaned to B who loaned to C who loaned to D, and so on. The failure on the part of a distant person on this chain had a ripple effect in rural society, affecting a number much higher than a couple of people or NGOs.

During my research, I saw that credit-related strife among members and their families were routine occurrences. Women would march off together to scold the defaulting woman, shame her or her husband in a public place, and, when she could not pay the full amount of the installment, go through her possessions and take away whatever they could sell off to recover the defaulted sum. In those circumstances when the woman had failed to repay, which happened several times a month in the NGOs I studied, the group members would repossess the capital that the woman had built with her loans. This ranged from taking away her gold nose ring (a symbol of marital status for rural women) to cows and chicks to trees that had been planted to be sold as timber to collecting rice and grains that the family had accumulated as food, very often leaving the family with no food whatsoever. The women who committed these acts did so at the exhortations of NGO officers, but they also considered these acts to be "protecting their investments," and the defaulting woman as someone who had "broken faith with the community." These acts were committed with the full knowledge of NGO officers, but the officers did not participate in these collective acts of aggression. Instead, they threatened to withhold future loans from group members unless the defaulted money was recovered.

In instances where everything had been repossessed because of a large default, members would sell off the defaulting member's house. This is known as house breaking (*ghar bhanga*) and has a long history in rural society. It is considered as the ultimate shame of dishonor in rural society. In my research area, house breaking occurred several (six to seven) times, whereas smaller forms of public shaming occurred every week. In addition, there were a few incidents of suicide committed by men who had been shamed by their inability to protect the honor of their families. But these instances were rare and were often the result of multiple causes, such as flooding in low-lying areas that had pushed the family into delinquency. What is important to note though is how these preexisting coercive norms, house breaking for example, have become institutionalized as part of the NGO technologies of loan recovery.

The NGOs also used the apparatuses of the state, such as the police and courts, to harass these poor women to pay up. NGOs often filed cases against individual women who would be taken into police custody and kept as criminals (*ashami*) until the family repaid the defaulted sum. In Bangladesh where discourses of shame and modesty predominate, if a woman was held in police custody overnight not only had she brought shame on her husband as a criminal, she had also lost her virtue. When loan recovery techniques became entangled in existing social attitudes toward women, women who came into their affinal homes through marriage were often isolated as "outsiders" and blamed for bringing shame to their husbands and their families. I met with several of these women who were divorced by their husbands because they had "disgraced" their families by going to jail.[24] Husbands blamed their wives for shaming them and their families, although the husbands were the beneficiaries of these loans.

The question of rural women's complicity and dissent were important facets of how the practice of loan recovery worked in rural life. Women did try to increase the wealth of their family by monitoring other women. Being a provider of loans secured the woman's status within the family as long as she could forestall defaults and not shame her family. Women also tried to manipulate the NGOs by borrowing from multiple sources without letting their managers know. To prevent membership overlap, NGOs required that their borrowers remained faithful to one institution. To circumvent that policy, women sometimes traveled to neighboring villages to borrow from different NGOs. Often women would make their loan officer wait for several hours when they were unwilling to return the money. For women there were some positive aspects to NGO membership. NGO association had given them some limited forms of practical freedom. Now rural women had more reasons to be seen around town. They could take some time off from their housework to do "NGO business" that their in-laws could not interfere in. But these poor women were firmly inside an interlocking system of debt to multiple NGOs, kin, fellow borrowers, and traditional moneylenders. The more they expanded their circulation in these overlapping systems of borrowing (that is borrowing from one to pay off another), the more indebted they became.

With the spread of microcredit operations in rural economy, NGO managers too faced tremendous pressure from NGO headquarters to operate smooth loan programs. Failure on their part to collect the money from the women borrowers resulted in the NGOs' withholding money from their paychecks. Too many defaults in their area would result in their getting fired or never being promoted. Thus, NGO managers applied a range of tactics to recover money from the women such as cancellation and late fees that formed a safety net in the event of a default. These charges do not show up on the books, and can only be accessed by creating trust with the women.

The NGO officers were fully cognizant of the negative consequences on women of their actions to recover the money.[25] Yet they were unwilling to replace the notion of collective contracts with individual contracts. They realized that weakening the tight fiscal control of loan recovery would make them lose profit because recovery of loans would become quite difficult. When I mentioned some of my reservations about microcredit practices to a manager of the Grameen Bank, she pointedly said: "Why are you surprised? Grameen Bank is a business and not a charity."

The Female Petty Moneylender: Jahanara's Story

Contrary to the claims of the Grameen Bank and other NGOs that they have reduced traditional moneylending through microcredit NGOs, what we find instead is the reproduction of usury at multiple levels of society, and the normalization of that activity within a new group of actors: poor, Muslim women.[26] Through membership in NGO loan programs, the formerly assetless poor have been able to accumulate some assets which now make them creditworthy in the estimation of the moneylender. Thus, the net of usury is cast much wider, bringing all sorts of formerly poor and assetless people inside its web. In my research area, the traditional moneylenders often boasted that their business was better due to NGO loans. The neoliberal subject that has emerged out of this encounter between microcredit and rural social relations is the figure of the female petty moneylender.

Moneylending is prevalent in villages that are close to markets, for the obvious reason that traders seek out the women borrowers for loans. In my research area, this village was Krishnonagar, which was located next to a large market, and on the other side of the market was the town. In an informal survey of Krishnonagar, 100 households out of 230 NGO beneficiary households were engaged in moneylending. As a result of the proximity to the market, the women of Krishnonagar were visible in public spaces. Compared to women living in the interior villages, these women possessed a higher degree of physical mobility. Women here had more access to nonkin men because of the location of their village, and it was acceptable for them to talk to nonkin men. NGO-related activities had added to that mobility and had created some new pathways for these women to interact with the larger community. Grameen Bank, BRAC, Proshika, and ASA offices were spread through the town, and access to these offices meant a trek through town. The women of Krishnonagar told me that they had access to the market prior to joining these NGOs. Many of them had to walk through the market to get to other places. As they pointed out, NGO membership did not necessarily make them into more "mobile subjects," but it did give them more reasons to be seen around town without people necessarily casting aspersions on their moral character.

One morning in December 1998, I went with my research assistant in search of female petty moneylenders in Krishnonagar. I was told that Jahanara Begum was the most famous moneylender in this area. She had over 350,000 *takas* ($7,446) invested in moneylending.[27] What did it mean, I had wondered, for a woman to have amassed so much money? How did she get to become such a successful moneylender?

Jahanara's husband operated a tea shop with her money. Her husband was considered a "weak" man by villagers because his wife was so successful. Jahanara had two sons and two daughters. Her eldest daughter had studied up to grade seven, and she was training to be a moneylender. However, none of the younger children was enrolled in school. In her words, "What can they do with an education? Better to learn moneylending at a young age."

When we arrived, Jahanara came forward to meet us. She was dressed in a red sari and wore substantial amounts of gold on her person (nose ring, bangles, and a chain) for a rural person. A striking woman, Jahanara looked confident and well fed. She had already notified several of her neighbors that an elder sister from abroad was going to write about her in a book that would be read by many people, and soon a group of women gathered around us. They all admired Jahanara, and soon it was clear that they were all in debt to her.

Jahanara invested her money in four categories: short-term business, small businesses in the market, middle-level farmers, and NGO borrowers. Of this, the majority of the money was invested in short-term business; usually the profits were repaid after three to six months. The money was lent to traders who would buy local produce such as paddy, betel leaves, jute, and timber and take them by boat to other parts of the country where they fetched higher prices. Then they returned with produce from other parts of the country to sell it in their local market. People consider it a safe form of investment. They do not lose the money unless the boat capsizes with the goods, which, from what I was told, was a rare event.

Jahanara's day was not typical for a rural woman. She did not stay at home to do housework. Most of her time was spent collecting money from traders. She also spent considerable time going to NGO meetings to pay her dues or to collect new loans. When I asked Jahanara about her success, she began to share this with me:

> I have also taken out loans in my daughter's name and in the names of other people. I am teaching my daughter my trade. I take loans out by proxy. I pay these women 100 *takas* [approximately $2] each for letting

me take the loan. Now all the NGOs give me the highest loans possible. If they do not want to give me the kind of loan I want, I say to them, I will cross out my name and go elsewhere. There are so many NGOs, another NGO will give me money. (*Here she paused and laughed.*) They need me more than I need them. They do not want me to leave. I am a good investment. I have money so I always pay my installments on time.

This is how Jahanara described her success:

One has to run. If you sit around, nothing will happen. I go with the members to the NGO office when we have to get the loan. I get the money and leave. I don't stay in their office long. When I give money to NGO women borrowers, I have to be careful. These women are so needy. You cannot give them too much money; 1,000 or 2,000 *takas* [between $21 and $43] is about the maximum amount. If I give them too much money, then I have to walk around empty-handed later. They will not be able to pay back. I give them loans when they cannot pay their *kistis* or when there is an emergency.

At the end of our conversation, Jahanara said that she didn't think that other women could become like her. According to her,

They do not understand anything except their husbands. If I gave my earnings to my husband, he would use it all up. And I just invest my money in business. In the beginning, I never thought of getting food, clothes for my children. I was very careful with my money. If you go to the homes of these women on the day they get a loan from an NGO, you will find that for the next seven days they spend the money on fish and meat. My husband is also not like other men. He lets me have my way.

The following week, we met Jahanara at the Grameen Bank meeting. She was the Center leader of the Grameen Group in that village. Grameen Bank officers only collect the installments after everyone has assembled and paid up every single penny owed to Grameen. If any woman was missing, and that usually happened when she did not have the money to repay, then all the other women in the group had to wait. This coercive technique deployed by bank officers created a lot of friction among the women as they were forced to remain at the Center instead of returning home to do their housework.

At this meeting one woman called Kashai Bou (a butcher's wife) was not present. Kashai Bou lived several villages away, and the Grameen Bank officer took Jahanara as Center leader with him to collect the money from her. We went along with them. On the way to Kashai Bou's house, Jahanara proudly told us that she had broken many houses when members could not pay: "We know when they cannot pay, so we take a carpenter with us to break the house."

When I asked Jahanara, "Why do you break the houses of kin?" Jahanara became indignant at first. Her initial comment was: "Why shouldn't we? They have breached their trust with us. If they cannot pay, then we will have to pay. Why should I pay for them?" Then she became quiet and said after a while:

> It is not good to break someone's house, but we are forced to do it. This is how we get loans from Grameen Bank and other NGOs. They put pressure on us to recover the money, then we all get together and force the defaulting member to give us the money. We don't care how we do it.

Neutralizing Dissent: Power/Knowledge in Development

> "The texts of development have always been avowedly strategic and tactical—promoting, licensing, and justifying certain interventions and practices, delegitimizing others. . . . What do the texts of development not say? What do they suppress? Who do they silence—and why?" (Crush 1995, 5)

Why is it that what I have written in these pages is not legible as a public discourse? The answer to that question is that these critiques are *silenced* in NGO-dominated research spaces. Knowledge is power, but power also legitimizes what counts as knowledge, and NGOs are powerful institutions in Bangladesh. The hagiographic transcripts of the Grameen Bank have to be apprehended at the crux of power and knowledge in the context of Bangladesh. For example, in Bangladesh, there is only one English language academic publishing house of note called University Press Limited (UPL). Obviously, this gives its editorial board tremendous power over what gets published in the English language in Bangladesh. In contrast, the vernacular press is a rich source of NGO critiques, but Western donors and researchers do not have access to them. In NGO-dominated research spaces where donors and Western researchers gather, the medium of communication is English, and that keeps out the majority of Bangladeshis who cannot communicate in English. In fact, the use of English in NGO research spaces is ostensibly to accommodate the Western donors, but in reality it regulates who and what can be heard.

Similarly, in the absence of a responsible state or a progressive social movement, the rural poor have to rely on the goodwill of the NGOs. Villagers critique NGOs with the qualification that NGOs offer them services that they need, but that they want the terms of these loans to be more humane. NGO officials in their private scripts admit that development cannot take place solely through microcredit, but they censor this in their public scripts for fear of jeopardizing their jobs (Pereira 1998). The fragmented political left continues its critique of NGOs, but since the 1990s they have lost legitimacy as a political voice. The role of feminists is complicated because feminist organizations are now organized as NGOs. Furthermore, feminists find it more important to focus on other violent forms of aggression against women, such as acid burnings and rapes, and they try to keep a united NGO voice against the tyranny of the clergy.

On August 22, 1998, a conference was held in Dhaka titled "Yunusonomics," organized by a local professor. The intent of the conference was to offer microcredit as the new panacea in development economics. The conference papers were presented in English. When the floor was opened for questions, the first speaker was an angry retired doctor who said that he had expected the discussion to be carried on in a language that was accessible to him. He added that he would speak his opinion in Bengali. He often went to his village and found that most people were becoming poorer after several years of membership with Grameen Bank. He had calculated the interest charged by Grameen to be over 50 percent. He asked, "How could they claim that this was a new paradigm to be followed? How was this high interest helping the poor?" Yet not a single person among the speakers engaged with the doctor, an ordinary citizen who had come to the conference to engage in a dialogue. There were some donor representatives present at the conference, but it was unclear if they understood what the doctor was saying. Thus, critique of microcredit and Grameen Bank expressed in the vernacular language was effectively neutralized within an NGO-dominated research space.

In order to fully comprehend why this silencing occurs one has to understand how the Grameen Bank operates as a source of symbolic capital for the middle class in Bangladesh. For the first time, we, the people of Bangladesh—Henry Kissinger's "bottomless basket"—have given a gift to the Western development community. Now foreign dignitaries from the former US President Bill Clinton to Senator Hillary Clinton to Queen Sophia of Spain come to Bangladesh to study a development micracle, the Grameen Bank. The Grameen Bank is a source of tremendous national pride for many Bangladeshis, which makes it all the more difficult to critique its microcredit policies or its assertions about women's empowerment. Those who do are often labeled as "traitors within." When in 2006, Professor Yunus and the Grameen Bank went on to win the Nobel Peace Prize, it signaled Bangladesh's arrival as an equal with the West. Bangladeshis were euphoric over the Nobel Prize, and elites continue to cite Yunus as the most famous Bangladeshi in the world. Grameen Bank went on to gain more power and authority both locally and globally by linking women's empowerment to entrepreneurship to create "brave new worlds."

Notes

This chapter is reproduced by permission of SAGE from *Cultural Dynamics* 20, no. 1 (2008): 5–29, © 2008 SAGE.

1. The other three NGOs are Bangladesh Rural Advancement Committee (now called BRAC), Proshika Human Development Forum, and Association for Social Advancement (ASA). All of these NGOs work with slight variations on the Grameen Bank model. The Grameen Bank is officially registered as a bank under the Bangladesh Bank Ordinance (1983) but conceptually it is a nongovernmental organization. Therefore, in my analysis, I treat it as such.

   My research was conducted prior to the events that have engulfed Grameen Bank and its founder since 2011. The government of Bangladesh has removed Professor Yunus as the director of the Grameen Bank in 2011. The Grameen Bank Commission formed by the government in 2012 has recommended that the Bank should be split into 19 organizations with 51% of shares to be given to the government (currently it owns 3% of shares). URL accessed June 21, 2013. http://www .independent.co.uk/news/world/asia/fears-over-bangladeshs-bank-of-the -poor-grameen-bank-as-commission-says-it-should-be-split-up-8669179.html.

2. According to the websites of these NGOs (www.grameen.com, www.brac.net, www.asabd.org, www.proshika.org).

3. In Bangladesh, Western aid organizations channel most of their aid through the NGO sector, which they helped to create in the 1970s. In 1997, the European Union channeled 25 percent of its aid through the NGO sector.

4. This point will not necessarily hold for smaller NGOs in Latin American countries that have a long tradition of social movements.

5. To facilitate social engineering (or the marketing of products), NGOs and the Grameen Bank undertake information gathering of their clients on diet, health, education, consumption, etc. similar to the modern state.

6. The need for cheap labor from Third World countries has resulted in the out-

migration of rural people as labor overseas, first to the Middle East in the 1970s and 1980s, and later to Malaysia and South Korea in the 1990s. These circulations of people and capital have also brought new ideas into rural society.

7. I maintain that ethnography yields very different conclusions from survey research and focus-group interviews, the methodological tools of development economists. Ethnography requires a sustained amount of time with a community, building the members' trust, and observing what people do as opposed to what people say they do when they are asked questions in a survey.

8. Muhammad Yunus with Alan Jolis. 1998. *Banker to the Poor*. Dhaka: University Press Limited.

9. During 1975–90, Bangladesh was under military dictatorship.

10. Transparency International (TI) routinely lists Bangladesh as one of the most corrupt countries in the world.

11. The development NGOs support either/or of the two leading political parties, the Awami League and the Bangladesh Nationalist Party.

12. 'Nobel winner starts political party to tackle corruption in Bangladesh,' *The Guardian*, 22 Feb. 2007. URL (accessed June 21, 2013) http://www.guardian.co .uk/world/2007/feb/23/debtrelief.development/.

13. Since the rural population is largely illiterate, voters are taught the symbols of different political parties (fish, a sprig of wheat, the scales of justice, etc., that are the signs for various political parties) to identify the political party.

14. See Yunus, Muhammad. 2008. *Creating a World Without Poverty: Social Business and the Future of Capitalism*. Washington, DC: Public Affairs.

15. Bangladesh was not formed as a welfare state.

16. In my research I found that NGO managers blamed the borrowers and their husbands for their venture failures. For example, when 50 percent of breeder chickens died within a week of the borrowers' getting a breeder chicken loan and setting up operations, the NGO (BRAC in this instance) managers spoke of the failure as a fault of the "poor, illiterate village women," and not as BRAC's fault in targeting people who didn't have the wherewithal (the training, the facilities, and so on) to run a chicken farm from a tin shed inside their family compound.

17. The NGO definition of poor is a family of four with less than 0.5 acre of arable land and with a base income of $2 a day based on the Human Development Index.

18. Giving to kin has a double bind. It is expected that kin members will intercede and prevent a potential default in order to save the honor of the family. However, when the extended family is poor or has weak ties with the defaulting member's family, they ask the woman to find other means (such as borrow at 120 percent from a moneylender) to pay off the loan.

19. The leading NGOs have model villages, usually close to the capital, Dhaka, to showcase to international donors how well their money is being spent to train rural women in economic activities.

20. In my area, the local headmistress of a school, the wife of a lawyer, and wives of some of the richest merchants in town were members of microcredit NGOs.

NGOs prefer richer female members because they are less likely to default. Moreover, as high-status people in rural society, they can more easily influence poorer members to pay up.

21. All the NGOs I studied replicated this basic structure: group responsibility of individual loans, strict recovery through weekly (ASA and Grameen) or biweekly (BRAC) or monthly meetings (Proshika), and product tie-ins with loans (hybrid seeds with agricultural loans, breeder chickens for BRAC loanees). Since 2002, Grameen Bank moved to a new model called Grameen II where they removed group responsibility requirement for loans. But they retained the public repayment part of their previous model, hence keeping the public shaming aspect of loan recovery still in use.

22. At the time of my research, the Grameen Bank had decided to lower the payment schedule from fifty-two weeks to fifty weeks, which would mean an additional rise in the weekly amount (*kisti*) paid by the borrowers. For poor people, a weekly rise of a few *takas* (the unit of currency) was a tremendous hardship.

23. In development jargon this is euphemistically known as peer monitoring.

24. In my area, the NGO Proshika had filed seventy-four cases against its women members, and many of them were taken into police custody. According to the law of the country, people cannot be taken to jail for delinquency, but powerful NGOs violated these rules to meet their ends.

25. These incidents occurred in front of NGO officers. They would exhort the women to "collect the money or else. . . ." I brought several such incidents to the attention of NGO workers in my area, but they would dismiss my concerns by saying, "These are the work of illiterate people. We [the NGO] do not encourage this. Did you see us present at the event?"

26. Moneylending in Bengal was traditionally handled by a caste of Hindu moneylenders. In some instances, Hindu widows often participated in small-time moneylending. With the creation of Pakistan in 1947, and with the migration of Hindus from Bangladesh (formerly East Pakistan), a new group of Muslim male moneylenders have emerged. Muslims will often give up moneylending after performing the hajj. However, the entrance of poor Muslim women into the institution of moneylending is a new phenomenon.

27. Calculated at 47 *takas* (1998 rate) to $1.

PART III Feminist Social Movements and NGOs

art III begins with an essay by Saida Hodžić, who argues that the feminist critique of NGOs as neoliberal and de-politicizing is flawed. She points out that NGOs are often constitutive of women's movements and suggests that a nuanced analysis might better understand these NGOs as hybrid formations or assemblages of different movements and organizations formed by coalitions and collectives. Her critique is an important departure from the argument that neoliberalism has brought an end to a more progressive and radical feminist past. She reminds us of the complex history of women's movements, not all of which could be seen as uniformly progressive or radical, which scholars have studied in such complexity, variety, and detail, and which a "master narrative" of neoliberalism as depoliticization is supplanting. Hodžić also reminds us that not all states have similar trajectories and that the neoliberal politics of global capital become sutured to quite different local teleologies and temporalities, with distinct consequences for feminist activism.

The question of teleology is also taken up by Sabine Lang, who follows up on her earlier work that argued that NGOs have co-opted feminist movements. In her essay in this volume, Lang argues that as feminists have become part of the governance structures of the European Union (EU), forming part of the "Velvet Triangle," as it is called, those feminists and women who are outside of NGOs or are working in social movements have lost the ability to be heard. Lang sees this shift in the EU as a loss for the political possibilities of feminism, especially feminism's more innovative traditions of social and collective action.

Laura Grünberg's essay focuses on the struggle of one NGO to be heard in the context of Romania's transition from a dictatorship to a liberal state. She examines the relation between nationalism and NGO formation and reflects on the emergence and history of an NGO that came into existence in Romania when the nation was at a point of crisis. The NGO, she argues, reflects the history of the nation, so that within the NGO, as at the national level, attempts at democratization lead to bureaucratization. For the NGO, bureaucratization reduces its ability to develop innovative, local responses to emerging situations. Grünberg's essay, reflecting on the problems of feminism in postdictatorship Romania, demonstrates that local NGOs are captured by national histories in states in ways that require greater research and analysis. Nationalisms form subjects of NGOs and are intimately connected to questions of gender, sexuality, and feminism. Questions of women's empowerment are often framed within nationalist concerns. Thus no feminist NGO can ignore the nationalisms that enable it to emerge, yet may also present obstacles and constraints that impede its progress.

In the final essay, Sonia Alvarez revisits her earlier, groundbreaking research on the "NGO boom" in Latin America. Alvarez finds that feminist work has taken over NGOs to create some interesting and important forms of agency and activism. In short, the NGO form is being taken over by activists to work through feminist projects. Feminists, she argues, by reflecting on and analyzing what had gone wrong with NGOization in the 1990s, have attempted to bring back movement building and collective action to these NGOs, even as feminism may not be the only social movement that these collectives are embracing. Feminists now often become politically active through multiple issues and collaborations. As a result, feminism itself is changing to become a multidimensional project.

The feminist scholarship assembled here reveals both the power of the NGO form and its transnational circulation. The essays also reveal the liveliness of feminist projects and discourses and their dissemination through NGOs of various kinds. We suggest that the diversity of states and transnational and local contexts means that the NGO form and feminist teleology remain unstable and heterogeneous. The dynamic relationship between feminisms and NGOs is giving rise to new conflicts and collaborations. Our concluding essay in this volume addresses this point in more detail and offers some speculations about future directions.

Feminist Bastards
Toward a Posthumanist Critique of NGOization

Introduction

The Women's Manifesto for Ghana (The Coalition on the Women's Manifesto for Ghana 2004), an important political document produced by a coalition of Ghanaian organizations and feminists, has been celebrated as having transcended the limitations of NGO-ization (Mama, Tsikata, Mensah-Kutin, and Harrison 2005; Tsikata 2009). Praising it, the Ghanaian scholar and activist Dzodzi Tsikata highlights the successes of mass mobilization and coalitional work: "The Women's Manifesto project is a showcase of how broadbased political processes and partnerships involving mass membership organizations can enable small organizations to transcend their limitations, maximize their resources, create a productive division of labour and, most significantly, to give their projects legitimacy and grounding" (2009, 190). Feminist scholars will likely recognize the positive value attributed to coalitions, seen today as some of the most productive forms of politically engaged feminist organizing (Mohanty 2003; Butler 2004; Swarr and Nagar 2010). But what exactly is so dangerous about nongovernmental organizations (NGOs) that their limits need to be transcended? And do coalitions such as the Ghanaian Women's Manifesto indeed usher in a new era of political feminist organizing?

I take these questions as a point of departure for a critical engagement with feminist criticisms of NGOs, which I call the "NGOization paradigm." I will analyze the logic of this paradigm and trace its theoretical genealogies in order to probe, in Joan Scott's spirit of critique, the "blind spots that insure coherence and stability" (2008, 7). The NGOization paradigm now organizes feminist knowledge about NGOs, often constraining the space of analysis and critique. I suggest that it obfuscates power relations in feminist organizing as much as it reveals them, and that we need to pay close attention to the tropes of failure, fall, and contamination that haunt it. By bringing theoretical analysis in conversation with an ethnography of the Ghanaian Women's Manifesto (hereafter "Manifesto"), I attempt to think *otherwise* (Wiegman 2002a, 3) about new feminist formations and anti-institutional critiques.

In feminist scholarship, NGOization is defined as a "steady increase in the number of women's non-governmental organizations" and is understood as a dominant trend in feminist organizing (Jad 2007, 177). NGOization is not a descriptive, but an evaluative notion: it does not simply refer to the boom in NGOs, but understands this phenomenon as harmful for feminism. Critics of NGOization claim that NGOs have enabled the depoliticization of social and women's movements, their appropriation by donor-driven agendas, and a neoliberal co-optation of feminist practice. They understand NGOs as a fall from Eden—a teleological decline from an idealized age of revolutionary feminist activism to the contemporary era of professionalized organizations that function as donors' peons. Their arguments, I will contend, hinge on a valorization of earlier women's movements, producing a nostalgic and Eurocentric revision of feminist history and resuscitating an uncritically humanist vision of feminist organizing.

The NGOization paradigm has become institutionalized as a master narrative and now serves as a normative theory that structures the feminist field of knowledge about NGOs. We see the operations of this referential normativity in a range of recent historical and ethnographic analyses of regional women's and feminist movements. Scholarship on feminist activism, organizing, and NGOs is increasingly framed by the questions of whether NGOization happened and whether it affected feminism positively or negatively. We thus have examinations of NGOization in various countries and regions: Israel (Herzog 2011), Romania (Grünberg 2000a), the Czech Republic (Kapusta-Pofahl, Hašková, and Kolářová 2005), the former Yugoslavia (Bagic 2006), Bangladesh (Nazneen and Sultan 2009), and the Americas (Markowitz and Tice 2002). This paradigm now also structures entire ethnographies of NGOs, in which the question "Is the professionalized feminist NGO the most *appropriate* form of feminist political practice?" (Murdock 2011, 5; my emphasis) serves as the central point of analysis.

The normativity of the NGOization paradigm is also evident in feminist scholarship that disagrees with its assumptions and conclusions. Scholars seem compelled to address the NGOization paradigm to make their work intelligible, even when this paradigm restrains the nuance and reach of their analyses. Julie Hemment's ethnography of Russian women's organizing, for instance, attends to it by trying to "refuse the dichotomy of success/failure" (2007, 145) and arguing against the assertion that bureaucratized NGOs have stifled the wider participation of grassroots women in the newly professionalized world of feminist organizing.[1] Similarly, Sarah Phillips's study of Ukrainian women's social activism addresses the charges of professionalization and elite formation while arguing that a critique predicated on these terms prevents us from understanding the complexities of NGOs (2008, 140).[2] Of note here is that these scholars have to position their contextualized analyses in reference to a paradigm that is prefigured as universally valid.

I take issue with the NGOization paradigm because it hinges on an anti-institutional critique, while having itself become a stable and closed circuit of truth claims. Critics seem to know that NGOs are detrimental to women's movements and feminist politics. In their analysis of transnational feminism, Linda Peake and Karen de Souza thus write that it is "well documented" that "NGOs have become corporatized, acting as arms of the state and playing an active part in the downloading of labor and costs from the state to local communities" (2010, 110). Consensus about the depoliticizing effects of NGOs has been reached, but not on the basis of historicized or contextualized analyses in postcolonial or transnational contexts. Most notably, the NGOization paradigm disregards an entire field of ethnographic scholarship that offers substantive critiques of NGOs (Weisgrau 1997; Fortun 2001; Riles 2001; Magno 2002; Hemment 2007; A. Sharma 2008; S. Phillips 2008; Murdock 2008).[3] These scholars examine the articulations of NGOs, women's movements, and feminist organizing critically, but not in the evaluative and binary terms set by the NGOization paradigm; rather, they analyze the sociocultural and political life of NGOs, their forms, and their contradictory effects. The refusal to engage with this scholarship has contributed to the stability and impermeability of the NGOization paradigm. Bringing ethnography to directly bear on this paradigm, I suggest, opens new analytical spaces for feminist scholarship.

The NGOization Paradigm and Its Genealogies

The work of two critics has been central to the initial formation of the NGOization paradigm. Sabine Lang and Sonia Alvarez formulated the idea of the *shift* from collective and political women's movements to professional bureaucracies. Lang defined NGOization as a move from movements to projects: "NGOization entails a shift away from experience-oriented movement politics toward goal- and intervention-oriented strategies" (1997, 116). Alvarez marked bureaucratization and institutionalization as defining features of NGOization, writing about an "increased professionalization and specialization of significant sectors of feminist movements" (1998, 295). Subsequent critics have relied heavily on Alvarez, and in doing so, have singled out her negative assessments of NGOs and ignored her larger arguments.[4] NGOization becomes a "hazard facing mass movements" (A. Roy 2004, 41) that has depoliticized feminism: "Issues of collective concern are transformed into projects in isolation from the general context in which they are applied and without taking due consideration of the economic, social, and political factors affecting them" (Jad 2007, 177).

More recent theorizations point to the rise of NGOs in the global South and stress their imbrications in the development apparatus and neoliberal reforms. Tsikata characterizes NGOization "by the lack of a mass base, connection and accountability; donor dependence; the substitution of NGOs for civil society and mass movements; the prioritization of a professional technocratic approach over politics because NGOs cannot be overtly political or partisan; and a short-term project-based approach and the favouring of magic bullets over long-range broad agendas in the struggle for women's rights and gender equality" (2009, 186). Sangtin Writers and Nagar take the criticism further by casting NGOs as hegemonic organizations that prevent feminist oppositional politics. Because of NGOs, "development ideology is reproduced in the resistant spaces of political action—through homogenization, through the politics of funding, through the articulation of universalizing discourses of the modern state" (2006, 146). Rather than critiquing the development apparatus, in this view, feminists have been co-opted by it and have become antipolitical. Arundhati Roy states pithily: "The NGO-ization of politics threatens to turn resistance into a well-mannered, reasonable, salaried, 9-to-5 job. With a few perks thrown in" (2004, 45).

Though not completely overlapping, the above definitions of NGOization share both formal and substantive features. For the critics, NGOization is formally distinct because it entails an alleged historical shift from collective movements to organizations. As we shall see later, the differentiation between earlier anti-institutional women's movements and contemporary formalized NGOs is a defining feature of this paradigm. At the substantive level, this scholarship brings together concerns about professionalization, the proliferation of donor-driven agendas, and the dominance of development ideologies, all of which are understood as stripping away progressive political agendas from social and women's movements.

Critics of NGOization point out NGOs' imbrications in the nexus of discourse, power, and expert knowledge. Through the so-called gender mainstreaming and gender and development paradigms operationalized by states, donors, and NGOs, feminism is said to have become a gender technocracy (Alvarez 1998, 312; Sangtin Writers and Nagar 2006, 146). Critics see NGOs as stripping "gender" of its radical content and instead producing bureaucratic expert knowledge geared at population management (Alvarez 1998, 308; see also Hemment 2007, 83). The story is one of the contamination of originally progressive and autonomous feminist politics by the modernist and developmental state. This contamination is seen as having depoliticized and professionalized feminism, thus disempowering nonprofessional women. Critics are concerned about the formation of new elites, NGOs' lack of broader social base, and their stifling of grassroots women's voices (Jad 2007, 178; Sangtin Writers and Nagar 2006, 143). NGOs are said to have reformulated feminist goals, replacing sociopolitical transformation with complacent policy making. For critics, NGOs address only culturally and politically acceptable questions (Alvarez 1998, 306) and advocate for mere reform of the state—reform that might extend state power over women's lives and create new forms of dependence and regulation (Lang 1997, 112). Some critics also draw attention to the interstices between NGOs, the retrenchment of the welfare state, and the processes of privatization and liberalization, as well as the operations of NGOs as agents of the ostensibly democratic reforms imposed by the United States (Jad 2007).

To understand the logic and power of this paradigm, it is useful to trace some of its genealogies. The NGOization paradigm stands on the shoulders of three important strands of critical theory: critiques of the development apparatus, critiques of feminist affiliations with the neoliberal and masculinist state, and critiques of the institutionalization of women's studies and the field's concomitant failures. First, the NGOization paradigm extends Foucauldian analyses of power knowledge from development to feminist NGOs, building on Arturo Escobar's critique of developmental conjunctures of power and knowledge about the Third World. The development discourse, Escobar wrote, has "fostered a way of conceiving of social life as a technical problem, as a matter or rational decision and management to be entrusted to that group of people—the development professionals—whose specialized knowledge allegedly qualified them for the task" (1995, 52). James Ferguson also argued that "the 'development' apparatus" (1994: 15) propagates the "governmentalist" (1994: 36) dogma—the notion that the state can and will benevolently shape economy and society—while in fact expanding state control. To do so, the development apparatus constructs its own objects of knowledge and ways of knowing, reposing political questions in technical language (1994). By constructing poverty as an outcome of ostensibly inadequate local knowledge or "backward" rural traditions, for instance, it erases considerations of historical inequalities, transnational labor migration, and class and race relations. For critics of NGOization, women's movements have become just such an apparatus.

Another genealogy is what Robyn Wiegman calls "the late-twentieth-century feminist tradition of critiquing the state as the end logic of political reform" (2008, 51). Inspired by Wendy Brown's critique of "feminism's turn to the state to adjudicate or redress practices of male dominance" (1995, ix), this scholarship questions feminist alliances with state institutions, and in particular the turn to legal reforms that do not challenge state order itself. As Wiegman puts it, feminists identify "with social movements whose profound political force had a great deal to do with their ethos of anti-institutionalism" (2008, 54). The rise of human and women's rights paradigms and liberal feminism changed this dynamic in the 1990s, fostering demands for state protection, funding, and legislation. Brown articulated the concern about this shift, poignantly demanding that we pay attention to "the perils of pursuing emancipatory political aims within largely repressive, regulatory, and depoliticizing institutions that themselves carry elements of the regime (e.g., masculine dominance) whose subversion is being sought" (1995, x–xi). Consequently, critics of NGOization see NGOs as vehicles of state-oriented, reformist politics.

This poignant critique has a blind spot: its appeal to the universality of feminist dispositions leaves the issue of politics of location unaddressed. Meanwhile, the question of the feminist relationship to the state was long a point of conflict among feminists worldwide. Historically speaking, feminists based in the United States and Western Europe did not collaborate with the state, and took issue with women in socialist countries who did. Opposition to the state, then, has a particular valence in the global North but is not a universally privileged form of feminism. As we shall see later, African feminists do not see collaboration with the state as a betrayal of feminist principles.

Finally, the NGOization paradigm resonates with the critique of institutionalized academic feminism (Wiegman 2002; Joan Scott 2008). As feminism moved from street to university, in one account of the origin story (Wiegman 2008, 60), it began to suffer from the double binds of its successes and lost some of its "critical edge" (Joan Scott 2008, 6). Wiegman asks:

> Has academic feminism betrayed its radical political roots, substituting abstraction for action, legitimacy for risk? Have the emergent generations of professionally trained feminists abandoned their foremothers' tradition by making of feminism an academic career? Has our success, in short, engendered failure, transforming grassroots social movement and anti-institutional ethics to prototypically liberal and hence reformist, not revolutionary, ideals? (2002a, 3)

The NGOization paradigm mirrors critiques of academic institutionalization but lacks the latter's historicized analyses and more nuanced (and charitable) hermeneutics. Instead, when feminist scholars analyze the institutionalization of activism, failure is the dominant trope. Using NGOs as the mirror, then, allows academic feminists to deflect concerns about failure and the danger of professionalization onto the other institutionalized feminists, those working with NGOs.

Longing for Humanist Sisterhood: NGOization and Feminist Nostalgia

At the heart of the NGOization critique is the juxtaposition between women's movements and NGOs. As we have seen, the very definitions of NGOization are structured by the claim that feminist organizing has turned collective and political women's movements into professional NGO bureaucracies. For the critics, NGOs are everything that women's movements were not. The very concept of NGOization relies on a temporal logic according to which women's movements have given way, been subsumed under, or turned into NGOs. In Lang's words, "sisterhood has converged in what I shall call the establishment of NGOs instead of political movements" (1997, 106). Alvarez, in turn, refers to the critics' mourning the loss of original feminism and its radical character: "the heroic days of barricades and demonstrations seem to be over" (1998, 305, quoting Alicía Frohmann and Teresa Valdés).

The following table is a condensed and abstract rendition of the NGO-ization paradigm. Although I have tried to interpret the critics' claims responsibly and include only the language they used, tables cannot render arguments in full or give a complete account of scholars' claims.[5] My main purpose here is to reveal the contours of the oppositional framework at the core of the NGOization paradigm and to point out the limitations of the nostalgic imagination that guides the tropes of lack, fall, and contamination.

In this paradigm, women's and feminist NGOs are understood in reference to women's movements under the signs of contamination and formalization. Critics see NGOs and movements as antithetical to each other, to the extent that NGOization signals the end of everything in feminism that is politically progressive and radical. In this view, NGOs have led to the loss of "the possibility of forming broader networks and institutions that may indeed have the power to mobilize along central feminist issues" (Lang 1997, 114). This understanding leads to nostalgic laments for the romanticized "autonomous feminist groups or collectives of yesteryear" (Alvarez 1998, 306). Overall, the critics' assessments of NGOs are structured by a particular economy of value: they idealize women's movements while disapproving of and dismissing NGOs.

If NGOs have indeed replaced women's movements and taken the edge off feminist organizing, we can understand why they are depicted as hazardous. Yet at the core of this comparative framework is an uncritical conception of past women's movements that entails active acts of forgetting. When the critics paint a largely positive picture of the feminist past, they do not portray it as a concrete and historical referent but as a vortex of valued symbolic epithets. They romanticize earlier forms of feminism, invoking essentialized notions of wholesome, egalitarian, and politically unified collectives. In doing so, the critics obliterate feminist crises and the inherent divisions, inequalities, and blind spots of past women's movements, such as their reliance on women as stable subjects with shared experiences of patriarchy.

For instance, Islah Jad forgoes a sustained analysis of class, power, difference, and representation in earlier Arab women's movements, even though they were run by "highly cultured and educated upper-middle-class women" who met in literary salons and established charitable societies (2007, 184). Lang's (1997) and Myra Ferree's (1997) analyses of NGOization

From Women's Movements to the NGO Apparatus

WOMEN'S MOVEMENTS	NGOS
Collectives, organic social networks	Organizations
Feminist culture	Femocracy
Large, fluid, functionally undifferentiated	Small, disconnected, specialized
Broad, interconnected concerns	Issue-oriented, narrow focus
Informal; have cause, mission, conviction	Professional
Experience	Expert knowledge
Militant participants	Paid staff
Feminists	Genderists
Organizing, consciousness-raising	Projects, services, advocacy, interventions
Processes	Measurable outcomes
Mobilizing	Networking
Intimacy, connection, broad social base	Distanced from "real" grassroots women
Raise contentious issues, connect the local and personal to the structural and political	Depoliticize gender, work on politically acceptable questions
Gender as a critical, revolutionary concept	Gender as a grant
Autonomous, outside of capital	Dependent on donors or the state
Antihierarchical, egalitarian, shared power formation	Inequitable internal power structures, elite
Antagonistic to the state, leftist politics	Policy-oriented, cooperative with the state
Want to transform culture and politics	Want to reform the state
Face-to-face contact (public mobilization)	Modern communication methods (public relations)
Leftist oppose development ideology, challenge global inequality	"Free-market" feminists promote neoliberalism

and bureaucratization in postunification Germany are marked by a different erasure: they rely on an uncritically ethnocentric and state-organized framework of who counts as a proper subject of German womanhood and women's movements. While lamenting the effects of NGOization on "women as victims of unification" (Ferree 1997, 46), Lang and Ferree see only German Germans as "women" and ignore the women's movements' neglect of migrant women in their midst. Their analyses of encounters between East and West German feminisms presuppose heteronormativity, whiteness, citizenship, and unproblematic gendered subjectivity, leaving invisible the consequences of historical and contemporary feminist organizing on Germany's inappropriate/d others (Trinh 2005).

The idealized conceptions of a properly political and collective feminist past do not readily map onto actual histories. When scholars analyze NGOs in reference to particular histories of women's movements rather than their ideal-typic conceptions, the tropes of the fall and contamination reach their limits. For instance, Alvarez writes that Latin American women's movements subsumed the categories of class, ethnicity, race, indigeneity, and sexuality to those of gender (Alvarez 1998, 300–301). Hemment also questions the idealization of earlier women's movements as egalitarian, showing that feminism in Russia was never in the purview of the popular and undifferentiated masses (2007).[6]

The erasure of concrete historical referents provides an answer to the puzzle about the popularity and normativity of the NGOization paradigm. I contend that the nostalgic rewriting of feminist history has popularized the notion of NGOization by constructing a space for a positive memory making about earlier women's movements. Indeed, this paradigm may be one of few locations in critical feminist literature where women's movements are praised and celebrated. Feminist scholars are otherwise highly attuned to the fact that issues of power and inequality were not adequately addressed by Western women's movements prior to the third wave of feminism, and that they have not been resolved. The NGOization paradigm seems to provide a curious respite from self-critique.

Another problem with this memory work is that it builds on an uncritical humanist and organicist discourse. In constructing movements as collective and identity-based while portraying NGOs as technocratic machines, the NGOization paradigm makes it clear that only the former are valued. Movements are imagined as based on social communities and "the model of the organic family" (Haraway 1991, 151), in which everyone got along just fine. In contrast, NGOs are understood as organizations first and people second. "Here the constituency is not a *natural* social group," Jad laments (2007, 185; my emphasis). In other words, the organic women-centered movement has given way to an externally driven machine motivated by neoliberal ideology and directed by states and donors. In this vision, the neoliberal free-market, civil society and gender mainstreaming agendas have taken over feminist organizing. What is the problem with machines? They reproduce a logic that turns political questions into technical problems solvable by machines (Ferguson 1990). For politics, in contrast, we need humans—according to a humanist understanding of political agency.

However, for those of us who question humanism's single vision and ostensibly all-encompassing inclusion, machines are not necessarily monsters. I find it methodologically and theoretically important to question the ascription of positive valence to the "organic" women's movements and the ascription of negative valence to the NGO machine. Who counts as human in this paradigm? Who belongs in the "natural" social world of women's movements? Nature has long served as a boundary marker between citizens and subjects. The benefits of humanism have never been universal, and race, class, ethnicity, sexuality, and geopolitical citizenship have organized their distribution.

I suggest that Donna Haraway's metaphor of the cyborg—an early and poignant response to humanism—helps us develop a critical analysis of NGOs. The metaphor, or myth, of cyborgs is constructed in opposition to the humanist vision of the subject of politics and "does not dream of community on the model of the organic family" (Haraway 1991, 151). Unlike the idealized women's movements, NGOs are "completely without innocence . . . wary of holism, but needy for connection" (ibid., 151). A posthumanist cyborg theory does not draw normative boundaries between movements and NGOs; rather, it confounds them. The very idea of a cyborg is "an argument for *pleasure* in the confusion of boundaries and for *responsibility* in their construction" (ibid., 150, my emphasis). For cyborgs, distinctions—whether between species or, as in this case, between forms of feminist organizing—are not absolute, but "leaky" (ibid., 152). NGOs, I suggest, also embody "transgressed boundaries, potent fusions, and dangerous possibilities" (ibid., 154).

Like cyborgs, NGOs have ambivalent origins: "The main trouble with cyborgs, of course, is that they are the illegitimate offspring of militarism and patriarchal capitalism, not to mention state socialism. But illegitimate offspring are often exceedingly unfaithful to their origins. Their fathers, after all, are inessential" (ibid., 151). Who, then, are the parents of NGOs? The critics of NGOization rely on organicist and woman-centered kinship metaphors to depict NGOs as unwanted children of the women's movement, suggesting that the institutional takeover of feminism has produced illegitimate offspring that did not inherit the movement's legacy. In other words, if NGOs are the unwanted children of feminist mothers, then neoliberal states and donors are the dominant fathers to whom women's movements have succumbed. The horizontal feminist "sisterhood" (Lang 1997, 106) has died, and the bureaucratic, top-driven, and masculinist neoliberal state has given birth to feminist bastards.

But NGOs, like cyborgs, are not always faithful to their origins. By studying their practices, we shall see that where NGOs come from and which strange bedfellows they make need not be a dominant concern. Some NGOs transgress boundaries and produce new kinds of political engagements, however tentative and fraught.

I will argue that the emergence of NGOs is a prolifically productive phenomenon. Here, I build on Jean Comaroff's (2007) take on the Foucauldian notion of productivity. Comaroff invites us to consider spheres of cultural production independently of axiological questions or value judgments. In her analysis of HIV/AIDS related activism in South Africa, Comaroff argues that although few people would claim that the disease is a positive phenomenon, it has nevertheless been productive: "It has given birth to significant forms of sociality and signification, of enterprise and activism, both negative and positive. . . . Such conditions breed desperate forms of inventiveness, representation, and enterprise" (2007, 203). Ghanaian NGOs are productive in that they have breathed new life into feminist organizing, helping foment new spheres of political activism. Yet they are not innocent, and their effects are unpredictable and ambivalent.

Historicizing NGOs and Feminist Organizing in Ghana

I begin my analysis of Ghanaian articulations of NGOs and movements with a brief historical account, as I agree with Sarah Phillips that critiques of NGOs need to be set against the backdrop of specific contexts and histories (Phillips 2008, 140). Historicizing women's movements from the Ghanaian perspective challenges the master narrative of NGOization in two important ways. First, the history of the Ghanaian women's organizing teaches us that the term "women's movement" has never been innocent, and that "movements" should not be celebrated. Ghana has a long history of women's political activity and organizing,[7] but the first "women's movement" to receive that name was far from horizontal. The 31st December Women's Movement was an organization founded in 1982 by the military government, lending the state a "gender-progressive" hue and a "grand feminist illusion" (Prah 2003, 7) until its collapse in 2000. Although this organization had a mass base and a membership of dozens of thousands of women from all walks of life, it was a state-led structure, directed and controlled by the former first lady, Nana Rawlings. Scholars of Ghanaian feminism have criticized this ostensible movement for monopolizing the space of feminist activism and suppressing other kinds of women's organizing (Manuh 2007; Tsikata 2009; Viterna and Fallon 2008). This history reminds us that feminists and states rely on the symbolic capital of popular participation for their legitimacy and that the term "movement" is not an innocent category, but also an effect of a political discourse and governmental practice.[8]

Second, a contextual analysis teaches us that an anti-institutional stance is not universal to feminism. In Ghana and indeed across Africa, the boundaries between movements and institutions are porous. African women's movements are not always grounded in informal groups of loosely associated individuals but in various kinds of formal institutions. These include women's economic cooperatives, government organizations, and church groups (Mikell 1995), NGOs and women's associations (Tripp, Casimiro, Kwesiga, and Mungwa 2009; Fallon 2008) as well as coalitions (Tsikata 2009). My research also points to the coconstitutive emergence of contemporary Ghanaian feminism and NGOs in the waning years of the Rawlings regime.[9] Opportunities for feminist organizing increased with the return of democracy, the availability of funding for gender and development projects, and the emergence of international feminists as donors who support projects in Ghana. Among the several thousand domestic, Ghanaian-led NGOs that have women's empowerment as one of their central projects, there are a few dozen women's NGOs with politically radical agendas. Some of them, particularly those in large cities, refer to themselves as "feminist," while others eschew this name; all are directed by women but see men as collaborators, coworkers, and constituents. These NGOs stand out among the organizational structures that produce politically transformative feminist work.

I have seen Ghanaian activists in and out of NGOs get things done by working with, not against, the state. This is the case even when their work involves challenges to the state order or the ruling government (Hodžić 2009, 2010). Ghanaian feminists see no value in being oppositional for the sake of taking a pure stance. Rather, they attempt to regender the state and further their political agendas through strategic collaborations with specific institutions and individuals. African feminists think critically about these alliances, considering them both dangerous and generative.[10]

The Women's Manifesto for Ghana

The Manifesto also points to possibilities immanent in new feminist formations that transgress institutional boundaries. This document, which took Ghana by surprise and attracted a lot of enthusiasm, regenerated political activism against neoliberal reforms and animated demands for a neosocialist transformation of the state.

The Manifesto understands itself as a harbinger of a "movement" (The Coalition on the Women's Manifesto for Ghana 2004, 70), and its vocabulary bears the imprint of feminism, using notions of "struggle" and "collective action" (ibid., 9) and urging "solidarity" (ibid., 72). At the same time, the Manifesto coalition is a hybrid form that blurs the boundaries between institutions and activists. Initiated and "hosted" by an NGO called ABANTU for Development, the Manifesto brought together an assemblage of individual feminists, NGOs, and organizations ranging from traders,' teachers,' and agricultural workers' unions and associations that collaborated for over a year. (For the purposes of my argument, note that most of this work took place in Accra, where many of the coalition members are located.) They initially refused funding offered by donors in order to avoid the short-term "project logic" (Jad 2007, 178) and were later able to negotiate the terrains of funding and accountability on their own terms. Porous boundaries and the assemblage of forms marked the making of the Manifesto: it combined expertise and experience, thrived on the labor of paid staff and unpaid activists, promoted both advocacy and political mobilization, aimed at reforming policy as well as transforming the state and society, and measured its successes on the basis of both outcomes and processes.

The Manifesto was created in response to frustrations with the government's work on gender and development and with donor-hijacked empowerment efforts. Critiquing the depoliticizing effects of the development apparatus, the Manifesto takes issue with the NGOs' financial insecurity that constrains their autonomy and independence and "leaves them open for co-optation by donor priorities and donor-led initiatives" (The Coalition on the Women's Manifesto for Ghana 2004, 67). It also notes that the effects of "empowerment money" (Elyachar 2002), its far from transparent distribution, and the ensuing regulation of NGOs have engendered rivalry among NGOs and undermined collaborative processes.

As one of its critical interventions, the Manifesto historicizes the precarity of Ghanaian women. Critical of dominant understandings of poverty and Ghana's neoliberal economic policy, the Manifesto questions the government's foci on privatization, economic growth, and fiscal stability, which have "relegated social welfare, social security, and human development issues to the background in official thinking and action" (The Coalition on the Women's Manifesto for Ghana 2004, 23). It also places the causes of poverty and disempowerment in historical and global perspectives, linking critiques of inequality to the effects of underdevelopment (ibid., 10, 55). Rejecting modernist development ideology, the term used is "underdeveloped," not "undeveloped," and poverty is understood according to the Marxist view as an effect of politics, the expropriation of resources, and both colonial and postcolonial exploitation. In agreement with a number of Ghanaian NGOs, the Manifesto does not reject the term "development" but resignifies it as an aspiration for economic and social justice.[11]

Challenging the empowerment paradigm, the Manifesto builds on the legacy of African feminists who have argued that the situation of women in Africa cannot be addressed by prioritizing gender alone (Nnaemeka 1998). African feminists have paved the way for the Manifesto's simultaneous focus on gender and its deprivileging as the dominant category for explaining inequality in favor of contextualized and historicized analyses of power and difference. Nevertheless, the Manifesto holds that Ghanaian women are particularly vulnerable in the neoliberal context: they largely operate in the informal sector of the economy (The Coalition on the Women's Manifesto for Ghana 2004, 13), are often responsible for both household labor and social provision within households, and are imperiled by privatization (ibid., 24). The Manifesto therefore demands "social security arrangements" for "all working women and men in the formal and informal sectors and in rural and urban areas" (ibid., 15).

Since the Manifesto demands policy changes on the part of the government, it might be misread as a state-centric, "advocacy" document aimed merely at reform. As we have seen, the demands for state action and the attribution of state power over the social and the cultural trouble critics of NGOization, who see demands on the state as evidence of institutional co-optation. Yet the Manifesto aims not at the simple reform of the state or the continuation of the logic of empowerment as charity, but also at their transformation. Although the Manifesto was in part enabled by neoliberalism, it articulates a set of aspirations that escape the neoliberal "common sense" (Harvey 2005, 39) and formulates neosocialism as its ideological framework.

Moreover, in the Ghanaian context, demanding that the state redistribute resources is a political act in its own right. Scholars credit the Manifesto with fomenting popular disenchantment with neoliberal ideology that individualizes responsibility for social welfare and deflects it from the state: "All of a sudden, people were beginning to ask questions and make demands on the government to provide certain things" (Rose Mensah-Kutin, in Mama, Tsikata, Mensah-Kutin, and Harrison 2005). Aradhana Sharma's analysis of Indian NGOs also rearticulates the politics of demands: "The use of administrative or governance techniques such as empowerment paradoxically ends up producing a critical practice directed at state agencies; this is a politics of citizenship centered on demanding resources-as-rights from government bodies" (2008, xxii). In direct contrast to NGOization critics, who understand NGOs as doling out as "aid or benevolence what people ought to have by right" (A. Roy 2004, 45),[12] we see that the Manifesto subverts the logic of charity and mobilizes demands for resources-as-rights. Such demands for rights, however embedded in the logic of liberalism, can transcend the logic of reform because they have a social life of their own. The production of the Manifesto, scholars and activists argue, has exceeded the final product: "Collective processes have become much easier, and trust and goodwill have been built" (Dzodzi Tsikata, in Mama, Tsikata, Mensah-Kutin, and Harrison 2005).

Coalition on the Fast Track: An Ethnography of Inclusion

Feminist coalitional politics is not free from effects of power. The following ethnographic analysis of the coalition's efforts to include NGOs in northern Ghana's Upper East region will show that feminist organizing was circumscribed by national geopolitics. In this encounter at the cultural and geopolitical margins of the state, the Manifesto coalition reproduced difference, reinforced inequality, and limited the scope of political critique.

On a Friday morning in April 2004, I found myself in an air-conditioned conference room in Bolga, attending a "consultative workshop" on the Manifesto. This coalition-building effort took place against the backdrop of regional inequalities. Due to complex historical reasons that range from economic patterns of trade to warfare, colonial governance by difference, and neglect by the independent state, northern Ghana has been marginalized—culturally, economically, and politically. As a result, this region has become a vortex of NGO activity, much of it structured under the rubric of development. The several politically engaged women's NGOs in the region are at the fringes of the national women's movement. Few feminists from the national capital address the problem of regional inequality, and when they do, it is under the rubric of donor-suggested, liberal efforts at inclusion. These geopolitical and historical constellations of feminism and development turn inclusion and coalition building into a site of conflict and the "cunning of recognition" (Povinelli 2002).

The coalition-building effort was shaped by preexisting inequalities and donor-recipient relations. Since Accra-based NGOs and coalitions are more visible and have easier access to economic and symbolic capital than northern NGOs, they are often seen as donors. At cross-regional meetings, for instance, northern NGOs commonly ask NGOs from Accra for funding. The Manifesto workshop was marked by more literal donor-recipient relations, as it was convened by an international NGO End to Poverty Ghana (a pseudonym). Although technically an NGO and a member of the Manifesto coalition, in practice, this organization functions as a donor and funds a range of regional "partner" NGOs. As these NGOs were the main workshop participants, other feminists from the region were left out.

The conference room was packed with NGO directors who were bound by obligations to their donor, even though the organizers had knocked on their doors just the night before. I was accompanying Elizabeth, the director of one of the Bolga-based women's NGOs where I conducted part of my research. The workshop was facilitated by Vida, who presented herself as occupying multiple positions: as a committed activist and a member of the coalition, a senior officer for End to Poverty with authority over resources, and a "fellow Northerner" who grew up at the margins of the state. She was joined by Abena, a staff member from another Accra-based NGO. Vida began the meeting by taking credit for the impetus to organize consultations, saying that she had personally initiated them. At first, she explained, the coalition had rested on the notion that everybody was invited and could participate equally. In reality, however, NGO activists from northern Ghana find it difficult to travel to the cosmopolitan cities in the south of the country, as these trips take anywhere from eight to over thirty hours. To remedy this, Vida initiated the meetings in northern Ghana and emphasized her personal commitment to this process: "I wear my official cap and my Northerner cap. As a Northerner, I felt obliged to do the consultations in the North." She returned to this point throughout the day, emphasizing her background and her desire to create a "gender network for the northern regions, as our issues are uniquely different."

Vida knew that she would have to appease the local NGOs for turning to them at such a late stage—the coalition had been organized in the previous year, and at this point the final draft of the document was already formulated. To preempt charges of having ignored the northern NGOs, Vida claimed that they had in fact been represented—by proxy. "Were you involved as women from Bolga?" she asked rhetorically, and answered the question herself: "Yes, because your District Assembly women and political parties represented you." Nevertheless, she stressed that she personally found this level of representation insufficient and that she wanted to have the perspectives of NGO-based activists.

Despite this framing, tensions flared up before Vida even handed out copies of the Manifesto. When Vida demanded that the participants say why the Manifesto was an important document, Elizabeth suggested that perhaps it was not. "We have been working on a similar document here in Bolga," Elizabeth said, simultaneously revealing the lack of knowledge Vida had about local efforts as well as hinting at the more "local"—and therefore legitimate—character of that document. Vida retorted: "This is a document that comes from the grassroots, not from 'Auntie Elizabeth because she is who she is.'"

This conflict over the scope of "grassroots" needs to be unpacked. Elizabeth and Vida each characterized the other as elitist and exclusionary, and used the definitional turf of the "local" and "grassroots" idioms to wage their battle over leadership and vision in the Ghanaian women's movement. While Elizabeth questioned the need for the Manifesto and criticized the coalition for ignoring the local efforts of Bolga activists, Vida suggested that a document coming from Bolga could not be "grassroots" because it would have been directed by Elizabeth, a well-educated expert. By simultaneously acknowledging Elizabeth's position as an important leader and accusing her of masterminding the local efforts, Vida skillfully shifted the critique away from the Manifesto. Her position as a donor and workshop convener allowed Vida to dictate the terms of debate and to set limits to the critique that others were allowed to voice.

Later in the day, she made it clear that her definition of what counts as "grassroots" was the right one. "When you invite people to a workshop, make sure they represent others," she said. "A woman from a village does not mean a grassroots woman. A District Assembly woman from a village does." In other words, grassroots women were those that the Manifesto coalition had designated as such early on.

The very terms of inclusion and recognition of northern NGOs also produced an impasse. The meeting had the common format of a one-day workshop: it was quick and superficial. This format meant that nothing radically new could be debated. Representatives of NGOs were given only one hour to read and comment on a few chapters of the Manifesto, which is written in an academic style. As this linguistic register is not easily accessible to nonelite NGO workers, they were not able to engage with it deeply. Moreover, the Manifesto's underlying paradigm was unfamiliar to most NGOs in Bolga. The Manifesto rearticulates causes of women's problems by pointing to their structural, historical, and global origins and considers neoliberal policies as an impediment to livelihood and economic justice. This radical break with the established NGO discourse was impossible to "popularize" in a few hours. Unfamiliar with this discourse and called on to present "their unique issues," in the ensuing group conversation representatives of local NGOs listed cultural particularities and resorted to the common culture-blaming discourses about patriarchy in northern Ghana.

Diana, one of the well-known women's leaders from Bolga, started off the discussion of the "Women's Economic Empowerment" section by raising the issue of microcredit. The Manifesto criticizes microcredit programs, seeing them as fostering an informal, deregulated economy that leaves women without access to health care and social security. For Diana and others in the group, these criticisms were new and unappealing. They saw microcredit as good—just not good enough for women. "Women can't even access credit because of lack of house ownership," Diana said, adding that "microcredit schemes should be improved." Her vision of economic empowerment was to extend microcredit, not to curtail it. One could argue that her stance was a pragmatic one, based on the situation she observes on a daily basis, since rural and urban women in the region favor microcredit. Indeed, the most frequent complaint I heard from rural women was that they did not get enough loans.[13] The subsequent conversation made it clear that the Manifesto's alternative vision of economic justice was both unfamiliar and difficult to engage with. Moreover, by coupling her support of microcredit with the issue of "cultural" impediments to economic empowerment, Diana opened the door to the familiar discourse of cultural pathologies, saying that "all cultural barriers to ownership should be removed" and telling a story of a woman who lost the possession of her housing after her husband's death.

"A widow in Garego was asked to marry her late husband's brother," Diana said. "She refused and they burned her rooms." Others quickly picked up on this story: "Was anybody arrested?" "How did you find out?" "Oh, but the village women don't report to the police." The discussion turned to the issue of cultural discrimination against women, without returning to the Manifesto. Eventually, the group representative wrote Diana's remarks on a flip chart. Later in the day, it became evident that other groups also framed culture as the main cause of women's problems. Group reports and flip charts highlighted various aspects of cultural discrimination against women and emphasized it as the main impediment to empowerment.

Given the workshop format of the encounter, representatives of northern NGOs responded to the Manifesto in ways that resonated with their idea of what workshops call for. Many NGOs see "traditional patriarchy" as the only kind of power that structures women's lives in northern Ghana, and culturalism is the dominant governmental framework for organizing knowledge about gender inequality. This discourse is learned and practiced at NGO workshops. The workshop format is a machine that dictates not only how the "business" of NGOs is conducted, but also what is said. Workshop contributions follow a common script, and the resulting flip charts tend to look alike.[14]

Neither was the coalition able to learn anything new from the encounter with Bolga NGOs. The very terms of inclusion of northern NGOs hinged on the recognition of their cultural difference and self-identification as the nation's "others." Hence, rather than being attuned to the subtext of Diana's commentary, which addressed the greater precarity of rural women, the coalition learned only what it expected to hear: northern culture discriminates against women and is the main impediment to empowerment. The terms of inclusion, then, reanimated the common discourses about the cultural pathology of marginalized groups rather than articulating new frameworks for understanding gender inequality in northern Ghana.

The encounter also limited the scope of political critique. Despite the Manifesto's bold self-definition as "a political document" (The Coalition on the Women's Manifesto for Ghana 2004, 5), at this meeting, Vida refused to engage with local understandings of politics. She censored Evelyn, another women's leader from Bolga, when she started criticizing regional inequality in the state's distribution of resources.

"The Women's Ministry has not been decentralized," Evelyn lamented. "In the North, we don't know what she [the minister] is doing. The Women's Ministry is a political office. It belongs to those of the NPP.[15] It's not for everybody. They are there for their own people."

By criticizing the government's gender politics, Evelyn articulated a common set of grievances about regional inequalities and the unequal distribution of resources that is structured by party politics and individual patronage. Vida and Abena quickly silenced her.

"When you go talk to the women, please don't get political. No NPP, no NDC," said Abena. Vida quickly added: "This Manifesto does not belong to any government, any party. . . . The document is completely antipolitical. Let us not be political."

Evelyn's critique of the government's gender politics and the regional and party-based practices of resource distribution was stopped because it was deemed too "political." Unpacking the discrepancy between the Manifesto's self-representation as a political document and this erasure of politics requires a consideration of the larger context of marginalization of northern Ghana by the state, as well as its spectral reflections on partisanship and politics. Ruling governments are understood as prioritizing the regions in which they have most support, and the Ministry of Women's and Children's Affairs was founded by the NPP government, which was seen as favoring southern Ghana. In addition, northern Ghanaians often remarked that their marginalization resulted from the state's refusal to "decentralize" its resources.

Although Evelyn's criticism was directed only at the government, it may have been understood as an attack on southern privilege. Her comments were perceived as dangerous because they were performative in the sense that she was saying more than was obvious (Ebron 2007). Evelyn's critique of regional inequalities was perhaps too close to the question of inequalities within the women's movement, and this was not a debate that the coalition was ready to have. Equally important, Evelyn's commentary about resource distribution was grounded in a popular critique of the state that the Manifesto avoids. Although the Manifesto voices an academic and leftist critique of the neoliberal retrenchment of the state, it does not challenge the informal practices of resource distribution that many Ghanaians object to. In other words, the Manifesto coalition wanted to transform the state but was not willing to engage with the critique of the state-as-lived.

Finally, the aftermath of the workshop brings into sharp relief the impasses of inclusion that do not challenge larger regional inequalities. Here, End to Poverty played bait and switch with the representatives of northern NGOs. Vida promised them funding, requesting proposals for workshops with local women. Stipulating that these regional consultations should be quick, efficient, and cheap, Vida put a serious strain on local NGOs. In three weeks, they would have to read and understand the Manifesto; write proposals; negotiate the budget; reserve workshop locations; organize lodging and food service; invite workshop participants, both by mail and in person; hold the actual workshop; write workshop reports; and compile receipts and endorsements of the Manifesto. Some workshop participants immediately objected to this time frame. Seidu, a senior official of End to Poverty's regional office, said: "Why are we rushing to have this done by the 15th? You said it's not just for the 2004 campaign." Vida retorted: "The consultations will continue afterward." But Seidu insisted: "But why rushing?" Abena put an end to the criticism: "You're a Ghanaian, I'm a Ghanaian. If we're given a hundred years, we'll never finish."

Seidu knew not to push this topic further, but his colleague from the northern region, Akolbire, returned to the same issue in the evaluation of the workshop, criticizing the limited time for the consultations. It is not surprising that the criticism came from within the organization's ranks, and from two men who are both in senior positions. While representatives of women's NGOs learn to keep their criticism in check in order not to alienate donors, these two men had no such constraints. They felt free to criticize their colleague, who was a woman and similar in rank to them.

Representatives of local NGOs, on the other hand, could only protest "with their feet"—by refusing to comply with Vida's request. Elizabeth did not think that would be wise, however, since they "might not receive money again." Given power relations between the NGOs and donors, declining to hold the workshops was not an option. Hence, Elizabeth put other projects on the back burner and planned the workshops Vida requested. Conflicts emerged when Elizabeth and her colleagues revealed that they did not want to completely follow End to Poverty's plan. Elizabeth proposed an additional workshop for men only, in order to get them on board at the outset. This aspiration reflects a divide between the vision of many northern NGO activists and the Manifesto coalition. The basic premise of the coalition is that gender issues are not a women's question, and that the Manifesto belongs to "all women and men in Ghana who can identify with its demands" (The Coalition on the Women's Manifesto for Ghana 2004, 70). Yet Elizabeth and representatives of other northern

NGOS say that they cannot wait for men to begin to identify with their demands—they want to bring them on board at the inception of each project.

In the end, Elizabeth's proposal was not approved. Moreover, word came that "there had been a misunderstanding"—Vida had never wanted local women's NGOs to organize further workshops, she said. This attempt at a graceful exit convinced no one, ending the coalition building around the Manifesto in the region for the time being. The northern groups would later take up common projects again, as they are among the NGOs that "cannot afford to assume a purist position" (Hemment 2007, 142).

This bait-and-switch approach was neither the first nor the last time that women's NGOs from Bolga were consulted by NGOs and coalitions from Accra at the last minute, or asked to write proposals by donors who subsequently turned them down. These haphazard attempts at inclusion are not an exception but reflect the order of things. In the course of my fieldwork, I attended a number of meetings at which representatives of NGOs from Accra came to northern Ghana for "consultations," only to reveal that all the important decisions had already been made. Mary, one of Elizabeth's colleagues, resignified the notion of "gender mainstreaming" to critique this phenomenon. "Southern NGOs and donors don't include the North in the project from the beginning," she said. "They do something last minute here, and are then surprised when it fails. It's the same thing with gender—people don't mainstream it into their projects at the beginning, and then they wonder why it doesn't work."

These kinds of criticism are usually voiced in informal conversations and are rarely uttered in the presence of those whom they target. In other words, listening to the subtext of critical remarks, rather than censoring them, would have been the only opportunity for members of the Manifesto coalition to grasp the dissatisfaction of northern activists with the liberal terms of inclusion that end up marginalizing them.

How do we understand this outcome in relationship to the NGOization paradigm? Given the structures of "empowerment money" and Vida's reliance on development forms such as last-minute workshops, it is easy to read the coalition's impasse as evidence of failure of NGOization. I suggest a counterintuitive interpretation. The impetus for this effort as well as the impasse on which it foundered were structured by the same forces: the geopolitical contexts of Ghanaian feminist organizing and the porous boundaries between NGOs and coalitions. Recall that the outreach effort was driven by a donor activist, not by the larger movement. As a person from northern Ghana and as a donor with experience in this region, Vida was more attuned to regional inequalities than many Accra-based members of the coalition. Her fusion of capital, subjectivity, and experience led the coalition to attempt to broaden its base—but did it also stop her from challenging the sedimented effects of marginalization? A critical understanding of regional inequalities, I suggest, was prevented both by the form of the encounter as well as by the liberal terms of recognition offered to the participants. Northern NGOs were asked to voice their concerns, but the only readily available position was that of cultural difference, and the only shared language that of its impediment to empowerment.

Conclusion: Rethinking NGOization

My aim in this chapter has been to decenter the NGOization paradigm as the organizing structure for feminist analyses of NGOs in order to widen our conceptual frameworks. This paradigm glosses over feminist crises and inequalities in past women's movements, and, I suggest, persists precisely because of its nostalgic valorization of anti-institutional feminist autonomy. We cannot conclude with questioning professionalization of feminist thought and practice; we need to examine anti-institutionalism itself. The NGOization paradigm assumes a universal traction but stops short of situating anti-institutional critique in time and place. By taking note of its location in the global North and in the academy, this essay attends to some of its epistemological and geopolitical implications. Anti-institutionalism also prevents us from recognizing that various organizations have been constitutive of women's movements in Ghana and elsewhere. The possibilities of shifting feminist configurations will remain invisible if we insist on anti-institutionalism as the only proper form of feminist politics.

How, then, do we think "*otherwise*" about new feminist formations (Wiegman 2002a, 3)? My analysis points to the value of historicizing and contextualizing the work of NGOs rather than contrasting them to ideal-typic women's movements. Feminist politics means—and should mean—different things in different contexts. I also suggest that we would be better served by neither dismissing NGOs nor celebrating movements, but by examining the articulation of their forms, as well as their blind spots and productive possibilities. Neither NGOs nor coalitions are pure, and the tropes of purity and contamination are not useful for analyzing emerging feminist formations.

This essay is therefore an exercise in a posthumanist critique of NGO practices that moves beyond Eurocentric anti-institutionalism. Rather than denouncing NGOs as illegitimate offspring of feminism, I have suggested the cyborg as a metaphor that harnesses the productive potential of transgressed boundaries. A cyborg theory does not draw normative boundaries between movements and NGOs; instead, it confounds them. The notion of cyborgs helps us see that the form of feminist organizing (be it movement, NGO, or coalition) does not determine whether its politics are progressive. NGOs, I have shown, are tied to neoliberalism, but they are also constitutive of political organizing that challenges neoliberal discourses and practices. Coalitions are situated in the same milieu and are embedded in the equally problematic structures of capital, power, and inequality. It is these structures, rather than the institutional forms of feminist organizing, that shape the outcomes of feminist politics. The Manifesto coalition reached an impasse because the larger women's movement has yet to address regional inequality outside the discourses of liberal inclusion and cultural difference as an impediment to development.

Like cyborgs, the kind of critique I offer here is not innocent, either. NGO-based activists from northern Ghana may agree with my analysis, but they "make do" and move on. As they consider explicit and public critique of power and inequality neither gracious nor pragmatic, I take responsibility for its dangers and implications.

Notes

1. Hemment counters the "main charges leveled at NGOs"—the depoliticization of resistance, the formation of new elites, and co-optation by donors (2007, 142–44)—while calling for nuanced accounts of women's agency, NGO workers' own critiques, and reflection on the politics of feminist knowledge production. Her solution is to link critique to "constructive political projects" in conversation with Russian women (ibid., 142).
2. See also Yakin Ertürk's positioning in her study of women's political organizing in Turkey (2006, 99).
3. The ethnographic literature is vast, so I have only cited monographs.
4. Critics quote Alvarez selectively to validate their evaluations of NGOization, ignoring her arguments about the productive influences of NGOs on feminist politics and organizing (Alvarez 1998, 1999). Meghan Simpson writes: "Local and global 'feminisms' alike have undergone a process of 'NGOization,' bringing movements to a broader political stage, but also effectively closing the door to a wider participation of women" who are not in the professionalized NGO circles (2009, 144). Amy Lind claims that "feminists from all strands have become

disillusioned to varying degrees by the bureaucratization, 'partyization,' and/or 'NGOization' of feminist struggles" (2003, 197). Jael Silliman writes that NGOization "distanced the priorities and organizing imperatives of women's NGOs and networks from the grassroots concerns of local women" (1999, 40), turning NGO activities into "narrow, state-centric strategies that appeared to respond more to the logic of patriarchal domination than to an alternative feminist worldview" (1999, 47).

5. Here, I focus on the work of scholars who attempt to define and theorize NGOization, including Lang (1997), Alvarez (1998), Jad (2007), and Sangtin Writers and Nagar (2006). Although they do not agree on everything, their work has established a scholarly paradigm that is widely cited and accepted.

6. Russian women's movements of the 1970s had also been the purview of "elites," Hemment argues, and were propelled by educated and urban women (2007, 76). This is neither a celebration nor a lament, but an observation that questions the basis on which we assess the effects of NGOs.

7. Although Ghanaian women's associations and groups were often repressed by colonial and postcolonial regimes (Mikell 1995), women participated in the country's political movements (against colonial economic policies, in the independence movement, and in protests against military regimes and the state's regulation of markets) and were represented in political parties.

8. Ghanaians are well aware of this economy of value: one NGO has recently changed its name from "Widows and Orphans Ministry" to "Widows and Orphans Movement." This NGO expunged the Christian connotations of the term "ministry," replacing it with the word "movement" that appeals to its current feminist supporters and donors.

9. Ghanaian understandings of the term "NGO" are varied. Organizations are formally recognized as NGOs when they apply for and receive the requisite government designation. In popular culture, however, NGOs are differentiated from associations (NGOs serve the general public, while associations are primarily accountable to their members) and community-based organizations (which are registered as NGOs but are based in small, often rural communities, and identify themselves as CBOs). NGOs are also seen as belonging to the larger category of "civil society," which is understood to include associations, unions, and also, interestingly, state institutions.

10. The South African feminist Sisonke Msimang wants to "ensure that feminism is not killed by its diluted sister—GAD [gender and development]" (2002, 13) but sees her professional work as valid and generative: "Many of us are feminists by profession and our 'experience' and analysis comes from having worked on projects that employ the terminology of Gender and Development" (2002, 12).

11. While living in Ghana, I too began to refer to "development" as an aspiration in this particular sense. This experience, as well as my larger ethnographic project, have taught me that we cannot assume that NGO workers uncritically accept development and neoliberal discourses, even if they use the same terminology.

Anna Tsing's articulation of "awkward engagements" captures well the gaps and frictions in global encounters: "Words mean something different across a divide even as people agree to speak" (2005, xi). Terminology can be resignified, these resignifications can also be co-opted, and working meanings are revealed only in lived practices and specific encounters.

12. Arundhati Roy writes: "NGOs give the impression that they are filling the vacuum created by a retreating state. And they are, but in a materially inconsequential way. Their real contribution is that they defuse political anger and dole out as aid or benevolence what people ought to have by right" (2004, 45).

13. The microcredit practices in northern Ghana are run by local NGOs and are neither predatory nor violent like those described by Lamia Karim (2011), which is not to say that they are successful or unproblematic.

14. See also Kay Warren's discussion of frameworks as "selective constructions, conveyed in fields of social relations that also define their significance" (1998, 178).

15. NPP is the New Patriotic Party, which ruled from 2000 to 2008; the National Democratic Congress (NDC) was then in opposition.

Lived Feminism(s) in Postcommunist Romania

Introduction

For more than fifteen years I have "done" and lived feminism in Romania: as the leader of a prestigious Romanian nongovernmental organization (NGO), AnA Society for Feminist Analyses;[1] as editor-in-chief of *AnaLize: Journal of Gender and Feminist Studies*;[2] as a professor of gender studies; and as a woman, wife, and mother in postcommunist Romania.

For years, on my personal post-its of "urgent things," AnA was a priority. For years, I socialized in various national and international contexts, making contacts for the organization, participating in the implementation of various projects, promoting the need for professional discourse on women's issues in Romania, and making the voice of the Romanian women's movement heard abroad. I grew up intellectually and evolved as a person, a leader, and a citizen, alongside Romanian postcommunist activism and academic feminism.

Over the years that I have spent practicing feminism in Romania, I have learned a long series of personal lessons about innocence and pragmatism, enthusiasm and bureaucracy, and successes and failures; about contradictions between theoretical and applied feminism; and about women, femininities, the women's movement, and Balkan and postcommunism transitions.

After practicing feminism in Romania on a daily basis for so long, I felt the need to critically review this period, to compare organizational theories with the concrete experiences of creating organizations and making them work, to understand my own feminism in comparison with that of others I have met during this journey, and to share my experiences.

This is how a book on the lived history of AnA was born (Grünberg 2008). It is a book about the private life of this NGO, officially registered in Romania in 1993, very active, visible, and connected to the civic movement of Romania until 2008. A private life should be, in my opinion, added to the public, official history of any NGO. What follows are some reflections and comments based on that book that I wrote and lived, presented in the form of contextualized storytelling and analysis.

AnA in Context

AnA was one of many NGOs created in Romania after 1989 that proved reliable at the national, regional, and international levels. It was committed to acting as a bridge between academics and the activist women's movement in Romania; to contributing to the professionalization of gender discourse and practice in Romanian NGOs; to developing and providing training and policy-oriented research on gender issues for different target groups; to developing and maintaining a multimedia resource center on women's and gender issues; to disseminating gender-sensitive information and data through various means, including the only feminist journal in Romania, *AnaLize: Journal of Gender and Feminist Studies*; and to getting involved in the national and international women's movement.

AnA has an official, solid curriculum vitae (CV): good projects designed and successfully implemented; a series of useful services offered (including consultancy, trainings, publications, and documentation facilities); international recognition; and important rewards. But just as important as the official CV is the unofficial one. For more than fifteen years, AnA was a school for learning democracy; a milieu for socializing, learning, and growing up; a space for friendships; an environment that allowed women to pursue their career ambitions and to stand out; and, especially, a context for women's solidarity, involvement, caring, and creativity. Unfortunately, due to financial constraints, AnA had to close its center in 2007; it is currently active mainly through the individual participation of its members in projects implemented by other organizations and institutions but has plans for a "come back."

Only a combined story of both the private and public lives of an NGO can offer a vivid image of that organization. Only a contextualized story—one that pays due attention to the various economic, political, social, national, or global contexts in which an NGO develops—can be an authentic account of its existence.

On a more general level, understanding feminism and the women's movement in Romania means, on the one hand, looking outward at the circumstances in which they both evolved after 1989. That means having an idea of pre- and post-1989 Romania in general and its civil society in particular. On the other hand, it suggests looking inside the movement at the process of institutionalizing gender equality in Romania after 1989 and to the people involved in the movement—mostly women, whose daily lives and personal biographies mixed with its daily existence.

I have been an activist in a particular postcommunist Eastern European context—Romania—that is known in general for the totalitarian regime imposed by Nicolae Ceaușescu and in particular for its "pronatalist policies." Forty years of communism and another twenty years of transition to capitalist society placed Romania in a profound economic, social, and moral crisis. Over the past decade, Romania has been experiencing a transition, a process of transformation that involved changing the economic, social, and political systems inherited from the communist era. Romanian society has undergone basic and complex processes of transition: from a closed society to an open one; from a nation in a military association (the Warsaw pact) to a nation without guaranteed external security (until November 2002, when it was invited to join the North Atlantic Treaty Organization); from an all-embracing state economy to a mixed economy; from a society with a single political party to a pluralistic one; from an isolated country to one included in the European Union (EU), since 2007; and others. In our post-1989 society, the market economy itself, European integration, the McDonald's-ization of cultural society, and feminism have all been experienced as major risks. Confronted with those risks, Romanians have proved to have, in Geert Hofstede's (1998) terminology, a strong uncertainty avoidance tendency (Interact, 2005).

I have been an activist in a country that, after 1989, also had to relearn the meaning and practice of civil society. First we had to delegitimize the collectivist, homogeneous discourse and start talking about individualization and human rights. The discourse and implicit practices of civil society somehow remained in the area of negative freedoms ("freedoms from"), to the detriment of positive ones ("freedoms to").

As the majority of studies of Romania indicate, even today the country has a weak network of associations, an underdeveloped NGO sector in comparison with other former communist countries, and only tenuous involvement in voluntary work (Voicu 2005). A study from 2006 shows that out of twenty-three million inhabitants, only 6 percent were members of an NGO and only 8 percent undertook any voluntary activities (FDSC, 2006). As the 2007 Euro barometer on discrimination shows, only 7 percent of European Union members believe NGOs have a role in combating discrimination (EC, 2007). Romania, an acceding country at this time, could not have been far from this tendency. The situation has improved lately but the citizen's confidence in public institutions and their involvement in such organizations is still low. In 2012, 34% of the Romanians declared a high level of confidence in NGOs, 79% considered that an NGO may influence decisions at local and regional level but only 20% were members of such an organization (half of them being union members) (FDSC, 2013).

Romanian society still has contradictory attitudes toward civil society. On the one hand, it idealizes NGOs: it expects too much from them, considers them to be a sort of panacea for the hidden diseases of our young democracy, or sees them as *the* promoters of democracy. As a consequence, NGOs end up being judged by idealistic standards that create a gap between expectations and performance. On the other hand, for all these years NGOs have been a kind of institutional minority that has been discriminated against. Companies looked at them with distrust, public institutions despised them, and the state in general treated them like commercial businesses. So if they are not idealized, then they are considered as possible black markets—sites for nearly illegal, or at least personal, affairs; a kind of comfortable refuge for people who are unwilling or unable to have a normal job. The fact that some politicians created and used some NGOs for their own political agendas and especially for their own pragmatic interests also deteriorated the public image of NGOs.

The nongovernmental movement in Romania had neither the time nor the favorable environment to become routine. If for other institutions coming out of totalitarianism, routine was a handicap, for us it would have been a sign of success. Romanian NGOs were running a race for which they did not have adequate breath, sports shoes, coaches, or psychological trainers. Nor did Romanian NGOs manage to finish that race or to rejoice in their small victories because the rules were immediately changed. In all those years they had no help settling down (finding a space, covering higher and higher expenses, finding competent management). The global economic crisis of the last period of time also negatively influenced the development and sustainability of the sector. The bureaucratic constrains of some of the national and international donors also discouraged creativity and the creation of new NGOs. As a result, an overabundance of sterile seminars, round-table discussions, conferences, and training courses appeared. Meanwhile, new government institutions were created in order to conform to the EU standards and demands, leaving the NGOs with even less support and without envisaging any sort of know-how transfer between existing NGOs and such new entities. Because of this atmosphere, many of the once-successful NGOs did not find their way and many others disappeared.

Financially dependent and manipulated, lacking an adequate environment and proper economic stimulus to support themselves (even though they created jobs and paid taxes to a state that did little for them), the Romanian activists adapted to the normative model imposed from abroad. They used eclectic, foreign, copied-and-pasted, often impossible-to-translate language, and they worked as hard as they could to represent a significant alternative public voice. But in the long run, they have not yet been able, in my opinion, to establish themselves in the country as a powerful, stable social partner. With few exceptions, they are marginal.

Feminism and Women's Movements in Postcommunist Romania

I developed myself professionally as a woman activist and gender expert in a country where the totalitarian period had interrupted a good interwar tradition of feminism. What followed after 1989 should be seen "not simply as a break with the past but also in part a continuation of it" (Gal and Kligman 2000b, 6). After that year, feminism and the women's movement reinvented themselves, not on the basis of the close or distant past, but with the help of a Western past. But this import had perverse effects, too.

Doing feminism in this period of postcommunist transition, and profound structural change was difficult. People were having a hard time absorbing changes that they perceived as happening too quickly; achieving stability in their lives was far from easy, so they were inclined to just rebuild what had existed. Feminism—as an effort to destabilize power relations between women and men, demand equal-opportunity policies, and institute a gender-friendly democracy—was perceived as dangerous or useless.

A lot has been written about the East-West partnership, essentially based on relationships of domination and the imposition of priorities, methods, and assessment criteria on the local democracies of former communist countries. Can the "others" really understand who we are and what we have been going through? Can we and the "others" (even if they are women like us) talk the same language and learn from each other's experiences? In 1995 I was part of the Romanian delegation at the Beijing World Conference on Women. On the opening day, in an immense stadium, an impressive ceremony involving thousands of beautiful Chinese children was performed for us. Surrounded by American women, I could clearly hear their enthusiasm and astonishment. For them it was just an extraordinary, incredible parade. For me, having experienced throughout my childhood weeks of stupid, military-like instruction in order to produce similar shows for Ceauşescu, it was an awful moment of remembrance. They were smiling; I was angry. How can any communication between two different worlds start from such a point?

This is just one example I bear in mind each time I read or hear about the West-East gaps or communication tensions. My personal memories could produce more examples like this. Immediately after the Romanian revolution, at the end of 1989, my foreign relatives sent me some packages of Pampers for my four-month-old son. Disposable diapers were new for me. I decided to keep them for later, for emergencies, and to continue to use cloth diapers that I washed with my mother. Later on, one Sunday, I decided to use the Pampers. I tried to put one on my son, but it was much too small for him. Reading the instructions more carefully, I saw that they fit only children under a certain weight. I should have used them as soon as they arrived, when my son was the right weight. I felt very "eastern" at that moment.

In a way, this is what happened when feminism was first imported from the West. It came with no clear instructions (for us) on how to use it. And we, being in a hurry to make up for the time we had lost, sometimes misused it or overreacted to it.

In a different research context (Grünberg 2000b) I pointed out the lack of clear objectives, the collectivist and centralizing tendencies, and the marginalization of the women's movement inside the Romanian civil movement. I noted tensions between activist and academic realms and between generations, as well as regional discrepancies. With time, some of the problems amplified, while others modified. Today for example instead of the gap between an activist women's movement and academic feminism, I would say that in Romania there is an academic women's activism, as the majority of those actively involved in NGOs are highly educated women. The marginalization of the women's movement is not so visible as before. Women's organizations are more inclusive now, collaborating more often with human rights groups or with NGOs dealing with Roma, sexual minorities or ecologist issues. Intersectionality as a strategic approach is present, gender being often treated (at least at the level of discourses) as a multidimensional category of analysis.

For a long period of time after 1989 women and women's problems have reentered public discourse, but in ways that do not always favor the emancipation policies that we hoped for. Women are often seen as victims (of violence, trafficking, poverty, and sexual harassment) and helpless (as single women, poor women, older women, or disabled women). They are represented as a marginal group that needs support, or as glamorous, sexy bodies that exist but do nothing significant with their heads. Governmental and nongovernmental institutions, along with the mass media, peddle those images to the exclusion of positive figures: women as agents and as involved, responsible, and competent social partners.

In 1989 the NGO activists in the women's movement entered an ideologically mined territory, full of stereotypes and unfavorable cultural clichés and stuffed with imported terms, concepts, strategies, and experiences—many of them lacking any significance in the space dominated by the clones of Master Manole and his sacrificial Ana.[3]

Mihaela Miroiu, a leader of academic feminism in Romania, argues that at that moment we failed to transfer our civic and academic feminism into a political feminism, and now we are practicing a sort of timid feminism, one that is marginal and camouflaged. Miroiu also talks about a "room-service feminism"[4] (2004) that was copied and pasted, suggesting that we are now witnessing a state feminism that lacks a solid foundation and financial resources, one that appears as mere window dressing for very European laws and policies (Miroiu 2006). Eniko Magyari-Vincze, another gender expert, argues that in postsocialist Romania,

> the public thinking on equal opportunities for women and men has been structured by two major mechanisms. On one hand, the idea of equality for women and men was delegitimized by a permanent appeal to communist memories and, on the other hand, equal-opportunity discourse was totally accepted as a requirement for entering the EU. Thus, two extreme positions—either rejection or unconditional acceptance—marked the institutionalization of gender issues in Romania. (2002, 7)

The integration of the country in the EU produced an interesting special category of people—the "opportunist nonsexists"—those accepting formally the gender equality discourses because this was the new trend, because being *mysogin* or sexist was no more socially desirable in the civilized communities of the EU countries. I would add the cultural perspective to this type of critical analysis. It is clear that simply importing, without adapting, successful models of gender equality from individualistic cultures to collectivist ones, from cultures oriented toward the future to cultures oriented toward their past[5], between cultures with different degrees of respect for the "written laws" (oral *vs.* written cultures) will not work, producing distortions and perverse effects.

We could say that immediately after 1989 in Romania there was a period of exaltation, of emotions, that attempted to make up for the past—for women and the women's movement in general (in the embryonic state it was in then). Our bodies had been politically and ideologically invaded,[6] and now we were happy that we could have as many abortions as we wanted, and where we wanted them. We had had enough (at least numerically speaking) women in positions of power, but the majority of them had been incompetent, selected for their obedience and their unattractive appearance.[7] So we refused this model and got involved with others in a way that had been unfamiliar to us: civil society. I remember the period of 1992–95 as one in which, apart from the suspicions among us due to a latent generational conflict, there was a special organizational unrest and idealistic approach that no longer exists today.

Later came a period of professionalization and latent accumulations. The women's movement initially rejected and then in various ways interpreted and internalized the Western discourse on women's issues, women's rights, gender, equal opportunities, feminism, and so forth. Romanian society also had assimilated (with and without the help of the women's movement) new cultural codes connected to other types of social partnerships, suggested by Western models. The activists started to speak a common language. Books and articles were written, feminism and gender studies began to be taught in schools, and gender experts appeared on the scene. But investing time in acquiring knowledge and know-how about gender issues meant a period of more reduced public visibility. Only recently this situation is slowly changing as a more self confident, playful, tech savvy, eager to show off feminism, involving the young generation of activists, could be noticed.

Since 1990 many things have happened all over Europe, including in Romania, in the area of feminism and the women's movement. Looking at the Romania of today through the lens of gender, one can easily see a series of initiatives to promote gender equality in Romania. The country's constitution, penal code, and laws concerning work have been revised; they now contain provisions for equal opportunities for women and men. Important gender-sensitive laws have been introduced (for example, a parental leave law; a domestic violence law; legal provisions for addressing sexual harassment; and, very important, an equal-opportunity law that contains, in addition to other aspects, a reference to the concept of multiple discrimination). In addition, new institutions and mechanisms to support equal opportunities for men and women have been created: the National Agency for Equal Opportunities, established in 2002 and responsible for elaborating national strategies in the area (it was transformed at a short period of time into a small department within the Ministry of Family and Social Protection); the National Council for Combating Discrimination; the Parliamentary Commissions for Equal Opportunities; and many women's NGOs, networks, and coalitions. It is also worth mentioning that important human resources have been created and mobilized particularly to help develop careers and jobs in the field of gender equality, hoping that the new market will absorb experts in this area. In 1998 the National School for Political and Administrative Studies in Bucharest started a master's program in gender studies in the Faculty of Political Sciences. Other major university centers (Cluj or Timişoara) have established similar programs. One of the major printing houses in Romania (Polirom) has, since 2000, published a special series in gender studies. Consequently, locally trained gender experts have produced a significant amount of national-focused studies and research together with various trainings in the area.[8]

From the perspective of academic feminism, development is obvious. From the perspective of Romanian feminist activism and its impact on society, the picture is different. Both quantitative and qualitative data show that in spite of the positive results, gender equality is still more of a desire than a reality. Data from the latest Gender Equality Index produced by the European Institute for Gender Equality situates Romania on the hindmost position among the 27 European countries in all areas investigated (work, money, knowledge, time, power, health) (EIGE, 2013). Various national data indicates also that there are still significant gender gaps in sectors such as employment, health, and education, and, maybe more important, a conservative cultural gender model still exists in society. According to different statistics, the average life expectancy of women in Romania is below that in Europe as a whole; women earn less money than men, and are victims of domestic violence and human trafficking, the balance between family life and career is just wishful thinking; less than 10 percent of the members of the Romanian Parliament are women. Furthermore, there are visible hierarchies and discrimination among women. Some groups of women (Roma women, elderly and rural women, single mothers, adolescents, and lesbians) face more problems than do other, more privileged women.[9]

Some Glimpses into the Lived History of a Women's NGO

Feminism in Romania coexisted uneasily with politics, inflation, corruption, preparing for and entering the European Union, the development of Internet communications, and individuals' changing life stories. In this Romania, this specific civil society, and the women's movement that I briefly described above, in this world AnA lived for more than fifteen years. So did I.

Everything started in 1992 as a game, in the pleasure of dialogue during nice evenings of reading and discussion, during a specific period of postcommunism disorientation, and because of some feminist literature that a very good friend of mine, Mihaela Miroiu, stumbled across during one of her trips to the West.

Passionate about the domain she had discovered—feminism—Mihaela gave me some books. She knew I had a degree in a field that I was not made for (mathematics), and that I would have preferred to study in another department (sociology), which had been closed because of totalitarian realities. Mihaela was working toward a doctoral degree in feminist philosophy, with my father as an adviser. She used to come by the house in the afternoons and argue with style on issues like whether women did or did not have an epistemic privilege; whether ecofeminist theories and radical feminist epistemologies are valid; and whether men can be empathetic to other beings, plants, and nature in general. I listened and got interested.

It's hard to say how we became official from there, but we formalized our chats under the name of "The Society for Feminist Analyses," or AnA. We chose the name for its various significations: for its visual symbolization of the classical A-nonA dichotomy, so critically discussed in feminism, and also for its reference to one of the fundamental myths of our culture that I have already mentioned: the legend of Master Manole, whose wife's name was Ana.

Then came twenty-one signatures officially requested for the list with "Founder members." (I can't remember today some of the people who signed it. Some of them were involved in the movement at that moment but some others were just friends, friends of friends, relatives who accepted to sign quickly "whatever" was needed). We hurriedly found out a copy of an NGO status, one among other few that were informally circulating around Bucharest (many NGOs established at that time had almost similar statuses. Nobody was paying much attention to the content of these documents. Only later on we realized the importance of each paragraph, as we needed to revise them). We quickly adapted the document to our specific types of activities, submitted a dossier and then received the official certificate from the Ministry of Culture. Then came our logo, flyers, a website, employees, reports, and the implementation of different programs focused on key words imposed by foreign financing bodies.

We learned activism by doing it. We started writing project proposals for various donors. At the beginning, our programs fit their sections on "women's rights." Then the word "gender" started appearing on the priority list. Then the magic phrase bringing potential financial support became "community development," followed by "sustainable development." After some time "social capital" appeared, and it became obvious that a women's program for women, with women, must be set up or at least formulated so that it could be assessed from the perspective of its impact on the development of social capital in Romania. Financial assistance was then redirected to the area of "community acquis implementation."[10] After that, doing projects for "Roma women" became popular; then "gender mainstreaming" became the ticket to funding. As I write now, women- or gender-focused programs are no longer so popular; now ecology programs are the chief beneficiaries of financial support. At this moment in the area of gender equality, Roma issues are still on the top of the agenda. Other key words and concepts imposed by the donor community would nowadays be "hate speech," "trafficking of women," "sexual minorities rights," "intersectionality of gender" or "gender as a transversal theme within projects."

On this perpetual shifting ground, AnA, like any other NGO, lived its life. First there was a period of infancy, full of credulity, naiveté, and childish mistakes. It was a time of pure enthusiasm that was not yet clouded over by pragmatism, but it was also a period when we were cheated and even robbed. For example, at one point we discovered that a university professor, a member of our organization, was collecting organization "fees" in our name from young students, promising them scholarships, and participation in international events. We expelled her from the organization. Another time our first accountant—a man—used and misused our funds, buying secondhand computers while claiming they were new, and stealing our stamp to use for his own purposes, thus creating major financial problems for all of us.

Then AnA grew up, became mature, settled down, found a "room of its own"—an apartment where the Multimedia Resource Center for Women was developed. Those were, formally, the glory days when we could boast of important projects, good results, a stable financial situation, the expansion of the organization, three to four full-time employees, and international visibility and rewards. It may seem paradoxical, but I consider this period a time of failure because bureaucracy somehow killed us step by step (Grünberg, 2003). Little by little, creativity was replaced with routine, enthusiasm with "coming to work" out of a sense of obligation, to meet deadlines, file reports, and fulfill other responsibilities. "Doing things" became "implementing activities," and showing results meant more stiffly worded reports and complicated financial justifications for each small acquisition, instead of keeping in touch with and being sensitive and empathetic to gendered realities. The core group never truly accepted the bureaucratization process. Because the majority of us had official bureaucratic jobs outside AnA, we could not bear to continue the same pattern at AnA. Explicitly and implicitly we constantly protested the bureaucratization of the organization, but unfortunately we found no alternative.

After a while, AnA became more virtual. Fewer meetings happened on the spot; face-to-face discussions were less common; and more decisions, even resignations, were made through e-mail. AnA became less about doing things together and more about networking with the national and international community in an intangible world often rich in information and financial resources. If and how clicktivism[11] helps and breeds social revolutions is a debatable issue. The virtual management of an NGO, virtual activism itself, and the gendered dimensions of online communications are complex issues beyond the scope of this essay. But in brief, online activism definitely means broader access, but it also implies a lack of corporal dialogue; it means that accessibility replaces profoundness and that people do communicate more but rarely meet (Breton 1995, 16). From AnA's point of view, human relations, not virtual relations, proved to be more vital for group social cohesion. In the virtual space, AnA got lost.

During this time, each of our projects had its own history beyond official evaluation reports and budgets. Each one was a complex mixture of enthusiasm, idealism, concrete objectives, schedules, and activities, as well as components of international agencies gender programmes and moments in our own biographies and in national and global economic, political, and social contexts.

In 1995 we launched a Phare[12] program called Toward a Nonsexist Education, which allowed us to, for the first time in Romania, analyze textbooks, talk to professors, and design training modules for nonsexist education. But when we wanted to continue it at the national level, we could not get any more funding because international donors were already moving from education to other key democratic topics. In 1998 we implemented the Together at Foişor Program for Community Development, which got our neighbors who lived in the same district in Bucharest involved with AnA. Although successful, the pilot project could not be further replicated because the "community development" theme, in two years, was no more a priority for donors. In 2006, we produced *Cartea neagră a egalității de şanse între femei şi bărbați în România* [Black book on equal opportunities between women and men in Romania]—a diagnosis of the state of affairs in the field in Romania (Borza, Grünberg, and Văcărescu 2006). Contrary to the general enthusiasm for the entering of the country in the EU (that happened in 2007) we were critical at that moment with respect to the creation, over night, of some governmental bodies only for fulfilling, on paper, certain European requirements, without consultations or using the already existing expertise in the area of gender equality. At first glance, there was sometimes a certain disconnect between what we were doing and the realities outside the organization. In the beginning of the 1990s, when Romania was confronted with strong internal political tensions, we were analyzing textbooks from a gender perspective. In 1995 my father died, and in 2004 a member of AnA had a cerebral stroke. We had to deal with these types of political and personal problems while also trying to manage deadlines and responsibilities at AnA. Love, divorce, studying for graduate degrees, pregnancies, menopause, and our children's school exams, along with an unstable political system, the 9/11 shock, and so forth formed the context in which projects were implemented—in concordance or dissonance with the rest of the world, out of step or in line with major events, and mixed with our own daily existence and problems.

Explicit and implicit, gender has been part of what made this organization, and in this sense, in the spirit of Joan Acker's definition of a gendered institution (Acker 1999), we can say that AnA was not only a feminine organization (with women in the majority or with a feminine attitude toward the instrumental and impersonal features of bureaucracy) but also a gendered one.

As an insider, it is hard for me to decide what exactly AnA was and still is. According to the *Romanian Official Gazette*, it is an NGO, which means, by law, "a private or public Romanian legal entity of public interest, nonpolitical, nonprofit, a legal person, not invested with state power, and not part of the public administration system" (1997, my translation). In conformity with our official statute, AnA is defined as "an autonomous scientific cultural society, nonpolitical, nonprofit, which gathers together philosophers, sociologists, psychologists, journalists, and students with interests and activities in promoting women and women studies in Romania." Experts would consider it a mediator of financial and human resources that helps cultivate citizenship and develop what Amitai Etzioni would call "democracy's muscles" (Etzioni, 2002, 15, my translation).

However, like any organization, AnA was a cognitive community that not only responded to certain social trends but had a special interest in generating knowledge and self-knowledge in a specific area. AnA was also a "space" in all of the three dimensions that Henri Lefevre (1991) identifies: a concrete physical space, a place of ideas and thoughts, and a lived space. For many years we had a place, an address where computers, books, telephones, files, employees, visitors, and so on could be found. With or without this place we had ideas, plans, concepts, and strategies on how to professionalize the discourse on women's issues in Romania, how to support a particular group of women, and how to make a difference in the area of gender equality in Romania. AnA was a concrete and abstract space for experiencing transition, democracy, and civil society. AnA meant Mihaela, Anca, Cecilia, Laura, Ioana, Florentina, and others—many women whose destinies crossed not because of duty but because of the pleasure of being together and having a common interest in a special type of social program that promoted gender equality in Romania.

AnA's story should be read in context and in a multidimensional frame of analysis in which individual, local, regional, and even global flavors mixed. AnA—like the transition to democracy itself—has been, at individual and collective levels, an educational project for its members and its beneficiaries. Inside AnA we learned the art of democratic association; we became not only spectators but players in the new political and social environment after 1989. Outside AnA the beneficiaries of our services were familiarized and confronted with issues linked to the gendered dimension of society and were encouraged to promote, in their private and public lives, the principles of equal opportunities for women and men in Romania.

At this moment, due to a lack of resources, we no longer have "a room of our own" or the minimal administrative staff to develop our departments and projects. Nevertheless, I could not say that AnA is dead. Beyond money, rooms, computers, files, an Internet connection, tables, and chairs, the spirit of AnA is still out there. The majority of its members are implicitly continuing the mission of the organization in other contexts. I still constantly receive e-mail messages from various members suggesting ways to continue to do something. Many of us are teaching gender studies, passing on our knowledge and experience. Under the umbrella of AnA, certain collaborations and partnerships are still taking place, especially within EU-funded projects, where gender expertise and sensitivity to issues of equal opportunities are a must in terms of evaluation criteria. This is an important lesson that I learned from AnA: death does not come easily for an NGO.

In the context of the women's movement in Romania, looking critically at AnA's destiny, which was also my destiny, I could present a fairly long "black list."[13] At the level of discourse on women and gender, there was and is still the perpetuation of unclear terminology and linguistic inconsistency; the usage of generalizations and overgeneralizations that lead to the erasing (within specific policies and programs, legislative initiatives, and so on) of the diversity between and within women's and men's groups; a copy-and-paste way of doing things; and quite often the use of an almost magical, alienated, specialized language or the development of a new wooden language within feminist discourse encouraged especially by the wooden language requested by donors.

From the perspective of the institutions created, there is a human, institutional, legislative, financial, and conceptual dilution and segmentation in the area of equal opportunities. There are some bureaucratic creations but little to no content or funds. Gender-sensitive politics exist on paper but are not written into the budget. There is a lack of continuity; there are good laws, but they are either not known or not applied! There is also a lack of accountability in the field of equal opportunities for women and men. And finally, there are still many more monologues (across institutions, inside institutions, and by both women and men) than dialogues.

At the level of women's NGOs, one may see that the field of study and research on gender issues is tolerated but not exactly recognized by the academic community in Romania. Gender knowledge is part of a separated, somehow marginalized curriculum (gender studies programs) but hardly mainstreamed in other disciplines (see Văcărescu 2011). There is a "brain drain" instead of a "brain gain" at the level of local feminism. Male involvement is low, due either to the marginalization of men in the women's movement or to cultural stereotypes of gender-sensitive men, especially those who declare themselves feminists. There is also an underdeveloped collaboration and cooperation culture among the feminist NGOs and women's organizations, and there are fewer and fewer women's NGOs each year. To top it off, as I already mentioned before, there is less of a grassroots women's movement and more of an academic activist movement.

The list could go on. The lack of powerful or trustworthy female role models (in school manuals, newspapers, politics—Romania has never had a female president!) is another deterrent to the development of a solid women's movement and the gender-equal representation in politics. What is probably needed at this moment, at least in Romania, for the successful institutionalization of gender equality is exactly what is happening: the emergence of a new generation of young feminists able and willing to propose an all-inclusive type of feminism, one that includes more than it excludes without diluting its objectives.[14] The much-debated intersectional approach to gender should be put into practice. Gender issues at the theoretical and practical level should include age, ethnicity, sexual orientation, living standard, and so on. By taking this approach on a larger scale, we will better understand not only the general problems of women (and men) but also the problems that are specific only to some of them. In this way what we will know will not necessarily be better but it will for sure be more.

It's likely that some or many of the above-mentioned dissatisfactions are pertinent outside the Romanian context, too, because the country is not an isolated island in Europe or the world. My black list shows in fact that the women's movement and feminism in Romania are searching for a path, struggling with the endless chaos of transition, the lack of trust in the role of civil society, the global economic crisis, the normal human attempt to avoid any major cognitive discomfort (and feminism may provoke that!), and the demands of daily existence on each woman (and man) in our local and global economic crisis.

For more than fifteen years I have done and lived feminisms in Romania. In my opinion, a lived history is more instructive than a purely theo-retical, historical approach. We learn more easily from what we live and from the mistakes we make than we do from the abstract theories and good practices presented by others. I read and learned about civil society from Aristotle, Kant, Hegel, Rousseau, Habermas, Rawls, Arendt, and Tocqueville, but, with all due respect, I learned even more from doing, giving birth, mothering, and even burying AnA.

What I learned from this experience of life called AnA is that change happens no matter what, but that you can push it in the right direction by doing something instead of just endlessly criticizing what is happening.

Notes

1. For the rest of the article I will refer to it as AnA. See www.anasaf.ro.
2. www.analize-journal.ro
3. The legend of Master Manole says that he was hired to build the most beautiful monastery in the country. But everything he built each day crumbled the follow-ing night, until he had a dream in which he was told that in order to succeed, he had to wall in someone he loved very much. The next day he immured his wife Ana in the walls of the church.
4. She defines "room-service feminism" as the imposition of gender-sensitive legis-lation in Central and Eastern Europe through the authority of international po-litical actors, including European ones, before the internal public recognition of a need for such legislation.
5. I refer here to the well-known Hofstede (2001) typology.
6. *Four Weeks, Three Months, and Two Days* (Mungiu, Cristian, 2007), the Roma-nian movie that won the Palme d'Or at the Cannes Festival in 2007.
7. One unspoken criterion for promotion during those times was to be unattractive, if possible uglier than Elena Ceaușescu, the powerful wife of the president who was known for her lack of education and culture, for interfering in the decisions of her husband, and for disliking any kind of feminine competition.
8. For details about the Polirom series, see www.polirom.ro, Colecția Studii de gen (gender studies series) and the recently created database http://www.fragen.nu /aletta/fragen (database with digitized feminist texts from 27 EU countries and Turkey).
9. In 2007 AnA, in collaboration with the National Institute for Scientific Research in the field of Labour and Social Protection, (AnA/INCSMPS, 2008) produced the *Multiple Discrimination in Romania National Report.*
10. Community acquis or *acquis communautaire*, sometimes called the EU acquis, is the accumulated legislation, legal acts, court decisions that constitute the body of EU law.
11. Term introduced by the journalist Micah White in 2010 in an article in the *Guardian.*

12. Phare is one of the major programs financed by the European Union to assist countries in Central and Eastern Europe as they prepare to join the European Union.

13. For an extensive discussion of the positives and negatives in the area of institutionalizing gender in Romania, see Borza, Grünberg, and Văcărescu (2006). The full "black list" can be found in English on www.anasaf.ro. Extracts and comments are also published in (Grünberg, 2009).

14. There are some good signs of a revival. I mention only the Filia Center-www.centrulfilia.ro; FRONT Association; Feminism in Romania-www.feminism-romania.ro, Association for Liberty and Gender Equality-ALEG-www.aleg-romania.eu, and other powerful feminist web platforms or blogs, such as Meduza-blogul-medusei.blogspot.ro.

CHAPTER 10

Sabine Lang

Women's Advocacy Networks

The European Union, Women's NGOs, and the Velvet Triangle

Introduction

The European Union (EU) is considered to be one of the more gender-friendly governance bodies of the early twenty-first century. With the Amsterdam Treaty of 1999, gender equality policy was established as a mainstreaming strategy to be included in all EU decision making (Vleuten 2007; Kantola 2010; Abels and Mushaben 2011). Equality directives for labor markets and work-life balance, inclusion of gender-equality norms in accession negotiations with new member states, and the recent establishment of the European Institute for Gender Equality in Vilnius speak to some success in putting gender on the EU agenda. Yet these measures have not been conceived strictly within the confines of the European Commission or Parliament. Instead, they can be attributed to women's advocacy networks, in which different constellations of feminist actors from inside and outside EU institutions joined forces to achieve policy goals. Developing a theoretical understanding of these advocacy networks has become one of the challenges of recent feminist research (Zippel 2006; Roth 2007; Montoya 2008; Lang 2009a and 2009b; Ahrens 2011). Earlier studies focused on classifying the types of actors involved in these networks. Alison Woodward has coined the concept of the "velvet triangle," in which EU-level femocrats, feminist academics, and experts, as well as women's movement activists, collaborate (2004; see also Locher 2007). Use of the term "velvet triangle" highlights routinized communication and interaction among institutional and civil society actors in the European gender arena. It provides frequent formal and informal contexts for discussion, for developing strategic alliances, and ultimately for more inclusive decision making. In contrast to Theodore Lowi's notion of an "iron triangle" (1979), in which politicians, bureaucrats, and interest groups monopolize political power behind closed doors, the term "velvet triangle" suggests a more fluid, less rigidly shielded exercise of power among feminist institutional and non-institutional political actors. One important aspect of this fluidity is biographical: members of velvet triangles often share parts of their professional biographies. They might have moved from movement activism into academia and then into the EU bureaucracy, or they might join the board of a women's nongovernmental organization (NGO) after serving in the EU Directorate for Employment, Social Affairs, and Inclusion. They tend to be critical of closed corporatist political processes and prefer instead to work in networks of trusted relationships that allow them to develop pragmatic alliances across institutional affiliations and positional power. The strength of the "velvet triangle" concept was that it—quite early in the EU policy network debate—identified the win-win relationship in the "patterned dance of needy bureaucrats, dedicated activists and eager academics" (A. Woodward 2004, 76). Bureaucrats gain access to academic and NGO expertise and can feel the pulse of their imagined constituencies. Activists acquire material and insider procedural knowledge and thus might gain more institutional leverage. And academics profit from interactions in which their academic work is being valued, which makes them part of an applied research process and allows them to acquire insider knowledge.

The "velvet triangle" concept has been pathbreaking in mapping the exchange-based relationships between different actors in EU policy making; yet it has also been challenged. The triangulation frame has been criticized as too static and limiting for policy network analysis. Some argue for an expansion of the existing policy triad of bureaucrats, movement actors, and academics to include other actors such as the media (Godemont and Motmans 2006) and professionalized gender consultancy firms. Others challenge the stability that the velvet triangle suggests and insist that women's policy networks are spatially and temporally unbounded, leading in effect to much broader—and thus more unruly—network concepts such as "women's cooperative constellations" (Holli 2008, 169) or "women's fields of advocacy" (Bereni 2011, 1). Still others sharpen the distinction between actors who participate in formal or informal policy networks (Ahrens 2011), highlighting the difference between official and regularized forms of interaction and loose, unofficial, and irregular networking occasions among women's equality actors in the European Union. Finally, research points to the power asymmetries in these networks and their effects on policy (Montoya 2008).

This is not the place to fully explore different iterations or alterations of the "velvet triangle" concept. Instead, the argument here focuses on one set of players that remains a constant in all documented shapes of women's advocacy networks: the coalitions of women's NGOs that tend to represent women's movements in the early twenty-first century. Although feminist research in recent years has emphasized the collaborative structure of successful networks (McBride Stetson and Mazur 2008) and the central role of insider-outsider coalitions in pursuing an equality agenda (Banaszak, Beckwith, and Rucht 2010), what has remained underexplored is the organizational form and the ties that bind its actors. Organizational structure influences rules, norms, behavior, and ultimately collective action. This essay examines the connection between the organizational form and scope of action of NGOized women's advocacy networks in the European Union.

I argue that the political opportunity structure of EU governance tends to give an advantage to specific formalized kinds of women's movement actors: those formally organized as NGOs. I have called this earlier an NGOized movement structure (Lang 1997; see also Lang 2013). This is not a normative claim but an empirical observation, and it should not be understood as proclaiming the selling out of a feminist agenda. It points to the fact that while EU institutions provide formal and informal venues for women's advocacy networks, they also shape actors and their choice of actions. In particular, operating within a specific network creates opportunities for some modes of advocacy while sidelining others. In the case of the European Union, I argue, one of the main filters of advocacy concerns the kinds of public engagement options available to women's advocacy networks.

The argument proceeds in three steps. First, I submit that the NGOization of European women's movements has altered the movements' form, mission, and means of engagement. This point critically engages with voices that take these changes merely as indicating a period of "abeyance," in which movements "sustain themselves in non-receptive political environments" (Taylor 1989, 761; see also Valiente 2009). Instead, I show that the European Union during the past decade has indeed presented quite a receptive environment for gender agendas. Therefore, the women's movement's lack of visibility in public affairs across Europe cannot be attributed to the need for a period of abeyance. Instead, I point to some more principled and long-term consequences of changes in form, mission, and strategies of women's activism in relation to supranational governance. Second, I argue that nonprofit legal stipulations as well as the political economy of women's NGOs fuel preferences for institutional advocacy as well as for topics and engagement venues prefigured by the goals of the European Commission. In effect, legal and economic challenges serve as barriers against effective public engagement by channeling the energy of movement activists toward institutional advocacy. Third, I engage with Sonia Alvarez's argument that some women's movements have moved "beyond NGOization" (see Alvarez's chapter in this volume) in order to reinvigorate their political presence and increase their public outreach. I submit that for European women's movements in 2011, such efforts were few and far apart, yet they indicate resistance among some women's movement actors against joining the mainstreamed paths of influence in the Brussels beltway.

The European Union, Civil Society, and the Nongovernmental Sector

The European Union, like most states and other transnational governance bodies, is a relative newcomer to the processes of interacting with civil society and European publics. As recently as a decade ago, the European integration literature as well as EU practitioners did not even refer very often to civil society (Smismans 2006, 4). Yet willingness to incorporate consultation processes with civic actors into the EU governance structure has increased in recent years (Warleigh 2003). Some attribute this openness to the "advocacy void" created by weak European political parties (Aspinwall 1998, 197). Others highlight the necessity to convince rather than regulate since in the past decade, much EU policy making has shifted from strict regulations to soft norms, from so-called hard law to soft law (Locher 2007). Soft law relies on discursive means of communication and on forming alliances that promote and disseminate EU intentions within member states, regions, and localities. Who would be better equipped to perform such tasks than civil society actors who draw legitimacy from having close ties to grassroots constituencies? It is "precisely the promotion of such informal practices and norms" in which civic actors are "most influential" (Checkel 1999, 554). NGOs are seen as key transmitters of soft law into society.

The European Union has come to rely on NGOs for communication with civil society in two ways: First, NGOs are perceived to be transmitters of institutional norms; they carry EU policy into the arenas of civil society where they operate. Second, they are seen as aggregates of citizens' voices and serve as a proxy for the European public (Lang 2009a and 2009b). This dual dimension of EU–civil society relations has been acknowledged in the European Commission's *The Commission and Non-Governmental Organizations: Building a Stronger Partnership* (2000). Cooperation between EU institutions and the nongovernmental sector is encouraged in order to foster a "more participatory democracy both within the European Union and beyond" (ibid., 4). NGOs are perceived as ideal partners because they are able "to reach the poorest and most disadvantaged and to provide a voice for those not sufficiently heard through other channels" (ibid., 5). By stimulating the formation of European NGO networks, the European Commission intends to foster the formation of a European public opinion (ibid., 5). Hence, NGOs and their networks are perceived to be prima facie expressions of civil society and key players in an emerging European public sphere (ibid.).

However, it is not clear whether European NGOs can live up to these wide-ranging expectations. Neither of these claims takes into account the specific and often complicated situatedness of NGOs between grassroots involvement and transnational action, between highly professionalized expertise and community outreach, and between insider status and outsider voice. Women's NGOs face these challenges in more pronounced ways than NGOs in other EU policy sectors. They operate with fewer resources than advocacy organizations in most other fields; they work in intersectionally complex policy environments; and they are confronted with increasing gender fatigue by politicians, bureaucrats, and European societies at large (Foundation Women in Europe 2010).

Women's NGOs in the European Union

There are at least four obvious ways in which women's NGOs engage with the European Union. Some get directly funded through various EU programs. Some are linked via national representatives to a transnational women's network such as the European Women's Lobby.[1] Some are part of policy networks that want to influence EU policy. Some shape national policy by using EU-level governance arenas, thus creating the boomerang (Keck and Sikkink 1998) or ping-pong (Zippel 2006) effect that fuels transnational advocacy. A common denominator of all four relationships is that they reward institutional communication skills and consultation and prefer organized to loosely networked activists. Women's NGOs cannot apply for EU funds if they are not incorporated legally as charitable organizations. If they seek to influence policy, they are increasingly being asked to prove the representativeness of their claims. Thus, in contrast to second-wave feminist movements' promotion of an antibureaucratic form that valued "informality, spontaneity, low degrees of horizontal and vertical differentiation" (Offe 1987, 73), EU governance attracts actors who have established organization, formal processes, and division of labor between horizontal and vertical units. Formally organized public interest representation within the European Union relies overwhelmingly on confederated structures, meaning associations of associations that generally do not even admit individuals as members. But even in less formal contexts, women's activists gain recognition primarily by exhibiting expertise and institutional communication skills rather than principled normative positions and public advocacy skills (J. Greenwood 2007). Movement actors turned NGOs are endowed with a specific set of insights and perspectives related to what Birgit Locher calls "testimonial knowledge" (2007, 91). Feminist NGOs are generally credited with providing institutional actors with the perspective of authentic experiences that are drawn from their base in grassroots movements and local organizations (Keck and Sikkink 1998, 19–20).

Women's NGOs have altered their formal and informal structures not just in order to adapt to EU governance. Yet whereas the NGOization process from the late 1980s up to the mid-1990s was primarily provoked by a mix of personal-biographical, economic, and national political stimuli (Lang 1997 and 2013), the political opportunity structure of the European Union added considerable impetus to pursue vertical integration, organizational transparency, institutional competence, and financial accountability.[2] These trends have been also significant in Central and Eastern European countries, where much of the women's movement's civic infrastructures in the 1990s developed during the period when national governments prepared their applications for joining the European Union. Bozena Choluj (2003) has argued that in Poland, about 300 women's groups—most of which were created in the 1990s—were ignored by state actors until EU accession negotiations demanded the creation of a national council of women's organizations as an advisory body for gender matters in the negotiations. Moreover, the greater access to EU funds after 2000 strengthened the position and political agency of Polish women's NGOs, solidifying their institutional structures, and opening up possibilities for transnational cooperation (Regulska and Grabowska 2008). At the same time, access to EU funding contained its own set of limitations, favoring large and well-organized women's NGOs over smaller groups without matching funds and limited grant writing skills and capacities (Roth 2007, 473; see also Graff 2009). In effect, Silke Roth (2007) claims that about 90 percent of smaller Central and Eastern European women's groups did not have access to EU funds, thus producing new lines of exclusion among women's movement actors.[3] As a result, local and regional movements' visibility has shrunk across Europe. Among feminist academics and movement actors, this has been fueling renewed debates about the consequences of European governance for women's movement building and politicization strategies (Fodor 2006; Outshoorn and Kantola 2007; Squires 2007), the central question being whether the specific form of inclusion of women's advocacy in the European Union does not in fact contribute to downsizing the scope and fervor of feminist activism.

Marian Sawer and Sarah Maddison (2009) have argued that the present global restructuring of the women's movement is an indicator of abeyance rather than of substantial and enduring shifts in mobilization capacity. The concept of abeyance goes back to Verta Taylor's analysis of the US women's movements between the 1920s and the 1960s, in which she recommends a less natalistic approach ("movements are born and they die" [1989, 761]) to movement research. Abeyance refers to a period in between other periods of strong movement visibility. It represents a time when a movement contracts but still provides "continuity from one stage of mobilization to another" (Taylor 1989, 761). In abeyance periods, social movement activity is generally low. It can either be carried on by surviving organizations (Taylor 1989) or, as Celia Valiente (2009) has shown for Spain under Franco, by new organizations or individuals with a formerly low feminist profile. Thus, one could potentially interpret the predominance of institutional modes of EU advocacy by women's NGOs as an indicator of an abeyance period for movement building and public advocacy.

I am not convinced that the NGOized European women's movement is in abeyance. Instead, my argument highlights the degree to which Europen women's movements actually adapted their form to become partners in European governance. Moreover, there is no earlier period of mobilization among European women that abeyance could have interrupted. Even though European women's groups engaged in international cooperation as early as the nineteenth century, organizing in Brussels within an integrated economic and increasingly interdependent political space poses a new and untested challenge to women's activism. It calls for activism that addresses existing cleavages and fosters new transnational and transversal solidarities. Hence, it calls for new mobilization repertoires that cannot rely on activating past iterations of mobilizations. Evidence of the struggle with crafting such new transnational and transversal mobilization repertoires is omnipresent in the current EU economic crisis. While women in Greece and Spain have taken to the streets to protest the gendered effects of austerity policies, feminist publics in Northern member states appear subdued and ill equipped to give voice to the critical juncture that the gender equality agenda in the EU currently faces.

Developing "citizen practice" (Wiener 1998) in the European Union demands establishing a refined set of skills and adapting to the highly scripted openings that the EU governance structure creates. At this time, there is much evidence that it systematically produces disincentives to public advocacy while establishing preferences for institutionalized action (Lang 2013). In addition, today's women's advocacy networks operate with a completely new communication repertoire, whereas abeyance indicates a lull between two relatively similar protest cultures. The US women's movement in the 1920s and in the 1960s used similar repertoires: street protests and boycotts, consciousness-raising and solidarity groups, and acts of civil disobedience. The later movement could reactivate traditions and practices that seemed time-tested and effective, while adapting them to its own political and social contexts. Today, any smooth adaptation of older movement repertoires seems questionable, as technology has radically altered mobilization (Bennett and Iyengar 2008). European engagement patterns are increasingly defined by the Internet and social media (Bennett, Lang, and Segerberg 2013), relying less on common organizational backgrounds and more on spontaneous and fluid forms of web-mediated action. The highly professionalized advocacy that European institutions endorse clashes with this new repertoire and its user networks. EU institutions demand fast and structured input that is aligned with pre-set agendas, and in general they favor the expertise of large advocacy organizations over input from diverse and loose alliances. Margot Wallstrom, a former commissioner for institutional relations and communication strategy and a staunch advocate of bringing more nonorganized women's voices into EU civil dialogue, has seen her agenda sidelined since she left office. In sum, NGOized European women's movements operate under governance conditions that tend to discourage public voice. Economic and legal constraints compound the problem.

Economic and Legal Constraints of Women's NGOs

Women's NGOs rely on organizational continuity, and continuity in turn depends on sustainable legal and economic frameworks. Gender activists form an NGO because they assume that legal incorporation will give their concerns public recognition and legitimacy, that private donors as well as governments will treat the organization as a professional entity, and that its status as a charity will enhance their ability to raise funds. Yet both the economic and legal implications of NGOization pose challenges for movement actors.

Even though gender equality has been identified as key to democratic participation and economic sustainability, women's NGOs in the European Union and worldwide still operate at the periphery of the international donor community. A report issued by the Association for Women's Rights in Development (AWID) explores the difference in finances between well-established, large, international NGOs and women's NGOs with a telling example: "In 2005, World Vision International, the world's largest Christian international development organization, and one with no mandate to support emergency contraception and abortion, had an income of almost USD 2 billion. In that same year, 729 of the leading women's rights organizations worldwide had a collective income of a paltry USD 76 million, not even 4 percent of World Vision's budget" (Kerr 2007, 20). And whereas women's NGOs in the global North somewhat improved their funding situation early in the new millennium as compared to the 1990s,[4] women's organizations in the Middle East, North Africa, Latin America, the Caribbean, and Central and Eastern Europe had more difficulty raising funds between 2000 and 2005 than in previous years (AWID/Kerr 2007, 15).

The European Union is the largest donor agency in Europe. It defines its financial situation in framework programs that span several years. From 2001 to 2005, the European Union financed the Fifth Community Action Program for the implementation of gender equality with a total of fifty million Euros. The main objectives of this framework strategy on gender equality were to raise awareness, to improve analysis and evaluation, and to develop the "capacity for players to promote gender equality" (European Commission 2001, 2). Yet it would be far from the truth to envision the bulk of these funds as going to women's NGOs. As a matter of fact, actors who have access to these program funds are explicitly mentioned in the initiative, and NGOs are fifth in a list of institutional actors that begins with: (1) member states (meaning the governments of member states); (2) local and regional authorities; (3) bodies promoting gender equality; and (4) social partners (European Commission 2001, 6).[5] The final report on the fifth framework states that in the category of "raising awareness," only 7 percent of these funds went to NGOs; in the category of "transnational cooperation," only 25 percent of the funds did (European Commission 2008). The majority of funds for raising awareness about gender were made available to government actors (30 percent) and social partners, such as business associations and large welfare associations (22 percent).

This indicates that the European women's nongovernmental sector received a very small portion of the funding of the central EU program on gender equality. In this area, funding of established political and social institutions trumps funding for women's NGOs. In effect, specific project missions are defined and structured to a large degree by government actors, and if NGOs participate, they often must do so under predefined conditions that were set by institutional politics. The primacy of institutional funding sets agendas and employs frames that women's NGOs need to adapt to.

This bias toward institutional funding continued in the next program period, called Progress, which lasted from 2007 to 2012. Progress reserved a total of 433 billion Euros to spend on sustainable development goals and projects, including research programs, education, and social and labor market policy initiatives. Within these parameters, Progress merged several key programs of the social agenda of the European Union for the purposes of synergy effects and mainstreaming gender equality. The part of Progress that explicitly funds activities related to gender equality received about the same amount of funds as those activities had been given in the Fifth Community Action Program, and the program design as well as the kinds of activities it promoted continued to cater to institutional actors such as governments, universities, and unions (Progress 2007).

Not only specifically gender-oriented EU funds are awarded with an institutional bias. The funding situation for women's NGOs in other EU policy domains exposes similar pulls. In 2007, for example, the largest women's fund in Europe, the Netherlands-based Mama Cash, called for signatures to petition the European Commissioner for Development and Humanitarian Aid, demanding an increase in support by the European Commission for women's projects (Mama Cash 2007). At the time, according to Mama Cash, the European Union was spending just 0.04 percent of its aid funds for women's projects (ibid.). In the same spirit, the report issued by AWID recommended that European women's projects pay more attention to their funding situation and "join forces to lobby for inclusion of women's rights in the development budget lines at country level and in the European Commission" (Kerr 2007, 77). Overall, AWID found the advocacy of European women's NGOs to be too focused on policy issues while the groups disregarded budget matters (ibid.). Moreover, the kind of policy issues addressed seem to be set by the institutional agenda of the European Union, which prioritizes trafficking and labor market issues. These are the policy issues that receive the most funds; it is much more difficult to get financial support for women's organizing or for controversial policies like sex workers' rights (Kerr 2007, 36). The AWID report substantiates the finding above that the European Union prioritizes larger women's NGOs, noting that "it is easier for them [the European Union] to administer fewer big grants" and that "proposals to the EU are extremely onerous and therefore cut out most women's rights groups" (ibid., 36). Thus, European women's NGOs must be professionalized if they are to receive funds from the European Union. They compete with established actors from unions, business associations, and the field of women's policy. Very few women's NGOs have the resources and means to match those of these solidly funded institutions.

This already difficult financial situation for European women's NGOs becomes even more precarious during times of economic crisis. AWID found that over half of the NGOs it surveyed received less funding in 2005 than in 2000 (Kerr 2007, 17). Across Europe as well as North America, roughly two-thirds of surveyed women's NGOs found fund-raising to be much harder in 2005 than in 2000 (AWID and Kerr 2007, 24). More than half of these NGOs increased their staff and resources for fund-raising in the past five years (AWID and Kerr 2007, 25). During the global economic crisis, it is likely that this downward trend will persist. In sum, economic constraints produce donor-friendly agendas and encourage professionalized, nonagonistic behavior among women's NGOs. Public advocacy and politicization take a back seat and are counterproductive if economic survival is paramount.

Defining the Political

Besides economic constraints, women's NGOs in the European Union face a set of legal restrictions that—even though not specific to women's organizations—affect their role as movement actors engaging in public advocacy.[6] Women's movement actors will argue that both advocacy and politicization of gender issues are necessary, and that both lobbying and public engagement are ultimately essential for lasting policy success. Advocacy and politicization are twins in their orientation toward mobilization. Whereas advocacy means acting on behalf of someone or something, politicizing points to two interrelated, but different dimensions of inclusion. First, it implies raising political awareness or involvement and thereby the salience of issues—that is its participatory dimension. Second, it refers to the agonistic dimension of the political process, indicating conflict and debate (Mouffe 2005). NGOized women's movements across Europe struggle with both dimensions of politicization: with a lack of salience of gender issues that go beyond the EU-sanctioned labor market focus and correspondingly a lack of involvement of EU citizens in the overall inequality agenda; and with a lack of agonistic public debate about what gender equality in Europe means in the first place. Not being able to politicize gender equality on a larger scale has its roots in a number of realms, such as the media and political parties—both of which are still dominated by men. But it is also the result of the legal restrictions on NGOs' political activity.

NGOs receive a charitable tax status through national tax laws or not-for-profit laws. In the European Union, there is no overarching legal structure in place. The tax status of the charitable sector falls in the purview of each member state. Of specific interest to NGOized movement actors' mobilization repertoire is the definition of what constitutes acceptable activities, which generally involves both adherence to constitutional principles and the exclusion of political activities.

Adherence to constitutional principles means accepting not just a normative order, but also specific behaviors. In Germany, for example, a 1984 ruling by the Federal Finance Court established that an NGO could have its charity status revoked if it publicly announced nonviolent resistance in public spaces or refused to comply with policy orders during a demonstration.[7] All EU member states have laws that prevent NGOs from engaging in political activities if they want to keep their charitable status. Yet what constitutes a political activity is defined differently from country to country. The common denominator is that support for political parties is not allowed. Beyond that, Hungary prohibits involvement in all direct political activities, without specifying what is deemed political, whereas Latvia restricts only political activities that "are directed to the support of political organizations (parties)" (Moore, Hadzi-Miceva, and Bullain 2008, 12). All across Europe, the legal definitions of "political activity" are hazy. German law stipulates that an occasional attempt to influence public opinion is acceptable for a charity, but involvement in "daily politics" is not.

In effect, even though most countries' charity laws allow a certain degree of political activity, it is the unclear margins combined with severe repercussions for transgressions that make public mobilization a potentially hazardous activity for NGOs. Research on the nonprofit sector has shown that these restrictions on political activity tend to promote a culture of extreme self-censorship and ultimately limit the capacity of NGOs to advocate for social change and engage publicly with public policy (Berry and Aarons 2003). The hazy definitions of acceptable speech and action pose problems for women's NGOs interested in more than merely representing issues within governance contexts.

In some European countries, NGO status is causing debate. At the forefront of a movement to alter political restrictions on NGO activity is the United Kingdom, where the discrepancy between the encouragement of democratic participation by community organizations and the restrictions on their public voice is attracting much criticism. The traditional focus in the United Kingdom, as across Europe, has been to encourage "volunteering or grassroots community work rather than 'upward' activism through . . . forms of advocacy" (Dunn 2008, 53). English legislation on charities before the 2006 Charities Act defined activities of public benefit. Political aims clearly do not fall within this list. Political activities, according to the Charities Act, are "broadly defined and will cover any activity or purpose which furthers the interests of a political party or cause or which seeks to change the laws, policies, or decisions of UK or other governments" (quoted in Dunn 2008, 54). Again, the Charities Act leaves some territory undefined: consultative functions could be seen as nonpolitical activities. But, as noted above, vague language on what constitutes political action tends to lead NGOs to tread very cautiously around political issues in public. Moreover, it disproportionately tends to affect smaller NGOs that have fewer resources to withstand possible legal tax challenges (Dunn 2008; Berry and Aarons 2003; Lang 2009a, 2009b and 2013).

In 2007 a Government Advisory Group on campaigning and the voluntary sector was formed in the United Kingdom. It issued a report in which it called for "clarification of the law and for an opening up of the legal rules to allow all political activities save support of political parties" (quoted in Dunn 2008, 57). The report highlighted the relationship between engagement of the public and liberalized rules for political advocacy of NGOs. It concluded that the mission of the law should not be to protect the public from political activity by NGOs—in contrast, "the law should encourage the public to participate in democratic processes through such organizations" (ibid.). In new guidelines for the existing law issued in March 2008, the UK Charities Commission supported the Advisory Group's recommendations. It is noteworthy that no change was made in the overall legal framework for NGOs. Only the guidelines for interpreting what constitutes acceptable political activity in the United Kingdom have been clarified, thus allowing the NGO sector to speak with a stronger voice in public. To my knowledge, no other European country has followed suit so far.

Women's NGOs and Public Engagement

The European Union offers large and professionalized women's NGOs and their networks more participatory venues than most national governments do. Women's advocacy coalitions are involved in a substantial number of policy debates; NGOs are invited to participate because they are experts and are seen as representatives of wider EU civil society. This process is giving women's advocacy networks considerable clout. Yet one consequence of the focus on institutional advocacy is that policy success can be achieved to a large degree without public participation. As several case studies of gender policy campaigns have shown, they did not depend on public involvement or public voice. Analyses of successful European women's campaigns, such as Kathrin Zippel's (2006) study of the campaign to include sexual harassment in the 2002 Equal Treatment Directive and Barbara Helfferich's and Felix Kolb's (2001) research on the introduction of gender mainstreaming in the Amsterdam Treaty, present evidence of institutional NGO activism producing gender-sensitive outcomes. Neither of these cases included strong public advocacy campaigns. The lesson for gender activists in Europe could thus simply be that mobilizing gender for European women's NGOs means developing the expertise and insider knowledge to gain access to and remain included in formal and informal contexts of institutional EU advocacy.

I have documented elsewhere that major European-based women's networks devote most of their time and energy to staying on top of policy developments, consulting with fellow stakeholders in the area of women's issues, and carrying their demands to the institutions of the European Union (Lang 2009b and 2013). Their capacity for public outreach, in contrast, is limited. In an analysis of five major European women's networks between 2006 and 2007, I established that they provided relatively few opportunities for interested citizens to interact with them through online means. The data I collected pointed to the dominance of informational over activating web content in all of the networks. Whereas most of them offered information about how to subscribe to newsletters, become a member, and make a donation, they very rarely gave voice to members and interested parties through such means as blogs and discussion forums. Comparatively low-cost means of public outreach remained thus underused (Lang 2009b). Within the scope of institutional advocacy, being able to activate large constituencies does not seem to be very important.[8] Instead, network identity was constructed on the basis of being gender experts and of providing information platforms. A newsletter analysis of the same set of EU-based women's networks corroborated these earlier findings. Only 5 percent of all newsletter coverage of the networks presented itself as "actionable," meaning coverage that invited citizens to participate in a future action taken by a network (ibid.). The vast majority of the newsletter content was devoted to purely informational accounts of past events and actions taken solely within the professional confines of the network.

Yet some women's networks seem to have become wary of the institutionally confined advocacy of European NGOs. This has prompted efforts to move "beyond NGOization" (see the chapter by Alvarez in this volume) and to the search for alternative venues for mobilization. The most visible attempt to create a European feminist movement outside or alongside existing women's NGOs was launched in 2006. The European Feminist Forum (EFF) was founded on grounds that "feminists in Europe are not acting as a movement to effect necessary changes" (European Feminist Forum 2007, see also European Feminist Forum 2009). The focus of the EFF was to "re-politicize the feminist movement in Europe" (European Feminist Forum 2009, 10) by establishing an ongoing dialogue, culminating in a face-to-face meeting; building new alliances and networks; and specifically fostering more East-West communication. Initial funding from the Open Society Institute and Mamma Cash, among others, allowed the EFF to develop an extensive and input-oriented online presence in four languages. Affinity groups were created, and a "travelling circus" (Lohmann 2009, 49) provided contacts between EFF activists and local projects across Europe. It is not as though the EFF was operating without NGO support; in fact, among the founding members of the EFF were KARAT, a network of Central and Eastern European women's NGOs, and Women in Development Europe, a large umbrella network of women's

NGOs working in development. Yet it is indicative of the disenchantment of many members of these established European women's networks that they helped launch an initiative that was clearly directed at activities outside of their regular business and that was more interested in public engagement than their own organizations were, or could be.

Initially, over 3,000 activists subscribed to the EFF's newsletter, joined affinity groups, and contributed to the debate it sponsored. But what looked like an impressive start came to an abrupt end in 2008. Due to financial difficulties, the core event for European activists, planned to take place in Poland, had to be canceled and the project was terminated. In its final assessment of the project's end, the organizers stated: "KARAT Coalition, the host organization in Poland, and the IIAV where the European Feminist Forum secretariat is housed, invested extensive personal and institutional resources in the fundraising efforts, which included visiting potential funders in Scandinavia, Poland and Brussels. . . . Funder after funder made clear this activity could not be funded from their limited budgets. It was not fundable by local or State governments (because it went over State boundaries), it was not a priority for many development aid budgets and it did not fit in to European Union tenders and calls. The lack of funds for this type of new initiative is an indication of the current difficult context in Europe for the feminist movement" (European Feminist Forum 2008).

Even though European women's NGOs and their networks are pulled into arenas of institutional advocacy, the search for new forms of movement building and cooperation indicates their discontent. The launch of the EFF on a European scale as well as of nationally focused initiatives like the UK feminista network in the United Kingdom[9] indicates ambivalence about tailoring advocacy solely toward institutional women's network strategies. Yet moving "beyond NGOization" also poses risks. Lack of public attention and of funds for the development of public advocacy repertoires inhibits these attempts.

Conclusion

The road signs directing women's movement activity across Europe seem to be pointing toward institutional advocacy. Incentives to participate in institutional governance by far outweigh those found in public advocacy contexts. It is not just the European Union that has opened its doors to civil society actors and that offers formal and informal access to selective women's movement actors; national governments have also discovered the value of civic consultations and NGO-driven expert forums. With their participation in institutionalized settings, European NGOized women's movements gain recognition, legitimacy, and knowledge they can use to acquire grants, and they can point to some impressive policy successes.

Economic and legal constraints contribute to the attraction of institutional advocacy arrangements. Since restrictions on NGOs' political activity are largely restrictions in regard to public political activity, women's NGOs' focus on advocating in institutionalized venues presents itself as a rational choice. Jutta Joachim and Birgit Locher, in their comparative work on NGOs in the United Nations and EU institutions, point to the potentially deradicalizing consequences of becoming institutional insiders: "NGOs rely on personal contacts and alliances with like-minded states for access, prefer lobbying strategies to symbolic or polarizing action, and make consensual proposals backed up by scientific expertise instead of engaging in radical criticism" (2009, 171).

In sum, the concentration of EU women's advocacy networks in the European Union on institutional governance has its costs. First, it diminishes the capacity for advocacy on behalf of underrepresented constituencies and issues and tends to sideline the public politicization of gender equality. The creation of the EFF was a testimony to this lack of emphasis on movement building, and its demise is a testimony to the difficulty of movement building without being able to rely on politicized feminist publics.

Second, the lack of public mobilization capacity at times endangers the forceful pursuit of institutional gender agendas. Since participation of women's NGOs in EU governance is organized around institutional needs and defined by institutional priorities, it will be employed only selectively. Several studies have pointed to a tendency within the European Union since about 2005 to subsume and sidetrack gender-equality issues under the broader markers of mainstreaming and diversity. Maria Stratigaki (2005) has analyzed the replacement of enforceable community action programs with a road map that lacks resources and remains vague. Jane Jenson (2008) has pointed out how the European employment strategy has slowly altered equality from a central pillar to a footnote. In both cases, NGOized women's advocacy networks have not been able to protect feminist agendas.

A third effect of NGOized advocacy networks is an increasing gap between insititutional insiders and outsiders as well as between transnational actors and local constituents. This "division of political labor whereby the professional feminist—the gender expert—has arrogated the global terrain to themselves without a clear basis of legitimation from local constituencies" (Mendoza 2002, 309)—is not just a European phenomenon; it has been observed by researchers from Latin America to Africa (Moghadam 2005; Adams 2006). And it can, as recent examples on the stages of the European Union have shown, lead relatively quickly to the formalized question of civil society actors' legitimacy.

The case of the European Union indicates that women's movements are not just coping with a period of abeyance, but that they face a set of institutional and structural shifts in mobilization capacity that are characterized by a focus on institutional governance, disincentives to public advocacy, and an increasing distance between insider status and public engagement. Women's movement actors demand that NGOs move toward a "conceptual shift from fundraising to agenda setting and movement building (Kerr 2007, 102). As advocacy becomes institutionally depoliticized and as selective NGOized movement actors become part of a policy-making process that has not been defined in participatory scenarios with affected communities, movement building and creating feminist publics across the European Union seems to be the most pressing task for the near future.

Notes

1. This is the umbrella organization for European women's NGOs. Its headquarters is in Brussels.
2. The United Nations and other governance bodies, as well as private foundation and donor funding, add to the pull toward NGOization. See, for example, Bagic (2006) for post-Yugoslavian, Mendoza (2002) for Latin American, and Jad (2007) for Arabic women's movements.
3. This is not to dispute the fact that some grant-savvy women's groups on the local level are well equipped to successfully apply for EU grants (see, for example, Guenther 2010).
4. The data are based on Joanna Kerr's survey of women's rights organizations worldwide in 2006. Over 1,400 organizations responded to the survey. The sample included 84 organizations from Western Europe and North America as well as 128 organizations from Central and Eastern European countries. Fifty percent of the organizations were founded in the 1990s and 39 percent after 2000 (Kerr 2007, 23). Two-thirds of the NGOs in this sample had budgets of less than $50,000 per year. Over two-thirds work primarily at the national (69 percent) and/or local levels (49 percent). Only 14 percent work at the international level.

5. The Council decided in 2004 to extend the fifth framework into 2006 in order to accommodate the accession of the ten new member states. The budget was increased to 61.5 million Euros.
6. Restrictions on political activities for NGOs are not unique to liberal democracies. In fact, such restrictions are much more severe in managed democracies like Russia and are used extensively to silence NGOs' voices in autocratic states.
7. Bundesfinanzhof 1984. Decision 29.08.1984, BStBl 1984 II p. 844.
8. Tatjana Pudrovska and Myra Marx Ferree (2004) add to this picture with their web-based analysis of women's networks, suggesting that European networks tend to refrain from a feminist agenda and use a more integrationist language.
9. See its website, at http://www.ukfeminista.org.uk; see also Banyard 2010.

Beyond NGOization?

Reflections from Latin America

This essay revisits what I referred to as "the Latin American feminist NGO boom" of the 1990s and offers some reflections on how and why, at least in that region of the world, we may be moving beyond it. As we know, NGOs became the subject of considerable controversy among feminists across the globe in the 1990s. While states, intergovernmental organizations (IGOs), and international financial institutions (IFIs) embraced NGOs as a "magic bullet" of which "nothing short of miracles" was to be expected (W. Fisher 1997, 442; Edwards and Hulme 1996), critical feminist discourses of the late 1990s, my own work included, problematized a process that feminists in both activist and scholarly circles dubbed "NGOization" (Alvarez 1998, 1999; Lang 1997; Silliman 1999; Schild 1998).

In Latin America, the debate over NGOs was particularly heated and often acerbic. In the eyes of their staunchest critics, NGOs were veritable traitors to feminist ethical principles that depoliticized feminist agendas and collaborated with neoliberal ones. Some contended that feminist NGOs were "institutionalized branches of the movement" that had been summarily "co-opted by the powers they once criticized (such as the state and transnational capital and their agents)" (Castro 2001, 17). NGOs' most strident detractors, the *feministas autónomas*, maintained that "to demand, reform, negotiate, and lobby," common practices among late-twentieth-century feminist NGOs, were "actions based on a liberal 'ethic' that make social movements as a whole into lifeless entities, subsidiaries and legitimators of the politics of domination and oppression" (Galindo 1997, 11). They vehemently condemned feminist NGOs for having "institutionalized" the women's movement and "sold out" to the forces of "global neoliberal patriarchy" (Bedregal 1997; Monasteiros 2007, 2008; Mujeres Creando 2005; Pisano 1996; see also Alvarez, Friedman, et al. 2003; Ríos Tobar, Godoy Catalán, and Guerrero Caviedes 2003).

I want to stress, however, that "blanket assessments of feminist NGOs as handmaidens of neoliberal planetary patriarchy" or development do-gooders failed to capture the ambiguities and variations in and among NGOs (Alvarez 1999, 200). The Good NGOs–Bad NGOs binary doesn't do justice to the dual or hybrid identity of feminist NGOs, their two facets, as technical-professional organizations that are at once integral parts of feminist movements (Alvarez 1999, 196). In this essay, I join scholars such as Julie Hemment (2007), Donna Murdock (2008) and Millie Thayer (2000, 2010) in moving beyond binary representations of NGOs. As Hemment rightly insists, in most feminist NGOs "the good and the bad are intertwined and interdependent" (2007, 68). She cautions, moreover, that "the critique of NGOs has resonated with anti-democratic and anti-human rights forces and led to the withdrawal of funds from rights-promoting projects" (2007, 142). Indeed, in contexts like Colombia, NGOs even became the targets of paramilitary forces who dubbed them "parasubversives"; former President Uribe himself accused human rights groups of being "defenders of terrorism" (Murdock 2008, 210), for instance. And feminist NGOs are not always spared harassment at the other end of the political spectrum, as Nicaraguan activists have learned since abortion was recriminalized under Daniel Ortega's reign and several NGO leaders have been charged with "illegal association to commit delinquency, *apologia* for the crime of abortion, complicity with the crime of sexual abuse," among other offenses.[1]

We need to move beyond unilateral condemnations of NGOs that have fed these kinds of antifeminist arguments and obscured the potential for agency and "wiggle room" even among those NGOs most beholden to global neoliberal gender agendas (Hemment 2007, 12–13; Sommer 2006; Alvarez forthcoming). In joining the critique of the 1990s critique of feminist NGOs, and therefore engaging in self-critique, I will first revisit the notion of NGOization, then review the crucial "movement work" performed by NGOs that was often obscured by that notion, and finally offer some reflections on how and why Latin American feminisms and other social movements may be beginning to move "beyond the Boom."

NGOization Revisited

I must begin by clarifying that my original use of the term "NGOization" was not intended as a synonym or shorthand for the proliferation of NGOS during the 1990s. NGOization during that decade was not simply about an increase in the numbers of more formally structured feminist organizations with paid, professional staff and funding from government, multilateral and bilateral agencies, and foreign donors. Rather, NGOization, in my view, entailed national and global neoliberalism's active promotion and official sanctioning of particular organizational forms and practices among feminist organizations and other sectors of civil society. And it was state, IGO, and IFI promotion of more rhetorically restrained, politically collaborative, and technically proficient feminist practices that triggered what I've called the "NGO Boom" of the 1990s in Latin America.

A number of national, regional, and global forces fueled NGOization in Latin America. As the region's neoliberal governments sought to administer the enormous social costs of draconian structural adjustment policies while cutting back state expenditures and social programs, many increasingly turned to those NGOS they deemed technically capable and politically trustworthy to assist in the task of "social adjustment." Since many of those programs targeted poor urban and rural women, governments enjoined feminist NGOS to "partner" with the state—often in the name of enhancing "women's citizen participation" in the policy process—and to lend their expertise in "gender matters" in executing (though rarely in formulating) them. As we know, donors also had a strong hand in pushing feminist organizations toward more professionalized, formal structures (Lebon 1998, 2006, 2010; Maier and Lebon 2010; Thayer 2000, 2010). Finally, the process of NGOization was further accentuated when the United Nations summoned feminist NGOS to participate in the Cairo Summit on Population and Development, the Beijing Women's Conference, and others in the string of Social Summits and the follow-up "+5" and then "+10" conferences it sponsored during the 1990s and 2000s (Alvarez 1998; Friedman 2000).

These trends unsettled the hybrid identities of many feminist NGOS in the region, leading some to place empowerment goals and a wide range of movement-oriented activities "on the strategic 'back burner,'" as Murdock suggests, and to put "demonstrable impact (or more bang for the development buck), garnered through short-term projects, large-scale workshops and forums, and more overt participation in the policy arena" on the "front burner" (2008, 3). By the late 1990s, NGOization had resulted from the confluence of three trends. First, as states and IGOs increasingly turned to feminist NGOs as gender experts rather than as citizens' groups advocating on behalf of women's rights, feminist cultural-political interventions in the public debate were often reduced to technical ones. Second, as neoliberal states and IGOs viewed NGOs as surrogates for civil society, feminist NGOs began to be (selectively) consulted on gender policy matters on the assumption that they served as "intermediaries" to larger societal constituencies. While many NGOs retained linkages to such constituencies, however, other actors in the expansive Latin American women's movement field—particularly popular women's groups and feminist organizations publicly critical of the neoliberal status quo—often were denied direct access to gender policy debates and thereby effectively politically silenced. Finally, as states increasingly subcontracted feminist NGOs to advise on or carry out government women's programs, NGOs' ability to critically monitor policy and advocate for more thoroughgoing feminist reform was sometimes jeopardized (Alvarez 1999, 183). Many organizations found themselves "caught up in the . . . NGO Boom—becoming more hierarchically organized, governed by corporate business management principles [becoming *empresas sociales*, or social companies], and increasingly focused on creating knowledge and policy" (Murdock 2008, 26, 48).

Feminist NGOs' Oft-Neglected "Movement Work"

What was often overlooked in scholarly and activist critiques of NGOization was the fact that, even at the height of the Boom, many if not most professionalized NGOs remained "true to their feminist roots" (Murdock 2008, 34) and often played a critical role in grounding and articulating the expansive, heterogeneous Latin American feminist fields of the 1990s and 2000s. As feminism was diffused among diverse subjects and into a wide range of spaces and places, it was reconfigured as *discursive fields of action* (Alvarez, Baiocchi, et al., unpublished manuscript). "Trickling up, down and sideways," as in Fiona Macaulay's (2010) apt depiction of Brazil's "multi-nodal women's movement" and "gender policy community," feminism in many, if not most, countries in the region today not only has been "mainstreamed" so that it extends vertically across different levels of government, traverses much of the party spectrum, and engages with a variety of national and international policy arenas; feminism also has been "sidestreamed," if you will, spreading horizontally into a wide array of class and racial-ethnic communities and social and cultural spaces, including parallel social movement publics. By producing feminist knowledges, disseminating feminist discourses, and serving as nodal points in the multiple political-communicative webs and networks that link diverse and dispersed feminist actors, NGOs—with their permanent headquarters, sizable budgets, functionally specific departments, specialized publications, and paid administrative, research, and outreach staff—became mainstays of feminist fields, helping to interweave disparate feminist actors and articulate them discursively.

First, many NGOs, as Vera Soares (1998) suggests, have been important producers of feminist knowledge. Some of the larger and better-resourced feminist organizations boast research departments that rival those of many university women's studies programs in the region. They churn out scores of position papers, monographs, and edited collections on topics ranging from gender and ethnic discrimination suffered by indigenous, peasant, and rural women workers to the poor quality of gynecological care offered by public health facilities and the widespread incidence of cervical cancer among working-class women to the courts' shoddy record in adjudicating domestic violence cases. The data and analysis generated by NGOs have provided vital foundations for more effective feminist advocacy in a variety of settings—from UN summits and national legislatures to local schools, neighborhood groups, and trade unions. And feminist NGO texts also often offer theoretical interpretations and conceptual innovations that contribute directly to that "fluid and continually evolving body of meanings that feminists think of when they ask themselves, 'Am I a feminist?'" and thus help forge what Jane Mansbridge has theorized as the "discursively created movement . . . that inspires activists and is the entity to which they feel accountable" (1995, 29).

A second critical way that NGOs have been central to sustaining movement fields, then, is as disseminators of feminist discourses. Though much of their knowledge production is explicitly aimed at influencing the policy process and is distributed widely to legislators, government bureaucrats, and other public officials, a good deal is also self-consciously directed at "the movement" and is often tapped and redeployed to a variety of ends by feminists active in other civil society organizations and social and political institutions. Embedded in feminist frameworks even when translated and tailored to suit particular audiences, the vast array of electronic and print journals, newsletters, training manuals, pamphlets, and other educational and audiovisual materials produced circulate widely among variously situated feminist activists through a range of media.

Feminist NGO products are also often used in educational and *conscientización* activities mounted by other (nonfeminist) social movements and civil society organizations, including many trade unions and grassroots groups. Moreover, as the vast constellation of knowledge products generated by NGOs wind their way through feminisms' multilayered political-communicative webs, they also often cross over into other (overlapping) networks of social movements, civil society organizations, and social and political institutions. Feminisms' discursive "baggage" thus sometimes travels "unaccompanied," so to speak. That is, even where there may be no bona fide "feminist activists" in sight, the communicative webs that NGOs help sustain work to disseminate feminist discourses indirectly into a variety of other publics. The multiple, if sometimes uncharted, routes traveled by feminist products and discourses, then, partly accounts for why "a diffuse feminism" has spread among a good number of popular women's organizations in many countries in the region (Feijoó 2000, 26; Di Marco 2006, forthcoming). That is, feminist NGOs work to mobilize ideas, not just people.

The discourses that inform feminist practices across a wide range of sites, moreover, flow through what Colombian feminist sociologist Magdalena León once referred to as a veritable "tangle of networks" (*"un enredo de redes"*)—both formal and informal. Indeed, Peruvian feminists Cecilia Olea Mauleón and Virginia Vargas describe "the movement" itself as a kind of "meganetwork" (Olea Mauleón and Vargas 1998, 147). The now pervasive feminist practice of *"enredarse"* or "getting entangled" consists of more formalized and institutionalized territorial, thematic, advocacy-focused, and identity-centered networks organized on a local, national, regional, or global scale, as well as more fluid, reticulated, and informal webs of interpersonal and interorganizational communication and interaction (Shepard 2003, 2006).

The 1990s was "the premier period" for the creation of new national and regional networks, fueled in part by Latin American feminists' unprecedented involvement in national consultation processes for the string of UN social summits that took place in the first half of that decade. Beyond Latin American feminisms' growing international entanglements in the 1990s and early 2000s, two further factors helped foster the spread of this more structured form of feminist *"enredos."* First, the decentering of feminisms itself seems to have prompted activists to devise more stable and predictable forms of articulation and collaboration across ever more diverse and dispersed organizational and geographical locations. The fact that networks became international donors' vehicle of choice for allocating funds in presumably more efficient and effective ways was a second crucial factor fueling the creation of numerous formalized feminist networks throughout the region. Throughout the 1990s, there was a veritable frenzy of donor funding for networks—particularly for UN-related women's rights advocacy networks—even as support for other types of NGO activities and for less institutionalized expressions of feminist activism dwindled in much of the region (Shepard 2003, 2006; Thayer 2010).

Movements Beyond the Boom?

The above outlined movement/field-sustaining work of NGOs was often obscured in critiques of NGOization prevailing during the Boom years. Moreover, in more recent times, growing numbers of NGOs arguably have again placed "movement work" on the front burner. Throughout Latin America, many are seeking to rearticulate local, national, regional, and global movement fields, engaging more vigorously in outreach and linking to other social movements and broader noninstitutional publics.

Several developments—internal and external to feminist fields—help account for the visible shifts under way among feminist NGOs and networks. Internally, there has been growing critical introspection and recognition of the limits of what Christina Ewig (1999) dubbed the "NGO-based social movement model." Not only had NGOization exacerbated power imbalances among feminists and sometimes dulled feminisms' more radical edge, but—many NGO professionals now maintain—that "model" also revealed limits for actually implementing hard-won policy gains, which requires public pressure, secured through changes in public opinion, not just through policy monitoring.

As the various "+ 5" conferences revealed that feminist and other progressive movements' project of influencing international policy arenas had yielded meager concrete results, many NGO activists grew ever more disillusioned with the fruits of their "expert" advocacy work (Vargas 2010). In a critical retrospective on feminist involvement in national and international policy monitoring, Peruvian activist Virginia Vargas, who headed the NGO preparatory process in the mid-1990s, argued that 2000 represented a critical turning point when "we reexamined ourselves, our conceptions and our political practices since the Beijing conference." Though there "undoubtedly were advances," she maintained,

> after our initial enthusiasm about everything that could be achieved with the fulfillment of the recommendations of the Platform, we moved to a much less seductive reality, not just because of what had not been fulfilled, but also because everything that we had achieved had been flattened and left doors open for retrogression. (2004, email correspondence)

Indeed, if it had been possible to incorporate some elements of feminist, human rights, or environmentalist agendas into the international accords and platforms of the 1990s, it also became increasingly apparent to many that any possibility for more significant changes in the rights and life conditions of most women and men was in effect blocked by the intensification of neoliberal globalization, the ever more dramatic rolling back of the state, structural adjustment processes, and the concomitant erosion of citizenship and social policies during that same decade (Alvarez, Faria, and Nobre 2004).

The obvious deficiencies of neoliberalism unleashed innovative and dynamic resistance movements at the turn of the present century. Involving an impressively broad array of nonstate actors, this revitalized "antisystemic" resistance spanned from mass mobilizations in Bolivia and Ecuador and novel forms of organizing among immigrants, indigenous, and Afrodescendant peoples to the innovative modalities of politics developed by Brazil's MST, Argentina's *piqueteros*, hip hop, and alternative media movements emergent throughout the region, and multiscalar networks growing out of the World Social Forum (WSF) and other recent national, regional, and global organizing processes (Alvarez, Baiocchi, et al. forthcoming; Johnston and Almeida 2006; Prashad and Ballvé 2006; Souza Santos 2007; Stahler-Sholk, Vanden, and Keucker 2008). If the UN-focused "global civil society" of the 1990s had mirrored the hegemonic international system and operated well within its discursive parameters, the 2000s witnessed the rise of counterhegemonic global social forces that found their point of articulation precisely in their radical opposition to the reigning global neoliberal regime—the antiglobalization movement or, as others would have it, the global justice and solidarity movement. Many feminist activists and networks were, from the very beginning, part of these ample, yet diffuse, new regional and global movements that found their most enduring expression in the WSF (Eschle 2005; Harcourt 2006; Alvarez 2012). Engagement with these counterhegemonic spaces has prompted growing numbers of NGOs to move away from the "project-centered logic" fueled by NGOization—in which feminist cultural-political interventions are "results-driven" and have clear beginning, middle, and end points—and (back) toward a "process-oriented logic," which is more fluid, open-ended, and continuous, though not linear (see L. Phillips and Cole 2009).

NGOization has been further rattled by factors external to movement fields: changes in national, regional, and global political economy and forms of governance now place political premiums and offer rewards for activist practices and organizational forms distinct from those that fueled the Boom. As anthropologist William Fisher predicted in an influential 1997 essay, "development has been a fickle industry, first embracing and then casting off a long series of enthusiastically touted new strategies. NGOs, now so widely praised, can anticipate becoming victims of the current unrealistic expectations and being abandoned as rapidly and as widely as they have been embraced" (443). The evident crisis of neoliberalism, which has swept much of Latin America since the late 1990s and has now enveloped the globe, could well shake the foundations of NGOization as new modalities of "development" are promoted to address crisis-riddled social formations.

Neoliberalism's crisis helped spark the current turn toward the left and center-left and the resurgence of the national-popular (or, according to some, the rise of neopopulism) which pose new challenges and offer fresh opportunities for feminist interventions in institutional and extra-institutional political arenas (Friedman 2007, 2010; Gago 2007). Governments of the so-called "Pink Tide"—spanning more or less intense shades of leftist "red" governments from Venezuela to Paraguay to Brazil to Chile and those backed, as in the cases of Bolivia and Ecuador, by previously marginalized ethno-racial majorities—are now often seeking and rewarding different sorts of NGO partners, those with stronger links to and capabilities for serving as intermediaries with broader civil society, especially popular-class-based, constituencies (on Latin America's turn to the left, see Hershberg and Rosen 2006; Prashad and Ballvé 2006; Ramírez Gallegos 2006; Castañeda and Morales 2008; Lievesley and Ludlam 2009; Weyland, Madrid, and Hunter 2010). NGOs still often provide "gender expertise" to governments of the Pink Tide, as has apparently been the case in

Chávez's Venezuela (Rakowski and Espina 2006; Espina 2007) and has certainly been true in Lula's Brazil and Bachelet's Chile, but they are less likely to serve as "surrogates for civil society" in such contexts.

As Elizabeth Monasteiros maintains is the case in Bolivia, indigenous women's groups (both rural and urban), women in neighborhood councils, and the mass-based Bartolina Sisa National Federation of Bolivian Peasant Women "have come to be perceived as the legitimate representatives of large women's majorities" while the legitimacy of "the technocratic middle class, particularly the NGOs" is being seriously questioned, thereby "changing who gets to represent women's interests and demands" (2007, 33; 2008, 181). Regaining that legitimacy might well entail a (re)transformation of NGOized NGOs into twenty-first-century variants of the "popular movement-assistance NGOs" of yesteryear (Alvarez 1993, 1997; Landim 1993; Teixeira 2003)—like the many NGOs that today specialize in advising participatory budget councils in PT-led cities throughout Brazil, for example. Particularly in the case of "more red" or mass-mobilization-based governments like those of Venezuala or Bolivia, moreover, NGOs that work with a demonstrable "mass base" are likely to fare better politically (and perhaps materially, in terms of government funding) than those that expend their energies in the corridors of the United Nations. And in Brazil under the PT governments of Lula and Dilma Rouseff, the proportion of NGO budgets coming from federal government sources nearly doubled, with more than 60 percent of NGOs reporting in 2007 that they had accessed federal funding, up from 36.6 percent in 2003 (Gouveia and Daniliauskas 2010, 29).

Even in a government on this "more pink," social democratic end of the Pink Tide, then, NGOs appear to have been rewarded for engaging in more "activist," movement-focused practices such as "popular education" and "*conscientização*," even as they continue to be summoned or subcontracted for the more technical, project-execution, and advisory activities that fueled the Boom of the 1990s. A new "participatory" brand of state feminism, inaugurated under Lula and continued under President Dilma Rousseff, helped tilt the political momentum within the feminist field in the favor of more activist practices (Sardenberg and Costa 2010). The feminist NGO Sempreviva Organização Feminista, or SOF, a key player in the global and national "anticapitalist camp" analyzed below, for example, was awarded a major contract by the Ministry of Agrarian Development's (MDA) Special Advisory Unit on Gender, Race and Ethnicity (*Assessoria Especial de Gênero Raça e Etnia*—AEGRE), for 2008 through 2010, which it implemented in eighteen states and fifty "territories of citizenship," poorer rural zones mapped out by the federal government for targeted intervention. Aimed at "contributing to the strengthening of [rural women] as political, social and economic subjects," as well as at "expanding and improving [their] access to the policies implemented by the MDA," the program employed "feminist methodologies" and deployed dozens of young feminists across Brazil's rural landscape, especially trained for the purpose of promoting the "training and articulation of rural women," strengthening their organizations, and bolstering their "productive economic activities based on a solidary and feminist economy" (Sempreviva Organização Feminista 2011).

Beyond NGOization?

Despite these recent trends, "NGOized" NGOs show few signs of going away in the near future. In fact, the 2000s also witnessed the consolidation of a sizable regional cadre of project- and policy-focused "gender expert" NGO professionals, BINGOs (big international NGOs), and networks that continue to specialize in policy monitoring and service delivery. In some cases, some of the most NGOized have actually morphed into private consultancy firms.

Still, by the turn of the 2000s, the increasing recognition of the limits of NGOization had led growing numbers of feminists to what Wendy Harcourt refers to as a "third moment" in their engagements with the global, regional, and national development discourses (2005, 34). "This third moment, which began in the late 1990s and continues to the present day," Harcourt suggests, "is marked by disengagement, or at least significant problematizing by the women's movement of the development discourse and apparatus and a decided shift toward interest in other sites of power and knowledge production." The growing recognition of the limits of NGOization has triggered revisioned advocacy strategies to expand those limits and renewed activist efforts to overcome them. The former have been taken on by people one of my interviewees facetiously referred to as "the orphans of the UN," products of the widespread disillusionment with the "postsocial summit" era; the latter, by activists I will call "the stepdaughters of neoliberalism," products of more recent forms of resistance to neoliberalism's reign. I want to stress that this distinction is not intended as a dichotomy; instead, these sometimes represent two facets of the same activist, organization, or network, two sides of the same feminist coin.

A number of the feminist NGOers most involved in the region's protracted engagement with the UN process have turned to alternative advocacy strategies more focused on intervening in cultural representations and the broader public debate, rather than centering their efforts more narrowly and technically on policy-making arenas. Disheartened by the limited effectiveness of transnational advocacy processes aimed at influencing IGOs and IFIs and critical of neoliberal and other "fundamentalisms," many have invested heavily in the World Social Forum process as an alternative arena for transnational activism, for example.

Several of the core feminist NGOs that spearheaded the Latin American parallel preparatory processes for the Cairo and Beijing UN conferences and their respective +5 "sequels," now grouped in a coalition called Articulación Feminista Marcosur (AFM, or Marcosur Feminist Articulation, a wordplay on Mercosur), have directed many of their energies toward participating in and influencing the WSF process, viewing it as an indispensable space of action for feminisms (Alvarez 2012; on feminist participation in the WSF, see León 2002; Faria 2003; Vargas 2003; Alvarez, Faria and Nobre 2004; Eschle 2005; Eschle and Maiguashca 2010; Phillips and Cole 2009). For the AFM, the WSF is a logical "world public" in which to pursue several of its core goals: "to strengthen the articulation between social movements, and in particular, to use the feminist presence established within these joint spaces to empower and influence the whole of society" (Articulación Feminista Marcosur 2002, 7). It views the WSF as "a plural space with proposals for an alternative globalization, where many new strategies and concerns of globalized social movements, such as feminism, converge" (AFM 2002, 14). But feminist pressure in the WSF process, the AFM insists, is crucial because "it is . . . a complicated site of alliances with other movements whose orientation to feminism is not always one of acknowledgement" (ibid.).

New ways of doing politics have grown out of feminist involvement in world summits, their preparatory and implementation processes, and the growing recognition of their limitations. One such innovation is the spread of national and transnational "campaigns" aimed as much at unsettling dominant cultural codes as they are at reforming legal ones, such as the Campaign for an Inter-American Convention on Sexual Rights and Reproductive Rights—launched in mid-2001 by a consortium of sixteen feminist NGOs, research institutes, and national and regional networks, including the AFM.

Uruguayan feminists Lucy Garrido and Lilian Celiberti—who formed part of an informal "web" of prochoice, reproductive rights activists from across the region who originally came up with the idea for this campaign—explained that, though it was in principle modeled after the 1994 Inter-American Convention on Violence against Women, they hardly expected the Organization of American States (OAS) to readily embrace the idea of a Sexual and Reproductive Rights Convention, much less that most national governments would endorse it in the short-to-medium term.[2] Instead, they said they wanted to "shake things up," to use the Inter-American system in "subversive" ways, to "provoke debate" in both activist and policy circles about "bodily and sexual rights" as core dimensions of democratic citizenship. The campaign also evinces an emphasis on "countercultural struggle": it declares that "the changes to which we aspire are both material and symbolic in nature. . . . It is in the cultural dimension where the right to have rights takes root, on the basis of differences and particularities of human beings" and advocates "a reconceptualization of the body in its political dimension" (Campaña por la Convención de los Derechos Sexuales y los Derechos Reproductivos 2006, 17). Also in evidence is a "postliberal" emphasis on the conditions that enable the exercise of rights:

> Rights cannot be conceived as something static nor can they be won once and for all. Historically, their development has taken place in an inconclusive and exclusionary manner. This was not a linear process but a process marked by fractures, setbacks, restoration of lost content, and the broadening and permanent invention of new dimensions. Today these new contents are restoring those aspects of human life and citizenship, which have been historically devalued or absent, silenced, naturalized, and prescribed for centuries. The most significant of these rights, in terms of their absence, are economic, social, and cultural rights and the rights that have faced the most resistance from conservative forces are sexual and reproductive rights. (Campaña 2006, 13)

Many of the Latin American feminists most invested in addressing the material consequences of globalization identify with what some have come to call "the anticapitalist camp" of the WSF and are among the folks I'm calling "stepdaughters of neoliberalism." The Brazilian branch of the World March of Women against Violence and Poverty (WMW), headquartered at the above-mentioned Sempreviva Organização Feminista (SOF), was centrally involved in the Forum process from the outset, for instance. In a flyer distributed during the 2003 WSF, the WMW declared that they were participating in the Porto Alegre event because they had "supported demonstrations that have taken place all over the world, which have been against militarism and the neoliberal politics denoting a commodification of life, because we believe feminism is fundamental to renew[ing] the sense of those fights. And it is within the process of fighting for everyone's freedom, that feminism rejuvenates [itself] each and every day."

New forms of "popular feminism" have taken shape among the various recent grassroots, anti-neoliberal movements, and often also engage with antiglobalization movements. Graciela di Marco has suggested, for example, that women *piqueteras*, workers in recovered enterprises (*fabricas recuperadas*), mothers who struggle against police brutality, and others in the popular movements that have blossomed since the economic debacle of late 2001 in Argentina, have found "their channel for expression in the Encuentros Nacionales de Mujeres [which attract close to 20,000 women each year], and in the marches, in the struggle for legal abortion and for freeing women imprisoned for participation in these movements" (di Marco 2006, 255). She maintains that the articulation of feminism and other social movements, "a contingent articulation of heterogeneous elements, of diverse demands that constitute the multiplicity of the movements (*piqueteras*, *obreras de empresas recuperadas*, *asambleístas*, *campesinas*, *indígenas*, and *feministas*) gave rise to a chain of equivalences, hegemonically represented in sexual rights, especially the right to abortion" that has led to the appearance of a collective identity, which, following Laclau, she dubs a "*pueblo feminista*" or "feminist people," based on the discursive construction of a common adversary, in this case the "carriers of traditional and patriarchal values" (di Marco, unpublished manuscript; see also Laclau 2005). Manifestations of that feminist *pueblo* are also amply evident at the WSF and other local and regional articulations of the "anticapitalist camp" such as the Vía Campesina—a global network of small agriculturalists in which popular feminism is arguably hegemonic.

And the expanding feminist *pueblo* is also apparent in the pronounced visibility and expressive expansion of what contributors to a recent anthology of the region's feminisms variously refer to as "Third Wave feminism," "complex identity feminisms," or "feminism of shifting identities" (Maier and Lebon 2010). The very women whom the "hegemonic feminism" of the so-called Second Wave viewed as "others"—poor and working-class women, Afro-descendant and indigenous women, lesbians—have translated and radically transformed some of its core tenets and fashioned "other feminisms," "*feminismos con apellidos*" (Ríos Tobar, Godoy Catalán, and Guerrero Caviedes 2003), that are deeply entwined, and some-times contentiously entangled, with national and global struggles against all forms of inequality and for social, sexual, and racial justice. These di-verse feminisms—together with young women from all social groups and classes who proclaim themselves *"feministas jóvenes"* with agendas dis-tinct from earlier generations—have produced effervescent movement currents that proffer trenchant critiques of enduring inequalities *among women*, as well as between women and men of diverse racial and social groups, thereby expanding the scope and reach of feminist messages and revitalizing women's cultural and policy interventions across the region.

By Way of Conclusion

At the height of neoliberal entrenchment, many feminist NGOs in Latin America, as elsewhere, were pulled into serving as surrogate representa-tives of civil society, developing gendered expertise in policy monitoring and project execution, and carrying out a variety of social programs for states. Professionalized, formally structured NGOs also abound among the diverse expressions of feminism that have flourished since the 2000s, in-cluding among some firmly rooted in the "anticapitalist camp." Yet many of the activities that get "frontburnered" today, I've tried to suggest, differ from those that prevailed at the height of the Boom.

Like most NGOs in feminist and other movement fields, those estab-lished by young women or black feminists typically engage in a range of cultural, educational, outreach, research, political, and other activities, and these may include policy- as well as movement-focused work. Thus, though professionalization and institutionalization (in the sense of rou-tinization) represent their own vexing challenges for internal democracy within and among movement groups, they do not *in themselves* determine the types of feminist practices that are prioritized by NGOs. As discursive fields of action, feminisms are dynamic, always changing, *on the move*. They are continually reconfigured by a mix of internal and external forces and have shifting centers of gravity. Which actors, discourses, practices, and organizational forms prevail or are most politically visible at any given time in a given sociopolitical context therefore necessarily vary. There is, in short, no twenty-first-century Iron Law of NGOization.

Notes

This chapter is reproduced by permission from *Development* 52, no. 2 (2009): 175–84. A more succinct version of this essay was presented at the eleventh International Forum of the Association for Women in Development, Cape Town, South Africa, November 14–17, 2008. My thanks to Andrea Cornwall and the Pathways to Women's Empowerment project for inviting me to join their panel on "The NGOization of Women's Movements."

All Spanish and Portuguese language original texts were translated by the author.

1. Quoted from anarlfem@caribe.net, e-mail, October 13, 2008. On Nicaraguan feminists' response to Sandinista assaults, see Kampwirth (2006, 2010), Gago (2007).
2. Personal communication during the Eighth Latin American and Caribbean Feminist Encuentro, held in Juan Dolio, Dominican Republic, November 1999.

Victoria Bernal and Inderpal Grewal

Feminisms and the NGO Form

Neither what we have called "the NGO form" nor any other form is or will be sufficient to contain feminist activism or to pursue feminist agendas in the coming decades. Feminist ideologies, agendas, and activism arise and are deployed in response to the enduring and emerging conditions of women's gendered lives. Today NGOs are a fact of women's lives around the globe. Furthermore, as the essays in this volume demonstrate, NGOs that are engaged with women or women's issues are part of the social context that constructs and defines "women." As such, NGOs are not simply vehicles for serving women or empowering them (however well or inadequately) but rather are themselves fields of gendered struggles over power, resources, and status. NGOs are simultaneously local and transnational, and ambiguously located in relation to states. NGOs may collaborate with, compete with, and sometimes act in place of states. The terrains of feminist struggles, thus, run through and across NGOs. The research in this volume has revealed the ambiguous and unstable synergies between feminisms and the NGO form.

As this body of research shows, NGOs themselves are not static. Within NGOs there is increasing awareness of many pitfalls and of the critiques leveled at NGOs as having been co-opted by powerful interests, including states, donors, corporations, and elites of various kinds. NGOs are growing more sophisticated in their collaborations with states, donors, and other NGOs. Although there remain NGOs that seem to be unconcerned with the dangers of agenda-setting by corporate, state, or donor sponsors, there are also NGOs that are developing strategies for maintaining independence even as they seek funding from powerful sources. For feminists, NGOs have brought new collaborations and uneasy partnerships with states and other institutions that are distinctly not feminist. NGOs' relationships to social movements are also variable and evolving, much as the links of advocacy networks are dynamic rather than stable. NGOs, moreover, often pursue complex agendas in projects that are not simply about gender but are also about class, race, religion, health, or environmental issues. As NGOs take on a number of issues along with addressing gender inequalities, such collaborations inevitably change the nature of feminist organizing. The results of these processes do not necessarily weaken feminism, but can serve to sustain it and extend its reach to wider constituencies and contexts.

In this anthology we started from the assumption that the proliferation of NGOs is deeply connected to the neoliberalism and privatization that emerge from the premise that "the welfare of the population and the improvement of its condition can best be served by 'non-state' actors" (S. Jackson 2005, 169). Lenders like the World Bank and the International Monetary Fund and development agencies and experts often have deemed states corrupt and inefficient, representing NGOs as more honest and direct providers of welfare. As Analiese Richard notes, "development experts have lauded NGOs as efficient conduits for aid, and pointed to the NGO 'boom' as an indicator of democratizing civil societies" (2009, 166). But, as the authors in this collection show, the operations of NGOs cannot be understood as separate from the travails of the state in the neoliberal present. NGOs are pliable and adaptable in some ways that government institutions are not, but this also makes NGOs highly manipulable, especially since they often depend on the resources of states and donors to sustain their activities. Furthermore, the proliferation of NGOs means that NGO activities can be disparate, piecemeal, and often rivalrous. At best, their interventions are often uncoordinated with those of other NGOs that are addressing the same or related issues; in the worst cases, they compete with one another for the same donor funds, constituencies, media attention, and other resources.

In terms of democracy and empowerment it is also important to remember that states, at least in principle, are held accountable to their citizens, and many states claim to be so. It is not always clear to whom NGOs are accountable. In practice, their most obvious accountability often is to their funders (these can be individuals, foundations, states, or corporations), since NGOs must report (for the most part) on how they used funds in order to sustain their funding. NGOs continue to proliferate and, as indicated by the expression "briefcase NGO," often require very little to get started. This fact also explains the appeal of the NGO form to women who may lack financial and social capital. At the same time, the low threshold for entry into the NGO field is countered by the pressures associated with growing state regulation of NGOs as well as the expansion of audit culture (Strathern 2000), oversight, and transparency promoted by donors. As a result, NGOs move closer to state-like bureaucratic practices.

Feminist struggles inside and outside of NGOs are ongoing, and our contributors reveal multiple unfolding stories based on their diverse research settings. Sonia Alvarez sees hopeful possibilities for Latin American feminisms through NGOs, whereas Sabine Lang sees NGOs as mainstreaming European feminisms in ways that may cut off more radical possibilities. These divergent perspectives reveal that the object of study and its context changes the view of the relationship between states, NGOs, and wider feminist constituencies, and these relationships indeed operate differently in the European Union's bureaucracy, for example, than in Latin American feminist circuits. Geopolitics and histories of colonialism have a role to play in these differences, even as new centers of power emerge globally. NGOs are often seen as innovators, forging new paths to development and democratization, but they are also constituted by their insertion into specific contexts and wider circuits. Often their personnel speak the language of international development or of Western corporate managerial practices. In fact, in order to successfully gain and maintain funding, NGO leaders must become fluent in these powerful discourses and attuned to shifting global trends (Merry 2001; J. Clark and Michuki 2009).

The emergence of the NGO form in relation to gender issues and women's empowerment suggests that feminism is indeed normalized in some institutional forms, yet feminism remains contentious and is neither fully integrated into nor contained by institutional boundaries of NGOs or states. The feminist activities of NGOs may provide the state with a justification for what it may not be able or want to accomplish. Feminist ideologies and practices, outside of statist, nationalist or organizational relations, may be ignored or repressed. At the same time, NGOs may have a significant role in advocacy, putting new problems and issues on the public agenda.

As the chapters in this volume reveal, NGOs work in concert with other institutions or in the spaces created by privatization, and in that sense they are partners of states, as much as they stand in opposition or contrast to states. States create the spaces within which NGOs operate, whether through the gaps created by state failure, retreat, privatization, and downsizing; through the regulations states impose on NGOs; or through the GONGOization process, whereby states and NGOs collaborate in ways that blur the meaning of "nongovernmental." States certainly remain powerful entities despite neoliberalization, although state power operates unevenly across regions and locations. In some sites, the state can seem invisible while NGOs may be active and ubiquitous. This may be the case where NGOs are present in locations that are rural or distant from the metropoles where state power may be most visible.

It is clear by now, however, that NGOs cannot serve as a substitute for the state, even in places where the state is in disarray. Jenny Pearce puts it succinctly: "It must be recognized, though, that increasing numbers of NGOs, however dedicated and efficient, could never offer rapid solutions to a problem on the scale of global poverty or even alleviate it sufficiently to ensure relative social stability" (2000b). The organization and reach of the state are significant, as is its putative accountability to citizens, even if practice often falls short of principle. NGOs may be held accountable by their donors, in practice, whether or not they feel accountable to the populations they seek to serve. In many cases, there is little tracking and accountability of NGOs, which means they can become corrupt or act for private gain. NGOs, thus, cannot in themselves provide the solution to the flaws of the state. It is clear, moreover, that we cannot analyze NGOs as separate from the state or from the global rise of neoliberal ideologies and privatization.

The NGO form has become so widespread because it is stable in appearance yet flexible in goals, internal organization, and in its constituencies. The NGO form is powerful because it easily serves as an intermediary, a bridge, and/or a translation across scales and forms, between levels of institutionalization, and between wider publics (particularly populations of political outsiders such as "grassroots" communities and women) and the political inside represented by state authorities and formal institutions. The gaps bridged by NGOs and the ways they translate between and across institutional and social boundaries are various, uneven, and shifting. To the degree that NGOs offer a low threshold of entry for women, they offer opportunities to advance feminist agendas in wider political arenas and to claim legitimacy and resources for women's demands.

We expect that state-NGO-private partnerships, whether or not they are named as such, will become more common. But this does not necessarily spell the demise of NGOs' potential for feminist organizing. Rather, it may suggest the need for a critical reassessment of the fetishism of "grassroots" and the gender politics associated with this construct, as well as the romanticization of private institutions as compared with government institutions. The professionalization of a class of women and gender "experts" is an achievement of NGOs that has not received the attention it is due, in part because of the focus on assessing NGOs' performance in relation to "grassroots" women. The proliferation of NGOs and their enmeshment in complex partnerships with other institutional forms may offer a means for women to enter more centrally into circuits of power and to integrate feminist concerns into government institutions. Scholars such as Janet Halley (2006) and Lang (in this volume) have documented examples of where this has happened.

In the absence of a feminist perspective, the emergence of this class of gender experts and technocrats within NGOs tends be viewed only in negative terms, as a sign of the increased distance of some women from the grass roots and as part of the production or reproduction of inequality (Schuller 2009, 85). What seems clear is that NGOs have provided employment for many women in both the global North and South. If many of these women are middle class or become middle class through this work, that fact should not only be a cause for criticizing NGOs. It may not be realistic to expect that all women will rise equally and simultaneously as result of any form of feminist activity. This emerging middle class may contribute to (re)producing inequality in society or within their organizations (Vasan 2004), yet their NGO work may be effective in advocating and securing greater rights and resources for women.

Gendered inequalities are persistent and entrenched yet subject to change, and NGOs are now often a catalyst of or a factor in such changes. As feminist research makes clear, gender can best be understood as relational and as always in process, and NGOs now play a role in the processes through which gender is constructed and reimagined. NGOs focused on gender issues or women are engaged in the process of constructing gender and producing certain kinds of "women" and "men" (NGOs focused on LGBTQ issues might produce other genders as well) in the course of doing and defining their work. Through these relations, some groups are produced as beneficiaries or recipients of resources and training, and their characteristics and needs are defined through these relations. Projects of

modernity and development have long histories of creating and consoli-
dating gendered categories, as have nationalist and postcolonial struggles
(Bernal 2001, 1994). In particular, the construct of "grassroots women" has
emerged as a powerful category in local and transnational contexts. More
recently, interventions in development discourse by Amartya Sen (1999)
and the work of Martha Nussbaum (2000) have produced new parameters for development in which notions of "capabilities" replace the concept
of "modernization" as the goal and project of development. As a result,
the "woman in development" has now become the subject of capability
associated with particular characteristics, roles, and outcomes. This suggests that a new universal norm of the woman of the global South is being
produced. Clearly NGOs are not simply addressing women or mobilizing
them but are engaged in constructing 'women,' whether as victims, beneficiaries, or as people with potential capability—or, most significantly for
feminism, as agents, organizers, and professionals.

Alongside the work of NGOs in producing "women" as a transnational
category of subordination, the project of making women into leaders and
professionalized experts is also taking place through NGO work. NGOs
collectively constitute a huge sector of employment. Neoliberal policies
have created spaces for NGOs to proliferate that offer employment and
self-employment opportunities to subjects defined as "women." Clearly
NGO work is not the same as state employment in terms of state pensions
or job stability—a difference that also contributes to the growth of NGOs
under neoliberalism. But the fewer obstacles facing women entering the
NGO sector and the fluidity of movement across job descriptions are offering new opportunities for many women. The close connections between
states and NGOs may make it possible for some women to move from
being gender advocates within NGOs to filling more influential official
positions of authority or at least to find more stable employment within
the state.

The field of engagement with gender is, moreover, elastic, fluid, and
flexible, and it is common for women to move to different jobs and institutions within this field—from working as an independent consultant to
holding a staff position in an NGO, to a position at the gender desk of a
donor agency or embassy, and so forth. This has brought into being a new
class of individuals who are "gender experts" and who possess professional
experience and expertise that are legible and marketable in a variety of
national and transnational circuits. In terms of gender, NGOs in many

locales may have given rise to a new class of experts and helped create a group of skilled, organized, and professional middle-class women who are the leaders and arguably the main beneficiaries of the NGO sector. These women, in fact, may be the women who are most empowered by NGOS, rather than the recipients or targets of NGO interventions. This reveals that NGOS may be "empowering" women in unanticipated ways—and very differently from Lauren Leve's example in Nepal (in this volume). This is a new level of professionalization that may help move some agendas as "women's causes" forward—or of some particular groups of women. If we look just at whether NGOS "empower" the "grass roots," as many NGOS claim to do, we may not be able to understand many of the consequences of the rise and spread of NGOS. NGOS not only are diverse, but contain contradictory processes. Thus, NGOS are reproducing class and gender hierarchies, even as they are also significant platforms of advocacy and organization.

One of the accomplishments of the NGO form is creating a sector of "empowered" middle-class women workers in the first world and the global South. This sector is gendered in some quite recognizable ways. Women working in the NGO sector get respect and prestige, they feel empowered by their work, and they command a new language of international gender work. These women gain a wider network of relationships, and often participate in transnational networks that enable cosmopolitanism and provide opportunities for mobility. These women produce knowledges about "the grass roots" and "women," as well as about government, governance, and development. They become experts, in part, by claiming their difference from state bureaucracies, corporations, and profit-making organizations and in this way they also construct the NGO form as superior.

NGOS may in some cases represent a professionalization of activists but NGOS may also create activists, as they draw more women into new entanglements with states, donors, and other groups of women. These local and global encounters give rise to new collaborations and conflicts. The constraints of NGO work may temper the radicalism of some feminists, while it serves to foster the development of new feminist perspectives among other women.

Quite often, NGOS have come to provide an institutional site from which women are not simply addressing "women's issues" but are helping to formulate what these issues are in a given context and articulating or demonstrating how conditions and policies might be improved. They may serve as "gender experts" or "policy experts" in the context of state policy as well as in transnational governance regimes within the United Nations or the European Union. Of course, in such situations, "gender" has become synonymous with "women," rather than with the broad range of genderings that the term might allow. In these processes of professionalization, NGOs are drawing different kinds of women into political participation and into relations with one another, so that within NGOs, inequalities may be reproduced, yet the NGO also serves as an arena in which these power relations (such as those between elite and subaltern women) come to be challenged. We see that relations among feminists and within NGOs are often hierarchical or contentious because "women" are not a natural, unitary interest group.

Feminists and women are not simply acting through NGOs or being served by them. The NGO as a transnational institutional form now participates in the processes that produce women as gendered subjects, and these processes also produce feminists. We suggest that, based on the evidence of the essays in this volume, feminist activism is flourishing across multiple agendas but may not always be recognized as such because the NGOs involved are not solely feminist in their membership or goals, nor do the ostensible purposes of the NGOs necessarily define the outcomes of their efforts. NGOs' collaborations with states and funders (national and foreign states, foundations, or corporations), as well as the processes of networking and professionalization, continue to generate new conflicts and struggles.

As we write this conclusion, we note an interesting shift away from the technocratic discourses of development and empowerment that characterized so many initiatives related to women in the past two decades toward new discourses that rely on moral terms in order to make emotional appeals on behalf of women. This is most evident in the salience of "sex trafficking" and the "trafficked woman" as contemporary global concerns. Nicholas Kristoff's one-man moral crusades are a good example of the new framing of women's subordination as a moral crisis. The "subaltern woman" or woman of the global South, in particular, is being written into a rescue narrative, allowing the global North to find redemption in new kinds of interventions of various sorts in the South.

This moral panic about women may be arising now, in part, as a response to the failure of neoliberal policies that promised to alleviate poverty, disenfranchisement, and inequality through the extension of market logics into every region and facet of life. But at the same time, the extension of the privatization logic of neoliberalism has created the spaces in which religious and secular moral claims have gained new traction in political arenas worldwide (Fassin 2012). The rise of moral arguments and emotional appeals seems to represent a turn away from the instrumental and technocratic rationales that underlay much of the NGO activity and the funding that sustained it in the recent past. In feminist terms, this moral turn poses particular new challenges since women's social and economic mobility have often been constrained on moral grounds, and women's access to the public sphere and their participation in politics have often been restricted in order to "protect" women who are constructed as easily victimized and vulnerable.

At the same time, the world has recently seen a series of struggles of antiauthoritarian, anticorporate, anti-neoliberal protest, including the so-called Arab Spring and Occupy movements. These suggest that the neoliberal paradigm and the states that adopted it will face increasing challenges from disparate sources. It seems unlikely that popular protests will vitiate the role of organizations, including NGOs, as vehicles for waging political struggles and promoting social welfare or will eliminate the need for feminist activism, in particular. The new political openings created by these mass actions cannot be acted on effectively without more-enduring structures of organization and coordination. For feminists the protests reveal that women's participation in public politics, whether official or alternative, remains fraught. Women in Egypt, most notably, continue to struggle to make their presence and their concerns felt within the Arab Spring and its aftermath. As the work of establishing democratic practices and of holding democratically elected governments accountable to the people continues, NGOs and feminist activism within and beyond NGOs will have significant roles to play.

Surveying the outcomes of feminist engagements with NGOs, we find no clear, unilinear line of progress, since the histories and configurations of struggle are diverse in different parts of the world. But, the nuanced analyses presented here reveal that the advocacy and advancement of feminist causes are taking place in varied ways on various fronts through NGOs, driven by a number of factors. NGOs have come to be strongly associated with women's issues and are themselves heavily populated by women members, workers, and constituencies. Feminists have a continued stake in engaging with NGOs and continuing to critique and strategize around the NGO form as women respond to the gendered politics of protest and to new discourses surrounding "women." Feminism in many forms, perhaps especially the NGO form, continues to be critical to geopolitics and to women's lives in the twenty-first century.

BIBLIOGRAPHY

Abels, Gabriele, and Joyce Mushaben. 2011. *Gendering the European Union.* Houndmills, UK: Palgrave Macmillan.

Abramson, David. 1999. "A Critical Look at NGOs and Civil Society as Means to an End in Uzbekistan." *Human Organization* 58 (3): 240–50.

Acker, Joan. 1999. "Gender and Organization." In *The Handbook of the Sociology of Gender,* edited by Janet Saltzman Chafetz, 177–94. New York: Plenum.

Adams, Melinda. 2006. "Regional Women's Activism: African Women's Networks and the African Union." In *Global Feminism: Transnational Women's Activism, Organizing, and Human Rights,* edited by Myra Marx Ferree and Aili Mari Tripp, 187–218. New York: New York University Press.

Afshar, Haleh, and Stephanie Barrientos, eds. 1999. *Women, Globalization and Fragmentation in the Developing World.* New York: St. Martin's.

Agarwal, Bina. 2001. "Participatory Exclusions, Community Forestry, and Gender: An Analysis for South Asia and Conceptual Framework." *World Development* 29 (10): 1623–48.

Agnihotri, Indu, and Vina Mazumdar. 1995. "Changing Terms of Political Discourse: Women's Movement in India, 1970s–1990s." *Economic and Political Weekly* 30 (29): 1869–78.

Ahearn, Laura. 2001. *Invitations to Love: Literacy, Love Letters, and Social Change in Nepal.* Ann Arbor: University of Michigan Press.

Ahmad, Q. K. 2007. *Socio-Economic and Indebtedness-Related Impact of Micro-Credit in Bangladesh.* Dhaka, Bangladesh: University Press Limited.

Aksartova, Sada. 2009. "Promoting Civil Society or Diffusing NGOs? U.S. Donors in the Former Soviet Union." In *Globalization, Philanthropy and Civil Society: Projecting Institutional Logics Abroad,* edited by David C. Hammack and Steven Heydemann, 160–91. Bloomington: Indiana University Press.

Alexander, M. Jacqui. 1997. "Erotic Autonomy as a Politics of Decolonization: An Anatomy of Feminist and State Practice in the Bahamas Tourist Economy." In *Feminist Genealogies, Colonial Legacies, Democratic Futures,* edited by M. Jacqui Alexander and Chandra T. Mohanty, 63–100. New York: Routledge.

Alexander, M. Jacqui, and Chandra Mohanty, eds. 1997. *Feminist Genealogies, Colonial Legacies, Democratic Futures*. New York: Routledge.

Alvarez, Sonia E. 1993. "Deepening Democracy: Popular Movement Networks, Constitutional Reform, and Radical Urban Regimes in Contemporary Brazil." In *Mobilizing the Community: Local Politics in the Era of the Global City*, edited by Robert Fischer and Joseph Klinger, 191–222. Newbury Park, CA: Sage.

———. 1997. "Reweaving the Fabric of Collective Action: Social Movements and Challenges to 'Actually Existing Democracy' in Brazil." In *Between Resistance and Revolution: Cultural Politics and Social Protest*, edited by Richard G. Fox and Orin Starn, 83–117. New Brunswick, NJ: Rutgers University Press.

———. 1998. "Latin American Feminisms 'Go Global': Trends of the 1990s and Challenges for the New Millennium." In *Cultures of Politics/Politics of Cultures: Re-Visioning Latin American Social Movements*, edited by Sonia E. Alvarez, Evelina Dagnino, and Arturo Escobar, 293–324. Boulder, CO: Westview.

———. 1999. "Advocating Feminism: The Latin American Feminist NGO 'Boom.'" *International Feminist Journal of Politics* 1 (2): 181–209.

———. 2012. "Globalized Localisms: The Origins, Travels and Translations of the World Social Forum Process." In *World Social Forum: Critical Explorations*, edited by Jai Sen and Peter Waterman. New Delhi: Open Word.

———. Forthcoming. *Feminism in Movement: Cultural Politics, Policy Advocacy and Transnational Activism in Latin America*. Durham, NC: Duke University Press.

Alvarez, Sonia E., Gianpaolo Baiocchi, et al., unpublished manuscript. "Interrogating the Civil Society Agenda, Reassessing Uncivic Contention: An Introduction." In *Beyond Civil Society: Social Movements, Civic Participation, and Democratic Contestation*, edited by Sonia E. Alvarez, Gianpaolo Baiocchi, Agustín Laó-Montes, Jeffrey W. Rubin, and Millie Thayer.

Alvarez, Sonia E., Evelina Dagnino, and Arturo Escobar. 1998. "Introduction: The Cultural and the Political in Latin American Social Movements." In *Cultures of Politics/Politics of Cultures: Re-Visioning Latin American Social Movements*, edited by Sonia E. Alvarez, Evelina Dagnino, and Arturo Escobar, 1–25. Boulder, CO: Westview.

Alvarez, Sonia E., Nalu Faria, and Miriam Nobre. 2004. "Another (Also Feminist) World Is Possible." In *World Social Forum: Challenging Empires*, edited by Jai Sen, Anita Anand, Arturo Escobar, and Peter Waterman, 154–61. New Delhi: Viveka Foundation.

Alvarez, Sonia E., Elisabeth Jay Friedman, et al. 2003. "Encountering Latin American Feminisms." *Signs* 28 (2): 537–79.

AnA/INCSMPS. 2008. *Multiple Discrimination in Romania. National Report*, Agora: Călăraşi. www.incsmps.ro-documente.

Andjelic, Neven. 2003. *Bosnia-Herzegovina: The End of a Legacy*. London: Frank Cass.

Appadurai, Arjun. 1986. "Is Homo Hierarchicus?" *American Ethnologist* 13 (4): 745–61.

———. 1998. "Disjuncture and Difference in the Global Cultural Economy." In *Modernity at Large: Cultural Dimensions of Globalization*, 27–47. Minneapolis: University of Minnesota Press.

———. 2000. "Grassroots Globalization and the Research Imagination." *Public Culture* 12 (1): 1–19.

———. 2001. "Grassroots Globalization and the Research Imagination." In *Globalization*, edited by Arjun Appadurai, 1–21. Durham, NC: Duke University Press.

———. 2002. "Deep Democracy: Urban Governmentality and the Horizon of Politics." *Public Culture* 14 (1): 21–47.

Arsenijević, Damir. 2010. *Forgotten Future: The Politics of Poetry in Bosnia and Herzegovina*. Baden-Baden: Nomos.

Articulación Feminista Marcosur. 2002. *Your Mouth Is Fundamental against Fundamentalisms*. Montevideo, Uruguay: Articulación Feminista Marcosur.

Asad, Talal. 2003. *Formations of the Secular: Christianity, Islam, Modernity*. Stanford, CA: Stanford University Press.

Aspinwall, Mark. 1998. "Collective Attraction: The New Political Game in Brussels." In *Collective Action in the European Union*, edited by Justin Greenwood and Mark Aspinwall, 196–213. London: Routledge.

Attwood, Lynne. 1997. "'She Was Asking for It': Rape and Domestic Violence against Women." In *Post-Soviet Women: From the Baltic to Central Asia*, edited by Mary Buckley, 99–118. Cambridge: Cambridge University Press.

Badran, Margot. 1996. *Feminists, Islam, and Nation*. Princeton, NJ: Princeton University Press.

Bagic, Aida. 2006. "Women's Organizing in Post-Yugoslav Countries: Talking about 'Donors.'" In *Global Feminism: Transnational Women's Activism, Organizing, and Human Rights*, edited by Myra Marx Ferree and Aili Mari Tripp, 141–65. New York: New York University Press.

Baines, Erin K. 2004. *Vulnerable Bodies: Gender, the UN and the Global Refugee Crisis*. Aldershot, UK: Ashgate.

Bakhtin, Mikhail. 1986. *Speech Genres and Other Late Essays*. Translated by Vern W. McGee. Austin: University of Texas Press.

Bakhtin, Mikhail, and V. N. Voloshinov. 1994. "Marxism and the Philosophy of Language." In *The Bakhtin Reader: Selected Writings of Bakhtin, Medvedev, Voloshinov*, edited by Pam Morris, 38–48. London: Arnold.

Banaszak, Lee Ann, Karen Beckwith, and Dieter Rucht. 2010. "When Power Relocates: Interactive Changes in Women's Movements and States." In *Women, Gender, and Politics: A Reader*, edited by Mona Lena Krook and Sarah Childs, 335–46. New York: Oxford University Press.

Banyard, Kat. 2010. *The Equality Illusion*. London: Faber and Faber.

Barry, Andrew, Thomas Osborne, and Nikolas Rose. 1996. "Introduction to." *Foucault and Political Reason: Liberalism, Neo-Liberalism, and Rationalities of Government*, edited by Andrew Barry, Thomas Osborne, and Nikolas Rose, 1–18. Chicago: University of Chicago Press.

Basu, Amrita. 2000. "Globalization of the Local/Localization of the Global: Mapping Transnational Women's Movements." *Meridians* 1 (1): 68–84.

Basu, Amrita, Inderpal Grewal, Caren Kaplan, and Liisa Malkki, eds. 2001. "Globalization and Gender." Special issue, *Signs* 26 (4).

Batliwala, Srilatha. 1994. "Defining Women's Empowerment: A Conceptual Framework." In *Population Policies Reconsidered: Health, Empowerment, and Rights*, edited by Gita Sen, Adrienne Germain, and Lincoln C. Chen, 127–38. Cambridge, MA: Harvard University Press.

Batliwala, Srilatha, and L. David Brown, eds. 2006. *Transnational Civil Society: An Introduction*. Bloomfield, CT: Kumarian.

Bauer, Dale, and S. Jaret McKinstry, eds. 1991. *Feminism, Bakhtin, and the Dialogic*. Albany: State University of New York Press.

Bebbington, Anthony. 2000. "Reencountering Development: Livelihood Transitions and Place Transformations in the Andes." *Annals of the Association of American Geographers* 90 (3): 495–520.

———. 2004a. "NGOs and Uneven Development: Geographies of Development Intervention." *Progress in Human Geography* 28 (6): 725–45.

———. 2004b. "Theorizing Participation and Institutional Change: Ethnography and Political Economy." In *Participation: From Tyranny to Transformation?*, edited by Samuel Hickey and Giles Mohan, 278–283. London: Zed.

Bebbington, Anthony, Samuel Hickey, and Diana C Mitlin, eds. 2008. *Can NGOs Make a Difference? The Challenge of Development Alternatives*. London: Zed.

Bedregal, Ximena. 1997. *Permanencia voluntaria en la utopía: El feminismo autónomo en el VII Encuentro Feminista Latinoamericano y del Caribe, Chile 1996*. Mexico City: Colección Feministas Cómplices.

Belloni, Roberto. 2001. "Civil Society and Peacebuilding in Bosnia and Herzegovina." *Journal of Peace Research* 38 (2): 163–80.

Benderly, Jill. 1997. "Feminist Movements in Yugoslavia, 1978–1992." In *State-Society Relations in Yugoslavia, 1945–1992*, edited by Melissa K. Bokovoy, Jill A. Irvine, and Carol S. Lilly, 183–209. New York: St. Martin's.

Bennett, Lynn. 1983. Dangerous Wives and Sacred Sisters: Social and Symbolic Roles of High-Caste Women in Nepal. New York: Columbia University Press.

Bennett, W. Lance. 1983. *News, the Politics of Illusion*. New York: Longman.

Bennett, W. Lance, and Shanto Iyengar. 2008. "A New Era of Minimal Effects? The Changing Foundations of Political Communication." *Journal of Communication* 58 (4): 707–31.

Bennett, W. Lance, Sabine Lang, and Alex Segerberg. 2012. "European Issue Publics Online: Citizen Engagement in EU versus National Level Advocacy Networks." In *The Europeanization of Public Spheres and the Diffusion of Ideas*, edited by Thomas Risse and Marianne van der Steeg. New York: Cambridge University Press.

Berdahl, Daphne. 1999. *Where the World Ended: Reunification and Identity in the German Borderland*. Berkeley: University of California Press.

Bereni, Laure. 2011. "Thinking the Transversality of Contentious Politics: The Field of Women's Advocacy." Unpublished manuscript.

Bernal, Victoria. 1994. "Gender, Culture, and Capitalism: Women and the Remaking of Islamic 'Tradition' in a Sudanese Village." *Comparative Studies in Society and History* (36) 1:36–67.

————. 2000. "Equality to Die For?: Women Guerilla Fighters and Eritrea's Cultural Revolution" *Political and Legal Anthropology Review* 23 (2): 61–76.

————. 2001. "From Warriors to Wives: Contradictions of Liberation and Development in Eritrea." *Northeast African Studies* 8 (3): 129–54.

Berry, Jeffrey M., and David F. Aarons. 2003. *A Voice for Nonprofits.* Washington: Brookings Institution.

Bhatia, Anju. 2000. *Women's Development and NGOs.* Jaipur, India: Rawat.

Bieber, Florian. 1999. "Consociationalism—Prerequisite or Hurdle for Democratisation in Bosnia? The Case of Belgium as a Possible Example." *SEER—South-East Europe Review for Labour and Social Affairs* 3:79–94.

Borneman, John. 1992. *Belonging in the Two Berlins: Kinship, State, Nation.* Cambridge, New York: Cambridge University Press.

Bornstein, David. 1996. *The Price of a Dream.* Dhaka, Bangladesh: University Press.

Borza, I., L. Grünberg, and Theodora Văcărescu. 2006. *Cartea neagră a egalității de șanse între femei și bărbați în România* [Black book on equal opportunities between women and men in Romania]. Bucharest: AnA.

Bose, Sumantra. 2002. *Bosnia after Dayton: Nationalist Partition and International Intervention.* Oxford: Oxford University Press.

Boserup, Esther. 1970. *Woman's Role in Economic Development.* New York: St. Martin's.

Bougarel, Xavier. 2006. "The Shadow of Heroes: Former Combatants in Post-war Bosnia-Herzegovina." *International Social Science Journal* 58 (189): 479–490.

————. 2007. "Death and the Nationalist: Martyrdom, War Memory and Veteran Identity among Bosnian Muslims." In *The New Bosnian Mosaic: Identities, Memories and Moral Claims in a Post-War Society,* edited by Xavier Bougarel, Elissa Helms, and Ger Duijzings, 167–92. Aldershot, UK: Ashgate.

Bowie, Katherine. 2008. "Standing in the Shadows: Of Matrilocality and the Role of Women in a Village Election in Northern Thailand." *American Ethnologist* 35 (1): 136–53.

Bratton, Michael. 1989. "The Politics of Government-NGO Relations in Africa." *World Development* 17 (4): 569–87.

Breton, Phillipe. 1995. *L'utopie de la communication: Le mythe du village planétaire.* Paris: La Découverte.

Bridger, Susan, Rebecca Kay, and Kathryn Pinnick. 1996. *No More Heroines? Russia, Women and the Market.* London: Routledge.

Bringa, Tone. 1995. *Being Muslim the Bosnian Way: Identity and Community in a Central Bosnian Village.* Princeton, NJ: Princeton University Press.

Brown, Wendy. 1995. *States of Injury: Power and Freedom in Late Modernity.* Princeton, NJ: Princeton University Press.

Burchell, Graham. 1996. "Liberal Government and the Techniques of the Self." In *Foucault and Political Reason: Liberalism, Neo-Liberalism, and Rationalities of Government,* edited by Andrew Barry, Thomas Osborne, and Nikolas Rose, 19–36. Chicago: University of Chicago Press.

Burghart, Richard. 1984. "The Formation of the Concept of Nation-State in Nepal." *Journal of Asian Studies* 44 (1): 101–25.

Butler, Judith. 1990. *Gender Trouble: Feminism and the Subversion of Identity.* New York: Routledge.

———. 1992. "Contingent Foundations: Feminism and the Question of 'Postmodernism.'" In *Feminists Theorize the Political,* edited by Judith Butler and Joan W. Scott, 3–21. New York: Routledge.

———. 1993. *Bodies That Matter: On the Discursive Limits of "Sex."* New York: Routledge.

———. 2004. *Undoing Gender.* New York: Routledge.

Campaña por la Convención de los derechos sexuales y los derechos reproductivos. 2006. *Manifiesto: Segunda versión (para el debate).* Lima: Campaña por la Convención de los derechos sexuales y los derechos reproductivos.

Carothers, Thomas. 1996. *Assessing Democracy Assistance: The Case of Romania.* Washington: Carnegie Endowment.

Castañeda, Jorge G., and Marco A. Morales, eds. 2008. *Leftovers: Tales of the Latin American Left.* New York: Routledge.

Castro, Mary García. 2001. "Engendering Powers in Neoliberal Times: Reflections from the Left on Feminisms and Feminisms." *Latin American Perspectives* 28 (6): 17–37.

Chambers, Robert. 1983. *Rural Development: Putting the Last First.* London: Longman.

———. 1997. *Whose Reality Counts? Putting the First Last.* London: Intermediate Technology.

Chandler, David. 2000. *Bosnia: Faking Democracy after Dayton.* London: Pluto.

Chatsumarn Kabilsingh. 1991. *Thai Women in Buddhism.* Berkeley, CA: Parallax.

Chatterjee, Partha. 1989. "Colonialism, Nationalism, and Colonialized Women: The Contest in India." *American Ethnologist* 16 (4): 622–33.

———. 2004. *The Politics of the Governed: Reflections on Popular Politics in Most of the World.* New York: Columbia University Press.

Checkel, Jeffrey. 1999. "Social Construction and Integration." *Journal of European Public Policy* 6 (4): 545–60.

Chodorow, Nancy. 1989. *Feminism and Psychoanalytic Theory.* New Haven, CT: Yale University Press.

Choluj, Bozena. 2003. "Die Situation der Frauen-NGOs in Polen an der Schwelle zum EU-Beitritt." In *Europas Toechter,* edited by Ingrid Miethe and Silke Roth, 203–24. Opladen, Germany: Leske and Budrich.

Clark, Ann Marie, Elizabeth J. Friedman, and Kathy Hochstetler. 1998. "The Sovereign Limits of Global Civil Society." *World Politics* 51 (1): 1–35.

Clark, Janine A., and Washeke M. Michuki. 2009. "Women and NGO Professionalization: A Case Study of Jordan." *Development in Practice* 19 (3): 329–39.

Clarke, Gerard. 1998. "Non-Governmental Organizations (NGOs) and Politics in the Developing World." *Political Studies* 46 (1): 36–52.

Cleaver, Frances. 2001. "Institutions, Agency and the Limitations of Participatory Approaches to Development." In *Participation: The New Tyranny?*, edited by Bill Cooke and Uma Kothari, 36–55. London: Zed.

The Coalition on the Women's Manifesto for Ghana. 2004. The Women's Manifesto for Ghana. (Hosted by ABANTU for Development). Accra, Ghana.

Cockburn, Cynthia. 1998. *The Space between Us: Negotiating Gender and National Identities in Conflict*. London: Zed.

———. 2007. *From Where We Stand: War, Women's Activism and Feminist Analysis*. London: Zed.

———. 2013. "Against the Odds: Sustaining Feminist Momentum in Post-war Bosnia-Herzegovina." *Women's Studies International Forum* 37: 26–35.

Cockburn, Cynthia, Meliha Hubić, and Rada Stakić-Domuz. 2001. *Women Organizing for Change: A Study of Women's Local Integrative Organizations and the Pursuit of Democracy in Bosnia-Herzegovina*. Zenica, Bosnia-Herzegovina: Medica Infoteka.

Collins, Chik. 1999. "Applying Bakhtin in Urban Studies: The Failure of Community Participation in the Ferguslie Park Partnership." *Urban Studies* 36 (1): 73–90.

Collins, Patricia Hill. 1990. *Black Feminist Thought*. New York: Routledge.

Comaroff, Jean. 2007. "Beyond Bare Life: AIDS, (Bio)Politics, and the Neoliberal Order." *Public Culture* 19 (1): 197–219.

Connors, Michael K. 2003. *Democracy and National Identity in Thailand*. Copenhagen: NIAS Press.

Cook, Nerida. 1998. "'Dutiful Daughters,' Estranged Sisters: Women in Thailand." In *Gender and Power in Affluent Asia*, edited by Krishna Sen and Maila Stivens, 250–90. London: Routledge.

Cooke, Bill, and Uma Kothari, eds. 2001. *Participation: The new Tyranny?* London: Zed.

Cornwall, Andrea. 2003. "Whose Voices? Whose Choices? Reflections on Gender and Participatory Development." *World Development* 31 (8): 1325–42.

———. 2004. "Spaces for Transformation? Reflections on Issues of Power and Difference in Participation in Development." In *Participation: From Tyranny to Transformation?*, edited by Samuel Hickey and Giles Mohan, 75–91. London: Zed.

Costa, LeeRay M. 2001. "Developing Identities: The Production of Gender, Culture and Modernity in a Northern Thai Non-Governmental Organization." PhD diss., University of Hawaii at Manoa.

———. 2008. "Gender, Sexuality and Nationalism in a Northern Thai Non-Governmental Organisation." *Asian Studies Review* 32 (2): 215–38.

Counts, Alex. 1996. *Who Needs Credit?* New Delhi: Research.

Cowen, Michael, and Robert Shenton. 1995. "The Invention of Development." In *Power of Development*, edited by Jonathan Crush, 27–43. London: Routledge.

Credit Development Forum. 1998. *Annual Yearbook*. Dhaka, Bangladesh: CDF.

Crewe, Emma, and Elizabeth Harrison. 1998. *Whose Development? An Ethnography of Aid*. London: Zed.

Crush, Jonathan, ed. 1995. "Imagining Development." In *Power of Development*, edited by Jonathan Crush, 1–27. London and New York: Routledge.

Dagnino, Evelina. 2008. "Challenges to Participation, Citizenship and Democracy: Perverse Confluence and Displacement of Meanings." In *Can NGOs Make a Difference? The Challenge of Development Alternatives*, edited by Anthony Bebbington, Samuel Hickey, and Diana C. Mitlin, 55–70. London: Zed.

Daniel, E. Valentine. 1987. *Fluid Signs: Being a Person the Tamil Way*. Berkeley: University of California Press.

Darunee, Tantiwiramanond, and Shashi Ranjan Pandey. 1987. "The Status and Role of Thai Women in the Pre-Modern Period: A Historical and Cultural Perspective." *Sojourn* 2 (1): 125–49.

———. 1991. *By Women, For Women: A Study of Women's Organizations in Thailand*. Singapore: ISEAS.

Das, Veena. 1995. "National Honor and Practical Kinship: Of Unwanted Women and Children." In *Critical Events: An Anthropological Perspective on Contemporary India*, edited by Veena Das, 55–83. Delhi: Oxford University Press.

Das, Veena, and Deborah Poole, eds. 2004. *Anthropology in the Margins of the State*. Santa Fe, NM: School of American Research Press.

De Sales, Anne. 2003. "The Kham Magar Country: Between Ethnic Claims and Maoism." In *Resistance and the State: Nepalese Experiences*, edited by David Gellner, 326–58. New Delhi: Social Science.

Dean, Mitchell. 1999. *Governmentality: Power and Rule in Modern Society*. London: Sage.

———. 2001. "'Demonic Societies': Liberalism, Biopolitics, and Sovereignty." In *States of Imagination: Ethnographic Explorations of the Postcolonial State*, edited by Thomas Blom Hansen and Finn Stepputat, 41–64. Durham, NC: Duke University Press.

Dej Poomkacha. 1995. "And Then What Next . . . Thai NGOs?" In *Thai NGOs: The Continuing Struggle for Democracy*, edited by Jaturong Boonyarattanasoontorn and Gawin Chutima, 88–96. Bangkok: Thai NGO Support Project.

Delcore, Henry. 2003. "Nongovernmental Organizations and the Work of Memory in Northern Thailand." *American Ethnologist* 30 (1): 61–84.

Denich, Bette S. 1976. "Urbanization and Women's Roles in Yugoslavia." *Anthropological Quarterly* 49 (1): 11–19.

Des Chene, Mary. 1996. "In the Name of Bikas." *Studies in Nepali History and Society* 1 (2): 259–70.

———. 1998. "Fate, Domestic Authority and Women's Wills." In *Selves in Time and Place: Identities, Experience, and History in Nepal*, edited by Debra Skinner, Alfred Pach III, and Dorothy Holland, 19–50. Lanham, MD: Rowman and Littlefield.

Desai, Manisha. 2002. "Transnational Solidarity: Women's Agency, Structural Adjustment, and Globalization." In *Women's Activism and Globalization: Linking Local Struggles and Transnational Politics*, edited by Nancy A. Naples and Manisha Desai, 15–33. New York: Routledge.

Desai, Sonalde B., et al. 2010. *Human Development in India: Challenges for a Society in Transition*. New Delhi: Oxford University Press.

Desjarlais, Robert. 2003. *Sensory Biographies: Lives and Deaths among Nepal's Yolmo Buddhists*. Berkeley: University of California Press.

Di Marco, Graciela. 2006. "Movimientos sociales y democratización en Argentina." In *De lo privado a lo público: 30 años de lucha ciudadana de las mujeres en América Latina*, edited by Nathalie Leblon and Elizabeth Maier. Mexico City: Siglo XXI.

———. Unpublished manuscript. "Social Movement Demands, Beyond Civil Society?" In *Interrogating the Civil Society Agenda: Social Movements, Civic Participation and Democratic Innovation*, edited by Sonia E. Alvarez, Gianpaolo Baiocchi, Agustín Laó-Montes, Jeffrey W. Rubin, and Millie Thayer.

Dobos, Manuela. 1983. "The Women's Movement in Yugoslavia: The Case of the Conference for the Social Activity of Women in Croatia, 1965–1974." *Frontiers* 7 (2): 47–55.

Dolhinow, Rebecca. 2010. *A Jumble of Needs: Women's Activism and Neoliberalism in the Colonias of the Southwest*. Minneapolis: University of Minnesota Press.

Doneys, Philippe. 2002. "Political Reform through the Public Sphere: Women's Groups and the Fabric of Governance." In *Reforming Thai Politics*, edited by Duncan McCargo, 163–82. Copenhagen: NIAS.

Dorsey, Ellen. 1997. "The Global Women's Movement: Articulating a New Vision of Global Governance." In *The Politics of Global Governance: International Organizations in an Interdependent World*, edited by Paul F. Diehl, 335–62. Boulder, CO: Lynne Rienner.

Dreze, Jean, and Harris Gazdar. 1997a. "Uttar Pradesh: The Burden of Inertia." In *Indian Development: Selected Regional Perspectives*, edited by Jean Dreze and Amartya Sen, 33–128. New Delhi: Oxford University Press.

Dreze, Jean, and Amartya Sen. 1997b. *Indian Development: Selected Regional Perspectives*. New Delhi: Oxford University Press.

Dumont, Louis. 1970. *Homo Hierarchicus: The Caste System and Its Implications*. Chicago: University of Chicago Press.

Dunlop, Joan, Mia Macdonald, and Rachel Kyte. 1996. "Women Redrawing the

Map: The World after the Beijing and Cairo Conferences." *SAIS Review* 16 (1): 153–65.

Dunn, Alison. 2008. "Charities and Restrictions on Political Activities: Developments by the Charity Commission for England and Wales in Determining the Regulatory Barriers." *International Journal of Not-for-Profit Law* 11 (1): 51–66.

Dyson, Tim and Mick Moore. 1983. "On Kinship Structure, Female Autonomy and Demographic Behaviour in India." *Population and Development Review* 9 (1): 35–60.

Eade, Deborah, "Preface" In *Development NGOs and Civil Society*, edited by Deborah Eade, 9–14. Oxford: Oxfam GB.

Ebron, Paula. 2007. "Constituting Subjects through Performative Acts." In *Africa after Gender*, edited by Catherine M. Cole, Takyiwaa Manuh, and Stephan F. Miescher, 171–90. Bloomington: Indiana University Press.

Edwards, Michael, and Fowler, Alan. 2002. "Introduction: Changing Challenges for NGO Management." In *The Earthscan Reader on NGO Management*, edited by Michael Edwards and Alan Fowler, 1–12. London: Earthscan Publications.

Edwards, Michael, and David Hulme. 1996. *Beyond the Magic Bullet: NGO Performance and Accountability in the Post–Cold War World*. West Hartford, CT: Kumarian.

———. 1998. "Too Close for Comfort? The Impact of Official Aid on Nongovernmental Organizations." *Current Issues in Comparative Education* 1 (1): 6–28.

EIGE, European Institute for Gender Equality. 2013. *Gender Equality Index*. Accessed on 10 June 2013. http://eige.europa.eu/sites/default/files/Gender -Equality-Index-Report.pdf.

Elyachar, Julia. 2002. "Empowerment Money: The World Bank, Non-Governmental Organizations, and the Value of Culture in Egypt." *Public Culture* 14 (3): 493–513.

Enslin, Elizabeth. 1998. "Imagined Sisters: The Ambiguities of Women's Poetics and Collective Actions." In *Selves in Time and Place: Identities, Experience, and History in Nepal*, edited by Debra Skinner, Alfred Pach III, and Dorothy Holland, 269–300. Lanham, MD: Rowman and Littlefield.

Erera, Pauline I., et al. 2002. "Why Don't They Marry? Never Married Women in Thailand." Chiang Mai University Women's Studies Center *Newsletter*, 2 (January 1).

Ertürk, Yakin. 2006. "Turkey's Modern Paradoxes: Identity Politics, Women's Agency, and Universal Rights." In *Global Feminism: Transnational Women's Activism, Organizing, and Human Rights*, edited by Myra Marx Ferree and Aili Mari Tripp, 79–109. New York: New York University Press.

Eschle, Catherine. 2005. "'Skeleton Women': Feminism and the Antiglobalization Movement." *Signs* 30 (3): 1741–60.

Eschle, Catherine, and Bice Maiguashca. 2010. *Making Feminist Sense of the Global Justice Movement*. Lanham, MD: Rowman and Littlefield.

Escobar, Arturo. 1995. *Encountering Development: The Making and Unmaking of the Third World*. Princeton, NJ: Princeton University Press.

———. 1996. "Constructing Nature." In *Liberation Ecologies: Environment, Development and Social Movements*, edited by Richard Peet and Michael Watts, 46–68. London: Routledge.

———. 2000. "Culture Sits in Places: Anthropological Reflections on Globalization and Subaltern Strategies of Localization." Paper presented at the Five Colleges Faculty Symposium on Globalization, Postdevelopment, and Environmentalism, Hampshire College, Amherst, MA, June 1–3.

———. 2008. *Territories of Difference: Place, Movements, Life, Redes*. Durham, NC: Duke University Press.

Espina, Giaconda. 2007. "Beyond Polarization: Organized Venezuelan Women Promote Their Minimum Agenda." *NACLA Report on the Americas* 40 (2): 20–24.

Esteva, Gustavo. 1992. "Development." In *The Development Dictionary: A Guide to Knowledge as Power*, edited by Wolfgang Sachs, 6–25. London: Zed.

Etzioni, Amitai. 2002. *Societatea monocromă*. Iași, Romania: Polirom. Translated by Mona Antohi.

European Commission. 2000. *The Commission and Non-Governmental Organizations: Building a Stronger Partnership*. Brussels: European Commission, January 18.

———. 2001. *Council Decision of 20 December 2000 establishing a Programme relating to the Community framework strategy on gender equality (2001–2005)*. (2001/51/EC). Brussels.

———. 2007. Discrimination in the European Union, *Special Eurobarometer* no. 263.

———. 2008. *Document de travail de la commission accompagnant le Rapport d'évaluation final de la stratégie-cadre et du programme d'action communautaire concernant la stratégie communautaire en matière d'égalité entre les femmes et les hommes*. Accessed June 24, 2013. http://eur-lex.europa.eu /LexUriServ/LexUriServ.do?uri=CELEX:52008SC2365:EN:NOT.

———. 2013. *Flash Eurobarometer 373*, Europeans' Engagement in Participatory Democracy. Accesed June 16, 2013. www.ec.europa.eu/public_opinion/flash /fl_373_en.pdf.

European Community. 2007. *Decision No. 1672/2006/EC of the European Parliament and of the Council of 10/24/2006 Establishing a Community Programme for Employment and Social Solidarity—PROGRESS*. Brussels.

European Feminist Forum. 2007. "Presentation on the European Feminist Forum." Accessed March 15, 2009. http://europeanfeministforum.org/spip.php?article 291&lang=en. See documentation of the EFF in the WaybackMachine at http:// web.archive.org/web/20070918163032/http://europeanfeministforum.org/ (access June 24, 2013).

———. 2008. "Announcement EFF June Conference in Poland Cancelled."

Accessed March 16, 2009. http://europeanfeministforum.org/spip.php?article
434&lang=en or http://www.wloe.org/European-Feminist-Forum.501.0.html.
————. 2009. The European Feminist Forum. A Herstory (2004–2008). Edited
by Aletta. Institute for Women's History. Amsterdam. Accessed June 24, 2013.
http://dare.uva.nl/document/174520.

Everett, Margaret. 1997. "The Ghost in the Machine: Agency in 'Poststructural'
Critiques of Development." *Anthropological Quarterly* 70 (3): 137–51.

Ewig, Christina. 1999. "The Strengths and Limits of the NGO Women's Movement
Model: Shaping Nicaragua's Democratic Institutions." *Latin American Research
Review* 34 (3): 75–102.

EWL European Women's Lobby. 2008. *Annual Report 2007*. Accessed February 14,
2009. www.womenlobby.org/SiteResources/data/MediaArchive/Publications
/EWL%20Annual%20Report%202007_EN.pdf.

Fakhro, Munira. 1997. "Civil Society and Non-Governmental Organizations in the
Middle East: Reflections on the Gulf." *Middle East Women's Studies* 11 (4): 1–3.

Fallon, Kathleen. 2008. *Democracy and the Rise of Women's Movements in Sub-
Saharan Africa*. Baltimore, MD: Johns Hopkins University Press.

Fals Borda, Orlando, and Muhammad Anisur Rahman, eds. 1991. *Action and
Knowledge: Breaking the Monopoly with Participatory Action Research*. New
York: Apex.

Faria, Nalu, ed. 2003. *Construir la igualdad: Debates feministas en el Foro Social
Mundial*. Quito: Red Latinoamericana Mujeres Transformando la Economía.

Fassin, Didier. 2012. *Humanitarian Reason: A Moral History of the Present*. Berkeley: University of California Press.

FDSC-Foundation for the Development of Civil Society. 2013. Fondul ONG in
Romania, Ghidul solicitanților, [NGO Fund in Romania. Solicitors guide],
www.fondong.fdsc.ro/unlopad/componenta1/GhidulSolicitantului.pdf.

————. 2006. Starea Sectorului Neguvernamental, [The situation of the NGO
sector], Bucharest.

Feijoó, Maria del Carmen. 2000. "El feminismo contemporáneo en la Argentina:
Encuentros y desencuentros en un escenario turbulento." In *Cuadernos de Investigación Social No. 3*. Lima: Departamento de Ciencias Sociales, Pontífica Uni-
versidad Católica del Perú.

Feldman, Shelley. 1997. "NGOs and Civil Society: (Un)stated Contradictions."
Annals of the American Academy of Political and Social Science (November):
46–65.

————. 2003. "Paradoxes of Institutionalisation: The Depoliticisation of Bangladeshi NGOs." *Development in Practice* 13 (1): 5–26.

Ferguson, James. 1990. *The Anti-Politics Machine: "Development," Depoliticization,
and Bureaucratic Power in Lesotho*. Minneapolis: University of Minnesota Press.

Ferguson, James, and Akhil Gupta. 2002. "Spatializing States: Toward an Ethnography of Neoliberal Governmentality." *American Ethnologist* 29 (4): 981–1002.

Fernando, Jude. 1997. "Nongovernmental Organizations, Micro-Credit, and the

Empowerment of Women." *Annals of the American Academy of Political and Social Science* 554 (November): 150–77.

Ferree, Myra Marx 1997. "German Unification and Feminist Identity." In *Transitions, Environments, Translations: Feminisms in International Politics*, edited by Joan W. Scott, Cora Kaplan, and Debra Keates, 46–55. New York: Routledge.

Ferree, Myra Marx, and Aili Mari Tripp, eds. 2006. *Global Feminism: Transnational Women's Activism, Organizing, and Human Rights*. New York: New York University Press.

Field Office Team. 1983. *Baseline Survey Report*. Kathmandu, Nepal: Development for All Field Office.

Fischer, Frank. 2006. "Participatory Governance as Deliberative Empowerment: The Cultural Politics of Discursive Space." *American Review of Public Administration* 36 (1): 19–40.

Fisher, Julie. 1998. *Nongovernments: NGOs and the Political Development of the Third World*. West Hartford, CT: Kumarian Press.

Fisher, William F. 1997. "Doing Good? The Politics and Antipolitics of NGO Practices." *Annual Review of Anthropology* 26: 439–64.

Fodor, Eva. 2006. "Gender Mainstreaming and Its Consequences in the European Union." *Analyst* 7 (September): 1–14.

Forbes, Ann Armbrecht. 1999. "The Importance of Being Local: Villagers, NGOs, and the World Bank in the Arun Valley, Nepal." *Identities* 6 (2–3): 319–44.

Fortun, Kim. 2001. *Advocacy after Bhopal: Environmentalism, Disasters, New Global Orders*. Chicago: University of Chicago Press.

Foucault, Michel. 1971. *Madness and Civilization: A History of Insanity in the Age of Reason*. Translated by Richard Howard. New York: Random House.

———. 1982. "On the Genealogy of Ethics: An Overview of Work in Progress." In *Michel Foucault: Beyond Structuralism and Hermeneutics*, edited by Hubert L. Dreyfus and Paul Rabinow, 229–52. Chicago: University of Chicago Press.

———. 1991. "Governmentality." In *The Foucault Effect: Studies in Governmentality*, edited by Graham Burchell, Colin Gordon, and Peter Miller, 87–104. Translated by Pasquale Pasquino. Chicago: University of Chicago Press.

———. 1995. *Discipline and Punish: The Birth of the Prison*. Translated by Alan Sheridan. New York: Vintage.

Foundation Women in Europe. 2010. "Europe Sensed vs. Europe Proclaimed— What Can European Women Expect from the EU?" *Symposium Flyer*, January 15. Frankfurt am Main, Germany.

Fowler, Alan. 1991. "The Role of NGOs in Changing State-Society Relations: Perspectives from Eastern and Southern Africa." *Development Policy Review* 9 (1): 53–83.

Fraser, Nancy. 1989. *Unruly Practices: Power, Discourse, and Gender in Contemporary Social Theory*. Minneapolis: University of Minnesota Press.

Freeman, Carla. 2000. *High Tech and High Heels in the Global Economy*. Durham, NC: Duke University Press.

———. 2001. "Is Local: Global as Feminine: Masculine? Rethinking the Gender of Globalization." *Signs* 26 (4): 1007–37.

Freire, Paolo. 1970. *Pedagogy of the Oppressed*. Translated by Myra Bergman Ramos. New York: Continuum.

———. 1997. *Pedagogy of the Oppressed*. Translated by M. B. Ramos. New York: Continuum.

Friedman, Elisabeth J. 2000. "Gendering the Agenda: Women's Transnational Organizing at the UN World Conferences of the 1990s." Paper presented at the Annual Convention of the International Studies Association, Los Angeles, CA, March 14–17.

———. 2007. "Introduction: How Pink is the 'Pink Tide'?" *NACLA Report on the Americas* 40 (2): 16.

———. 2010. "Seeking Rights from the Left: Gender and Sexuality in Latin America." In *Women's Movements in a Global Era: The Power of Local Feminisms*, edited by Amrita Basu, 285–314. Boulder, CO: Westview.

Friedmann, John. 1992. *Empowerment: The Politics of Alternative Development*. Cambridge, MA: Blackwell.

Funk, Nanette. 2006. "Women's NGOs in Central and Eastern Europe and the Former Soviet Union: The Imperialist Criticism." In *Women and Citizenship in Central and Eastern Europe*, edited by Jasmina Lukić, Joanna Regulaska, and Darja Zaviršek. Aldershot, UK: Ashgate.

Gagnon, V. P., Jr. 2003. "Liberal Multiculturalism: Part of the Problem?" In *Democracy Papers*, edited by Džemal Sokolović, 8–12. Konjic, Bosnia-Herzegovina: Institute for Strengthening Democracy.

Gago, Verónica. 2007. "Dangerous Liaisons: Latin American Feminists and the Left." *NACLA Report on the Americas* 40 (2): 17–19.

Gal, Susan, and Gail Kligman. 2000a. *The Politics of Gender after Socialism. A Comparative-Historical Essay*, Princeton, NJ: Princeton University Press.

———, eds. 2000b. *Reproducing Gender: Politics, Publics and Everyday Life after Socialism*. Princeton, NJ: Princeton University Press.

Galindo, María. 1997. "Tiempo saboteado en que nos toca vivir." In *Permanencia voluntaria en la utopía: La autonomía en el VII Encuentro Feminista Latinoamericano y del Caribe*, edited by Ximena Bedregal. Mexico City: Centro de Investigación y Capacitación de la Mujer.

Gandhi, Nandita, and Nandita Shah. 1992. *The Issues at Stake: Theory and Practice in the Contemporary Women's Movement in India*. New Delhi: Kali for Women.

Garcia, Veronica Vasquez. 2001. "Taking Gender into Account: Women and Sustainable Development Projects in Rural Mexico." *Women's Studies Quarterly* 29 (1–2): 85–98.

Gautam, Shobha. 2001. *Women and Children in the Periphery of the Peoples' War*. Kathmandu, Nepal: Institute for Human Rights Communications Nepal.

Gautam, Shobha, Amrita Banskota, and Rita Manchanda. 2001. "Where There

Are No Men: Women in the Maoist Insurgency in Nepal." In *Women, War and Peace*, edited by Rita Manchanda, 214–251, New Delhi: Sage.

———. 2003. "Where There Are No Men: Women in the Maoist Insurgency in Nepal." In *Understanding the Maoist Movement of Nepal*, edited by Deepak Thapa, 93–124. London: Sage.

Gautam, Shova, and Anjana Shakya. 1999. "Maoist Movement: Impact on Women." *Kathmandu Post*, October 28.

Gaventa, John. 2006. "Finding the Spaces for Change: A Power Analysis." *IDS Bulletin* 37 (6): 23–33.

Gellner, David. 2002. "Introduction: Transformations of the Nepalese State." In *Resistance and the State: Nepalese Experiences*, edited by David Gellner, 1–30. New Delhi: Social Science.

———, ed. 2003. *Resistance and the State: Nepalese Experiences*. New Delhi: Social Science.

George, Susan. 1990. *A Fate Worse Than Debt*. New York: Grove Weidenfeld.

Geske, Mary, and Susan Bourque. 2001. "Grassroots Organizations and Women's Human Rights: Meeting the Challenge of the Local-Global Link." In *Women, Gender, and Human Rights: A Global Perspective*, edited by Marjorie Agosin, 246–64. New Brunswick, NJ: Rutgers University Press.

Ghodsee, Kristen. 2004. "Feminism-by-Design: Emerging Capitalisms, Cultural Feminism, and Women's Nongovernmental Organizations in Postsocialist Eastern Europe." *Signs* 29 (3): 727–53.

———. 2005. *The Red Riviera: Gender, Tourism, and Postsocialism on the Black Sea*. Next Wave. Durham: Duke University Press.

Gibson-Graham, J. K. 1996. *The End of Capitalism (As We Knew It): A Feminist Critique of Political Economy*. Minneapolis: University of Minnesota Press.

Gilbert, Andrew. 2006. "The Past in Parenthesis: (Non) Post-Socialism in Post-War Bosnia-Herzegovina." *Anthropology Today* 22 (4): 14–18.

Godemont, Jozefien, and Joz Motmans. 2006. "The Velvet Triangle in the Flemish Field of Women's and LGB Movements: Networks, Strategies and Concepts." Paper presented at the Considering Encounters Seminar on Women's (Gender) Studies and Women's Movements, Panteion University, Athens, Greece, May 4.

Goetz, Anne-Marie, and Rina Sengupta. 1996. "Who Takes the Credit? Gender, Power and Control over Loan Use in Rural Credit Programs in Bangladesh." *World Development* 24 (1): 45–64.

Gouveia, Taciana, and Marcelo Daniliauskas. 2010. *ABONG: Panorama da Associadas*. São Paulo: Associação Brasileira de ONGs.

Government of India. 1997. *Mahila Samakhya (Education for Women's Equality): Ninth Plan Document 1997–2002*. New Delhi: Ministry of Human Resource Development, Department of Education.

Graff, Agnieszka. 2009. "The Trouble with NGOs." In *The Future of Gender Policies in the European Union*, edited by Agnieszka Grzybek, 33–37. Warsaw: Heinrich Boell Foundation.

Gramsci, Antonio. 1971. *Antonio Gramsci: Selections from the Prison Notebooks*, edited by Quintin Hoare and Jeffrey Nowell-Smith. New York: International.

Grandits, Hannes. 2007. "The Power of 'Armchair Politicians': Ethnic Loyalty and Political Factionalism among Herzegovinian Croats." In *The New Bosnian Mosaic: Identities, Memories and Moral Claims in a Post-War Society*, edited by Xavier Bougarel, Elissa Helms, and Ger Duijzings, 101–22. Aldershot, UK: Ashgate.

Greenwood, Davydd, and Morten Levin. 1998. *Introduction to Action Research*. London: Sage.

Greenwood, Justin. 2007. "Governance and Organised Civil Society in the European Union: The Search for 'Input Legitimacy' through Elite Groups." In *Governance and Civil Society in the European Union*, edited by Vincent Della Sala and Carlo Ruzza, 2:31–46. Manchester, UK: Manchester University Press.

Grewal, Inderpal. 2005. *Transnational America: Feminisms, Diasporas, Neoliberalisms*. Durham, NC: Duke University Press.

Grewal, Inderpal, and Caren Kaplan, eds. 1994. *Scattered Hegemonies: Postmodernity and Transnational Feminist Practice*. Minneapolis: University of Minnesota Press.

Grillo, Ralph D., and R. L. Stirrat. 1997. *Discourses of Development: Anthropological Perspectives*. Oxford: Berg.

Grødeland, Åse Berit. 2006. "Public Perceptions of Non-Governmental Organisations in Serbia, Bosnia & Herzegovina, and Macedonia." *Communist and Post-Communist Studies* 39 (2): 221–46.

Grünberg, Laura. 2000a. "NGO-ization of Feminism in Romania: The Failure of a Success." *Analize* 7:14–19.

———. 2000b. "Women NGOs in Romania." In Reproducing Gender: Politics, Publics and Everyday Life after Socialism, edited by Susan Gal and Gail Kligman, 307–336. Princeton, NJ: Princeton University Press.

———. 2003. "NGOization of Feminism in Romania: The Failure of a Success, *Interdisciplinary Political and Cultural Journal* no. 2. Lodz University, Poland: Versita.

———. 2008. *biONGrafie: AnA—istoria trăită a unui ONG de femei*. [biONGraphy: AnA—the lived history of a women's NGO]. Bucharest: Polirom.

———. 2009. "18 ans: L'âge du féminisme roumain," *Chronique Feministe*, special issue on Feminismes a l'Est," Université des Femmes, Bruxelles, Belgium, no. 102 (in French).

Guenther, Katja M. 2010. *Making Their Place: Feminism after Socialism in Eastern Germany*. Stanford, CA: Stanford University Press.

Guha, Ranajit. 1983. *Elementary Aspects of Peasant Insurgency in Colonial India*. Delhi: Oxford University Press.

Guijt, Irene, and Meera Kaul Shah. 1998. *The Myth of Community: Gender Issues in Participatory Development*. London: Intermediate Technology Development Group.

Gupta, Akhil. 1995. "Blurred Boundaries: The Discourse of Corruption, the Culture of Politics, and the Imagined State." *American Ethnologist* 22 (2): 375–402.

———. 1998. *Postcolonial Developments: Agriculture in the Making of Modern India*. Durham, NC: Duke University Press.

Gupta, Akhil, and Aradhana Sharma. 2006. "Globalization and Postcolonial States." *Current Anthropology* 47 (2): 277–307.

Hadžibegović, Ilijas, and Husnija Kamberović. 1997. "Građansko društvo u Bosni i Hercegovini: porijeklo i kontekst." *Revija slobodne misli* 99 (9–10): 48–56.

Hall, Stuart. 1988. *The Hard Road to Renewal: Thatcherism and the Crisis of the Left*. London: Verso.

Halley, Janet. 2006. *Split Decisions: How and Why to Take a Break from Feminism*. Princeton, NJ: Princeton University Press.

Hann, Chris, and Elizabeth Dunn, eds. 1996. *Civil Society: Challenging Western Models*. New York: Routledge.

Hansen, Thomas Blom. 1999. *The Saffron Wave: Democracy and Hindu Nationalism in Modern India*. Princeton, NJ: Princeton University Press.

———. 2001. *Wages of Violence: Naming and Identity in Postcolonial Bombay*. Princeton, NJ: Princeton University Press.

Hansen, Thomas Blom, and Finn Stepputat, eds. 2001. *States of Imagination: Ethnographic Explorations of the Postcolonial State*. Durham, NC: Duke University Press.

Haraway, Donna J. 1988. "Situated Knowledges: The Science Question in Feminism and the Privilege of Partial Perspective." *Feminist Studies* 14 (3): 575–99.

———. 1991. *Simians, Cyborgs, and Women: The Reinvention of Nature*. New York: Routledge.

———. 1992. "Ecce Homo, Ain't (Ar'n't) I a Woman, and Inappropriate/d Others: The Human in a Post-Humanist Landscape." In *Feminists Theorize the Political*, edited by J. Butler and J. W. Scott, 86–100. New York: Routledge.

Harcourt, Wendy, ed. 1999. *Women@internet*. London: Zed.

———. 2005. "The Body Politic in Global Development Discourse." In *Women and the Politics of Place*, edited by Wendy Escobar and Arturo Escobar, 32–47. Bloomfield, CT: Kumarian.

———. 2006. "The Global Women's Rights Movement: Power Politics around the United Nations and the World Social Forum." *United Nations Research Institute for Social Development: Civil Society and Social Movements*, Programme Paper Number 25.

Harcourt, Wendy, and Arturo Escobar. 2002. "Women and the Politics of Place." *Development* 45 (1): 7–14.

Harvey, David. 2000. "Cosmopolitanism and the Banality of Geographical Evils." *Public Culture* 12 (2): 529–64.

———. 2005. *A Brief History of Neoliberalism*. Oxford: Oxford University Press.

Hashemi, Syed, Sidney Schuler, and Ann Riley. 1996. "Rural Credit Programs and Women's Empowerment in Bangladesh." *World Development* 24 (3): 635–53.

Hearn, Julie Hewitt. 2007. "African NGOs: The New Compradors?" *Development and Change* 38 (6): 1095–10.

Helfferich, Barbara, and Felix Kolb. 2001. "Multilevel Action Coordination in European Contentious Politics." In *Contentious Europeans: Protest and Politics in an Emerging Polity*, edited by Douglas R. Imig and Sidney G. Tarrow, 143–62. Lanham, MD: Rowman and Littlefield.

Helms, Elissa. 2003a. "Gendered Visions of the Bosnian Future: Women's Activism and Representation in Post-War Bosnia-Herzegovina." PhD diss., University of Pittsburgh.

Helms, Elissa. 2003. "Women as Agents of Ethnic Reconciliation? Women's NGOs and International Intervention in Postwar Bosnia-Herzegovina." *Women's Studies International Forum* 26 (1): 15–33.

———. 2006. "Gendered Transformations of State Power: Masculinity, International Intervention, and the Bosnian Police." *Nationalities Papers* 34 (3): 343–61.

———. 2007. "'Politics Is a Whore': Women, Morality, and Victimhood in Post-War Bosnia-Herzegovina." In *The New Bosnian Mosaic: Identities, Memories and Moral Claims in a Post-War Society*, edited by Xavier Bougarel, Elissa Helms, and Ger Duijzings, 235–53. Aldershot, UK: Ashgate.

———. 2010. "The Gender of Coffee: Women and Reconciliation Initiatives in Post-War Bosnia and Herzegovina." *Focaal: Journal of Global and Historical Anthropology* 57: 17–32.

———. 2013. *Innocence and Victimhood: Gender, Nation, and Women's Activism in Postwar Bosnia-Herzegovina*. Madison, WI: University of Wisconsin Press.

Hemment, Julie. 2000. "Gender, NGOs and the Third Sector in Russia: An Ethnography of Russian Civil Society." PhD diss., Cornell University.

———. 2004. "Strategizing Development: Translations, Appropriations, Responsibilities." In *Post-Soviet Women Encounter Transition: Nation Building, Economic Survival, and Civic Activism*, edited by Kathleen Kuehnast and Carol Nechemias, 313–34. Washington: Woodrow Wilson International Center for Scholars.

———. 2007. *Empowering Women in Russia: Activism, Aid, and NGOs*. Bloomington: Indiana University Press.

———. 2011 "Global Civil Society and the Local Costs of Belonging: Defining Violence Against Women in Russia." In Anthropology at the Front Lines of Gender-Based Violence. Jennifer Wies and Hillary Haldane, eds. Nashville: Vanderbilt University Press.

Henderson, Carol. 1994. "Famines and Droughts in Western Rajasthan: Desert Cultivators and Periodic Resource Stress." In *The Idea of Rajasthan: Explorations in Regional Identity*, edited by K. Schomer, J. L. Erdman, D. O. Lodrick, and L. I. Rudolph, 2:1–29. New Delhi: Manohar.

Henderson, Sarah L. 2003. *Building Democracy in Contemporary Russia: Western Support for Grassroots Organizations*. Ithaca, NY: Cornell University Press.

Hershberg, Eric, and Fred Rosen, eds. 2006. *Latin America after Neoliberalism: Turning the Tide in the 21st Century?* New York: New Press.

Herzog, Hanna. 2011. "NGOization of the Israeli Feminist Movement: Depoliticizing or Redefining Political Spaces?" In *The Contradictions of Israeli Citizenship: Land, Religion, State*, edited by Guy Ben-Porat and Bryan S. Turner, 158–79. New York: Routledge.

Hickey, Samuel, and Giles Mohan, eds. 2004. *Participation: From Tyranny to Transformation?* London: Zed.

Hilhorst, Dorothea. 2003. *The Real World of NGOs: Discourses, Diversity, and Development*. London: Zed.

Hindess, Barry. 2004. "Liberalism—What's in a Name?" In *Global Governmentality: Governing International Spaces*, edited by Wendy Larner and William Walters, 23–39. London: Routledge.

Hirshman, Mitu. 1995. "Women and Development: A Critique." In *Feminism/Postmodernism/Development*, edited by Marianne H. Marchand and Jane L. Parpart, 42–55. New York: Routledge.

Hobart, Mark, ed. 1993. *An Anthropological Critique of Development: The Growth of Ignorance*. London: Routledge.

Hodžić, Saida. 2009. "Unsettling Power: Domestic Violence, Gender Politics, and Struggles over Sovereignty in Ghana." *Ethnos* 74 (3): 331–60.

———. 2010. "The Logics of Controversy: Gender Violence as a Site of Frictions in Ghanaian Advocacy." In *Domestic Violence and the Law in Colonial and Postcolonial Africa*, edited by Emily Burrill, Richard L. Roberts, and Elizabeth Thornberry, 220–38. Athens: Ohio University Press.

Hofstede, Geert, ed. 1998. *Masculinity and Femininity: The Taboo Dimension of National Cultures*. Thousand Oaks, CA: Sage.

———. 2001. *Cultures' Consequences: Comparing Values, Behaviors, Institutions and Organizations across Nations*. Thousand Oaks, CA: Sage.

Holli, Anne Marie. 2008. "Feminist Triangles: A Conceptual Analysis." *Representation* 44 (2): 169–85.

Hrycak, Alexandra. 2006. "Foundation Feminism and the Articulation of Hybrid Feminisms in Post-Socialist Ukraine." *East European Politics and Societies* 20 (1): 69–100.

Husanović, Jasmina. 2009. "The Politics of Gender, Witnessing, Postcoloniality and Trauma." *Feminist Theory* 10 (1): 99–119.

Hutt, Michael. 2004. *Himalayan People's War: Nepal's Maoist Rebellion*. Bloomington: Indiana University Press.

Inglis, Shelley. 1998. "Re/Constructing Right(s): The Dayton Peace Agreement, International Civil Society Development, and Gender in Postwar Bosnia-Herzegovina." *Columbia Human Rights Law Review* 30: 65–121.

Interact. 2005. *Studiu despre valorile comportamentul românilor din perspectiva dimensiunilor culturale după metoda lui Geert Hofstede* [Study on the values of Romanians behaviours from the perspective of the Geert Hofstede method]. Accessed March 15, 2011. www.training.ro/docs/studiu2.pdf.

Jackson, Cecile. 1993. "Doing What Comes Naturally? Women and Environment in Development." *World Development* 21 (123): 1947–63.

Jackson, Cecile, and Pearson, Ruth. 1998. *Feminist Visions of Development: Gender Analysis and Policy*. London: Routledge.

Jackson, Stephen. 2005. "The State Didn't Even Exist: Non-Governmentality in Kivu, Eastern DR Congo." In *Between a Rock and a Hard Place: African NGOs, Donors, and the State*, edited by Jim Igoe and Tim Kelsall, 165–96. Durham, NC: Carolina Academic.

Jacobson, Doranne. 1982. "Purdah and the Hindu Family in Central India." In *Separate Worlds: Studies of Purdah in South Asia*, edited by Hanna Papanek and Gail Minault, 81–109. Delhi: Chanakya.

Jad, Islah. 2007. "The NGO-ization of Arab Women's Movements." In *Feminisms in Development: Contradictions, Contestations, and Challenges*, edited by Andrea Cornwall, Elizabeth Harrison, and Ann Whitehead, 177–90. London: Zed.

Jancar, Barbara. 1985. "The New Feminism in Yugoslavia." In *Yugoslavia in the 1980s*, edited by Pedro Ramet, 201–23. Boulder, CO: Westview.

Jancar-Webster, Barbara. 1990. *Women and Revolution in Yugoslavia, 1941–1945*. Denver, CO: Arden.

Jandhyala, Kameshwari. 2001. "State Initiatives." In "Towards Equality: A Symposium on Women, Feminisms and Women's Movements," *Seminar* 505:31–35.

Jansen, Stef. 2006. "The Privatisation of Home and Hope: Return, Reforms and the Foreign Intervention in Bosnia-Herzegovina." *Dialectical Anthropology* 30 (3): 177–99.

Jeffery, Roger, and Patricia Jeffery. 1997. *Population, Gender and Politics: Demographic Change in Rural North India*. Cambridge: Cambridge University Press.

Jeffrey, Leslie Ann. 2002. *Sex and Borders: Gender, National Identity and Prostitution Policy in Thailand*. Honolulu: University of Hawaii Press.

Jenson, Jane. 2008. "Writing Women Out, Folding Gender In: The European Union 'Modernizes' Social Policy." *Social Politics* 15 (2) 131–53.

Joachim, Jutta. 2002. "Comparing the Influence of NGOs in Transnational Institutions: The UN, the EU and the Case of Gender Violence." Paper presented at the Annual Convention of the International Studies Association, New Orleans, LA, March 24–27. Accessed July 25, 2011. http://isanet.ccit.arizona.edu/noarchive/joachim.html.

Joachim, Jutta, and Birgit Locher 2009. "Worlds apart or worlds together? Transnational activist in the UN and the EU" in: Jutta Joachim and Birgit Locher (eds.) *Transnational Activism in the UN and the EU: A Comparative Study*. London: Routledge, 171–182.

John, Mary E. 1999. "Gender Development and the Women's Movement: Problems for a History of the Present." In *Signposts: Gender Issues in Post-Independence India*, edited by Rajeswari Sunder Rajan, 100–124. New Delhi: Kali for Women.

Johnston, Hank, and Paul Almeida, eds. 2006. *Latin American Social Movements: Globalization, Democratization, and Transnational Networks.* Landham, MD: Rowman and Littlefield.

Joshi, Varsha. 1995. *Polygamy and Purdah.* Jaipur, India: Rawat.

Kabeer, Naila. 1994. *Reversed Realities: Gender Hierarchies in Development Thought.* London: Verso.

————. 1996. *Gender, Demographic Transition and the Economics of Family Size: Population Policy for a Human-Centered Development.* Geneva: United Nations Research Institute for Social Development.

Kamat, Sangeeta. 2002. *Development Hegemony: NGOs and the State in India.* New Delhi: Oxford University Press.

————. 2004. "The Privatization of Public Interest: Theorizing NGO Discourse in a Neoliberal Era." *Review of International Political Economy* 11 (1): 155–76.

Kampwirth, Karen. 2006. "Revolución, Feminismo y Antifeminismo en Nicaragua." In *De lo privado a lo público: 30 años de lucha ciudadana de las mujeres en América Latina,* edited by Nathalie Leblon and Elizabeth Maier. Mexico City: Siglo XXI.

————. 2010. "Populism and the Feminist Challenge in Nicaragua: The Return of Daniel Ortega." In *Gender and Populism in Latin America: Passionate Politics,* edited by Karen Kampwirth, 162–79. University Park: Penn State University Press.

Kandiyoti, Deniz. 1991. "Identity and Its Discontents: Women and the Nation." *Millennium* 20 (3): 429–43.

Kantola, Johanna. 2010. *Gender in the European Union.* New York: Palgrave Macmillan.

Kaplan, Caren, Norma Alarcon, and Minoo Moallem, eds. 1999. *Between Woman and Nation: Nationalisms, Transnational Feminisms, and the State.* Durham, NC: Duke University Press.

Kapusta-Pofahl, Karen, Hana Hašková, and Marta Kolářová. 2005. "'Only a Dead Fish Flows with the Stream': NGO Formalization, Anarchofeminism, and the Power of Informal Associations." *Anthropology of East Europe Review* 23 (1): 38–52.

Karim, Lamia. 2001. "Politics of the Poor: NGOs and Grass-Roots Political Mobilization in Bangladesh." *PoLAR* 24 (1): 92–107.

————. 2004. "Democratizing Bangladesh: State, NGOs and Militant Islam." *Cultural Dynamics* 16 (2–3): 219–318.

————. 2011. *Microfinance and Its Discontents: Women in Debt in Bangladesh.* Minneapolis: University of Minnesota Press.

Karki, Arjun, and David Seddon. 2003a. "The People's War in Historical Context." In *The People's War in Nepal: Left Perspectives,* edited by Arjun Karki and David Seddon, 3–48. Delhi: Adroit.

————. 2003b. *The People's War in Nepal: Left Perspectives.* Delhi: Adroit.

Keck, Margaret E., and Kathryn Sikkink. 1998. *Activists beyond Borders: Advocacy Networks in International Politics.* Ithaca, NY: Cornell University Press.

Kernot, Sarah, and Manjita Gurung. 2003. *Insurgency and Displacement: Perspectives on Nepal.* Kathmandu, Nepal: South Asia Forum for Human Rights.

Kerr, Joanna. 2007. *The Second Fundher Report: Financial Sustainability for Women's Movements Worldwide.* Accessed April 30, 2013. http://www.awid.org /Library/The-Second-Fundher-Report-Financial-Sustainability-for-Women-s -Movements-Worldwide.

Kesby, Mike. 2005. "Retheorizing Empowerment-Through-Participation as a Performance in Space: Beyond Tyranny to Transformation." *Signs* 30 (4): 2037–65.

Khandaker, Shahidur. 1998. *Fighting Poverty with Micro-Credit: Experience from Bangladesh.* Dhaka, Bangladesh: University Press.

Kirsch, A. Thomas. 1982. "Buddhism, Sex-Roles and Thai Society." In *Women of Southeast Asia,* edited by Penny Van Esterik. Dekalb: Northern Illinois University, Center for Southeast Asian Studies.

———. 1985. "Text and Context: Buddhist Sex Roles/Culture of Gender Revisited." *American Ethnologist* 12 (2): 302–20.

Klees, Steven J. 1998. "NGOs: Progressive Force or Neoliberal Tool." *Current Issues in Comparative Education* 1 (1): 49–54.

Kligman, Gail. 2000. *Politica duplicității: Controlul reproducerii în România lui Ceaușescu* [The politics of duplicity: controlling reproduction in Ceaușescu's Romania]. Bucharest: Editura Humanitas.

Klima, Alan. 2004. "Thai Love Thai: Financing Emotion in Post-Crash Thailand." *Ethnos* 69 (4): 445–64.

Kothari, Uma. 2001. "Power, Knowledge and Social Control in Participatory Development." In *Participation: The New Tyranny?,* edited by Bill Cooke and Uma Kothari, 139–52. London: Zed.

Kudva, Neena. 2005. "Strong States, Strong NGOs." In *Social Movements in India: Poverty, Power, Politics,* edited by Raka Ray and Mary Fainsod Katzenstein, 233–66. Lanham, MD: Rowan and Littlefield.

Kumar, Nita, ed. 1994. *Women as Subjects: South Asian Histories.* Charlottesville: University Press of Virginia.

Kurtović, Larisa. 2012. "Politics of Impasse: Specters of Socialism and the Struggles for the Future in Postwar Bosnia-Herzegovina." PhD. diss., Berkeley, CA: University of California Berkeley.

Laclau, Ernesto. 2005. *On Populist Reason.* New York: Routledge.

Laclau, Ernesto, and Chantal Mouffe. 1985. *Hegemony and Socialist Strategy: Toward a Radical Democratic Politics.* London: Verso.

Landim, Leilah. 1993. *A invenção das ONGs: do serviço invisível à profissão sem nome.* Rio de Janeiro: Museu Nacional.

Lang, Sabine. 1997. "The NGOization of Feminism." In *Transitions, Environments, Translations: Feminisms in International Politics,* edited by Joan W. Scott, Cora Kaplan, and Debra Keates, 101–20. New York: Routledge.

————. 2000. "The NGO-ization of Feminism: Institutionalization and Institution Building within the German Women's Movement." In *Global Feminisms since 1945*, edited by Bonnie Smith, 290–304. New York: Routledge.

————. 2009a. "Gendering European Publics? Transnational Women's Advocacy Networks in the European Union." In *Media Agoras: Democracy, Diversity, and Communication*, edited by Bart Cammaerts, Inaki Garcia Blanco, and Sofie van Bauwel, 198–219. London: Routledge.

————. 2009b. "Assessing Advocacy: Transnational Women's Networks and Gender Mainstreaming in the European Union." *Social Politics* 16(3), 327–357.

————. 2012. *NGOs, Civil Society, and the Public Sphere*. New York: Cambridge University Press.

Laurie, Nina. 2005. "Establishing Development Orthodoxy: Negotiating Masculinities in the Water Sector." *Development and Change* 36 (3): 527–49.

Lebon, Nathalie. 1998. "The Labor of Love and Bread: Volunteer and Professionalized Activism in the São Paulo Women's Health Movement." PhD diss., University of Florida.

————. 2006. Introduction to *De lo privado a lo público: 30 años de lucha ciudadana de las mujeres en América Latina*, edited by Nathalie Lebon and Elizabeth Maier. Mexico City: Siglo XXI.

————. 2010. "Women Building Plural Democracy in Latin America and the Caribbean." In *Women's Activism in Latin America and the Caribbean: Engendering Social Justice, Democratizing Citizenship*, edited by Elizabeth Maier and Nathalie Lebon, 3–25. New Brunswick, NJ: Rutgers University Press.

Le Breton, David. 2001. *Despre tăcere* [On silence], translation Constantin Zaharia. Bucharest: All Educational.

LeFebvre, Henri. 1991. *The Production of Space*. Translated by Donald Nicholson-Smith. Malden, MA: Blackwell.

Lendvai, Noemi, and Paul Stubbs. 2009. "Assemblages, Translation, and Intermediaries in South East Europe." *European Societies* 11 (5): 673–95.

León, Irene, ed. 2002. *Retos feministas en un mundo globalizado: Foro Social Mundial, Porto Alegre 2002*. Quito: Agencia Latinoamericana de Información.

Leve, Lauren G. 1993. "1983–87 Takukot/Majh Lakuribot Adult Literacy Initiative: Five Year Retrospective Evaluation." Kathmandu, Nepal.

————. 2001. "Between Jesse Helms and Ram Bahadur: Women, NGOs, 'Participation,' and 'Empowerment' in Nepal." *PoLAR* 24 (1): 108–28.

————. 2004. "Nepal's Missing Middle and the US Search for Global Security." Paper presented at the South Asia Security Challenges for the New Millennium conference, University of Texas at Austin, April 29–30.

Leve, Lauren G., and Lamia Karim. 2001. "Privatizing the State: Transnational Capital, Development and NGOs." *PoLAR* 24 (1): 53–58.

Lewis, David. 2003. "NGOs, Organizational Culture, and Institutional Sustainability." *Annals of the American Academy of Political and Social Science* 590: 212–16.

Lewis, David, et al. 2003. "Practice, Power, and Meaning: Frameworks for Studying Organizational Culture in Multi-Agency Rural Development Projects." *Journal of International Development* 15 (5): 541–57.

Li, Tania Murray. 1991. "Compromising Power: Development, Culture and Rule in Indonesia." *Cultural Anthropology* 14 (30): 295–322.

———. 2007. *The Will to Improve: Governmentality, Development, and the Practice of Politics*. Durham, NC: Duke University Press.

Lievesley, Geraldine, and Steve Ludlam, eds. 2009. *Reclaiming Latin America: Experiments in Radical Social Democracy*. London: Zed.

Lind, Amy. 2003. "Gender and Neoliberal States: Feminists Remake the Nation in Ecuador." *Latin American Perspectives* 30 (1): 181–207.

Locher, Birgit. 2007. *Trafficking in Women in the European Union*. Wiesbaden, Germany: vs Verlag.

Lohmann, Kinga. 2009. "Feminist Resource Mobilization and Building Political Power." In *The European Feminist Forum. A Herstory (2004–2008)*, edited by Aletta. Institute for Women's History. Amsterdam, 39–52. Accessed June 24, 2013. http://dare.uva.nl/document/174520.

Lowi, Theodore. 1979. *The End of Liberalism*. New York: W. W. Norton.

Luthra, Bimla. 1976. "Nehru and the Place of Women in Indian Society." In *Indian Women: From Purdah to Modernity*, edited by Bal Ram Nanda. New Delhi: Vikas.

Macaulay, Fiona. 2010. "Trickling Up, Down and Sideways: Gender Policy and Political Opportunity in Brazil." In *Women's Activism in Latin America and the Caribbean: Engendering Social Justice, Democratizing Citizenship*, edited by Elizabeth Maier and Nathalie Lebon, 273–90. New Brunswick, NJ: Rutgers University Press.

MacFarlane, Alan. 2001. "Sliding Down Hill: Some Reflections on Thirty Years of Change in a Himalayan Village." *European Bulletin of Himalayan Research* 20 (1): 105–10.

MacKinnon, Catherine A. 1989. *Toward a Feminist Theory of the State*. Cambridge, MA: Harvard University Press.

———. 2007. *Are Women Human? And Other International Dialogues*. Cambridge, MA: Belknap Press of Harvard University Press.

Magno, Cathryn. 2002. *New Pythian Voices: Women Building Political Capital in NGOs in the Middle East*. New York: Routledge.

Maguire, Patricia. 1987. *Doing Participatory Research: A Feminist Approach*. Amherst: University of Massachusetts Center for International Education.

———. 1996. "Considering More Feminist Participatory Research: What Has Congruency Got to Do with It?" *Qualitative Inquiry* 2 (1): 106–18.

Magyari-Vincze, Eniko. 2002. *Prezente feminine, Studii despre femei în România*. Cluj, Romania: Desire.

Mahbub ul Haq Human Development Centre. 2000. *Human Development in South Asia 2000*. Karachi, Pakistan: Oxford University Press.

Mahmood, Saba. 2005. *Politics of Piety: The Islamic Revival and the Feminist Subject.* Princeton, NJ: Princeton University Press.

Maier, Elizabeth, and Nathalie Lebon, eds. 2010. *Women's Activism in Latin America and the Caribbean: Engendering Social Justice, Democratizing Citizenship.* New Brunswick, NJ: Rutgers University Press.

Mama, Amina, Dzodzi Tsikata, Rose Mensah-Kutin, and Hamida Harrison. 2005. "In Conversation: The Ghanaian Women's Manifesto Movement." *Feminist Africa* 4 (2005).

Mama Cash. 2007. "Petition to the Commissioner for Development and Humanitarian Aid." Accessed June 24, 2013. http://www.lygus.lt/mic2/1TC/news.php?id=916.

Manchanda, Rita. 1999. "Empowerment with a Twist." *The Hindu*, November 21.

Mansbridge, Jane. 1995. "What Is the Feminist Movement?" In *Feminist Organizations: Harvest of the New Women's Movement*, edited by Martin Ferree and Patricia Yancey Martin, 26–34. Philadelphia: Temple University Press.

Manuh, Takyiwaa. 2007. "Doing Gender Work in Ghana." In *Africa after Gender*, edited by Catherine M. Cole, Takyiwaa Manuh, and Stephan F. Miescher, 125–49. Bloomington: Indiana University Press.

March, Kathryn S. 2002. *"If Each Comes Halfway": Meeting Tamang Women in Nepal.* Ithaca, NY: Cornell University Press.

Marchand, Marianne, and Anne Sisson Runyan, eds. 2000. *Gender and Global Restructuring: Sightings, Sites and Resistances.* London: Routledge.

Markowitz, Lisa, and Karen W. Tice. 2002. "Paradoxes of Professionalization: Parallel Dilemmas in Women's Organizations in the Americas." *Gender and Society* 16 (6): 941–58.

Marriott, McKim. 1989. "Constructing an Indian Ethnosociology." *Contributions to Indian Sociology*, n.s., 23 (1): 1–39.

Marriott, McKim, and Ronald Inden. 1977. "Toward an Ethnosociology of South Indian Caste Systems." In *The New Wind: Changing Identities in South Asia*, edited by Kenneth David, 227–38. The Hague: Mouton.

Martens, Kerstin. 2002. "Mission Impossible? Defining Nongovernmental Organizations." *Voluntas: International Journal of Voluntary and Nonprofit Organizations* 13 (3): 271–285.

Massey, Doreen. 1994. *Space, Place, and Gender.* Malden, MA: Blackwell.

———. 2000. "Entanglements of Power: Reflections." In *Entanglements of Power: Geographies of Power/Resistance*, edited by Joanne P. Sharp, Paul Routledge, Chris Philo, and Ronan Paddison, 279–86. London: Routledge.

Mathur, Kanchan. 1999. "From Private to Public: The Emergence of Violence against Women as an Issue in the Women's Development Programme, Rajasthan." In *Institutions, Relations and Outcomes: A Framework and Case Studies for Gender-Aware Planning*, edited by Naila Kabeer and Ramya Subrahmanian, 288–311. New Delhi: Kali for Women.

Mawdsley, Emma, Janet Townsend, Gina Porter, and Peter Oakley. 2002. *Knowl-*

edge, Power and Development Agendas: NGOS *North and South.* Oxford: INTRAC.

Maycock, Matthew. 2003. *Whose Revolution: Can the Maoist Revolution in Nepal Lead to Women's Empowerment?* School of Oriental and African Studies (University of London). Msc Thesis.

Mbembe, Achille. 2000. "At the Edge of the World: Boundaries, Territoriality and Sovereignty in Africa." *Public Culture* 12 (1): 259–84.

McBride Stetson, Dorothy, and Mazur, Amy G. 2008. "Women's Movements, Feminism, and Feminist Movements." In *Politics, Gender and Concepts,* edited by Gary Goertz and Amy Mazur, 219–43. Cambridge: Cambridge University Press.

McClintock, Anne. 1993. "Family Feuds: Gender, Nationalism and the Family." *Feminist Review* 44(Summer):61–80.

McClintock, Anne, Aamir Mufti, and Ella Shohat, eds. 1997. *Dangerous Liaisons: Gender, Nation, and Postcolonial Perspectives.* Minneapolis: University of Minnesota Press.

McHugh, Ernestine. 2001. *Love and Honor in the Himalayas.* Philadelphia: University of Pennsylvania Press.

McKinnon, Katharine. 2007. "Post-Development, Professionalism, and the Politics of Participation." *Annals of the Association of American Geographers* 97 (4): 772–85.

Mehra, Rekha. 1997. "Women, Empowerment, and Economic Development." *Annals of the American Academy of Political and Social Science* 554 (November 1997): 136–49.

Mendelson, Sarah E., and John K. Glenn, eds. 2002. *The Power and Limits of* NGOS: *A Critical Look at Building Democracy in Eastern Europe and Eurasia.* New York: Columbia University Press.

Mendoza, Breny. 2002. "Transnational Feminisms in Question." *Feminist Theory* 3 (3): 313–22.

Menon, Nivedita. 1996. "The Impossibility of 'Justice': Female Foeticide and Feminist Discourse on Abortion." In *Social Reform, Sexuality and the State,* edited by Patricia Uberoi, 369–92. New Delhi: Sage.

Menon, Ritu, and Kamla Bhasin. 1993. "Recovery, Rupture, Resistance: Indian State and Abduction of Women during Partition." *Economic and Political Weekly* 28 (17): WS 2–11.

Menon-Sen, Kalyani. 2001. "The Problem." In "Towards Equality: A Symposium on Women, Feminisms and Women's Movements," *Seminar* 505:12–15.

Mercer, Claire. 2002. "NGOS, Civil Society and Democratization: A Critical Review of the Literature." *Progress in Development Studies* 2 (1): 5–22.

Merry, Sally Engle. 2001. "Women, Violence, and the Human Rights System." In *Women, Gender and Human Rights,* edited by Marjorie Agosin, 83–97. New Brunswick: Rutgers University Press.

Meyer, Mary K. and Elisabeth Prugl, eds. 1999. *Gender Politics in Global Governance*. Rowman and Littlefield.

Mikell, Gwendolyn. 1995. "African Feminism: Toward a New Politics of Representation." *Feminist Studies* 21 (2): 405–24.

Mills, Mary Beth. 1999a. "Enacting Solidarity: Unions and Migrant Youth in Thailand." *Critique of Anthropology* 19 (2): 175–91.

———. 1999b. *Thai Women in the Global Labor Force: Consuming Desires, Contested Selves*. New Brunswick, NJ: Rutgers University Press.

———. 2005a. "From Nimble Fingers to Raised Fists: Women and Labor Activism in Globalizing Thailand." *Signs* 31 (1): 117–44.

———. 2005b. "Women and Labor Activism: Struggle, Power and Pleasure." Paper presented at the Ninth International Conference on Thai Studies, Northern Illinois University, DeKalb, April 3–6.

———. 2008. "Claiming Space: Navigating Landscapes of Power and Citizenship in Thai Labor Activism." *Urban Anthropology and Studies of Cultural Systems* 37 (1): 89–128.

Mindry, Deborah. 2001. "Nongovernmental Organizations, 'Grassroots,' and the Politics of Virtue." *Signs* 26 (4): 1187–212.

Mines, Mattison. 1994. *Public Faces, Private Voices: Community and Individuality in South India*. Berkeley: University of California Press.

Miraftab, Faranak. 1997. "Flirting with the Enemy: Challenges Faced by NGOs in Development and Empowerment." *Habitat International* 21 (4): 361–75.

Miroiu, Mihaela. 2004. "State Men, Market Women: The Effects of Left Conservatism on Gender Politics in Romanian Transition." *Feminismo/s* 3 (June): 207–34. Accessed April 29, 2012. http://rua.ua.es/dspace/bitstream/10045/3243/1/Feminismos_3_14.pdf.

———. 2006. *Neprețuitele femei*. Bucharest: Polirom.

Mitchell, Timothy. 1999. "Society, Economy, and the State Effect." In *State/Culture: State-Formation after the Cultural Turn*, edited by George Steinmetz, 76–97. Ithaca, NY: Cornell University Press.

Moghadam, Valentine M. 2000. "Transnational Feminist Networks: Collective Action in an Era of Globalization." *International Sociology* 15 (1): 57–85.

———. 2005. *Globalizing Women: Transnational Feminist Networks*. Baltimore, MD: Johns Hopkins University Press.

Mohan, Giles, and Kristian Stokke. 2000. "Participatory Development and Empowerment." *Third World Quarterly* 21 (2): 266–80.

Mohanty, Chandra Talpade. 1991. "Under Western Eyes: Feminist Scholarship and Colonial Discourses." In *Third World Women and the Politics of Feminism*, edited by Chandra Talpade Mohanty, Ann Russo, Lourdes Torres, 51–80. Bloomington: Indiana University Press.

———. 2003. *Feminism without Borders: Decolonizing Theory, Practicing Solidarity*. Durham, NC: Duke University Press.

———. 1986. "Mobilization without Emancipation? Women's Interest, State, and

Revolution in Nicaragua." In *Transition and Development: Problems of Third World Socialism*, edited by Richard R. Fagen, Carmen Diana Deere, and Jose Luis Coraggio, 280–302. New York: Monthly Review.

Molyneux, Maxine. 1986. "Mobilization without Emancipation? Women's Interest, State, and Revolution in Nicaragua." In *Transition and Development: Problems of Third World Socialism*, edited by Richard R. Fagen, Carmen Diana Deere, and Jose Luis Coraggio, 280–302. New York: Monthly Review.

Monasteiros, Elizabeth, ed. 2006. *No pudieron con nosotras: El desafío del feminismo autónomo de Mujeres Creand*. Pittsburgh, PA: University of Pittsburgh Press.

———. 2007. "Bolivian Women's Organizations in the MAS Era." *NACLA Report on the Americas* 40 (2): 33–37.

———. 2008. "Bolivian Women's Organizations in the MAS Era." In *Real World Latin America*, edited by the D. S. Collective and NACLA, 33–37. Boston: Dollars and Sense.

Monitorul Oficial R.A. 1997, No. 14 [Official Journal of Romania].

Montoya, Celeste. 2008. "The European Union Capacity Building and Transnational Networks: Combating Violence against Women through the Daphne Program." *International Organization* 62 (1): 359–72.

Moore, David, Katerina Hadzi-Miceva, and Nilda Bullain. 2008. "A Comparative Overview of Public Benefit Status in Europe." *International Journal of Not-for-Profit Law* 11 (1): 5–35.

Morris, Pam, ed. 1994. *The Bakhtin Reader: Selected Writings of Bakhtin, Medvedev, Voloshinov*. London: Arnold.

Moser, Annalise. 2004. "Happy Heterogeneity? Feminism, Development, and the Grassroots Women's Movement in Peru." *Feminist Studies* 3 (1): 211–37.

Moser, Caroline O. N. 1993. *Gender Planning and Development: Theory, Practice, and Training*. London: Routledge.

Mosse, David. 2001. "'People's Knowledge,' Participation and Patronage: Operations and Representations in Rural Development." In *Participation: The New Tyranny?*, edited by Bill Cooke and Uma Kothari, 16–35. London: Zed.

———. 2005. *Cultivating Development: an Ethnography of Aid Policy and Practice*. London: Pluto.

Mouffe, Chantal. 2005. *On the Political: Thinking in Action*. London: Verso.

Msimang, Sisonke. 2002. "African Feminisms II: Reflections on Politics Made Personal." *Agenda* 54:3–15.

Mujeres Creando. 2005. *La virgen de los deseos*. Buenos Aires: Tinta y Limón.

Murdock, Donna F. 2008. *When Women Have Wings: Feminism and Development in Medellin, Columbia*. Ann Arbor: University of Michigan Press.

Nabar, Vrinda. 1995. *Caste as Woman*. New Delhi: Penguin.

Nagar, Richa. 2000. "Mujhe Jawab Do! (Answer Me!): Women's Grass-Roots Activism and Social Spaces in Chitrakoot (India)." *Gender, Place and Culture* 7 (4): 341–62.

————. 2006a. "Introduction: Playing with Fire: A Collective Journey across Borders." In *Playing with Fire: Feminist Thought and Activism through Seven Lives in India*, edited by Sangtin Writers and Richa Nagar, xxi-xlvii. Minneapolis: University of Minnesota Press.

————. 2006b. "Postscript: NGOs, Global Feminisms, and Collaborative Border Crossings." In *Playing with Fire: Feminist Thought and Activism through Seven Lives in India*, edited by Sangtin Writers and Richa Nagar, 132–55. Minneapolis: University of Minnesota Press.

Nagar, Richa, and Saraswati Raju. 2003. "Women, NGOs and the Contradictions of Empowerment and Disempowerment: A Conversation." *Antipode* 35 (1): 1–13.

Naples, Nancy A. 1998. *Grassroots Warriors: Activist Mothering, Community Work, and the War on Poverty*. New York: Routledge.

————. 2002. "Changing the Terms: Community Activism, Globalization and the Dilemmas of Transnational Feminist Praxis." In *Women's Activism and Globalization: Linking Local Struggles and Transnational Politics*, edited by Nancy A. Naples and Manisha Desai, 3–14. New York: Routledge.

Naples, Nancy A., and Manisha Desai, eds. 2002. *Women's Activism and Globalization: Linking Local Struggles and Transnational Politics*. New York: Routledge.

Nazneen, Sohela, and Maheen Sultan. 2009. "Struggling for Survival and Autonomy: Impact of NGO-ization on Women's Organizations in Bangladesh." *Development* 52 (2): 193–99.

Nepal South Asian Center. 1998. "Nepal Human Development Report." Unpublished manuscript submitted to the UN Development Programme, Nepal.

Nnaemeka, Obioma, ed. 1998. *Sisterhood, Feminisms, and Power: from Africa to the Diaspora*. Trenton, NJ: Africa World.

Nongyao Nawarat. 1996. "The Political Policies Concerning the Interests of Women in Local Politics in Thailand." MA thesis, University of York.

Noonan, Norma. "The Bolshevik Legacy and Russian Women's Movements." In *Russian Women in Politics and Society*, edited by Wilma Rule and Norma C. Noonan, 77–95. Westport, CT: Greenwood Press.

Nussbaum, Martha. 2000. "Women's Capabilities and Social Justice." In *Gender Justice, Development and Rights*, edited by Maxine Molyneux and Shahra Razavi, 45–77. New York: Oxford University Press.

Offe, Claus. 1987. "Challenging the Boundaries of Institutional Politics." In *Changing Boundaries of the Political*, edited by Charles S. Maier, 63–105. Cambridge: Cambridge University Press.

Olea Mauleón, Cecilia, and Virginia Vargas. 1998. "Los nudos de la región." In *Encuentros, (des)encuentros y búsquedas: El movimiento feminista en América Latina*, edited by Cecilia Olea Mauleón. Lima: Ediciones Flora Tristán: 139–172.

Ong, Aihwa. 1996. "Strategic Sisterhood or Sisters in Solidarity? Questions of Communitarianism and Citizenship in Asia." *Indiana Journal of Global Legal Studies* 4 (1): 107–35.

————. 2006. *Neoliberalism as Exception: Mutations in Citizenship and Sovereignty*. Durham, NC: Duke University Press.

O'Reilly, Kathleen. 2004. "Developing Contradictions: Women's Participation as a Site of Struggle within an Indian NGO." *Professional Geographer* 56 (2): 174–84.

————. 2006a. "'Traditional' Women, 'Modern' Water: Linking Gender and Commodification in Rajasthan, India." *Geoforum* 37 (6): 958–72.

————. 2006b. "Women Fieldworkers and the Politics of Participation." *Signs* 31 (4): 1075–98.

————. 2010. "Now Is the Time for the Smart: Adapting and Adopting Neoliberal Development." *Antipode* 42 (1): 179–200.

Our Water. 1999. *Leporello Leaflet*. Jaipur, India: Popular Printers.

————. 2000. *Proposal for Strengthening of the Programme Component Women's Participation in the Project*. Unpublished Manuscript.

————. 2002. *Achievements*. Unpublished Manuscript.

————. n.d. *Handbook on Women's Participation*. Unpublished Manuscript.

Outshoorn, Joyce, and Johanna Kantola, eds. 2007. *Changing State Feminism*. Houndmills, UK: Palgrave MacMillan.

Page, Ben. 2005. "Naked Power: Women and the Social Production of Water in Anglophone Cameroon." In *Gender, Water, and Development*, edited by Tina Wallace and Anne Coles, 57–74. Oxford: Berg.

Paley, Julia. 2001. *Marketing Democracy: Power and Social Movements in Post-Dictatorship Chile*. Berkeley: University of California Press.

Parvati, Comrade. 2003. "Women's Participation in the People's War in Nepal." In *The People's War in Nepal: Left Perspectives*, edited by Arjun Karki and David Seddon, 165–82. Delhi: Adroit.

Pasuk, Phongpaichit, and Chris Baker. 1995. *Thailand: Economy and Politics*. Kuala Lumpur: Oxford University Press.

Peake, Linda, and Karen de Souza. 2010. "Feminist Academic and Activist Praxis in Service of the Transnational." In *Critical Transnational Feminist Praxis*, edited by Amanda Lock Swarr and Richa Nagar, 105–23. New York: State University of New York Press.

Pereira, Jeffrey. 1998. "Those Who Think Microcredit Is the Only Key to Development Are Making a Huge Mistake [in Bengali]." *Adhuna*, January–March, 29–30.

Pettigrew, Judith. 2003. "Guns, Kinship, and Fear: Maoists among the Tamu-mai (Gurungs)." In *Resistance and the State: Nepalese Experiences*, edited by David Gellner, 305–25. New Delhi: Social Science.

Pettigrew, Judith, and Sara Schneiderman. 2004. *Women and the Maobaadi: Ideology and Agency in Nepal's Maoist Movement*. *Himal South Asian* 17 (1): 19–29. http://www.himalmag.com/2004/january/essay.htm.

Philipose, Pamela. 2001. "International Dimensions." In "Towards Equality: A Symposium on Women, Feminisms and Women's Movements," *Seminar* 505.

Accessed June 15, 2013. http://www.india-seminar.com/2001/505/505%20pamela
%20philipose.htm.

Phillips, Lynne, and Sally Cole. 2009. "Feminist Flows, Feminist Faultlines:
Women's Machineries and Women's Movements in Latin America." *Signs*
35 (1): 185–211.

Phillips, Sarah D. 2008. *Women's Social Activism in the New Ukraine: Development
and the Politics of Differentiation*. Bloomington: Indiana University Press.

Pigg, Stacy Leigh. 1992. "Inventing Social Categories through Place: Social Representations and Development in Nepal." *Comparative Studies in Society and History* 34 (3): 491–513.

———. 1993. "Unintended Consequences: The Ideological Impact of Development in Nepal." *Comparative Studies of South Asia, Africa and the Middle East*
13 (1–2): 45–58.

———. 1998. "'Found in Most Traditional Societies': Medical Practitioners
between Culture and Development." In *International Development and the
Social Sciences*, edited by Frederick Cooper and Randall M. Packard, 259–90.
Berkeley: University of California Press.

Pisano, Margarita. 1996. *Un Cierto Deparpajo*. Santiago, Chile: Ediciones Número
Crítico.

PoLAR, Symposium: Ethnographic Perspectives on NGOS, Vol. 33, Issue 2, November 2010.

Pongsapich, Amara. 1995. "Nongovernmental Organizations in Thailand." In
*Emerging Civil Society in the Asia Pacific Community: Nongovernmental Under-
pinnings of the Emerging Asia Pacific Regional Community*, edited by Tadashi
Yamamoto. Singapore: ISEAS.

———. 1997. "Feminism Theories and Praxis: Women's Social Movement in Thailand." In *Women, Gender Relations and Development in Thai Society*, edited by
Virada Somsawasdi and Sally Theobald, 1:3–51. Chiang Mai: Chiang Mai University Women's Studies Center, Faculty of Social Sciences.

Pongsapich, Amara, and Nitaya Kataleeradabhan. 1994. *Philanthropy, NGO Activities and Corporate Funding in Thailand*. Bangkok: Chulalongkorn University
Social Research Institute.

Poster, Winifred, and Zakia Salime. 2002. "The Limits of Micro-Credit: Trans-
national Feminism and US AID Activities in the United States and Morocco." In
*Women's Activism and Globalization: Linking Local Struggles and Transnational
Politics*, edited by Nancy A. Naples and Manisha Desai, 185–215. New York:
Routledge.

Povinelli, Elizabeth A. 2002. *The Cunning of Recognition: Indigenous Alterities and
the Making of Australian Multiculturalism*. Durham, NC: Duke University Press.

Prah, Mensah. 2003. "Chasing Illusions and Realising Visions: Reflections on
Ghana's Feminist Experience." Keynote speech at the CODESRIA Anniversary
Conference, Dakar, Senegal, December 10–12. http://www.codesria.org/IMG
/pdf/GA_Chapter-2_prah.pdf.

Prashad, Vijay, and Teo Ballvé, eds. 2006. *Dispatches from Latin America: On the Frontlines against Neoliberalism*. Cambridge, MA: South End.

Pudrovska, Tatjana, and Myra Marx Ferree. 2004. "Global Activism in 'Virtual Space': The European Women's Lobby in the Network of Transnational Women's NGOs on the Web." *Social Politics* 11 (1): 117–43.

Pugh, Michael. 2003. "Protectorates and Spoils of Peace: Political Economy in South-East Europe." In *Shadow Globalization, Ethnic Conflicts and New Wars: A Political Economy of Intra-State War*, edited by Dietrich Jung, 47–69. London: Routledge.

Pupavac, Vanessa. 2005. "Empowering Women? An Assessment of International Gender Policies in Bosnia." *International Peacekeeping* 12 (3): 391–405.

Radachowsky, Sage. 2003. "A View on the People's War in Nepal." *ZNet*. http://www.zcommunications.org/a-view-on-the-peoples-war-in-nepal-by-sage-radachowsky.

Raheja, Gloria, and Ann Gold. 1994. *Listen to the Heron's Words: Reimagining Gender and Kinship in North India*. Berkeley: University of California Press.

Rahman, Aminur. 1999. "Micro-Credit Initiatives for Equitable and Sustainable Development: Who Pays?" *World Development* 27 (1): 67–82.

———. 2001. *Women and Microcredit in Rural Bangladesh: An Anthropological Study of the Rhetoric and Realities of Grameen Bank Lending*. Boulder, CO: Westview.

Rahman, Lupin, and Vijayendra Rao. 2004. "The Determinants of Gender Equity in India: Examining Dyson and Moore's Thesis with New Data." *Population and Development Review* 30 (2): 239–68.

Rahnema, Majid, and Victoria Bawtree, eds. 1997. *The Post-Development Reader*. London: Zed.

Rakowski, Cathy A., and Giaconda Espina. 2006. "Institucionalización de la lucha feminista/femenina en Venezuela: Solidaridad y fragmentación, oportunidades y desafíos." In *De lo privado a lo público: 30 años de lucha ciudadana de las mujeres en América Latina*, edited by Nathalie Lebon and Elizabeth Maier. Mexico City: Siglo XXI.

Ramírez Gallegos, Franklin. 2006. "Mucho más que dos Izquierdas." *Nueva Sociedad* 205: 30–44.

Rankin, Katherine N. 2001. "Governing Development: Neoliberalism, Microcredit, and Rational Economic Woman." *Economy and Society* 30 (1): 18–37.

———. 2004. *The Cultural Politics of Markets*. Toronto: University of Toronto Press.

———. n.d. "The Politics of Subversion in Development Practice: An Exploration of Microfinance in Nepal and Vietnam." Unpublished manuscript.

Ray, Raka, and Mary Fainsod Katzenstein, eds. 2005. *Social Movements in India: Poverty, Power, and Politics*. Lanham, MD: Rowan and Littlefield.

Rees, Madeleine. 2002. "International Intervention in Bosnia-Herzegovina: The Cost of Ignoring Gender." In *The Postwar Moment: Militaries, Masculinities and International Peacekeeping, Bosnia and the Netherlands,* edited by Cynthia Cockburn and Dubravka Žarkov, 51–67. London: Lawrence and Wishart.

Regulska, Joanna and Magda Grabowska. 2008. "Will It Make a Difference? EU Enlargement and Women's Public Discourse in Poland." In *Gender Politics in the Expanding European Union,* edited by Silke Roth, 137–54. London: Routledge.

Richard, Analiese. 2009. "Mediating Dilemmas: Local NGOs and Rural Development in Neoliberal Mexico." *PoLAR* 32 (2): 166–94.

Richter, James. 1999. "Citizens or Professionals? Evaluating Western Assistance to Russian Women's Organizations: Report to the Carnegie Corporation." Unpublished manuscript.

Riles, Annelise. 2001. *The Network Inside Out.* Ann Arbor: University of Michigan Press.

Ríos Tobar, Marcela, Lorena Godoy Catalán, and Elizabeth Guerrero Caviedes. 2003. *Un nuevo silencio feminista? La transformación de un movimiento social en el Chile postdictadura.* Santiago, Chile: Centro de Estudios de la Mujer.

Robinson, Jenny. 2000. "Feminism and the Spaces of Transformation." *Transactions of the Institute of British Geographers* 25 (3): 285–301.

Rofel, Lisa. 1999. *Other Modernities: Gendered Yearnings in China after Socialism.* Berkeley: University of California Press.

Rose, Nikolas. 1996a. *Inventing Ourselves: Psychology, Power and Personhood.* New York: Cambridge University Press.

———. 1996b. "Governing 'Advanced' Liberal Democracies." In *Foucault and Political Reason: Liberalism, Neo-liberalism and Rationalities of Government,* edited by Andrew Barry, Thomas Osborne, and Nikolas Rose, 37–64. Chicago: The University of Chicago Press.

———. 1999. *Powers of Freedom: Reframing Political Thought.* New York: Cambridge University Press.

Roth, Silke. 2007. "Sisterhood and Solidarity? Women's Organizations in the Expanded European Union." *Social Politics* 14 (4): 460–87.

Routledge, Paul. 2003. "Voices of the Dammed: Discursive Resistance amidst Erasure in the Narmada Valley, India." *Political Geography* 22 (3): 243–70.

Rowlands, Gina. 1997. *Questioning Empowerment: Working with Women in Honduras.* Oxford: Oxfam.

Roy, Arundhati. 2004. *Public Power in the Age of Empire.* New York: Seven Stories.

Roy, Manisha. 1992. *Bengali Women.* With a new afterword. Chicago: University of Chicago Press.

Sachs, Wolfgang. 1992. *The Development Dictionary: A Guide to Knowledge as Power.* London: Zed.

Sacks, Karen. 1989. "Toward a Unified Theory of Class, Race and Gender." *American Ethnologist* 16 (3): 534–50.

Sampson, Steven. 1996. "The Social Life of Projects: Importing Civil Society to Albania." In *Civil Society: Challenging Western Models,* edited by Chris Hann and Elizabeth Dunn, 121–43. New York: Routledge.

———. 2003. "Weak States, Uncivil Societies, and Thousands of NGOs: Benevolent Colonialism in the Balkans." In *The Balkans in Focus: Cultural Boundaries in Europe*, edited by Sanimir Resić and Barbara Tornquist-Plewa, 27–44. Lund, Sweden: Nordic Academic.

Sangtin Writers and Richa Nagar. 2006. *Playing With Fire: Feminist Thought and Activism through Seven Lives in India*. Minneapolis, MN: University of Minnesota Press.

Sardenberg, Cecília M. B., and Ana Alice Alcântara Costa. 2010. "Contemporary Feminisms in Brazil: Achievements, Shortcomings, and Challenges." In *Women's Movements in the Global Era: The Power of Local Feminisms*, edited by Amrita Basu, 255–84. Boulder, CO: Westview.

Sassen, Saskia. 1998. *Globalization and Its Discontents*. New York: New Press.

———. 2000. "Spatialities and Temporalities of the Global: Elements for a Theorization." *Public Culture* 12 (1): 215–32.

Sawer, Marian, and Sarah Maddison. 2009. "Premature Obituaries: How Can We Tell if Social Movements Are Over?" Paper presented at the First ECPR Gender and Politics Conference, Belfast (January).

Schech, Susanne, and Jane Haggis, eds. 2002. *Development: A Cultural Studies Reader*. Oxford: Blackwell.

Schild, Verónica. 1998. "New Subjects of Rights? Women's Movements and the Construction of Citizenship in the 'New Democracies.'" In *Cultures of Politics/ Politics of Cultures: Re-Visioning Latin American Social Movements*, edited by Sonia E. Alvarez, Evelina Dagnino, and Arturo Escobar. Boulder, CO: Westview.

———. 2000. "Neo-Liberalism's New Gendered Market Citizens: The 'Civilizing' Dimension of Social Programmes in Chile." *Citizenship Studies* 4 (3): 275–305.

Schroeder, Richard A. 1999. *Shady Practices: Agroforestry and Gender Politics in the Gambia*. Berkeley: University of California Press.

Schroeder, Richard A., and Krisnawati Suryanata. 2004. "Gender and Class Power in Agroforestry Systems: Case Studies from Indonesia and West Africa." In *Liberation Ecologies: Environment, Development, Social Movements*, edited by Richard Peet and Michael Watts, 188–204. London: Routledge.

Schuller, Mark. 2007. "Seeing Like a 'Failed' NGO: Globalization's Impacts on State and Civil Society in Haiti." *PoLAR* 30 (1): 67–89.

———. 2009. "Gluing Globalization: NGOs as Intermediaries in Haiti." *PoLAR* 32 (1): 84–104.

Scott, James C. 1976. *The Moral Economy of the Peasant*. New Haven, CT: Yale University Press.

———. 1998. *Seeing Like a State: How Certain Schemes to Improve the Human Condition Have Failed*. New Haven, CT: Yale University Press.

———. 2006. "Cities, People, Language." In *The Anthropology of the State: A Reader*, edited by Aradhana Sharma and Akhil Gupta, 247–69. Malden, MA: Blackwell.

Scott, Joan W. 2008. "Introduction: Feminism's Critical Edge." In *Women's Studies on the Edge*, edited by Joan W. Scott, 1–13. Durham, NC: Duke University Press.

Seddon, David. 2001. "The Contradictions of Rural Transformation in Nepal." *European Bulletin of Himalayan Research* 20 (1): 117–23.

Sempreviva Organização Feminista. 2011. "Formação e Articulação de Mulheres Rurais nos Territórios de Cidadania." Accessed May 15, 2011. http://www.sof .org.br/.

Sen, Amartya. 1999. *Development as Freedom*. New York: Knopf.

Sen, Gita, and Caren Grown. 1987. *Development, Crises, and Alternative Visions*. New York: Monthly Review.

Serrano, Isagni R. 1994. *Civil Society in the Asia-Pacific Region*. Washington: Civicus.

Shah, Saubhagya. 2002. "From Evil State to Civil Society." In *State of Nepal*, edited by Kanak Mani Dixit and Shastri Ramachandran, 22–83. Kathmandu, Nepal: Himal.

Shakya, Sujita. 2003. "The Maoist Movement in Nepal: An Analysis from the Women's Perspective." In *The People's War in Nepal: Left Perspectives*, edited by Arjun Karki and David Seddon, 375–404. Delhi: Adroit.

Sharma, Aradhana. 2006. "Crossbreeding Institutions, Breeding Struggle: Women's Empowerment, Neoliberal Governmentality, and State (Re)Formation in India." *Cultural Anthropology* 21 (1): 60–95.

———. 2008. *Logics of Empowerment: Development, Gender, and Governance in Neoliberal India*. Minneapolis: University of Minnesota Press.

Sharma, Aradhana, and Akhil Gupta. 2006. "Introduction: Rethinking Theories of the State in an Age of Globalization." In *The Anthropology of the State: A Reader*, edited by Aradhana Sharma and Akhil Gupta, 1–41. Malden, MA: Blackwell.

Sharma, S. 2000. "Caar Jillaa Maovaadiiko Haatma [Four districts controlled by the Maoists]." *Himalayan Research Bulletin* 10 (7): 30–40.

Sharma, Ursula. 1978. "Women and Their Affines: The Veil as a Symbol of Separation." *Man* 13 (2): 218–33.

Sharp, Joanne P., Paul Routledge, Chris Philo, and Ronan Paddison, eds. 2000. *Entanglements of Power: Geographies of Domination/Resistance*. London: Routledge.

Shepard, Bonnie. 2003. NGO *Advocacy Networks in Latin America: Lessons from Experience in Promoting Women's and Reproductive Rights*. Miami: North-South Center, University of Miami.

———. 2006. *Running the Obstacle Course to Sexual and Reproductive Health: Lessons from Latin America*. Westport, CT: Praeger.

Shrestha, Nanda. 1995. "Becoming a Development Category." In *Power of Development*, edited by Jonathan Crush, 266–77. London: Routledge.

Silliman, Jael. 1999. "Expanding Civil Society: Shrinking Political Spaces—The Case of Women's Non-Governmental Organizations." *Social Politics* 6 (1): 23–53.

Simmons, Cynthia. 2010. "Women Engaged/Engaged Art in Postwar Bosnia: Reconciliation, Recovery, and Civil Society." *The Carl Beck Papers* 2005: 1–45.

Simpson, Meghan. 2009. "Intersectionalities of Gender and Class in the Wake of Kyrgizstan's March 2005 Events." In *Gender Dynamics and Post-Conflict Reconstruction*, edited by Christine Eifler and Ruth Seifert, 137–54. Frankfurt am Main: Peter Lang.

Sisson, Richard, and Leo E. Rose. 1991. *War and Secession: Pakistan, India and the Creation of Bangladesh*. Berkeley: University of California Press.

Skinner, Debra, Alfred Pach III, and Dorothy Holland, eds. 1998. *Selves in Time and Place: Identities, Experience, and History in Nepal*. Lanham, MD: Rowman and Littlefield.

Sklevicky, Lydia. 1984. "Karaktaristike organizirano djelovanja žena u Jugoslaviji u razdoblju do drugog svjetskog rata [Characteristics of Women's Organized Activity in Yugoslavia up to the Second World War]." *Polje* 308 (October): 415–17 and 309 (November) 454–56.

———. 1989. "Emancipated Integration or Integrated Emancipation: The Case of Post-Revolutionary Yugoslavia." In *Current Issues in Women's History*, edited by Arina Angerman et al., 93–108. London: Routledge.

Sluka, Jeffrey A. 2000. *Death Squad: The Anthropology of State Terror*. Philadelphia: University of Pennsylvania Press.

Smismans, Stijn. 2006. *Civil Society and Legitimate European Governance*. Cheltenham, UK and Northampton, MA: Edward Elgar.

Snitow, Ann. 1999. "Cautionary Tales." In *Proceedings of the 93rd Annual Meetings of the American Society of International Law*, 35–42. Buffalo, NY: W.S. Hein & Co.

Soares, Vera. 1998. "Feminismo e ONGs." In *O impacto social do trabalho das ONGs no Brasil*, edited by Associação Brasileira de Organizações Não Governamentais. São Paulo: Associação Brasileira de Organizações Não Governamentais.

Sob, Krishna, and Keith D. Leslie. 1988. "Participatory Development: A Case Study of the Nonformal Education Project in Takukot Panchayat of the Gorkha District." Kathmandu: Save the Children.

Sobhan, Rehman. 1997. "The Political Economy of Micro-Credit." In *Who Needs Credit? Poverty and Finance in Bangladesh*, edited by Geoffrey Wood and Iffath Sharif, 131–41. Dhaka, Bangladesh: University Press.

Sommer, Doris ed. 2006. *Cultural Agency in the Americas*. Durham, NC: Duke University Press.

Sorabji, Cornelia. 1994. "Mixed Motives: Islam, Nationalism and *Mevlud*s in an Unstable Yugoslavia." In *Muslim Women's Choices: Religious Belief and Social Reality*, edited by Camillia Fawzi El-Solh and Judy Mabro, 108–27. Oxford: Berg.

SOROS. 2006. Ancheta "România urbană" [Survey Urban Romania], Bucharest: SOROS.

Souza Santos, Boaventura de. 2007. *The Rise of the Global Left: The World Social Forum and Beyond*. London: Zed.

Sparr, Pamela, ed. 1994. *Mortgaging Women's Lives: Feminist Critiques of Structural Adjustment*. Atlantic Highlands, NJ: Zed.

Sperling, Valerie. 2000. *Organizing Women in Contemporary Russia: Engendering Transition*. Cambridge: Cambridge University Press.

Sperling, Valerie, Myra Marx Ferree, and Barbara Risman. 2001. "Constructing Global Feminism: Transnational Advocacy Networks and Russian Women's Activism." *Signs* 26 (4): 1155–86.

Spivak, Gayatri Chakravorty. 1988a. "Subaltern Studies: Deconstructing Historiography." In *Selected Subaltern Studies*, edited by Ranajit Guha and Gayatri Chakravorty Spivak, 3–34. Oxford: Oxford University Press.

———. 1988b. "Can the Subaltern Speak?" In *Marxism and the Interpretation of Culture*, edited by Cary Nelson and Lawrence Grossberg, 271–313. Urbana: University of Illinois Press.

———. 1996. "'Woman' as Theatre: United Nations Conference on Women, Beijing 1995." *Radical Philosophy* 75 (January–February): 2–4.

Springer, J. 2001. "State Power and Agricultural Transformation in Tamil Nadu." In *Social Nature: Resources, Representations, and Rule in India*, edited by Arun Agrawal and Kalyanankrishnan Sivaramakrishnan, 86–106. New Delhi: Oxford University Press.

Squires, Judith. 2007. *The New Politics of Gender Equality*. Houndmills, UK: Palgrave MacMillan.

Stahler-Sholk, Richard, Harry E. Vanden, and Glen David Kuecker, eds. 2008. *Latin American Social Movements in the Twenty-First Century: Resistance, Power, and Democracy*. Lanham, MD: Rowman and Littlefield.

Stein, Rachel, ed. 2004. *New Perspectives on Environmental Justice: Gender, Sexuality and Activism*. New Brunswick, NJ: Rutgers University Press.

Steinmetz, George, ed. 1999. *State/Culture: State-Formation after the Cultural Turn*. Ithaca, NY: Cornell University Press.

Strathern, Marilyn. Ed. 2000. *Audit Cultures: Anthropological Studies in Accountability, Ethics, and the Academy*. London: Routledge.

Stratigaki, Maria. 2005. "Gender Mainstreaming versus Positive Action: An Ongoing Conflict in EU Gender Policy." *European Journal of Women's Studies* 12 (2): 165–86.

Stromquist, Nelly. 2002. "NGOs in a New Paradigm of Civil Society." *Current Issues in Comparative Education* 1 (1): 61–67.

Stubbs, Paul. 1996. "Nationalisms, Globalization and Civil Society in Croatia and Slovenia." *Research in Social Movements, Conflicts and Change* 19: 1–26.

———. 1997. "NGO Work with Forced Migrants in Croatia: Lineages of a Global Middle Class?" *International Peacekeeping* 4 (4): 50–60.

———. 1999. "Social Work and Civil Society in Bosnia-Herzegovina: Globalisation, Neo-feudalism and the State." *International Perspectives on Social Work*: 55–64.

———. 2007. "Civil Society or *Ubleha?* Reflections on Flexible Concepts, Meta-

NGOs and New Social Energy in the Post-Yugoslav Space." In *20 Pieces of Encouragement for Awakening and Change: Peacebuilding in the Region of the Former Yugoslavia*, edited by Helena Rill, Tamara Šmidling, and Ana Bitoljanu, 215–28. Belgrade, Serbia: Center for Nonviolent Action.

Sunder Rajan, Rajeswari. 2003. *The Scandal of the State: Women, Law, and Citizenship in Postcolonial India*. Durham, NC: Duke University Press.

Swarr, Amanda Lock, and Richa Nagar, eds. 2010. *Critical Transnational Feminist Praxis*. Albany: State University of New York Press.

Tamang, Seira. 2002. "The Politics of Developing Nepali Women" in *State of Nepal*, edited by Kanak Mani Dixit and Shastri Ramachandran. Kathmandu, Nepal: Himal Books.

Tambiah, Stanley J. 1996. *Leveling Crowds: Ethnonationalist Conflicts and Collective Violence in South Asia*. Berkeley: University of California Press.

Taylor, Verta. 1989. "Social Movement Continuity: The Women's Movement in Abeyance." *American Sociological Review* 54 (5): 761–75.

Teixeira, Ana Claudia. 2003. *Identidades em construção: As organizações não-governamentais no processo brasileiro de democratização*. São Paulo: Annablume.

Thapa, Deepak. 2003. *Understanding the Maoist Movement of Nepal*. Kathmandu, Nepal: Martin Chautari.

Thayer, Millie. 2000. "Traveling Feminisms: From Embodied Women to Gendered Citizenship." In *Global Ethnography: Forces, Connections and Imaginations in a Postmodern World*, edited by Michael Burawoy, 203–33. Berkeley: University of California Press.

———. 2010. *Making Transnational Feminism: Rural Women, NGO Activists, and Northern Donors in Brazil*. New York: Routledge.

Timothy, Kristen. 2004. "Defending Diversity, Sustaining Consensus: NGOs at the Beijing World Conference on Women and Beyond." *Development Bulletin* 64: 34–36.

Tinker, Irene. 1990. *Persistent Inequalities: Women and World Development*. New York: Oxford University Press.

Todd, Helen. 1996a. *Cloning Grameen Bank: Replicating a Poverty Reduction Model in India, Nepal and Vietnam*. London: Intermediate Technology.

———. 1996b. *Women at the Center*. Dhaka, Bangladesh: University Press Limited.

Townsend, Janet, Gina Porter, and Emma Mawdsley. 2002. "The Role of the Transnational Community of Non-Government Organizations: Governance or Poverty Reduction?" *Journal of International Development* 14 (6): 829–39.

Trinh T. Minh-ha. 2005. *The Digital Film Event*. New York, NY: Routledge.

Tripp, Aili Mari, Isabel Casimiro, Joy Kwesiga, and Alice Mungwa. 2009. *African Women's Movements: Changing Political Landscapes*. New York: Cambridge University Press.

Tsikata, Dzodzi. 2009. "Women's Organizing in Ghana since the 1990's: From Individual Organizations to Three Coalitions." *Development* 52 (2): 185–92.

Tsing, Anna Lowenhaupt. 1997. "Transitions as Translations." In *Transitions, Environments, Translations: Feminisms in International Politics,* edited by Joan W. Scott, Cora Kaplan, and Debra Keates, 253–72. New York: Routledge.

———. 2005. *Friction: An Ethnography of Global Connection.* Princeton, NJ: Princeton University Press.

Umar, Badruddin. 2004. *The Emergence of Bangladesh: Class Struggles in East Pakistan (1947–1958).* New York: Oxford University Press.

United Nations Development Program. 2003. *Millenium Development Goals: A Compact among Nations to End Human Poverty.* New York: Oxford University Press.

Unnithan-Kumar, Maya. 1997. *Identity, Gender and Poverty: New Perspectives on Caste and Tribe in Rajasthan.* Providence, RI: Berghahn.

USAID. U. S. Agency for International Development. 2011. CSO *Sustainability Index for Central and Eastern Europe and Eurasia,* 167–174. Accesed on February 10, 2012. http://transition.usaid.gov/locations/europe_eurasia/dem_gov /ngoindex/reports/2011/2011CSOSI_Index_complete.pdf#page=167.

Văcărescu, Theodora. 2011. "Uneven Curriculum Inclusion: Gender Studies and Gender in Studies at the University of Bucharest." In *From Gender Studies to Gender in Studies: Case Studies on Gender-Inclusive Curriculum in Higher Education,* edited by Laura Grünberg, 147–185. Bucharest: UNESCO-CEPES.

Valiente, Celia. 2009. "Social Movements in 'Abeyance' and Political Regimes: The Feminist Protest in Franco's Spain (1930s–1975)." Paper presented at the First ECPR Gender and Politics Conference, Belfast, January 21–23.

Van Esterik, Penny. 1996. "Nurturance and Reciprocity in Thai Studies." In *State Power and Culture in Thailand,* edited by E. Paul Durrenberger, 22–46. New Haven, CT: Yale University Southeast Asia Studies.

Vargas, Virginia. 2003. "Feminism, Globalization and the Global Justice and Solidarity Movement." Cultural Studies 17 (6): 905–20.

———. 2004. "Beijing más diez: La larga y sinuosa marcha hacia la democracia en América Latina y el Caribe." *La Red Va.,* no. 324.

———. 2010. "Constructing New Democratic Paradigms for Global Democracy: The Contribution of Feminisms." In *Women's Activism in Latin America and the Caribbean: Engendering Social Justice, Democratizing Citizenship,* edited by Elizabeth Maier and Nathalie Lebon, 319–36. New Brunswick, NJ: Rutgers University Press.

Vasan, Sudha. 2004. "NGOs as Employers: Need for Accountability." *Economic and Political Weekly* 39 (22): 2197–98.

Verdery, Katherine. 1996. *What Was Socialism, and What Comes Next?* Princeton, NJ: Princeton University Press.

Virada Somswasdi. 1997. *Some Pertinent Legal and Social Issues on Women in Thailand.* Chiang Mai: Chiang Mai University Women's Studies Centre.

———. 2003. "The Women's Movement and Legal Reform in Thailand." Unpublished manuscript.

Viterna, Jocelyn, and Kathleen Fallon. 2008. "Democratization, Women's Movement, and Gender-Equitable States: A Framework for Comparison." *American Sociological Review* 73 (4): 668–89.

Vleuten, Anna van der. 2007. *The Price of Gender Equality: Member States and Governance in the European Union*. Hampshire, UK: Ashgate.

Voicu, Bogdan. 2005. *Penuria pseudo modernă a postcomunismului românesc* [The pseudo-modern scarcity of Romanian postcommunism]. Bucharest: Expert Projects.

Walker, David, John Paul Jones, Susan Roberts, and Oliver Froehling. 2007. "When Participation Meets Empowerment: The wwf and the Politics of Invitation in the Chimalapas, Mexico." *Annals of the Association of American Geographers* 97 (2): 423–44.

Walley, Christine. 1997. "Searching for 'Voices': Feminism, Anthropology, and the Global Debates over Female Genital Operations." *Cultural Anthropology* 12 (3): 405–38.

Walsh, Martha. 1998. "Mind the Gap: Where Feminist Theory Failed to Meet Development Practice—A Missed Opportunity in Bosnia and Herzegovina." *European Journal of Women's Studies* 5 (3–4): 329–43.

Warleigh, Alex. 2003. "Informal Governance: Improving EU Democracy?" In *Informal Governance and the European Union*, edited by Thomas Christensen and Simona Piattoni, 22–35. Cheltenham, UK: Edward Elgar.

Warren, Kay B. 1993. *The Violence Within: Cultural and Political Opposition in Divided Nations*. Boulder, CO: Westview.

———. 1998. "Indigenous Movements as a Challenge to the Unified Social Movement Paradigm for Guatemala." In *Cultures of Politics/Politics of Cultures: Re-Visioning Latin American Social Movements*, edited by Sonia E. Alvarez, Evelina Dagnino, and Arturo Escobar, 165–95. Boulder, CO: Westview.

Watson, Peggy. 1997. "Civil Society and the Politics of Difference in Eastern Europe." In *Transitions, Environments, Translations: Feminisms in International Politics*, edited by Joan W. Scott, Cora Kaplan, and Debra Keates, 21–29. New York: Routledge.

Wedel, Janine R. 1998. "Informal Relations and Institutional Change: How Eastern European Cliques and States Mutually Respond." *Anthropology of East Europe Review* 16 (1): 4–13.

———. 2001. *Collision and Collusion: The Strange Case of Western Aid to Eastern Europe*. New York: Palgrave.

Weisgrau, Maxine. 1997. *Interpreting Development: Local Histories, Local Strategies*. Lanham, MD: University Press of America.

West, Guida, and Rhoda Lois Blumberg, eds. 1990. *Women and Social Protest*. Oxford: Oxford University Press.

West, Guida, and Rhoda Lois Blumberg. 1990. "Introduction: Reconstructing Social Protest from a Feminist Perspective," In *Women and Social Protest*, edited by Guida West and Rhoda Lois Blumberg, 3–35. Oxford: Oxford University Press.

Weyland, Kurt, Raúl Madrid, and Wendy Hunter, eds. 2010. *Leftist Governments in Latin America: Successes and Shortcomings*. New York: Cambridge University Press.

Wiegman, Robyn. 2002a. "Introduction: On Location." In *Women's Studies on Its Own: A Next Wave Reader in Institutional Change*, Robyn Wiegman ed., 1–44. Durham, NC: Duke University Press.

———, ed. 2002b. *Women's Studies on Its Own: A Next Wave Reader in Institutional Change*. Durham, NC: Duke University Press.

———. 2008. "Feminism, Institutionalism, and the Idiom of Failure." In *Women's Studies on the Edge*, edited by Joan W. Scott, 39–66. Durham, NC: Duke University Press.

Wiener, Antje. 1998. *European Citizenship Practice: Building Institutions of a Nonstate*. Boulder, CO: Westview.

Williams, Brackette, ed. 1996. *Women out of Place: The Gender of Agency and the Race of Nationality*. New York: Routledge.

Williamson, John. 1990. "What Washington Means by Policy Reform." In *Latin American Adjustment: How Much Has Happened*, edited by John Williamson, 7–38. Washington: Institute for International Economics.

Woodward, Alison. 2004. "Building Velvet Triangles: Gender and Informal Governance." In *Informal Governance and the European Union*, edited by Thomas Christensen and Simona Piattoni, 76–93. London: Edward Elgar.

Woodward, Susan L. 1985. "The Rights of Women: Ideology, Policy, and Social Change in Yugoslavia." In *Women, State, and Party in Eastern Europe*, edited by Sharon L. Wolchik and Alfred G. Meyer, 234–54. Durham, NC: Duke University Press.

World Bank. 2002. "Bosnia and Herzegovina: Local Level Institutions and Social Capital Study." Washington, D.C.: World Bank.

World Education. 1989. Naya Goreto: The Nepal National Literacy Campaign. Boston, MA and Kathmandu, Nepal.

Yang, Mayfair, ed. 1999. *Spaces of Their Own: Women's Public Spheres in Transnational China*. Minneapolis: University of Minnesota Press.

Young, Kate. 1993. *Planning Development with Women: Making a World of Difference*. London: Macmillan.

Yunus, Muhammad, and Alan Jolis. 1998. *Banker to the Poor: Micro-Lending and the Battle against World Poverty*. Dhaka, Bangladesh: University Press.

———. 2008. *Creating a World without Poverty: Social Business and the Future of Capitalism*. Washington, DC: Public Affairs.

Yuval-Davis, Nira. 1999. "What Is 'Transversal Politics'?" *Soundings* 12:94–98.

———. 2006. "Human/Women's Rights and Feminist Transversal Politics." In *Global Feminism: Transnational Women's Activism, Organizing and Human Rights*, edited by Myra Marx Ferree and Aili Mari Tripp, 275–95. New York: New York University Press.

Zabelina, Tat'iana. 1996. "Sexual Violence Towards Women." In *Gender, Generation and Identity in Contemporary Russia,* edited by Hilary Pilkington, 169–86. London: Routledge.

Zhang, Lu. 2009. "Chinese Women Protesting Domestic Violence: The Beijing Conference, International Donor Agencies, and the Making of a Chinese Women's NGO." *Meridians* 9 (3): 66–99.

Zippel, Kathrin. 2006. *The Politics of Sexual Harassment: A Comparative Study of the United States, the European Union, and Germany.* Cambridge: Cambridge University Press.

Zvizdić, Memnuna. 1996. "The Workshop." *Surviving the Violence: War and Violence against Women Are Inseparable,* by Medica Zenica, 32–33. Köln: Medica Mondiale.

Sonia E. Alvarez is the director of the Center for Latin American, Caribbean, and Latino Studies and Leonard J. Horwitz Professor of Political Science at the University of Massachusetts, Amherst. Before coming to UMass, she taught politics and Latin American studies at the University of California, Santa Cruz. Alvarez has written extensively on social movements, feminisms, NGOS, transnational activism, and democratization. She has taken part in Latina/women of color feminist, social justice, international solidarity, and antiracist activism since the 1980s and since then also has maintained manifold connections with Brazilian, Latin American, and global feminist movements, while theorizing with and about them.

Victoria Bernal is an associate professor of anthropology at the University of California, Irvine. Her interests include feminist theory, African Studies, diasporas, Islam, war and militarism, civil society, citizenship, and new media. Her book, *Nation as Network: Diaspora, Cyberspace, and Citizenship* exploring transformations of sovereignty and citizenship associated with migration and digital media will be published by the University of Chicago Press in 2014. She is the editor of an anthology designed for teaching anthropology, *Contemporary Cultures, Global Connections: Anthropology for the 21st Century*.

LeeRay M. Costa is director of the Gender and Women's Studies Program and an associate professor of anthropology and of gender and women's studies at Hollins University. She is currently working on a project exploring feminist pedagogies of civic engagement.

Inderpal Grewal is a professor in and chair of the program in Women's, Gender, and Sexuality Studies at Yale University. Her research concerns feminism and postcolonialism, transnationalism, cultural studies, and South Asia.

Laura Grünberg is president of a Romanian nongovernmental organization, AnA Society for Feminist Analyses, and an associate professor at the Faculty of Sociology and Social Work at the University of Bucharest. She has published in the area of sociology of gender, sociology of the body, gender and education, and women's movements. She has also written children's books.

Elissa Helms is currently an assistant professor in the Department of Gender Studies at the Central European University in Budapest, Hungary. Her research, publications, and teaching focus on the gendering of nationalism, NGO activism and donor aid, gender and ethnic violence, and gendered dynamics of social change after significant ruptures such as war or the collapse of state socialism. She is the author of *Innocence and Victimhood: Gender, Nation, and Women's Activism in Postwar Bosnia-Herzegovina* and coeditor, with Xavier Bougarel and Ger Duijzings, of *The New Bosnian Mosaic: Identities, Memories and Moral Claims in a Post-War Society.*

Julie Hemment is an associate professor in the Department of Anthropology at the University of Massachusetts, Amherst. Her research interests include gender and postsocialism, NGOs and global civil society, youth, social welfare, and citizenship. She is the author of *Empowering Women in Russia: Activism, Aid, and NGOs*; her articles have appeared in journals such as *Signs, Slavic Review* and *Anthropological Quarterly* and in anthologies. She is currently working on a book that explores themes of youth, gender, and nationalism in postsocialist space by examining Russia's new state-run youth organizations.

Saida Hodžić is an assistant professor of anthropology and of feminist, gender, and sexuality studies at Cornell University. She received a PhD in medical anthropology from the University of California, Berkeley and San Francisco. Her publications explore global inequalities that constrain the work of African feminists; the theoretical pitfalls of framing the struggles over women's rights in terms of the binary between liberal impositions and popular resistance; and the discursive and performative fields on which Ghanaian activists wage their battles over expertise and legitimacy.

Lamia Karim is an associate professor of anthropology at the University of Oregon. Her research interests include globalization, gender, human rights, and social movements. She has published numerous scholarly articles in anthropology journals (*Cultural Dynamics, PoLAR*, and *Contemporary South Asia*) on gender and globalization, and chapters in edited volumes.

Sabine Lang is an associate professor of international studies at the Henry M. Jackson School of International Studies of the University of Washington. Her research on multilevel governance and women's advocacy has appeared, among others, in the journals *Social Politics* and *German Politics*. Her latest book, *NGOs, Civil Society, and the Public Sphere*, has been published by Cambridge University Press in 2013.

Lauren Leve is an associate professor of religious studies at the University of North Carolina at Chapel Hill. She is the author of *The Buddhist Art of Living in Nepal:*

Ethical Practice and Religious Reform and various articles and book chapters focusing on development, gender, human rights, and religious innovation in Nepal.

Kathleen O'Reilly is an associate professor in the Department of Geography at Texas A&M University. She studies the social and environmental impacts of development projects, especially those working on drinking water, sanitation, poverty, and gender. She is interested in the ways that development interventions restructure social, environmental, and spatial relations in rural communities in India. Her work has been published in major geographical, women's studies, and anthropological journals, including the *Annals of the Association of American Geographers, Geoforum, Economic Geography, Signs*, and *Human Organization*.

Aradhana Sharma is an associate professor of anthropology and feminist studies at Wesleyan University. She is the author of *Logics of Empowerment: Development, Gender, and Governance in Neoliberal India* and coeditor of *The Anthropology of the State: A Reader*. Her work, focusing on gender, development, neoliberalism, the state, governance and activism in India has also appeared in the journals *Cultural Anthropology, Current Anthropology*, and *Citizenship Studies*.

ABANTU for Development, 234–36
abeyance in NGOs, global restructuring
of feminism and, 268–69, 272–74
abortion: Latin American feminist
activism for, 296–99; in postcommunist Romania, 255–57; recriminaliza-
tion in Nicaragua of, 296
academic feminism: in Bosnia-
Herzegovina, 19, 21–46; critiques of,
227; in Romania, 253–57, 263–64; in
Russia, 125–28
Achievements 2002, 148–49
Acker, Joan, 260–61
activism: impact of NGOs on, 304–10;
Latin American feminist NGOs and,
288–91; NGOization paradigm and
nostalgia for, 227–32; perceptions
in Bosnia-Herzegovina of, 29–37; in
Romania, 257–62; of Thai women,
167–68; unofficial GONGO participation in, 101–6. *See also* elite activism;
social justice movements; women's
movements
activist mothering movement (Thailand), 178–81, 191n14, 191n16
Adult Literacy Centers, Nepalese establishment of, 59–60
advocacy: by Bosnian women's NGOs,
36–37, 40–43; European Union disincentives to, 272–74; political constraints on women's NGOs for, 276–
79. *See also* transnational advocacy
networks
affinity groups, women NGOs and creation of, 280–81
Afghanistan, NGO activity in, 38
African feminism, Ghanaian Women's
Manifesto analysis of, 234–36
Afro-descendant groups, mass mobilization in Latin America of, 292–95
Aga Khan Foundation, 13
agency: women's empowerment in
Nepal and, 65–74; of women's NGOs
in EU, 271–74
Agency for Gender Equality (Bosnia-
Herzegovina), 47n8
agriculture, in rural Nepal, 56–60
Ahearn, Laura, 66–67
aktiv žena (women's activities) groups,
in Bosnia-Herzegovina, 32–33, 43,
47n13
alternative media movement, 292
Alvarez, Sonia, 1, 46, 220, 224–28, 230,
245n4, 269, 285–99, 303
American Bar Association, 119
Amnesty International, 119
Amsterdam Treaty of 1999, 266, 279
AnA Society for Feminist Analyses
(AnA), 248; history of, 257–64; post-
communist creation of, 248–52

AnaLize: Journal of Gender and Feminist Studies, 248–49

Andric-Ružicic, Duška, 36

Anti-Fascist Women's Front (Antifašisticki Front Žena, AFŽ), 32, 48n16

anti-institutionalism, NGOization paradigm and, 244–45

Appadurai, Arjun, 193–94

Arab Spring, 309

Argentina, women's movements in, 292, 298–99

arranged marriages in Nepal, women's empowerment and role of, 67–68, 76–81

Articulación Feminista Marcosur (AFM), 296–99

Asad, Talal, 74–76

Asia Foundation, 169

Asia Pacific Forum for Women, Law, and Development, 170

Assessoria Especial de Gênero Raça Etnia (AEGRE) (Brazil), 294–95

Association for Social Advancement (ASA), 215n1, 217n21

Association for Women's Rights in Development (AWID), 274–76

"association of women," in Bosnia-Herzegovina, 32–37

autonomy: in feminist scholarship, 90n49; in Indian activism, 96–98

"Babylution" demonstrations (Bosnia), 41

Bachelet, Michelle, 294

Bakhtin, Mikhail, 55, 153–54, 163–64

Bangladesh: microcredit program in, 193–215; NGO activity in, 215n3; political history of, 199–201; power/knowledge institutions in, 213–15; sexual politics and regulation in, 207–9; women moneylenders in, 210–13, 217n26

Bangladesh Rural Advancement Committee (BRAC), 215n1, 216n16, 217n21

"banking" learning method, in Nepalese literary program, 58–60

Banskota, Amrita, 52

Bartolina Sisa National Federation of Bolivian Peasant Women, 294–95

Basu, Anrito, 12–13

Batra, Seema, 100–101

battered women's movement, local initiatives in, 122–25

Bebbington, Anthony, 163

Begić, Aida, 40

Beijing Women's Conference. *See* World Conference on Women in Beijing

Bennett, Lynn, 76

Bernal, Victoria, 1–18, 301–10

Bhattarai, Baburam, 85

"bikās" (development) in rural Nepal, 66–67, 70–74, 81–86, 90n42

Bolivia, movement mobilization in, 292–95

boomerang effect in women's advocacy networks, 270–74

Bordia, Anil, 96, 108–9

Bosanka (Bosnian NGO), 30–37, 39

Bosnia-Herzegovina: "claim-bearing label" of NGOs in, 27–29; effects of NGO boom in, 43–46; postwar feminist organizing in, 19, 21–46; postwar NGOs established in, 21–24; rape camps in, 123; uncertainty of support for NGOs in, 37–43

Bosnian League of Women Voters, 39–43

Bosnian Women's Initiative, 26–27

Bowie, Katherine, 190n3

Brazil: neopopulism in, 293–94; women's movement in, 288–92, 297–99

breastfeeding, Thai government promotion of, 191n16

"briefcase NGOs," 303

British Embassy, 119

Brown, Wendy, 110, 226

Buddhism, Thai women's activism and influence of, 180–81

bureaucratization: Indian GONGO subversion of, 101–12; Latin American "movement work" and, 289–91; NGOization paradigm and, 224–27; in Romanian NGOs, 259–64; state/non-state work identities in hybrid GONGO/NGO structure and, 99–106; velvet triangle concept and, 267–69; women's NGOs in EU and, 270–74, 303

Burma Women's Day, 177–78

Cairo Summit on Population and Development, 287–88

Campaign for an Inter-American Convention on Sexual Rights and Reproductive Rights, 296–99

capability concept of development, 306

capitalism: as catalyst for revolution, 62–65; Latin American feminists' campaign against, 296–99; microcredit systems and influence of, 193–96, 214–15; NGOization paradigm and role of, 231–32

Cargo cults, 46n2

Cartea neagră a egalității de șanse între femei și bărbați în România (Black book on equal opportunities between women and men in Romania), 260

caste system, Indian GONGO subversion efforts concerning, 102–6

Ceaușescu, Elena, 264n7

Ceaușescu, Nicolae, 250, 253

Celiberti, Lilian, 296–97

Center for Social Work (Bosnia-Herzegovina), 43

Central Europe, women's groups in, 271–74

Charities Act of 2006 (United Kingdom), 278–79

charity laws, political constraints on women's NGOs as result of, 277–79

Chatterjee, Partha, 109–10

Chávez, Hugo, 294

Chiang Mai University, Women's Studies Center, 184

Chile, neopopulism in, 293–94

Choluj, Bozena, 271–72

Chorigaon region (Nepal), 55–60; empowerment and agency in, 65–74

Christianity, NGOs and promotion of, 87n13

citizenship: in European Union governance structure, 273–74; neoliberal concepts of, 194–96; Romanian women's cultivation of, 261–64

civil society: in Bosnia-Herzegovina, 25–27, 33–37; European Union policies and, 269–70; framing of gendered violence issues and, 138–40; global and local aspects of, 119–40; Indian GONGO-NGO partnerships and, 94–95, 109–12; international advocacy for, 12; neopopulist movements in Latin America and, 293–95; NGOization paradigm and role of, 231; NGO promotion of, 4–6, 8–18; in postcommunist Romania, 250–52; in postsocialist countries, 47n7; Thai women's activism and discourses of, 175; women's advocacy networks and development of, 266–69

"claim-bearing label" for NGOs, in postwar Bosnia-Herzegovina, 27–29

class hierarchies: cultural preservation initiatives and, 176–78; Ghanaian Manifesto critique of, 240–44; Indian caste system and, 113n12; in microcredit programs, 216n20; NGOization and, 168–72, 228, 230, 305–10; Thai feminist discourse and, 181–86; Thai women's activism and, 172–74, 180–81; transnational feminist solidarity and, 187–90

clientilistic networks: hybrid GONGO/NGO structure and, 100–106; postwar Bosnian NGOs and, 48n22

Clinton, Bill, 215

Clinton, Hillary, 215
coalition building: activist mothering and, 179–81; feminist critique of, 219–20; Ghanaian ethnography of inclusion and, 236–44; Ghanaian Women's Manifesto project and, 221–23; Thai women's activism and, 169–72
Coalition on the Women's Manifesto for Ghana, 221–23, 234–36
Cockburn, Cynthia, 40
coercion, hybrid GONGO/NGO structure and risk of, 99–106
collective empowerment strategies: feminist activism in postliberal India and, 106–12; feminist critique of, 219–20; Latin American feminist movements and, 289–91; in Mahila Samakhya project, 96–98; NGOization paradigm as shift from, 224–27; in postcommunist Romania, 250–52; in Romanian women's organizations, 261–64
collective transformation, Thai feminist solidarity and, 189–90
Collins, Chik, 161
Colombia: Latin American "movement work" and, 290–91; NGOs in, 286
colonialism, NGOs in context of, 303–10
Comaroff, Jean, 232
The Commission and Non-Governmental Organizations: Building a Stronger Partnership, 270
"community aquis" *(acquis communautaire)* implementation, 258–59, 264n10
community-based integrated rural development (CBIRD), in Nepalese literacy program and, 58–60
community development: Our Water project in India, 148–65, 165n1; in Romania, 260–64; Thai women's programs for, 170–78; women's associations in Bosnia-Herzegovina and, 27–29, 32–37, 43, 47n13

Comprehensive Peace Agreement (2006) (Nepal), 83–86, 91n52
confederated structures, women's NGOs in EU and, 271–74
conscientization theories, 60–65; empowerment model and, 88n33; Latin American "movement work" and, 290–91, 294–95; Mahila Samakhya project design and, 96–98
Convention on the Elimination of All Forms of Discrimination Against Women, 12, 141n5; Bosnia-Herzegovina as signatory on, 24
Cook, Nerida, 172–73
Cooke, Bill, 146–48
Cornwall, Andrea, 147–48
corporate sector: as NGO donor resource, 10–11; NGOization paradigm and, 223; NGO structure in relation to, 7, 15–18; in postcommunist Romania, 251–52; structural violence of development and, 60–65; Third World economic sovereignty and hegemony of, 196–97
corruption in government: in Bangladesh, 199, 216n10; Nepalese rural revolution and role of, 51
Costa, LeeRay, 116, 166–92
Credit Development Forum, 204–6
crisis center model: economic discrimination priorities and, 129–32; gendered violence in Russia and rise of, 125–28, 141n15; Russian *vs.* western concepts of, 133–38
critical development geography, Indian women's NGOs and, 147–48
cross-cultural commonality: transnational advocacy and costs of, 123–25; women's activism and, 119
Crothers, Thomas, 47n7
cultural preservation and production: educational reforms and, 177–78; Ghanaian regional inequalities and issues of, 239–44; NGOization para-

digm and, 232; in postcommunist Romania, 250–52; rural activism and, 175–78; Thai feminism and challenges of, 182–86

CURE (Girls), arts in Bosnia-Herzegovina of, 40–42

cyborg metaphor, NGOization paradigm and, 231–32, 245

Das, Veena, 90n48

Dayton Peace Agreement, impact on NGOS of, 24

debt-related dependency, microcredit systems and, 198–99

defaults in microcredit systems, group responsibility for, 206–9

democratization: Bosnian NGOS and interest in, 33–37; empowerment and agency and role of, 68–74; gender equality linked to, 124–25, 140n4, 274–76; Nepalese state failure and absence of, 81–86, 89n38; in postwar Bangladesh, 200–201; in Romania, 249–52, 261–64; state accountability and, 302–3; structural violence of development and, 61–65; Thai women's activism and, 169–72, 181–86

dependency: in Bangladesh, dependency on NGOS, 201; chain of, in microcredit systems, 207–9; of NGO donor funding in Bosnia and, 37–43; of Romanian NGOS, 251–52; strategies for avoiding, 302–10

depoliticization of NGOS: in Bosnia-Herzegovina, 32–37, 48n14; economic development and, 138–40; feminist critique of, 219–20; future of women's advocacy and role of, 282–83; in Ghanaian Women's Manifesto, 234–36, 240–44; NGOization paradigm and, 223–27; in Russian women's organizations, 245n1

Desai, Manisha, 181

Desjarlais, Robert, 77

De Souza, Karen, 223

development programs: alternatives to, 144–45; attitudes in Nepal towards, 91nn50–51; gender equality issues and, 305–10; in Ghana, 237–44, 246n11; global and political changes in, 293–95; growth of women's participation in, 160–65; microcredit systems and, 213–15; Nepalese rural revolution and failure of, 50–86; NGO integration in, 4–6, 10–11; NGOization paradigm and, 224–27; in postwar Bangladesh, 199–201; Thai feminist discourse in, 184–86; in Thailand, feminist solidarity and, 186–90; transnational advocacy and costs of, 124–25, 186–90; violence against women as issue in, 122–25; violence as result of, 60–65, 88n26; women's political activism as result of, 52–55

dharma, Hindu concept of, 76, 80–81

dialogic exchange: growth of women's participation through, 160–63; in Indian women's NGOS, 143–65; micropolitics of, 152–54; spatial practices and, 154–60

difference: rural Thai women activist and, 187–90; Thai women's activism and politics of, 166–90; transborder feminist solidary in face of, 188–90

domestic violence: NGOS in Bosnia for combatting, 31–37; Russian vs. Western crisis center models and role of, 129–32, 134–38; in Soviet-era Russia, 126–28; transnational campaigns against, 121–25

donor institutions: Bangladeshi NGOS and, 195–96; Bosnian NGOS' dependency on, 37–43; Bosnian women's NGOS and initiatives of, 33–37; "claim-bearing label" of NGOS in Bosnia and, 27–29; credibility of women's groups with, 28–29; development agendas of, 144–45; Gha-

donor institutions (*continued*)
naian Manifesto coalition and obligations to, 237–44; Ghanaian women's movement critique of, 234–36; microcredit operations and, 204–6; NGOization paradigm and agendas of, 10–18, 225–27; in postwar Bosnia-Herzegovina, 24–27; Russian crisis center models and, 125–28, 137–38; spatial practices and influence of, 157–60
Dorsey, Ellen, 132
dukka (suffering), Nepalese concept of: empowerment among women and, 71–74; marriage in context of, 76–81

Eastern Europe, women's groups in, 271–74
East-West communication: public engagement issues for women's NGOs and, 280–81; Romanian feminism and issues of, 252–53
economic issues: in Bangladesh, 199–201; depoliticization of, 138–40; economic constraints of women's NGOs, 274–76; future of women's advocacy and, 281–83; gendered violence and, 124–25, 142n22; Ghanaian regional inequality and, 236–37; Ghanaian Women's Manifesto analysis of, 234–36; Indian women's NGOs and, 150–65; Latin America women's movements and, 287–88, 298–99; microcredit and political economy of shame, 197–99; Nepalese literacy program as tool for, 57–60; Russian women's groups prioritization of, 129–32, 142n22; Thai women's activism and, 176–78, 182–86, 192n12; Third World economic sovereignty and, 196–97; women's marginalization from, 120–21
Ecuador, mass mobilizations in, 292–95

education: Indian hierarchies of, 113n12; Indian women's NGOs and role of, 150–51; Maoist movement suspicion of, 91n53; marriage in Nepal as interruption of, 78–81; Nepalese women's empowerment and, 63–74, 88n21; NGOs in, 19–20; Romanian nonsexist education program, 260; Thai women's activism concerning, 177–78; transnational feminist solidarity and, 187–90
electoral politics: Bosnian NGOs' activism concerning, 39–43; Thai feminism and, 185–86, 192n22. *See also* political agendas
electrification, in rural Nepal, 56
elite activism: NGOization paradigm and, 222–23; in Thailand, 172–74
employment: in Bangladesh NGOs, 201; in Bosnia-Herzegovina NGOs, 30–31, 36–37, 47n11; discrimination in Romania and, 255–57; European Union gender equality policies involving, 266; opportunities in NGOs for, 14, 305–10; in rural Nepal, 56–60; Russian discrimination of women in, 129–38; in Thai women's activism, 180–81. *See also* labor migration
empowerment: feminist discourses on, 175; governmentalization of, in postliberal India, 107–12; political consciousness and rethinking of, 81–86; subversion of state repression and, 95; theoretical evolution of, 62–65. *See also* women's empowerment
"Empowerment with a Twist" (Manchanda), 52
Encuentros Nacionales de Muheres, 298
"enredarse" practices, Latin American feminist movements and, 290–91
equality: economic equality, lack of prioritization for, 129–32; gender equality in Bosnia-Herzegovina,

43–46, 47n8; gender equality in Romania, 256–57, 260–64; lack of prioritization in NGOs for, 123–25

Equal Treatment Directive, 279

Escobar, Arturo, 226

ethnic identity: in Nepal, 56–60, 87n11; in postwar Bosnia-Herzegovina institutions, 24–27

ethnic minority returnees, Bosnian NGOs for, 33–37

ethnographic research: on Maoist movement in Nepal, 53–55; methodologies of, 216n7; NGOization paradigm and, 223

Etzioni, Amitai, 261

Europe, battered women's movement in, 122–25

European Commission, 269–70

European Commissioner for Development and Humanitarian Aid, 275–76

European Feminist Forum (EFF), 280–81

European Institute for Gender Equality, 256–57, 266

European Union (EU): Bangladesh aid from, 215n3; economic power of, 274–76; feminists and governance structure of, 219–20; funding priorities and biases of, 274–76, 281–83; gender politics and, 14, 281–83; nongovernmental sector relations with, 269–70; norms and regulations of state duties under, 38–43; Phare programs of, 260, 265n12; political constraints on women's NGOs within, 276–79, 303; postwar Bosnia-Herzegovina and aid from, 25, 44–46; public engagement and women's NGOs under, 279–81; Romanian membership in, 250, 252, 254–55, 260, 262; women's advocacy networks and, 266–83; women's NGOs in, 270–74

European Women's Lobby, 270–74

Ewig, Christina, 291

exchange-based relationships, velvet triangle concept in, 267–69

"failed development" thesis: political consciousness and, 81–86; rural revolution in Nepal and, 52–55, 86n4; violence and development and, 60–65

failed states: Bangladeshi NGOs and, 195–97; NGOs and, 10–11

"false consciousness" paradigm, rural revolution and, 82–86

female genital mutilation, campaigns against, 122–25

feminismos con apellidos (other feminisms), 298–99

feministas autómas, 285–86

feministas jóvenes, 299

feminist organizations: academic feminism and, 221–28; Bangladesh rural credit systems and, 214–15; in Bosnia-Herzegovina, 26–27, 31–37, 45–46, 48n16, 48n20; coalition building and, 168–72; gendered personhood concept and, 90n45; in Ghana, 221–23, 232–34; Indian state partnerships with, 95; indigenous groups' exclusion from, 172–74; international policy monitoring by, 291–99; Latin American critique of, 285–86; Latin American "movement work" and, 287–91, 294–95; neoliberalism and, 10–11; NGOization paradigm critiqued by, 221–23, 285–88; NGOs as catalyst for, 1–11, 19, 301–10; professionalization of, 30–31, 36–37, 170–72, 180–86, 224–27, 246n10; public engagement issues for, 279–81; in Romania, 248–64, 265n14; Russian crisis center proliferation and role of, 125–28; Russian economic crises in competition with, 120–21, 129–32, 141n13; social movements and, 219–20; spatial practices and agenda of, 157–60; Thai women's activism and,

feminist organizations (*continued*)
166–68, 175, 181–86; "third moment"
development in, 295; women's advocacy networks, 266–83
Ferguson, James, 226
Ferree, Myra Marx, 228, 230, 284n8
Fifth Community Action Program,
274–76, 284n5
film, Bosnian women directors in, 40
Finland, activities in postwar Bosnia-
Herzegovina, 25
Fisher, William, 293
Ford Foundation, 119, 141n6
foreign intervention agencies: Bangladeshi NGOs and, 195–96; Bosnian NGOs and role of, 24–27, 41–43,
45–46; terminology and definitions,
46n4; Thai women's activism and, 174
Foucault, Michel, 94–95, 112n4; NGO-
ization paradigm and power/knowl-
edge theory of, 225–26; participatory
research and, 147–48; productivity
theory of, 232
Frederich Ebert Stiftung, 169–72
freedom: development and promotion
of, 61–65; in feminist scholarship,
90n49; Nepalese women's concepts
of, 74; in postcommunist Romania,
250–52
Freire, Paolo, 58–60, 62–65
fundamentalist Islam: Bosnian women's
critique of, 40; freedom and autonomy concepts in, 90n49
funding strategies of NGOs: economic
equality as focus for, 132; political
motivations and, 6; Russian crisis
center models and, 125–28, 137–38;
women's NGOs in EU and, 270–74
Funk, Nanette, 44

Gandhi, Indira, 96–97
Gandhi, Rajiv, 96–97
Garrido, Lucy, 296–97
Gautam, Shobha, 52

gay rights, activism in Bosnia-
Herzegovina concerning, 40–43,
48n21
Gender Center of the Federation
(Bosnia-Herzegovina), 47n8
Gender Center of the Republika Srpska,
47n8
gender equality: Bosnia-Herzegovina
NGOs, lack of involvement in, 25–27,
31–37; Bosnian feminist perspectives on, 40–43, 47n8; community
development/cultural preservation
discourses and activism on, 176–78;
conscientization theory and role of,
63–65; democratization's impact on,
124–25, 140n4; economic context
for, 129–32, 274–76; European Union
policies concerning, 266–83; feminist discourse on, 303–10; gender
mainstreaming, 14, 96, 143, 225, 231,
243, 258–62, 279; Ghanaian Women's
Manifesto analysis of, 234–36; Indian
micropolitics and, 152–54; Indian
women's NGOs and paradox of,
143–65; Latin American NGOization
and, 287–88; legal context for, 274–
76; Maoist movement agenda and
inclusion of, 70–74; microcredit and,
193–96; Nepalese rural revolution
and role of, 52–55; NGO agendas for,
302–10; NGOization paradigm and,
3–11, 225–27, 231; personhood concepts and, 74–81; political constraints
on women's NGOs concerning, 276–
79; post-Cold War politics and, 14;
in Romania, 250–52, 255–59, 262–
64; in Russia, 120–21, 125–28; spatial
practices and women's empowerment and, 156–60; Thai feminist
discourse on, 181–86; transnational
anti-violence campaigns and, 122–
25
Gender Equality Agency (Bosnia-
Herzegovina), 25

Gender Equality Index, Romanian development and, 256–57

generational changes: Bosnian feminism and, 41–43, 49n23; in Latin American feminism, 299; in Romanian feminism, 263–64

geopolitics: Indian women's NGOs and, 143–65; NGOs in context of, 8–11, 303–10; transnational feminist solidarity and, 187–90

German feminism: political constraints on women's NGOs and, 277–79; in postunification Germany, 230; Russian feminists and, 129; support for Bosnian women's organizations from, 26, 28, 31–37, 39–40, 42–43

Ghana: coalition building and ethnography of inclusion in, 236–2344; NGO historicization and feminist organizing in, 232–34; regional economic inequality in, 237–44; women's coalitions in, 221–23

ghuunghat practices, Indian women's NGOs and role of, 151

globalization: abeyance of women's movement and, 272–74; feminist activism and, 128, 219; Latin American movement work as response to, 292–99; microcredit in Bangladesh and, 193; NGO as shadow state and, 196–97; NGOization in Latin America and, 287–88; Thai feminist discourse and, 184–86; Thai women's activism and issues of, 176–78; transnational advocacy and, 119–40; women's activism and, 120–21

global North: campaigns against gendered violence in, 122–25; economics for women's NGOs in, 274–76; NGOization paradigm and role of, 244–45; NGO structure in, 7–11; Third World feminism in discourse of, 182–86, 192n23

global South: campaigns against gen-

dered violence in, 122–25; economics for women's NGOs in, 274–76; NGOization paradigm in, 224–25; NGO structure in, 7–11; subaltern woman in, 308–10; Third World feminism in discourse of, 192n23

Gold, Ann, 151

Gorbachev, Mikhail S., 125

Gorkha district (Nepal): literacy rate in, 66–67; population statistics for, 87n11; unification in, 87n10; women's empowerment in, 52, 55–60

governmentality and governance structures: deradicalization of Indian GONGO/NGO activism, 109–12; feminist activism and, 219–20; Foucault's concept of, 112n4; future of women's advocacy and role of, 282–83; Ghanaian Women's Manifesto demands for, 235–326; Latin American "movement work" and, 289–91; NGOization paradigm and influence of, 283n2; NGOs and, 5–6; women's NGOs in EU and, 270–74; work identities in Indian GONGO/NGO structure and, 99–106

Government Organized Non-governmental Organizations (GONGOs): anthropological research on, 112n7; in Bosnia-Herzegovina, 20; in Ghana, 233–34; in India, 94–95; work identities in, 98–106

Grameen Bank, 193–215; Bangladeshi women moneylenders and, 212–13; critiques of, 214–15; Grameen II model, 217n21; payment schedule in, 217n22; political economy of shame and, 195–99; restructuring of, 215n1

Gramsci, Antonio, 195

grassroots activism: feminism and, 11–18; Ghanaian regional inequality and role of, 237–44; governmentalization of, in postliberal India, 107–12;

grassroots activism (*continued*)
microcredit systems and, 193–96;
neoliberal ideology and, 94–95;
NGOization paradigm and shift from,
200–201, 223–27; in Romania, 263–
64; state involvement in, 97; Thai
class hierarchies and, 172–74, 183–86,
190n2, 191n8; in United Kingdom,
278–79; women's NGOs in EU and,
271–74
grassroots organizations (GROs), 46n3
Greece, women's organizations in,
273–74
Grewal, Inderpal, 1–18, 301–10
group responsibility, in microcredit
operations, 206–9, 217n21
Grown, Caren, 182
Grünberg, Laura, 220, 248–64
guerrilla groups (Nepal), women's
participation and leadership in, 52
Guha, Ranajit, 65

Hague Tribunal, 123
Halley, Janet, 305
Haraway, Donna, 50, 231–32
Harcourt, Wendy, 295
health services, in rural Nepal, 56–60
Hegel, G. W. F., neoliberal and conscien-
tization models and, 65
Heinrich Böll Foundation, 184
Helfferich, Barbara, 279
Helms, Elissa, 19
Hemment, Julie, 115, 119–40, 223, 230,
245n1, 246n6, 286
Hickey, Samuel, 146–48, 162–63
Hilhorst, Dorothea, 27–28
Hindu culture: dharma in, 76; in Nepal,
56–60; women moneylenders in,
217n26
hip hop movement, 292
Hirshman, Mitu, 182
historicization of NGOs, Ghanaian femi-
nist organizing and, 232–34, 244–45,
246n7

HIV/AIDS activism, productivity concept and, 232
Hodžić, Saida, 16, 219, 221–45
Hofstede, Geert, 250
homosexuality: NGOs for sexual rights
and, 15–18. *See also* gay rights
honor codes, political economy of
shaming and, 198–99
horizontal integration, Latin American
feminist movement and, 288–91
hotline systems, Russian *vs.* Western
crisis center models and, 135–38
house breaking *(ghar bhanga)*: Bangladeshi women moneylenders and, 213;
Bangladesh practice of, 208–9
housewife groups, in rural Thailand,
170, 178–79, 191n7
housing crisis, gendered violence in
Soviet-era Russia and, 126–28
"How to Create a Women's Crisis
Center," 128
humanist feminism, NGOization paradigm and, 227–32
humanitarian NGOs, local efforts in
Bosnia-Herzegovina and, 30–31
human rights organizations: generic humanity and, 74–81; in Latin
America, 286; NGO structure and,
12–18; in Romania, 250–52, 254; Thai
women's movements and, 175, 181–
86, 191n18; women's rights linked to,
123
human trafficking issues: NGO involvement in, 308–10; women's advocacy
programs against, 37, 40, 44, 137, 254,
257–58, 276
Hungary, political constraints on
women's NGOs in, 277–79
hybridity in NGOs: feminist critique
of, 219–20; Ghanaian Women's
Manifesto and, 234–36; Ghanaian
women's organizations' embrace
of, 232–34; Latin American NGO-
ization and, 285–88; Mahila Sama-

khay project as both NGO/GO, 93–98; work identities in, 98–106

hypermasculinity of state institutions, Indian GONGO resistance to, 103–6

immigrants, mass mobilization in Latin America by, 292–95

imperialism: NGOs as agents of, 4–6; structural violence of development and, 60–65

inclusion, NGOization paradigm and ethnography of, 236–44

Independent Russian Women's Movement, 125–28

India: dowry deaths campaign in, 122; feminist activism in postliberal era, 106–12; GONGO advocacy for women's empowerment in, 93–106; Our Water project in, 148–65; state-civil society partnerships in, 93–95; women's NGOs in, 20, 143–65, 171–72, 189–90

indigenous groups: cultural preservation and developmental impact for, 177–78; mass mobilization in Latin America of, 292–95

individual responsibility: group responsibility vs., 206–9; neoliberal discourse on, 203; political discourse on, 178, 180–81; in postcommunist Romania, 250–52; in Romanian women's organizations, 261–64; spatial practice and, 153–55; Thailand social hierarchy and, 174; women's participation and, 145–46

inequality: Ghanaian coalition building and regional inequalities, 237–44; transnational advocacy and disregard of, 123–25

Infoteka, 31, 36, 42–43

INGO, Nepalese women's political activism linked to, 52–55

institutional credit, NGOs in Bangladesh as source of, 200–201

Inter-American Convention on Violence against Women, 297

interest rates, in Bangladeshi microcredit systems, 207–9

intergovernmental organizations (IGOs): in Latin America, 285–86; NGOization paradigm and, 287–88

internal refugees, in Nepal, 51, 86n2

International Conference on Thai Studies, Women's Forum of, 166–67

international financial institutions (IFIs): NGOization in Latin America and, 285–86; NGOization paradigm and, 287–88, 302–10

international institutions: in Bosnia-Herzegovina of, 24–25, 29–37; employment discrimination of women and, 130–31; EU funding bias in favor of, 274–76; EU-NGO civil society initiatives and, 269–70; future of women's advocacy within, 281–83; Ghanaian Manifesto coalition and, 237–44; lack of public engagement in, 279–81; NGOization in Thailand and, 169–72; NGOs and, 16–18; Russian vs. Western crisis center models and policies of, 137–38; Thai feminist discourse in, 184–86; transnational women's advocacy and, 266–83; violence against women as priority for, 122–25; women's NGOs in EU and, 270–74

International Monetary Fund (IMF), 131, 302; Thai economic crisis and, 176; Third World economic sovereignty and, 196–97

International Women's Day, Bosnian women's groups' celebration of, 32–34

Internet, transnationational advocacy and role of, 142n21

intersectionality: in Romanian feminism, 263–64; Thai women's activism and, 168 intervention agencies: credibility of women's groups with, 28–29; diversity of, in Bosnia-Herzegovina, 43–46; gendered intervention, women's empowerment and, 160–65; in postwar Bosnia-Herzegovina, 25–27, 42–43, 47n6

Iraq, NGO activity in, 38

"iron triangle," Lowi's concept of, 267

Islamic NGOs: in Middle East, 13; NGOization paradigm and, 228, 230; support of Bosnian women from, 33, 44–46, 47n5

Jad, Islah, 228, 230–31

jana andolan (People's Movement), failure of democratization following, 51

jana yuddha ("People's War") (Nepal), 50–51

Jansen, Stef, 46n4

John, Mary, 106–7

Joshi, Varsha, 151

kanyadān (obligation), Nepalese concept of, marriage and, 78–81

KARAT Coalition, 280–81

Karim, Lamia, 116, 193–215, 247n13

Kataleeradabhan, Nitaya, 170

Keck, Margaret, 12, 122

Kerr, Joanna, 283n4

Kesby, Mike, 162–63

keyword techniques, in Nepalese literary program, 58–60

Khan, Tasneem, 150

kinship structures: formal *vs.* practical practices of, 90n48; microcredit operations and, 204–6, 216n18; Thai women's activism and, 169–72, 190n3

Kishore, Prabha, 98–99

Kissinger, Henry, 214–15

knitting projects, of Bosnian women's NGOs, 35

knowledge production: Latin American feminist movements and, 289–91; NGOization paradigm and, 225–26; power and, 213–15; Romanian women's organizations generation of, 261–64

Kolb, Felix, 279

Kosovo, NGO activity in, 38

Kothari, Uma, 146–48

Kristoff, Nicholas, 308

Kumari, Gyan, 66

Kvinna til Kvinna (Women to Women), 47n9

labor migration: from Gorkha district (Nepal), 57–60; microcredit systems and, 194–96; in Third World countries, 215n6. *See also* employment

Laclau, Ernesto, 298

land issues, Indian GONGO activism concerning, 102–6

Lang, Sabine, 1–2, 14, 219, 224–28, 230, 266–83, 303, 305

Latin America: factors in NGOization in, 287–88; movement work as alternative to NGOization in, 291–99; "movement work" of feminist NGOs in, 288–91; NGOization of women's movements in, 220, 230, 285–99; post-NGOization feminism in, 295–99; state-sanctioned violence in, 122

Latvia, political constraints on women's NGOs in, 277–79

Lefevre, Henri, 152–54, 261

legal constraints of women's NGOs, 274–76; charity and tax laws and, 276–79

legislative reforms: Bosnian NGO involvement in, 39–46; "community aquis" *(acquis communautaire)*, 258–59, 264n10; in postcommunist Romania, 256–57

legitimacy issues, hybrid GONGO/NGO structure and, 99–106

León, Magdalena, 290–91

Ler-Sofronić, Nada, 48n20

Leve, Lauren, 5, 19–20, 50–86

Lewis, David, 163–64

liberal theory: gendered violence in Russia and skepticism of, 126–28; NGOization paradigm as retreat from, 224–27; NGO scholarship and, 5–11

Lind, Amy, 245n4

linguistic practices: Ghanaian Manifesto coalition and issue of, 238–44, 246nn8–9; power/knowledge dissemination and, 213–15; Romanian gender equality issues and, 262–64; Thai women's activism and, 179–81

literacy programs: empowerment and agency Chorigaon (Nepal) and, 65–74; in Gorkha district (Nepal), 56–60, 88n21; marriage practices and impact of, 89n37; Nepalese women's empowerment and, 63–65; political activism linked to, 52–55

local feminist movements: battered women's movement initiatives, 122–25; community-level associations in Bosnia-Herzegovina as, 27–29; competing economic issues in Russia with, 129–32; Ghanaian regional inequality and role of, 237–44; global civil society and, 119–40; Indian Our Water project and, 149–65; Indian women's NGOs and, 146–48; in Latin America, 293–94; NGOs and emergence of, 12–18; in post-Soviet Russia, 126–28; in postwar Bosnia-Herzegovina, 23–24; Russian vs. Western crisis center models and, 133–38; transnational advocacy networks and, 119–21; women's NGOs in EU and, 271–74

local governments, suspicion of NGOs in Bosnia-Herzegovina by, 28–29

Locher, Birgit, 271

Lowi, Theodore, 267

Lula da Silva, Ignacio, 294

Macaulay, Fiona, 288–91

Maddison, Sarah, 272

Magyari-Vincze, Eniko, 254

Mahila Samakhya project (MS), 20, 93; GONGO structure of, 95–98; neoliberal theory and goals of, 106–12; relative obscurity of, 112n8; state/nonstate work identities in, 98–106

Mahmood, Saba, 90n49

mai-baap (mother-father), Indian state institutions classed as, 100, 112n10

majjā (fun), Nepalese concept of, 79

Majstorović, Danijela, 40

Mama Cash, 275–76, 280–81

Manchanda, Rita, 52–54, 60, 62–65

Mani, Kaveri, 97

Maoist movement (Nepal): criticisms of, 89n39; developmental failure and role of, 50–86; emergence of, 19–20; empowerment and agency and role of, 68–74; Forty Point Demands of, 71, 86n11; political consciousness and social identity in, 81–86; political demands of, 91n52; structural violence of development and, 61–65; violence against teachers by, 91n53; women's participation and leadership in, 52

March, Kathryn, 73–74

Marco, Graciela di, 298

markets: Nepalese literacy program and ideology of, 57–60; NGOization paradigm and role of, 7–11, 15–18, 231; rural activism as tool for, 200–201

marriage: Indian women's NGOs and role of, 150–51; Nepalese women's subjectivization as result of, 76–81, 89n37, 90n40; rituals and customs in Nepal for, 90nn46–47

Massey, Doreen, 152–54

mass mobilization, as alternative to NGOIZATION, 292–95

Master Manole (Romanian legendary figure), 254, 257, 264n3
maternalism in women's movements, 178–81, 191n14
Mauleón, Cecilia Olea, 290
meaning creation, micropolitics and, 153–54
Medica Mondiale, 35, 38
Medica Zenica, 26, 28, 31–37, 39–40, 42–43
Merjem (Bosnian NGO), 33–37
Merry, Sally Engle, 12
microcredit schemes: of Bosnian NGOs, 33–37; critiques of, 214–15; demystification of, 193–215; in Ghana, 239–44, 247n13; Grameen Bank model, 201–6; group responsibility model, 206–9, 217n21; kinship structures and, 204–6; Nepalese women's empowerment and, 63–65; political economy of shame and, 195–99; in postwar Bosnia-Herzegovina, 26–27; in rural Nepal, 56–60; surveillance mechanisms in, 206–9; usury expansion linked to, 210–13; violence as result of, 88n26; women as scapegoats in, 216n16
middle-class women: activist Thai women as, 181–86; in NGOs, 14
Middle East, Islamic NGOs in, 13
military counterinsurgency campaigns, Nepalese rural revolution and role of, 51
military service, Gorkha district (Nepal) enrollment in, 57–60
milk song, Thai women's activism and double meaning in, 179–80, 191n16
Mills, Mary Beth, 183
Miroiu, Mihaela, 254, 257, 264n3
Mitchell, Timothy, 7
mjesna zajednica (neighborhood-level administrative units), 47n13
Mohan, Giles, 146–47, 162–63
Mohanty, Chandra, 171–72, 186–87

Monasteiros, Elizabeth, 294
moneylending in Bangladesh, women's involvement in, 210–13, 217n26
moral arguments, NGO activism and, 308–10
Moser, Annalise, 187
movementization of NGOs, in postwar Bosnia-Herzegovina, 22–24, 38–42
Msimang, Sisonke, 246n10
Multimedia Resource Center for Women (Romania), 259
multinational corporations, Third World economic sovereignty and, 196–97
Murdock, Donna, 286, 287–88
Muslim moneylenders, 217n26

Nagar, Richa, 171–72, 188, 189–90, 224
Naples, Nancy, 176, 179
Naš Most (Our Bridge), 32–33, 39
National Agency for Equal Opportunities (Romania), 256–57
National Council for Combating Discrimination (Romania), 256–57
National Front of the Working People, 48n16
nationalism: in Nepal, 55–60; NGO formation in Romania and, 220; postcolonial feminism and, 17–18; in postwar Bosnia-Herzegovina, 26–27; Thai women's activism and, 175, 177–78
"Naya Goreto" (New Path) curriculum, 63; in Nepalese literacy program, 58–60
neoliberalism: feminist critique of NGOs and, 219–20; Ghanaian Women's Manifesto critique of, 235–36; hybrid NGO/GO structures and, 94–95, 106–12, 113n11; Latin American movement work and crisis in, 292–99; Latin American NGOization and, 285–88; microcredit in Bangladesh and, 193–215; Nepalese literacy program and,

57–60; NGOization paradigm and, 4–6, 8–11, 169–72, 224–27, 302–10; participation in development projects linked to, 146–48; postcolonial paradigms of, 115–17; postwar Bosnia-Herzegovina NGOs and influence of, 25–27, 37, 44–46, 48n18; structural violence of development and, 61–65, 88n26, 88n33; "third moment" feminism and resistance to, 295–99; transnational advocacy and hegemony of, 124–25, 141n10

neopopulism, rise in Latin America of, 293–95

Nepal: failed development and rural revolution in, 50–86; feminism and NGOs in, 19–20; rural social networks in, 87n8; unification of, 87n10

Network of East-West Women listserv, 142n21

NGO Affairs Bureau (Bangladesh) (NGOAB), 195–96

NGOization paradigm: anti-institutionalism and, 244–45; critical research on, 245n4, 246n5; current research involving, 287–88; feminist coalition building and, 168–72; genealogy of, 224–27; Ghanaian NGO historicization and feminist organizing and, 232–34; Ghanaian transcendence of, 221–23; humanist feminism and, 227–32; inclusion and coalition building and, 236–44; lack of public engagement as result of, 280–81; in Latin America, 220, 285–99; political constraints on women's NGOs and, 276–79; posthumanist critique, 221–45; process-oriented logic as alternative to, 293–95; transborder feminist solidarity and, 186–90; velvet triangle concept and, 267–69; women's NGOs in EU and, 270–74

"NGO-speak," "claim-bearing label" of NGOs in Bosnia and, 27–29

Nicaragua, women's NGOs in, 286

Nobel Peace Prize, 197–98, 215

nonformal adult education (NFE): empowerment and agency and role of, 65–74; in rural Nepal, 57–60

nongovernmental organizations (NGOs): as agency for activism, 16; class and group marginalization and, 16; cooptation of feminist movements by, 219–20; debates over future of, 16–18; disbursement statistics for, 1; European Union policies and, 269–70; feminism and structure of, 301–10; feminist activism integrated into, 8–18; feminist research concerning, 1–2; feminist social movements and, 219–20; form of, 6–11; globalization and shadow state status of, 196–97; normalization of, 1; postcolonial neoliberal paradigms and, 115–17; in postcommunist Romania, 250–52; proliferation of, 2; regional trends in, 3; scholarship divisions concerning, 3–6; structure and form of, 3–18, 301–10. See also women's NGOs

nonprofit status, political constraints on women's NGOs and, 276–79

North Atlantic Treaty Organization (NATO), 250

nostalgic feminism, NGOization paradigm, 227–32

Nussbaum, Martha, 306

Occupy movement, 309

Office of the High Representative, 24, 47n6

Omu, Kisang, 77

Ong, Aihwa, 123–24, 194, 200–201

online communications, Romanian women's organizations and, 259–64

Open Society Institute, 119, 280–81

O'Reilly, Kathleen, 116, 143–65

organicist discourse, NGOization paradigm and, 230–32

Organization for Security and Cooperation in Europe (OSCE), 24, 47n6

Organization of American States (OAS), 297

Ortega, Daniel, 296

Other: rural Thai women activist and, 187–90; Thai women's activism and politics of, 166–90

Our Water project, Indian women's participation in, 148–65

Parliamentary Commissions for Equal Opportunities (Romania), 256–57

participatory action research (PAR), 142n23; dialogic exchange and, 160–63; gendered paradox of, in Indian women's NGOs, 145–48; spatial practices and, 154–60

participatory goals of NGOs, Nepalese literacy program and, 57–60

Pathak, Sunita, 93–94, 97

Peake, Linda, 223

Pearce, Jenny, 304

pedagogical theory: empowerment framework and, 94–95; in Nepalese literary program, 58–60, 88n21

People's Army (Nepal), 53, 55–56

personhood, gendered concepts of, 74–81, 90n45

Peru, feminist organizations in, 290

Pettigrew, Judith, 83–84

Phare program (EU), 260, 265n12

Phillips, Sarah, 46n1, 223, 232

Pigg, Stacy, 66–67

ping-pong effect in women's advocacy networks, 270–74

"Pink Tide" in Latin America, 293–95

piqueteras movement (Argentina), 292, 298–99

"+5" conferences, Latin American feminism and, 291–93, 296–99

Poland, women's organizations in, 271–72

PoLAR (2010), 4

police intimidation and brutality: Indian GONGO resistance to, 103–6; Latin American feminism and, 298–99; microcredit systems and use of, 208–9, 217n24; Nepalese rural revolution and role of, 51

Polirom (Romanian publisher), 256

political agendas: "claim-bearing label" for NGOs as separation from, 28–29; depoliticization of Bosnian NGOs and, 32–37, 48n14; deradicalization of Indian GONGO/NGO activism and subversion of, 109–12; electoral activism of Bosnian NGOs, 39–43; empowerment in context of, 81–86; EU-based women's NGOs and restrictions on, 276–79, 284n6; in Ghanaian Manifesto, 240–44; Indian state and women's empowerment and, 93–112; Indian women's NGOs, micropolitics and, 152–54; of Latin American feminists, 296–99; NGOization paradigm and shift from, 225–27; of NGOs, 6, 13–18; in postwar Bangladesh, 200–201; Thai feminism and, 184–86, 190n3. See also electoral politics

political economy of shame, microcredit systems and, 195–99

Pongsapich, Amara, 170

"popular feminism," in Latin America, 296–99

postcolonial neoliberalism: citizenship in context of, 194–96; nongovernmental organizations and, 115–17

post-Enlightenment political theory: neoliberal and conscientization models and, 65; secular personhood in relation to, 75

postsocialist Europe, Bosnian NGOs and climate of, 45–46

poststructuralism, NGO scholarship and, 5–6

poverty: Ghanaian Women's Manifesto analysis of, 235–36; Nepalese rural revolution and role of, 51; violence linked to, 60–65

power-sharing mechanisms, in postwar Bosnia-Herzegovina, 24

power structure: in Bangladesh, 213–15; Indian GONGO subversion of, 102–6; Indian women's NGOs and, 143–48; integration of NGOs into, 8–11; knowledge and, 213–15; Nepalese women's participation and leadership in, 52–60; NGO-based social movement model and, 291–99; NGOization paradigm and power/knowledge theory, 225–26; NGOs in relation to, 1–6; secular personhood in relation to, 74–75; spatial practices and women's participation in, 154–60; Thai women's activism and influence of, 166–90; in women's advocacy networks, 267–69

primitivization paradigms, gendered violence issues and, 138–40

private networks, gendered violence in Russia and role of, 127–28

privatization: framing of gendered violence issues and, 139–40; of gendered violence, 124–25; Ghanaian Women's Manifesto critique of, 235–36; Indian neoliberal degovernmentalization and, 113n11; NGOization paradigm and, 8–11, 165–72, 225–27, 302–10

process-oriented logic, as NGOization alternative, 293–95

professional NGO bureaucracies: Arab women's movements and, 228, 230; distance from grassroots and, 305–10; employment in Bosnia-Herzegovina of, 30–31, 36–37; lack of public engagement and, 279–81; in Latin America, 299; NGO-based social movement model and, 291–99; NGOization paradigm and, 222–27, 306–10; in postcommunist Romania, 255–57; in Russia, 133–38, 246n6; Thai

women's activism and, 170–72, 180–86; velvet triangle concept and, 267–69; women's NGOs in EU as, 271–74

Progress Program (EU), 275–76

Project for Tomorrow (PFT), 167, 176–78

property rights and arrangements, gendered violence in Soviet-era Russia and concepts of, 126–28

Proshika Human Development Forum, 215n1, 217n21, 217n24

Psychosocial therapy, Bosnian NGOs' focus on, 35

public engagement, women's NGOs in EU and, 279–81

Pudrovska, Tatjana, 284n8

pueblo feminista (feminist people), 298–99

purdah practices, Indian women's NGOs and role of, 151

Queer (arts) Festival (Sarajevo), 48n21

race and racism, NGOs and, 14–15

radne akcije (work actions), 30

Raheja, Gloria, 151

Rani, Meena, 93

rape survivors: NGOs in Bosnia for, 31–37. *See also* sexual violence

Rawlings, Nana, 233–34

reconciliation institutions, in postwar Bosnia-Herzegovina, 26–27, 47n6, 47n9

reconstruction efforts, in postwar Bosnia-Herzegovina, 26–27

refugee services, in postwar Bosnia-Herzegovina, 26

representation, Thai women's activism and politics of, 172–74

reproductive rights, Latin American feminist activism for, 296–97

resistance movements, in Latin America, 292–99

Richard, Analiese, 302

rituals and customs: Indian women's NGOs and role of, 150–51; Nepalese women's adherence to, 71–74

Roma issues, Romanian women's activism on behalf of, 258–59

Romania: democratic transition in, 220; gender equality in, 256–57, 260–64; postcommunist feminism in, 248–64; US policy in, 47n7

Romanian Official Gazette, 261

"room-service feminism," Romanian concept of, 254–55, 264n4

Roth, Silke, 272

Rouseff, Dilma, 294

Rowlands, Jo, 162

Roy, Arundhati, 224, 247n12

rural activism: capitalism as catalyst for, 62–65; class hierarchies and marginalization of, 169–72; community development/cultural preservation discourses and, 175–78; community development discourse and, 175; exclusion in Thai scholarship of, 172–74; financial dependency on NGOs and, 201; hybrid GONGO/NGO structure and, 99–106; Indian women's empowerment and, 93–112; labor migration and, 215n6; microcredit systems and, 193–96, 204–6, 214–15; Nepalese developmental failure and rural revolution, 50–86; oppositionality with urban feminism and, 187–90; political consciousness and, 81–86; structural violence of development and, 61–65; Thai feminist discourse and marginalization of, 181–86; of Thai women, 166–90, 190n3; village social networks in Nepal and, 87n8

Russia: crisis center model in, 133–38; feminist activism in, 125–28; gender violence issues in, 138–40; prioritization of economic change over feminism in, 129–32; women activist organizations in, 119–21, 223, 245n1

sacrifice, Thai women's activism and concept of, 180–81

Sampson, Steve, 43

Sangtin Writers, 171–72, 189–90, 224

Sawer, Marian, 272

Schild, Verónica, 64, 75

Scott, James, 82–83

Scott, Joan, 222

second-wave feminism, in socialist-era Bosnia-Herzegovina, 38

self-censorship, political constraints on women's NGOs and, 278–79

self-realization: depoliticization of economic equality and, 138–40; in Soviet-era Russia, 126; Thai women's activism and ideology of, 176–78

Sempreviva Organização Feminists (SOF), 294–95, 297–98

Sen, Amartya, 306

Sen, Gita, 182

service-oriented NGOs, neoliberal encouragement of, 141n10

sexual politics: of Latin American feminists, 296–99; NGOs and, 14–15; political economy of shaming and, 198–99; in rural Bangladesh, 206–9; Thai feminist discourse on, 181–86

sexual violence: local Russian women's groups, attitudes concerning, 129–32, 142n16; NGO mobilization in postwar Bosnia-Herzegovina and issues of, 26–27, 36–37; Russian *vs.* Western crisis center models and role of, 136–38; transnational campaigns against, 121–25. *See also* domestic violence; rape survivors

Shah, Gyanendra, 55, 71, 91n52

Shah, Prithvinarayan, 55

Shah, Saubhagya, 83–84

Shah dynasty (Nepal), 55

shaming: in microcredit enterprises loan recovery program, 207–9, 217n21; as social control instrument, 198–99

Sharma, Aradhana, 14, 20, 22, 93–112, 236

Sikkink, Kathryn, 12, 122

Silliman, Jael, 245n4

Simpson, Meghan, 245n4

Sixteen Decisions (Grameen Bank), 204–6

Soares, Vera, 289–91

social engineering, by Bangladesh NGOs, 215n5

social gatherings, of Bosnian NGOs, 33–37

socialist feminism: "association of women" in Bosnia-Herzegovina and, 32–37; post-Cold War capitalism and, 14; Russian women's organizations and, 125–28, 141n13

social justice movements: Bosnian NGOs and mobilization for, 36–37; feminist discourses on, 175; feminist social movements and, 219–20; literacy programs as catalyst for, 60; NGO-based social movement model and, 291–99; NGO collaborations with, 302–10; Thai feminist perspectives on, 184–86, 191n18; transnational advocacy for, 120–21

social media, gender issues in Bosnia on, 41

social services NGOs: in Bosnia-Herzegovina, 28–37; Indian Our Water project and, 149–65; overview of, 10–11; reinforcement of patriarchal assumptions through, 41–43

soft law practices, European Union policies and, 269–70

songs, Thai women's activism and double meaning in, 179–80, 191n16

Sophia (Queen of Spain), 215

Soviet Women's Committee, 125, 140n2

Spain, women's organizations in, 272–73

spatial practice: in Indian women's

NGOs, 146–48; micropolitics of, 152–54; of Romanian women's organizations, 261–64; women's participation and empowerment and, 154–60

Spivak, Gayatri Chakravorty, 50, 65, 141n8

Srebrenica genocide survivors, activism of women's groups for, 36–37, 48n17

STAR (Strategies, Training, Advocacy for Reconciliation) Project, 47n9

state-as-giver paradigm, Indian hybrid GONGO/NGO programs and, 101–6, 112n9

"state effect" of NGOs, 7–11

state institutions: in Bangladesh, 200–201; in Bosnia-Herzegovina, 24, 37–43; democratization and empowerment accountability of, 302–3; economic discrimination of women in, 130–32; gendered violence committed by, 122–25; Ghanaian Women's Manifesto demands from, 234–36; Ghanaian women's movements and, 233–34; hybrid GONGO/NGO collaboration in India and, 93–112; Latin American NGO collaboration with, 292–99; local practices of, impact on NGOs of, 13; Mahila Samakhya project partnership with, 96–98; microcredit systems and use of, 208–9; neoliberal degovernmentalization and, 113n11; Nepalese developmental failure and, 50–86; NGO collaboration with, 1–11, 20, 124–25, 304–10; NGOization paradigm and collaboration with, 196–97, 226–27, 287–88; in postcommunist Romania, 254–57; state-civil society partnerships and, 94–95; structural violence of, 62–65; subversion of empowerment and activism by, 101–6; Thai women's activism and role of, 170–72; violence in Nepal committed by, 70–74. See also Government Orga-

state institutions (*continued*) nized Non-governmental Organizations (GONGOs)

Stokke, K., 146–47

"strategic sisterhood," critique of, 123–24

structural violence, development as form of, 60–65

subalternity: Indian GONGO/NGO structure and, 100–106, 109–12; neoliberal and conscientization models and, 65; Nepalese developmental failures, 50–52; NGO activism and, 308–10; political consciousness and, 82–86

subjectification, gendered concepts of personhood and, 75–81

"successful development" thesis, rural revolution in Nepal and, 54–55

suffering, subjectivizing force of, gendered personhood and, 74–81

sukha (ease and comfort), Nepalese concept of: empowerment among women and, 71–74; marriage in context of, 76–81

support groups, Russian *vs.* Western crisis center models and role of, 136–38

surveillance mechanisms, in microcredit systems, 206–9

Tamang women in Nepal, empowerment among, 73–74

Tanzania, NGO coalitions in, 11

tax laws, political constraints on women's NGOs as result of, 277–79

Taylor, Verta, 272

technocratic ideology, NGO activism and, 308–10

teleology: feminist activism and, 219–20; of NGOization paradigm, 222–23

"testimonial knowledge," of women's NGOs in EU, 271

textile production, Thai cultural preservation initiatives and, 176–78

Thailand: activist mothering movement in, 178–81; community development/cultural preservation discourses and activism in, 175–78; feminism and human rights in, 181–86; NGOization in, 169–72, 191n6; scholarship on women's activism in, 172–74, 191n9; transborder feminist solidarity with women in, 186–90; women's activism in, 166–90

Thayer, Millie, 45, 286

"third moment" feminism, 295

third sector institutions, in postwar Bosnia-Herzegovina, 25–27

Third Wave feminism, in Latin America, 298–99

Third World feminism: First World feminist discourse on, 182–86; NGOization paradigm and, 226; NGO structure and, 7–11; structural violence of development and, 60–65

31st December Women's Movement, 233–34

Together at Foișor Program for Community Development (Roman), 260

top-down project implementation: participation in development projects and, 146–48; Thai women's activism and, 176–77

Toward a Nonsexist Education, 260

transnational advocacy networks: class-related access to, 183–86; critique of paradigms within, 138–40; divisions and tensions within, 119–21; economic issues as focus of, 132; EU funding access for, 274–76; European Union role in, 269–70; future issues for, 281–83; gender equality policies and, 266–83; Indian women's empowerment programs and, 95–98; Latin American "move-

ment work" and, 289–91; NGOization paradigm and, 4–6, 12–18, 223;
post-NGOization feminism in Latin
America and, 296–99; public engagement and, 279–81; Russian feminist
activism and, 121–25, 141n7; Russian *vs.* Western crisis center models
and, 133–38; Thai women's activism
and, 170–72, 186–90; velvet triangle
concept and, 266–69; women's NGOs
and European Union, 270–74, 307–10
transnational social movements
(TSMS), anti-violence campaigns by,
123–25
transversal politics, Thai feminist solidarity and, 188–90
Tribhuvan University, Center for Educational Research, Innovation, and
Development, 58
Tsikata, Dzodzi, 221–23, 224
Tsing, Anna, 246n11
Tver, Russia, crisis center model in,
133–38

UK Charities Commission, 279
Ukraine: NGO boom in, 46n1; women's
social activism in, 223
UN High Commission on Human
Rights, 123
United Kingdom, political constraints
on women's NGOs in, 278–79
United Nations: conferences on women,
8, 11–12; human rights conferences
of, 123; impact on NGOs of, 17–18;
Latin American feminist movements
and, 290–91, 295–99; Latin American
NGOization and, 287–88; NGOization
paradigm and influence of, 283n2;
state-civil society partnerships promoted by, 94–95, 292–95; Thai feminist discourse in, 184–86; violence
against women issues at, 122–25
United States: abeyance in women's

movement in, 272–74; battered
women's movement in, 122–25; NGO
structure in, 7
universalism, feminism and theme of,
119
University of Sarajevo, gender studies
at, 41
University Press Limited (UPL), 213–15
UN Millennium Development Goals, 12
Uruguay, feminist movements in, 296–
97
US Agency for International Development (USAID): Bangladesh programs
of, 200–201; in Bosnia-Herzegovina,
26–27, 47n9; empowerment initiatives of, 60–65; Nepalese women's
empowerment unit in, 62–65
usury practices: Bangladeshi women's
involvement in, 207–9; microcredit
and expansion of, 210–13

Valiente, Celia, 272
Vargas, Virginia, 290, 291–92
Vati, Leela, 99
velvet triangle, transnational women's
advocacy and, 219–20, 266–69
Venezuela, neopopulism in, 293–94
vernacular press, in Bangladesh, 213–15
vertical integration, Latin American
feminist movement and, 288–91
Village Development Committees
(VDCs) (Nepal), 55–60
Village Women's Development Committee (Khanakammakaan phad-
thana satrii muu baan) (Thailand),
170–72
violence: absence of development and,
81–86; development as catalyst for,
60–65; in Gorkha district of Nepal,
55–56, 89n39; Nepalese developmental failure and role of, 50–51; Russian *vs.* Western crisis center models
and framing of, 136–38; transnational

violence (*continued*)
campaigns against, 121–25, 141n5. *See also* domestic violence; sexual violence
virtual management of NGOs, 259–64
volunteerism: in postcommunist Romania, 251–52; skepticism in Bosnia-Herzegovina concerning, 29–37, 47n13, 48n19; in Thai women's activism, 179–81; in United Kingdom, 278–79

Walley, Christine, 172–74
Wallstrom, Margot, 273–74
Warsaw Pact, 250
Watson, Peggy, 126
Western feminism: Russian crisis center models and, 125–26; Russian Soviet-era connections with, 120, 140n2; socialist feminists and, 14; Third World feminism and, 182–86; transborder critiques of, 186–90
Wiegman, Robyn, 226–27
Woman and Politics, 185
Women and the Constitution Network, 185
Women in Development Europe, 280–81
women-in-development (WID) paradigm, in postwar Bangladesh, 199–201
Women's Development Programme (WDP), 95
women's empowerment: activist mothering movement (Thailand) and, 178–81; Bangladeshi women moneylenders and, 210–13, 217n26; Bosnian NGOs and emergence of, 39–43, 48n14; dialogic exchange and growth of, 160–63; economic equality as focus in, 129–32; feminist discourse on NGOs and, 303–10; Ghanaian Women's Manifesto analysis of, 234–36; Ghanaian women's organizations and, 233–34; group responsibility model, in microcredit systems, 206–9; in India, state-government collaboration on, 93–112; Indian NGOs and facilitation of, 151–65; mainstreaming of, as development strategy, 63–64, 107–8; Nepalese rural revolution and role of, 52–86; participation in development projects linked to, 145–48; political agency in Nepal and, 65–74; rural activism as tool for, 169–72; shaming as tool for, 198–99; spatial practices and creation of, 154–60; state accountability for, 302–3; suffering as subjectivizing force and, 74–81; unofficial GONGO advocacy for, 101–6

Women's Manifesto for Ghana (The Coalition on the Women's Manifesto for Ghana), 221, 234–36; coalition building and inclusion agenda of, 236–44

women's movements: emergence in Bosnia-Herzegovina of, 29–37, 40–43; feminist framework in India for, 95–98; Ghanaian Women's Manifesto and, 221, 234–36, 245n7; historicization of, in Ghana, 232–34; Latin American feminist NGOs and, 288–99; maternalism in, 178–81, 191n14; Nepalese developmental failures and, 50–86; NGOization inhibition of, 223, 227–32; professionalization of, 224–27; in Romania, 249–57; in Russia, 119–21; Russian crisis center model and, 125–28, 141n13; in Thailand, 166–68; women's advocacy networks, 266–83

women's NGOs: Bangladesh microcredit operations and, 206–15; Bangladesh women moneylenders and, 210–13, 217n26; credibility in Bosnia-Herzegovina of, 28–29; economic and legal constraints of, 274–76; emergence of, 1, 11–18; European Union and, 270–74; feminism and structure of, 301–10; fundraising difficulties of, 274–76; Ghanaian historicization and feminist organizing of, 232–34; in India, gendered paradoxes in, 143–65, 189–90; "movement work" in Latin America and, 288–91; NGOization paradigm and, 221–23, 228–32; political constraints on, 276–79; in postwar Bosnia-Herzegovina, 21–27; public engagement and, 279–81; in Romania, 257–64; Thai women's activism and, 166–90; theory and critique of participation in, 145–48; transborder feminist solidarity with Thai women and, 186–90; transnational agendas regarding, 13–18; women's development programming in Nepal and, 57–60

Woodward, Alison, 266–67

work identities in hybrid GONGO/NGO structure, Mahila Samakhya project in India and, 98–106

World Bank, 302; NGOs and, 17–18, 47n6, 48n22; state-civil society partnerships promoted by, 94–95; Third World economic sovereignty and, 196–97

World Conference on Women in Beijing, 11–12, 123, 141n8, 173–74, 253, 287–88

World March of Women against Violence and Poverty (WMW), 297–99

World Social Forum (WSF), 292–95, 296–99

Yami, Hisala, 85

youth issues, Thai women's activism concerning, 177–78

Yunus, Muhammad, 197–200, 214–15, 215n1

Yuval-Davis, Nira, 188–89

Žbanić, Jasmila, 40

Zenica, Bosnia-Herzegovina, local women's organizations in, 23–24

Zhenskii Svet (Women's Light), 129–40

zhesovety (Soviet-era women's organizations), 125, 140n2

Zippel, Kathrin, 279